The Communicator's Commentary

**Hosea, Joel, Amos
Obadiah, Jonah**

THE COMMUNICATOR'S COMMENTARY SERIES
OLD TESTAMENT

Lloyd J. Ogilvie

General Editor

The Communicator's Commentary

**Hosea, Joel, Amos,
Obadiah, Jonah**

Lloyd J. Ogilvie

WORD BOOKS, PUBLISHER • DALLAS, TEXAS

Library of Congress Cataloging in Publication Data
Main entry under title:

The Communicator's commentary.

      Bibliography: p.
      Contents: OT20. Hosea–Jonah / by Lloyd J. Ogilvie
      1. Bible. O.T.— Commentaries. I. Ogilvie, Lloyd John. II. Ogilvie, Lloyd J.
BS1151.2.C66 1986 221.7'7 86–11138
ISBN 0-8499-0426-9 (v. OT20)

Printed in the United States of America

0 1 2 3 4 9 AGF 9 8 7 6 5 4 3 2 1

Contents

Amos

Obadiah

Jonah

Publisher's Preface

Hosea–Jonah contains some of the richest material in the Bible for our understanding of God's justice and mercy. This important volume in the Communicator's Commentary on the Old Testament is written by Lloyd John Ogilvie, senior pastor of the First Presbyterian Church of Hollywood, California, and general editor of the Communicator's Commentary series.

Lloyd Ogilvie is widely known and respected for his dedication to faithful Bible exposition and for his pastor's heart which is revealed in his concern and care for people. His ministry reflects these traits, whether in the pulpit, in his books, or in his "Let God Love You" television program. Moreover, in this day of disillusionment and skepticism toward those who would seek to bring a "word from the Lord," his life is a faithful representation of the message he communicates.

It is then appropriate that he should provide this commentary on five of those books commonly referred to as the Minor Prophets. From Hosea's strong declaration that God desires "mercy and not sacrifice" and his admonition to God's people to "observe mercy and justice, and wait on your God continually," to Amos's stirring words, "Let justice run down like water, and righteousness like a mighty stream," we are brought face to face with our need for repentance and faithfulness to God today. We also hear afresh in these pages the invitation from Joel to "return to the Lord your God, for He is gracious and merciful, slow to anger, and of great kindness." In Obadiah, the shortest of the biblical books, we encounter the Lord's searching word: "For the day of the Lord upon all the nations is near." And we receive in the book of Jonah the wonderful assurance that God's justice is tempered by His mercy and grace.

Lloyd Ogilvie, working with this rich material, provides compelling commentary that calls the church to give up her adulterous ways, to return to her merciful God, and to courageously serve others in His name.

This commentary is intended for use by Bible students, teachers, and ministers in personal study, teaching, and preaching. You will find it a practical tool as well as a scholarly resource. We commend Lloyd Ogilvie's excellent work to you and, with him, prayerfully offer it to the church for the work of ministry.

CHARLES KIP JORDON
PUBLISHER

Author's Preface

God has called all of His people to be communicators. Everyone who is in Christ is called into ministry. As ministers of "the manifold grace of God," all of us—clergy and laity—are commissioned with challenge to communicate our faith to individuals and groups, classes and congregations.

The Bible, God's Word, is the objective basis of the truth of His love and power that we seek to communicate. In response to the urgent, expressed needs of pastors, teachers, Bible study leaders, church school teachers, small group enablers, and individual Christians, the Communicator's Commentary is offered as a penetrating search of the Scriptures of the Old and New Testament to enable vital personal and practical communication of the abundant life.

Many current commentaries and Bible study guides provide only some aspects of a communicator's needs. Some offer in-depth scholarship but no application to daily life. Others are so popular in approach that biblical roots are left unexplained. Few offer impelling illustrations that open windows for the reader to see the exciting application for today's struggles. And most of all, seldom have the expositors given the valuable outlines of passages so needed to help the preacher or teacher in his or her busy life to prepare for communicating the Word to congregations or classes.

This Communicator's Commentary series brings all of these elements together. The authors are scholar-preachers and teachers outstanding in their ability to make the Scriptures come alive for individuals and groups. They are noted for bringing together excellence in biblical scholarship, knowledge of the original Hebrew and Greek, sensitivity to people's needs, vivid illustrative material from biblical, classical, and contemporary sources, and lucid communication by the use of clear outlines of thought. Each has been selected to contribute to this series because of his Spirit-empowered ability to help people live in the skins of biblical characters and provide a "you-are-there" intensity to the drama of events of the Bible which have so much to say about our relationships and responsibilities today.

The design for the Communicator's Commentary gives the reader an overall outline of each book of the Bible. Following the introduction, which reveals the author's approach and salient background on the book, each chapter of the commentary provides the Scripture to be exposited. The New King James Bible has been chosen for the Communicator's Commentary because it combines with integrity the beauty of language, underlying Hebrew and Greek textual basis, and thought-flow of the 1611 King James Version, while replacing obsolete verb forms and other archaisms with their everyday contemporary counterparts for greater readability. Reverence for God is preserved in the capitalization of all pronouns referring to the Father, Son, or Holy Spirit. Readers who are more comfortable with another translation can readily find the parallel passage by means of the chapter and verse reference at the end of each passage being exposited. The paragraphs of exposition combine fresh insights to the Scripture, application, rich illustrative material, and innovative ways of utilizing the vibrant truth for his or her own life and for the challenge of communicating it with vigor and vitality.

It has been gratifying to me as editor of this series to receive enthusiastic progress reports from each contributor. As they worked, all were gripped with new truths from Scripture—God-given insights into passages, previously not written in the literature of biblical explanation. A prime objective of this series is for each user to find the same awareness: that God speaks with newness through the Scriptures when we approach them with a ready mind and a willingness to communicate what He has given; that God delights to give communicators of His Word "I-never-saw-that-in-that-verse-before" intellectual insights so that our listeners and readers can have "I-never-realized-all-that-was-in-that-verse" spiritual experiences.

The thrust of the commentary series unequivocally affirms that God speaks through the Scriptures today to engender faith, enable adventuresome living of the abundant life, and establish the basis of obedient discipleship. The Bible, the unique Word of God, is unlimited as a resource for Christians in communicating our hope to others. It is our weapon in the battle for truth, the guide for ministry, and the irresistible force for introducing others to God.

A biblically rooted communication of the Gospel holds in unity and oneness what divergent movements have wrought asunder. This commentary series courageously presents personal faith, caring for individuals, and social responsibility as essential, inseparable dimensions of biblical Christianity. It seeks to present the quadrilateral Gospel in its fullness which calls us to unreserved commitment to Christ, unrestricted self-esteem in His grace, unqualified love for others in personal evangelism, and undying efforts to work for justice and righteousness in a sick and suffering world.

A growing renaissance in the church today is being led by clergy and laity who are biblically rooted, Christ-centered, and Holy Spirit-empowered. They have dared to listen to people's most urgent questions and deepest needs and then to God as He speaks throughout the Bible. Biblical preaching is the secret of growing churches. Bible study classes and small groups are equipping the laity for ministry in the world. Dynamic Christians are finding that daily study of God's Word allows the Spirit to do in them what He wishes to communicate through them to others. These days are the most exciting time since Pentecost. The Communicator's Commentary is offered to be a primary resource of new life for this renaissance.

It has been very encouraging to receive the enthusiastic responses of pastors and teachers to the twelve New Testament volumes of the Communicator's Commentary series. The letters from communicators on the firing line in pulpits, classes, study groups, and Bible fellowship clusters across the nation, as well as the reviews of scholars and publication analysts, have indicated that we have been on target in meeting a need for a distinctly different kind of commentary on the Scriptures, a commentary that is primarily aimed at helping interpreters of the Bible to equip the laity for ministry.

This positive response has led the publisher to press on with an additional twenty-one volumes covering the books of the Old Testament. These new volumes rest upon the same goals and guidelines that undergird the New Testament volumes. Scholar-preachers with facility in Hebrew as well as vivid contemporary exposition have been selected as authors. The purpose throughout is to aid the preacher and teacher in the challenge and adventure of Old Testament exposition in communication. In each volume you will meet Yahweh, the "I AM" Lord who is Creator, Sustainer, and Redeemer in the unfolding drama of His call and care of Israel. He is the Lord who acts, intervenes, judges, and presses His people into the immense challenges and privileges of being a chosen people, a holy nation. And in the descriptive exposition of each passage, the implications of the ultimate revelation of Yahweh in Jesus Christ, His Son, our Lord, are carefully spelled out to maintain unity and oneness in the preaching and teaching of the Gospel.

This volume on the first five of the Minor Prophets and Walter Kaiser's volume on the other seven deal with some of the most challenging Scriptures of the Old Testament. I often think of a comment I heard about the study of these prophets.

"We were going along just fine until we hit the Minor Prophets," a man said. "Then we really got bogged down. Those grim greybeards are difficult to understand and what I did understand was hard to apply to life today!"

This honest comment was made to me at my banquet table in Kansas City where I was the speaker. The man told me about a Bible study course he and his wife were taking together. He couldn't say enough about what the comprehensive, in-depth study meant to his spiritual growth. Though he had been a Christian for years, he had never spent much time in the Old Testament. He found it all very stimulating and inspiring, except for the Minor Prophets.

The man's sentiments are echoed by many church members, and not a few preachers and teachers. Pastors sometimes preach from isolated texts from the Minor Prophets but seldom tackle verse-by-verse, passage-by-passage exposition of them in a prolonged series of messages. Nor are the Minor Prophets often selected as the content of Bible study classes, except on the seminary level. The demanding discipline for the teacher is often considered too great for weekly preparation.

The purpose of this commentary is to provide a combination of resources for the contemporary preacher and teacher so that moving through these books will be both understandable and applicable to life today.

This volume was written by a communicator for communicators. It is not meant to be only a scholarly treatise, though I hope disciplined scholarship is not lacking at any point. Nor is it designed to be only a popular treatment of profound Scripture, though I pray that preachers and teachers will find practical help in the demanding task of illustrating these Scriptures. I have tried to keep in mind what I need when I sit down to prepare a message or class. I need a thorough analysis of the biblical text, including etymological studies of the words, background on the context, an approach that stimulates my own thinking about ways to help my listeners apply the main thrust of the passage or verse. Whenever possible I have tried to include all of these elements in my treatment of each portion of these biblical books.

I must confess that it would have been easier either to add to the many scholarly works on the Minor Prophets or to simply compile a series of sermons. Rather, I have tried to be faithful to the goal of Communicator's Commentary Series that the publishers and I set some seven years ago, to combine in-depth scholarship with incisive application and illustration.

There were times that I would have enjoyed the luxury of staying in the eighth century B.C., dealing with what a prophet said and what it meant in his circumstances. The "what does this mean to us today?" question often presented the greatest challenge. At this point I was spurred on by the thought that every preacher or teacher of the Minor Prophets grapples with the same problem.

I have made a concentrated effort to vary the method of dealing with the passages. Sometimes I begin with our contemporary scene and move into the text. Other times, application follows straight exposition. I hope each of these chapters will serve as a guide for preaching or teaching an exhaustive—but not exhausting—series of messages or classes.

The Minor Prophets call us to return to our holy God with righteous living and social justice. What they have to say about God's judgment rattles our teeth and shakes us in our boots. They confront the shallowness of religion without personal and social obedience. And the prophet's messages are not homilies for hermits. The corporate people of God are confronted with the cost of being chosen. The prophets bring us to that frightening place where we see ourselves clearly and we honestly cry out for Calvary to experience grace with greater healing than ever before.

The church in America and everywhere needs the bracing messages of the Minor Prophets. We need the "thus says the Lord" blast of the trumpet to fire our blood and shake us from our lethargy.

Renewal happens when we see ourselves and our churches as God sees us and we repent. The Minor Prophets expose our false gods, our willfulness, and our pride. They help us think majestically about God and His choice to be our God and give us a new beginning.

LLOYD OGILIVIE

Introduction to the Book of Hosea

THE TIMES OF HOSEA

Hosea and his contemporary Amos were active in the middle of the eighth century B.C. Although Amos was from Judah, both spoke primarily to the northern kingdom, Israel. A few years later Isaiah and Micah would address the southern kingdom, Judah, with a similar message.

Amos probably began his ministry a few years before Hosea and completed his prophecy within the reign of Jeroboam II of Israel. Hosea began his prophecy in the last years of that king and continued into the turbulent years leading up to the collapse of the northern kingdom. His ministry apparently ended some years before the destruction of Israel's capital, Samaria, in 722 B.C.

POLITICAL BACKGROUND

The long reign of Jeroboam II (786–746 B.C.) was a time of prosperity for Israel, as it was for Judah during the contemporary reign of Uzziah (783–742 B.C.). Israel and Judah were able to subdue neighboring nations and extend their borders nearly to the outlines of Solomon's kingdom (2 Kings 14:25; cf. 1 Kings 8:65). The larger powers of Egypt and Assyria were preoccupied with problems closer to home, so that Palestine was free from foreign domination, though this was soon to change.

With the extended territory and the conditions of peace, Israel and Judah enjoyed increased trade and the revenue generated by controlling major trade routes. Archaeological evidence confirms the wealth of Samaria during this period. Israel and Judah were at their economic and political peak.

Such a climate was bound to breed optimism and a confidence in the prospects for the future. The nations doubtless regarded prosperity as a sign of God's favor and a confirmation of their policies and practices. The prophets Amos and Hosea gave a vastly different evaluation of the situation and predicted the catastrophe, which would come with surprising quickness.

After the death of Jeroboam II, Israel fell into political chaos. Jeroboam's son, Zechariah, was assassinated after only six months on the throne. His assassin, Shallum, ruled for one month before falling to the sword of Menahem.

In addition to the internal collapse, external conditions spelled disaster for Israel. The Assyrian king Tiglath-Pileser III (745–727 B.C.) proved to be a vigorous ruler, able to subdue enemies close to home and extend Assyria's influence far beyond. His conquests were also different in character from earlier Assyrian exploits, which were mainly tribute-gathering raids. Now Assyria was bent on full conquest. Any nation that failed to submit faced deportation, a policy that Tiglath Pileser III pursued more consistently than any previous ruler.

Menahem offered tribute to Assyria during one of Tiglath Pileser's early campaigns, hoping that Assyrian power would help him consolidate his hold on the throne of Israel (2 Kings 15:19–20). No doubt, the resulting head tax was resented in Israel. After Menahem's death, his son Pekaiah lasted only two years before he was murdered by Pekah.

Pekah joined Damascus and the Philistines in an anti-Assyrian coalition. When they attacked Judah because Judah would not join, King Ahaz appealed to Assyria for help (2 Kings 16:5–8). In 734 B.C. Tiglath Pileser III attacked the Philistine cities, then moved against Israel and took Damascus in 732 B.C.

The Assyrians took most of Israel's land outside the Samaritan highlands and deported the population (2 Kings 15:29). At this time Hoshea murdered Pekah and surrendered to the Assyrians. A few years later Shalmaneser V (727–722 B.C.) became the new Assyrian king. Hoshea used the change of throne as an opportunity to withhold tribute. The Assyrian retaliation came in 724 B.C. Samaria fell in 722 B.C.; the population was deported, and the northern kingdom of Israel was no more.

Although it is difficult to identify historical occasions for Hosea's prophecies, since he never gives names, the references to series of kings (8:4) and palace intrigues (7:3–7) reflect the chaotic period following Jeroboam's death. One popular view contends that the conflict with Judah during Pekah's reign forms the background for Hosea 5:8–14. There is no evidence in the book that Hosea witnessed the downfall of Samaria, an omission that probably points to his death before that time.

Social Background

Contrary to the egalitarian tendencies of the covenant stipulations and the tribal league, conditions under the monarchy had brought extremes of wealth and poverty. This was particularly true in Israel, where the native Canaanite population with its feudal background had a much stronger influence than in Judah. Amos in particular rails against the breakdown of the social structure and the constant injustices.

Religious Background

Syncretism characterized the religious order of the day. The worship of the Canaanite god Baal diluted Israel's worship of Yahweh to a great extent. *Baal*, meaning "lord" or "husband," was the name commonly given to the Canaanite storm god, Hadad. He was often represented as a bull, the symbol of fertility. The bull images built by Jeroboam I at Dan and Bethel (1 Kings 12:28–33) no doubt provided another occasion for assimilating the worship of Yahweh to the worship of Baal.

Canaanite religion, like most in the ancient world, connected gods and goddesses with forces in the natural world and considered that their course could be influenced by the devotion and rituals of worshippers. Religion then takes on a magical quality as an attempt to manipulate the gods, which is characteristic of perverted religion in any place and time. Rituals aim to ensure the foundations for life, such as the rain necessary for crops in Palestine and the success of animal and human reproduction.

Along with this was the view that sexual relations between gods and goddesses were responsible for some of the initial and continuing processes in nature. Based on this idea and a concept of imitative magic, sacred prostitution was a prominent part of the cult. Worshipers would engage in sexual intercourse with cult prostitutes at the shrines hoping to influence the gods to do likewise, and thus ensure continuing fertility.

Religious devotion was hardly lacking in this age. The question was the quality of that devotion. Certainly the acts of Yahweh were celebrated in the cult, but too often these were taken as a sign of unconditional support for the status quo. The covenant obligations were either blurred or understood as completely fulfilled by the rituals (Amos 5:21–24).

Prophecy in Eighth-Century Israel and Judah

The eighth century B.C. witnessed the beginning of the classical or literary prophets in Amos, Hosea, Isaiah, and Micah. This does not mean that they wrote, but that collections of their sayings were preserved in written form.

In many ways they continued the traditions of their great predecessors such as Samuel, Nathan, Elijah, and Elisha. They counseled and rebuked kings and called for reforms in political, social, and religious life as messengers of Yahweh's word.

A major distinctive of the eighth-century prophets rose from the situation they faced. Until this time the political existence of Israel was not really in question. The nation endured only temporary humiliation, primarily from the small states nearby. The new Assyrian might combined with the policy of deportation threatened national survival as never before.

Faced with this situation and the continuing rebellion against Yahweh, the prophets asserted that Yahweh could destroy the nation and its institutions just as He had created them. Promises to the fathers were no guarantee of national existence in view of persistent rejection of Yahweh's word.

Though the prophets had an unpopular message in their day, their message was vindicated when the disaster they predicted was accomplished. At that point, the words of the court prophets who predicted that all would be well would seem especially empty. However, the significance of the classical prophets is much greater than their correct predictions of disaster.

They offered hope that God still had a purpose for His people who were refined through the judgment. Therefore, they offered a vision of renewed prosperity and peace for the community, though often far in the indefinite future. Their words spoken to eighth-century B.C. Israel and Judah were applied later when Judah faced defeat and exile in Babylon. The prominent prophets of that later day, Jeremiah and Ezekiel, spelled out afresh the conditions for the continuation of the people of God as a living community through the disasters of losing land, cult, and political state.

This perspective on the sovereignty and freedom of Yahweh and His way with the chosen people was a large reason that Israel, at least in the remnant of Judah, persisted as a distinct community of faith in contrast with the inhabitants of other small states in Palestine. For Israel refined through exile, existence as a community of faith depended solely on Yahweh and His word. Yahweh was free to offer or take away other gifts of land, king, and temple in His time.

The Prophet Hosea

Hosea is the only classical prophet from the northern kingdom. Amos also prophesied to Israel, but he was from Judah. Except for Hosea's father's name and his marriage, we know little about his life. We are told neither his birthplace nor his profession nor the circumstances of his call to prophecy. No inaugural visions like Isaiah's or Jeremiah's appear in this book.

The only personal detail of importance in the book is Hosea's marriage. His marriage and the children born become powerful symbols and vehicles to communicate God's word to Israel. While other prophets such as Jeremiah and Ezekiel used marriage as a symbol of God's relationship with Israel and Judah, no other prophet was called to experience the agony of a failed marriage as a vehicle of communication.

The Message of Hosea

In order to understand the message of Hosea, we must not only become familiar with the political and religious background of his times, but also with what was his source of authority. Hosea based his message on the Pentateuch, and Deuteronomy in particular. This presupposes that the Pentateuch was available to the prophet and that it was not compiled in the seventh and sixth centuries B.C. as some scholars contend.

The events leading up to the Sinai covenant, the covenant itself, and the blessing and curses of the Mosaic Law provide the objective standard for Hosea's oracles to eighth-century Israel. From these the prophet drew his strong convictions of the election of Israel to be God's chosen people and the requirements of being His holy people. Exodus and Deuteronomy were the main source of Hosea's rich images of God's plan and purpose for His people.

Two prominent figures are used by Hosea to remind Israel of Yahweh's election and call. First, the people were Yahweh's son. This was rooted in Exodus 4:22, "Israel is My Son, My first born." With prevenient initiative grace, Yahweh had chosen His people centuries before through the covenant with Abraham. He had called His "son" out of bondage in Egypt and had faithfully brought them to Sinai. "When Israel was a child, I loved him, and out of Egypt I called My son," (Hos. 11:1). The relationship between Yahweh and Israel was one of gracious love for His son.

At Sinai, the key image changes from sonship to marriage. For Hosea, it was there that Israel was betrothed to Yahweh. The emphasis remains on initiative election. Yahweh chose His bride Israel. He bonded Himself to His people with His promise to be their God and expected faithfulness and obedience in the bonds of love. The image of sonship stressed Yahweh's election and the image of marriage stressed the free choice of Israel to enter into a covenant relationship. Election and free will are held in harmonious balance in Hosea's understanding of Israel's relationship with Yahweh.

In his own marriage to Gomer, Hosea was put through an existential experience of Yahweh's relationship with Israel, His bride of Sinai. As we shall see, Hosea was able to understand Israel's defection from her Sinai betrothal through rebellion, apostasy, and syncretism by what he went through personally with Gomer's unfaithfulness. When the prophet was called by Yahweh to love Gomer despite her sin, he realized from excruciating firsthand experience the depth of God's love for Israel.

Yahweh gave Hosea a word to express the fullness of His love for Israel. The word is *hesed*, communicating initiative grace and complete loyalty. Yahweh had elected and called Israel to be His bride out of unqualified love and desired from His people unfaltering loyalty.

6

Where He had kept His covenant indefatigably, Israel had responded with infidelity. She had been unfaithful by committing adultery with false gods. Hosea's turbulent relationship with Gomer in his own marriage pressed his heart next to the torment in the heart of God over Israel. The prophet is forced to live with the soul-sized issues of holiness, justice, mercy, and forgiveness.

Deuteronomy 4:20–31 is the historical perspective of Hosea's message, Moses words of warning and prophecy to the people of Israel give progression to the prophet's thought. Israel was chosen. She must never forget the covenant, for God is a consuming fire and a jealous God. If the people turned to false gods, God would punish them and take them from the promised land. They would be exiled and suffer for their sins. Then the people would repent and call on the Lord and obey Him. And out of mercy He would not forsake His people nor forget the covenant He made with their fathers. Hosea's prophecy follows the five stages of Moses' prediction of what would actually happen to the people prior to, during, and after the exile.

The blessings and curses passages of Deuteronomy are applied extensively by Hosea as he presents the case against Israel for her apostasy. He serves as Yahweh's litigator in pressing the charges.

The book of Hosea has profound implications for our own personal relationship with God. We are confronted with our own false gods, spiritual adultery, and God's judgment for our denial of the covenants of Sinai and Calvary in Christ's blood. We have received *hesed* in full measure in Christ and yet often are unfaithful disciples. As part of the bride of Christ, the church, we have been called to holy living and yet must confess our corporate lack of first love commitment to the Bridegroom. And in our relationships with people we are challenged by the call to love again those who have hurt and misused us.

As individuals and as the church, a study of Hosea is disturbing before it is comforting. We are drawn irresistibly into the book and find ourselves inside the skin of Hosea as he endures the pain of his marriage and realizes the anguish of God. But we will also be forced to identify with Israel and be led into a deeper realization of our own need to return to the Lord.

An Outline of Hosea

I. Title: The Word of Yahweh: 1:1
II. The Word of Yahweh to and through Hosea: 1:2–14:8
    A. Yahweh's Word in Hosea's Family: 1:2–3:5
        1. Hosea's Family and Israel: 1:2–2:23
            a. Hosea's Wife and Naming and Renaming the Children: 1:2–2:1
                (1) Hosea's Family—Omens of Judgment: 1:2–9
                (2) Israel Restored: 1:10–2:1
            b. Judgment and Restoration of Israel: 2:2–23
                (1) Yahweh's Exasperation with Israel: 2:2–13
                (2) Yahweh's New Marriage with Israel: 2:14–23
        2. The Love of Yahweh and Hosea: 3:1–5
    B. Hosea's Prophecies: 4:1–14:8
        1. Yahweh's Charge against all Israel: 4:1–3
        2. Yahweh's Charge against all the Priests: 4:4–19
        3. Israel's Leaders—a Snare: 5:1–7
        4. Ephraim and Judah in Conflict: 5:8–15
        5. A Call to Return: 6:1–3
        6. Yahweh's Desire for Loyalty: 6:4–6
        7. Surrounded by Their Deeds: 6:7–7:2
        8. Domestic Politics without Yahweh: 7:3–7
        9. International Politics without Yahweh: 7:8–16
        10. Apostasy in Cult and Politics: 8:1–14
        11. No more Festivals: 9:1–9
        12. Rebels Rejected by Yahweh: 9:10–17
        13. No more Cult or King: 10:1–8
        14. Destroyed by War: 10:9–15

CHAPTER ONE

Confrontive Grace

Hosea 1:1–2:1

1:1 The word of the Lord that came to Hosea the son of Beeri, in the days of Uzziah, Jotham, Ahaz, and Hezekiah, kings of Judah, and in the days of Jereboam the son of Joash, king of Israel.

Hos. 1:1

"Is there any word from the Lord?"

These words were scrawled on the back of a postcard and sent to me. I had asked my congregation and people in our radio and television audiences to write me their most urgent questions. This one caught my attention. It's really the ultimate question beneath all our other questions.

We long to know what God has to say about our needs, frustrations, and problems. We yearn for His guidance, wisdom, and vision. Sometimes, He tells us more than we are ready to hear or follow. He not only assures us of His love and mercy, but He confronts us with things that need to be changed in us, our relationship with Him, or our society. He constantly seeks to show us the truth about our lives and helps us to do something about it.

We have been elected to be saints, people who belong first and foremost to God. He has chosen, called, and cherished us. Our status is secure because of His faithfulness and unmerited favor toward us. God will not let us go nor forsake us.

At the same time, we are programmed for growth. God loves us as we are but never leaves us as we are. Not us or the people to whom we seek to communicate. And as communicators God often does in us what He wants to do through us. Our lives become the laboratory in which we discover new truth and learn how to communicate with empathy. We can lead people only so far as we've grown ourselves.

Often our growth takes place in profound but traumatic experiences of God's judgment. He confronts us with our own set of false gods, our lust for success, or our inconsistency in living what we preach or teach. Only then do we have the credentials to be prophetic about idolatry in the church or the unrighteousness in our society.

Most important of all is our need to rediscover how much we mean to God. He created us to know, love, and obey Him. He has pursued us with tenacious persistence. He has wooed us to Him through the revelation of His indefatigable love in Jesus Christ and His cross. He has worked in our minds and hearts to enable us to respond and claim His grace and forgiveness. He has filled us with His Spirit and has given us the gift of prayer to know Him intimately, discern His will, and be faithful sons and daughters.

Then God has called us to be part of His family, the church, the people of God. He has nurtured us and cared for us. Out of sheer grace, not because we were either worthy or deserving, He appointed us to be leaders in the church and gave us the awesome responsibility to be sensitive to His Spirit and listen for His word for the people of God. What He wants to say to them through us, He first says to us for our own lives. And in the process, He allows our hearts to be broken by the things in us and our churches that break His heart.

The one thing God will not accept from us or His people is second place. He will not be one of the many gods of our own making or faking. He demands to be sovereign of all and not just the source of strength to accomplish our plans and purposes. He must be Lord of all or will not be Lord at all.

We have been called to be leaders at a time when God is calling His people to deeper holiness, purity, and faithfulness. He is renewing His church. And out of unchanging love, He communicates His bracing judgment and His unqualified forgiveness. Our response can be nothing less than, "Renew your people, Lord, beginning with me!"

UNBROKEN LOVE FROM A BROKEN HEART

Now we can live in Hosea's heart. Our hearts can beat with his as in his own way he longed for a word from the Lord. He felt acutely the sins of his people. Then one day the word of the Lord came to him. It was not just a message to proclaim but a call to experience the unbroken love of God from His broken heart.

The book of Hosea begins with a title like that of many prophetic books. The first words characterize the book as the word of Yahweh. We need to see this in the context of the ancient understanding of *word* and the particular meaning of *the word of Yahweh* in Israel.

The ancient world regarded words not merely as vehicles to communicate information or instruction between people, but as agents of power. On the human level, words of blessing and curse had the power to influence the course of events. Once words were uttered, they seemed to take on life of their own and could not be canceled, as in the blessing of Jacob and the cursing of Esau (Gen. 27:32–38).

On the divine level, we see the creative power of God in the first chapter of Genesis where God speaks and orders the natural world to come into being (Ps. 33:6, 9). Certainly, the word of Yahweh does communicate information, making known His will. Yet that word is at the same time a power that is involved in accomplishing the will of Yahweh (Isa. 55:10–11) and actively shaping the course of history, particularly in the prophetic use of the term. The word God speaks is inseparable from the impact of His Spirit which He imparts. Hearing the word is at the same time an encounter with God Himself.

It is this powerful and creative word of Yahweh that comes to Hosea. It affects His own personal situation profoundly, as we shall see, but it is not intended just for him. The word of Yahweh is spoken to Hosea in the context of a very specific need at a particular period of Israel's history. The reference to Judean and Israelite kings indicates that this word of Yahweh was not given in a vacuum, but in the crucible of the final years of the prosperous reign of Jereboam II of Israel and beyond, as shown by the list of Judean kings (see Introduction to the book of Hosea). The prominence of the numbers of Judean kings points to the final collecting and editing of Hosea's prophecies in Judah, probably after the collapse of the northern kingdom in 722 B.C.

A STARTLING AND SHOCKING WORD

The word of Yahweh to Hosea is startling and shocking. *"When the Lord began to speak by Hosea, the Lord said to Hosea, 'Go, take yourself a wife of harlotry and children of harlotry, for the land has committed great harlotry by departing from the Lord'"* (Hos. 1:2).

How could God command such a thing? And to one of His faithful prophets, no less. It was after the Lord had begun to speak through Hosea that this seemingly abhorrent command of the Lord came to him. Other prophets engaged in radical symbolic actions, such as Isaiah walking naked through Jerusalem (Isa. 20), or Ezekiel refusing to mourn his dead wife (Ezek. 24:15–18). This command to Hosea, however, seems to violate Yahweh's own standards of morality.

Because of this difficulty, some have tried to explain the passage as mere allegory or vision with no basis in Hosea's life. This is not a satisfactory explanation of the text. The account of marriage to a specific woman (Hos. 1:3) and the subsequent narrative about the birth of the children indicate that this is the record of the concrete experience of Hosea.

In our interpretation of this verse, we must bear in mind that Hosea was called by God to experience an actual recapitulation in his own marriage, of God's betrothal of Israel as His bride of Sinai. So the woman Hosea is called to marry was either sexually pure, as Israel was spiritually pure before committing apostasy in adultery with other gods, and committed adultery after marriage, or she was already involved in some form of adultery, or Hosea, expressing God's consistent love for Israel in spite of its spiritual adultery, was commanded to marry a prostitute.

A further factor to keep in mind is that the construction *wife of harlotry* is found only here in the Bible. The word used for harlotry is a general word for sexual misconduct, which need not imply that of an unmarried prostitute but could include adultery as well. In fact, it is used in parallel with *adultery* in 2:2. Moreover, the common words for prostitute or cult prostitute are not used here. "Harlotry" is translated from the Hebrew word *zĕnûnîn*, from the verb, *zānâ*, "to commit fornication, to be a harlot." So, we wonder, exactly what does "wife of harlotry" mean?

Various alternatives have been proposed by expositors of this text. Andersen and Freedman in *The Anchor Bible* propose that the woman was sexually pure when she married Hosea and later defiled the marriage by being unfaithful.[1] Hans Walter Wolff suggests that ordinary Israelite women who worshiped Baal would engage in an act of "sacred" fornication prior to being married. Thus the woman Hosea was to marry could have been a sexually defiled Israelite, but not a prostitute in the professional or cultic sense.[2] James Luther Mays, on the other hand, considers that the woman was a cult prostitute from the worship of Baal.[3] Certainly her immoral lifestyle before and after marriage to Hosea would have been a part of the ethos of the general promiscuity engendered by the flourishing Baal fertility cults of the time.

We must also ask whether the woman is the same person as the unfaithful wife of chapter three. God tells Hosea, *"Go again, love a woman who is loved by a lover and is committing adultery"* (Hos. 3:1).

The simplest solution to this question and the various alternatives we have cited is to take the text of Hosea as it stands. God told Hosea to take a *wife of harlotry*, to marry a woman who was involved in some form of prostitution and after marriage returned to her former lifestyle. It is certainly tempting to read into the text that she was a cult prostitute, even though a strong case cannot be proven from the text itself.

The salient point is that Hosea was called to make the same choice that was before God. The prophet was commanded to select and marry a woman who was involved in physical adultery just as God was confronted with the choice to be faithful to the people of Israel who were committing spiritual adultery by departing from the Lord.

Here we have the first clear rendition of the central theme that will reoccur constantly throughout the symphony of unqualified grace in the book of Hosea. It is the haunting, pulsating theme of unbroken love from a broken heart. God cannot give up His bride of Sinai regardless of what unfaithfulness she has committed.

We must linger to listen to this theme and allow it to capture our minds. It must become like a familiar song that we hear and then cannot get out of our minds for days. The theme of the unqualified love of God grips our repetitive thought patterns for a lifetime—for eternity. God chooses to choose us even when we have rejected His faithfulness. There are no depths to which we can sink where He will not find us and seek to woo us back into a right relationship with Himself.

This is not "cheap grace." It demands that God's mercy outreach His righteous judgment. And this is the other heartrending theme that adds counterpoint to the grace notes of the symphony of the book of Hosea. We hear both themes throughout the book, almost as if they are competing for dominance. We hear surges of yearning love (what the Scots call "leal love," love that is loyal, lasting, indefatigable, faithful) superseded and at times mingled with crashes of the tympany of wrath and the trumpet call for obedience.

Over the years, as I have preached or taught the Book of Hosea, I have found that it is crucial early on to personalize the dilemma of God in dealing with Israel's unfaithfulness by talking about the cross in the heart of God. There was a cross of judgment and forgiveness in God's heart before there was a cross on Calvary. Golgatha revealed God as both the just and the justifier (Rom. 3:26).

This becomes very real when we consider honestly God's problem with each of us. He cannot wink at our sin that separates us from Him or our sins that express our rebellion. At the same time, He must find a way to confront us and heal us. The astounding realization is that He persistently chooses to be our God regardless of what we've done or been. Amazing love, indeed. But love that we can never take for granted. Trifling with that grace will not change God, but it can change us — we can drift so far that we no longer cherish being chosen and become incapable of confession and absolution.

HOSEA'S CHILDREN AND GOD'S CHILDREN

That's exactly what happened to Israel. The naming of Hosea's children is a stark reminder of this. We will consider the names of the children as evidence of God's judgment on Israel's descent into the morass of apostasy. In directing Hosea to name his first son "Jezreel" God says, *"Call his name Jezreel, for in a little while I will avenge the bloodshed of Jezreel on the house of Jehu and bring an end to the kingdom of the house of Israel. It shall come to pass in that day that I will break the bow of Israel in the Valley of Jezreel"* (Hos. 1:4–5).

The name *Jezreel* carries a double meaning. Literally, it means "God sows," conveying the image of God as the giver of life. Jezreel is also the name of the valley-plain between the mountain ranges of Samaria and Galilee and of a city at the valley's southern edge at the foot of Mount Gilboa. Jezreel was the scene of Gideon's victory over Midian (Judg. 6–7). More relevant to its use here in Hosea, Jezreel was a scene of bloody atrocities by Ahab and subsequently, in retaliation, by Jehu. Some background is helpful.

Ahab and his queen, Jezebel, had a second palace at Jezreel. Their land adjoined a vineyard owned by a man named Naboth. It had been handed down to him from the generations. Ahab coveted the vineyard, and when Naboth would not sell it to him, Jezebel took things into her own hands. She arranged for Naboth to be honored at a feast, accused by false witnesses of blaspheming God and the king, and stoned to death (1 Kings 21). For this and her other evil acts, Jezebel came under the judgment of God. 2 Kings records that Jehu, King of Israel, after he had killed Ahaziah, her son and king of Judah, ordered eunuchs to throw Jezebel out of a window. Her blood was splattered and her body eaten by dogs. But Jehu's bloodshed did not stop there. He also had the seventy sons of the king beheaded and slaughtered the forty-two brothers of the king. The atrocities then turned to all the priests and worshipers of Baal. But in reality, Jehu was no more faithful to the law of God than those he had slain. He too came under God's judgment and died after reigning twenty-eight years.

So the name *Jezreel* was synonymous with one of the bloodiest periods in the history of Israel, a period abhorrent to God. The name *Jezreel* was tantamount to violence, murder, and the wanton shedding of blood. And now, according to God's own commentary on the name in these verses, the descendent of Jehu, Jereboam II, would be punished, there would be an end to the kingdom of Israel when her military might, the "bow of Israel," would be broken. This prophecy was fulfilled when in 733 B.C. Tiglath-Pileser III swept across the entire Galilean territory. At the time of Hosea's prophecy, it was still a warning. Jereboam II and the people could have repented. But they were in the spiritual stupor of the prosperity of the times.

The name given to the second child, a daughter, carries the impact of judgment on the lack of response to the name given to the first child. Once again God assigns and explains the name: *"Call her name Lo-Ruhamah, for I will no longer have mercy on the house of Israel, but I will utterly take them away"* (Hos. 1:6).

The name *Lo-Ruhamah* (*lōʾ ruḥāmâ*) literally means "not pitied" or "not loved." The Hebrew root *rhm* (*reḥem*-womb), as Wolff explains, communicates "the natural love parents have for their children, a close tie that joyfully and unconditionally embraces the child as the weaker person, especially in time of need."[4] The translation "pity" does not do justice to the deep and unconditional nature of the love expressed. The construction of the word could be, "She has not been shown mercy." The name, like that of Jezreel becomes what Mays calls a "message-name,"[5] a living symbol of the reality of God's judgment.

But what is the judgment? It is to give Israel what she wanted, as indicated in action and word: to live independently from God. She had not wanted to be loved by Yahweh and had squandered her love on false gods. In essence God said, "You have told Me in a million ways you do not want My love, My mercy; now I will call you by the name that expresses what you apparently have desired all along—to not be loved or bear the responsibilities of being My cherished people. Therefore I will call you 'not loved.'" As Andersen and Freedman put it, "Since Yahweh is always, in His deepest being *rahûm*, the negation of His love cancels His most basic relationship with His people."[6]

The people of Israel no longer acknowledged their sin or sought forgiveness. In response, the Lord said that He would no longer have mercy on them. The expressions are emphatic with "never again" and the combination of the infinitive and the imperative verb "lift up and take away," which is usually translated "forgive" here taken as an elliptical expression for "take away sin." In reality, God could not forgive what the people would not acknowledge. Awesomely, God gave them the desires of their heart.

Think of it on a human level. If in a marriage one of the persons consistently rejects the other's overtures of love, affection, and care, and acts with bristled resistance to affirmation and encouragement, refusing to give any sign of loving in return, he or she should not be surprised if one day the mate says, "Well, you act like you don't want my love, so from now on, you shall have what you've told me you want: no love!" The same could be true of friendship in which people refuse the gifts of love offered and receive what they have communicated they desired.

In a more profound way, in our relationship with God, what are we telling Him about our need for His love and mercy? Do we really want Him to be our God? If so, why are our prayers so short and shallow? Why do we resist His guidance? And why is there so little evidence of social righteousness and personal holiness in our daily lives? Why do we expect so little and are satisfied with even less? And what about the church? Could it be that the tradition-bound, culture-captured church of our time is exactly what we want it to be? Shocking? Yes.

Verse seven seems at first to be a relief from the severity of the judgment of Israel. God's word about Judah: *"Yet I will have mercy on the house of Judah, will save them by the Lord their God, and will not save them by bow nor by sword or battle, by horses or horsemen."*

17

How shall we interpret this very different attitude toward Judah? Many believe that it was the word of the Lord through Hosea as a warning and an assurance of mercy to Judah in preparation for threatening events to come. Others have suggested that this verse is an addition by an editor in Judah after the fall of Israel in 722 B.C. If so, the deliverance referred to for Judah probably is the miraculous escape of Jerusalem from destruction when under siege from Sennacherib in 701 B.C. during Hezekiah's reign. When the Assyrians were camped outside of Jerusalem, one night 185,000 of the army died, and Sennacherib returned to Nineveh. The Lord had intervened in answer to the prayers of Hezekiah and the ministry of Isaiah.

But remember that 115 years later, in 586 B.C., Jerusalem did fall in keeping with Isaiah's prophecy concerning the southern kingdom spoken at the time of the siege of Jerusalem. The years that followed, except for the reign of Josiah, were a steady decline in Judah leading up to the destruction of Jerusalem and the Babylonian exile. Judah did not hear the word of the Lord either from Hosea or Isaiah.

This points up our proclivity to assume that the judgment of God is meant for others but not for us. Pride and self-justification prompt us to slip out from under the impact of what the Lord is saying.

Recently, a woman came out of worship in my church in Hollywood after I had tried to be unescapably clear about God's call to repentance.

She said to me, "Right on, Pastor. That was a barn burner. Just what these people need. Hope they heard what you said to them!"

Why was she not among the large gathering of people on their knees in prayer at the front of the sanctuary? The same reason Israel did not listen to Hosea and Judah, assuming that what the prophet had said to them could never be true of Judah. But it was!

THE FINAL STAGE OF JUDGMENT

The name given to Hosea's second son and third child articulated the final stage of the judgment of God upon His people. If they were not startled by the shocking news that the kingdom would come to an end or that God's mercy would be cut off, there was little God could do but call them by a name that should shatter their spiritual pride in being God's chosen people. *"Now when she had weaned Lo-Ruhamah, she*

*conceived and bore a son. Then God said: 'Call his name Lo-Ammi, for you
are not My people and I will not be your God'"* (Hos. 1:8–9).

Lo-Ammi literally means "not My people" (*lō' 'ammî*). This message-
name should have stabbed Israel awake from her somnolent self-satisfaction. It should have been a stunning blow, for there was nothing more
fundamental to Israel's national identity than the covenant promises
of Yahweh: *"I will walk among you and be your God, and you shall be My
people"* (Lev. 26:12). And yet, Israel had chafed under the loyalty that
God demanded, the faithfulness required. The leaders and the people
resolutely tried to escape from being God's holy people. The naming
of this child told Hosea and should have warned the people that for a
time God will disown His people. They will be, *"not My people."*

Before we press on with the last two verses of chapter 1 of Hosea
and the future restoration of Israel, again we need to pause to allow
the full impact of the message-names of Hosea's children to sink in.

The book of Hosea alternates between severe judgment and tender
mercy. Our temptation as communicators is to move quickly to the
mercy passages and neglect the disturbing judgment. Our natural
inclination is to respond to our listeners who are facing hard times
and reach out to them with the mercy of God. In so doing, we may
neglect the people whose self-satisfaction may be keeping them from
God's best for their lives. Often we say to ourselves, "People already
know how bad they are; they need to hear how great is God's grace."
We can no longer get away with that simplistic approach to the
gospel. You and I are teaching and preaching at a time that matches
the spiritual conditions in Israel more than we may want to acknowledge. Our communication of assurance to those who are caught in the
syndrome of self-condemnation as a result of the psychological con-
ditioning of childhood or growing years, must be coupled with confrontation with the truth of what God demands of all His people.
Persistent self-condemnation and self-complacency are both defenses
against the Spirit of God and refusals to be whole.

God has called His people to greatness. That greatness is to be
expressed in our character, our relationships, and our servanthood in
both church and society. The refusal to accept our calling to greatness
as God's people is expressed in our commitment to smallness of
vision for ourselves and the church.

The names God called Hosea to give his children not only reveal
God's judgment of Israel in the eighth century B.C. but expose the

progressive drift from Him in any age. That results in what Jesus called the unforgivable sin (see Matt. 12:22–37). It begins with the pride of refusing to accept our own spiritual emptiness and insulate ourselves against admitting our need. Then this pride progresses to the stage where we think we have nothing to confess. Usually we try to justify our handling of failures or inadequacies, or we blame others, life, and circumstances for our failures, or we cover our failures by trying harder to be adequate. Finally, we become closed to God's Spirit. We resist claiming Christ as the source of our strength for the challenges and difficulties we encounter in life.

Our first "no" to the Holy Spirit is a traumatic refusal. But after that, it becomes easier to withhold ourselves from intimate fellowship with God. Ultimately, we become self-satisfied and mediocre. We are calloused toward the ministry of the Lord's Spirit.

That is why Jesus called the unforgivable sin the blasphemy against the Holy Spirit. This callousness led the Pharisees and scribes in Jesus' day to denigrate His work by saying that Jesus was possessed by Beelzebub, the prince of demons. These legalists were so insensitive to God's goodness and mercy that they were able to insult and defame God.

For us, it's possible to say "no" to God so long that we are no longer capable of saying "yes," much less receive His remedial judgment. That was the condition of the spiritual and moral life of Israel in Hosea's day. Sadly, it is no less true of our own day. Today, however, the situation is complicated by the fact that personal piety is often separated from the responsibilities of Christian living and actually is used as a basis of self-justification and resistance to judgment. People feel that if they believe in Christ, pray their prayers, and participate in church activities that they have become "good Christians" and have fulfilled their obligations. Many are not growing in their faith, leading others to Christ, or involved in ministry to heal the sores of suffering in our society. The frightening thing is that we can resist so long that we no longer desire to respond to what God is calling us to be and to do. It causes pain in the divine heart of God.

This is what Paul called grieving the Holy Spirit of God. *"And do not grieve the Holy Spirit of God, by whom you were sealed for the day of redemption"* (Eph. 4:30). The Greek word Paul uses for "grief" is a very poignant human term to express sorrows. The admonition is set in the midst of a list of things we are to do or refuse to do because Christ is

Lord of our lives. Paul is very specific about the implications of sainthood. He calls for absolute love, holiness, purity, honesty, and integrity and challenges us to be to others what God has been to us. "And be kind to one another, tenderhearted, forgiving one another, even as God in Christ also forgave you" (Eph. 4:32).

Paul's use of the word *grieve* to describe God's reaction to our resistance to His love is consistent with His exposure of His yearning heart revealed through Hosea. We can identify with that grief. We all have people in our lives over whom we grieve. We feel the conflicting emotions of wanting the best for them and, at the same time, experience the frustration over having our efforts to help them resisted.

A friend of mine whose son resists and rejects both his affirmation and his correction, was aching over what to do. "You know," he said with anguish, "for the first time in my life, I think I understand the heart of God. I know what it's like to grieve over someone I love."

When we suffer that kind of pain over difficult people in our lives, we sense how God feels when we resist being loved by Him or refuse to obey His guidance. By identifying our hurt when people we love stiff-arm our love or turn their backs on our caring, we can empathize with God's grief for us.

And what grieves Him? Anything that blocks the free flow of His love and forgiveness. Any idolatry that elevates the people, possessions, or positions of our lives to the status of being gods in our lives. Any defection from our calling to serve God by being servants of people and their needs. Any tolerated injustice or unrighteousness in our society.

Whenever we speak of the judgment of God, it is so crucial to make very clear what He expects so that we can measure our lives by His standards. Early in my ministry, a parishioner said to me, "Lloyd, I sense your dissatisfaction in your people, as if you want us to become something more than we are. But you are not giving us a clear vision of what we are to become."

The man was on target. Prophetic teaching and preaching is not grumbling about people or using the word *judgment* as a general catchall for their unclarified inadequacies. It is only in the light of what we are meant to be that we can experience God's authentic judgment. Here, at least for openers, is what I sense God desires and longs to inspire in His people today:

1. An unmitigated acceptance of His absolute sovereignty over our lives and our calling to know, love, and obey Him as our Father,

2. An unreserved acceptance of His love and forgiveness through Jesus Christ His Son, our Lord, and an experience of repentance, conversion, and rebirth to new life in Him,

3. An unlimited commitment to Christ as Lord and a wholehearted dedication to be His disciples,

4. An unfettered infilling of the power of His Spirit, a character molded by the fruit of the Spirit, and a life equipped by the gifts of the Spirit,

5. An unswerving dedication to daily prayer and Bible study to discern and receive strength to do the will of God,

6. An unhindered participation in the worship, study, and fellowship of the church and a willingness to share in the renewal of the church as the people of God,

7. An unqualified response to the call to be ministers to serve the needs of others,

8. An unrestrained willingness to share our faith and introduce others to Christ,

9. An unimpeded involvement in mission to the suffering, the hungry, and the poor in body or spirit in the community, nation, and world, and

10.   An unstinting stewardship expressed in tithing and giving beyond the tithe for the Lord's work and to individuals in need.

These are only rudiments of basic biblical faith. Too much to expect? It would seem so among many Christians and churches today. And yet, God expects so much more as an expression of an intimate relationship with Him and our awesome calling as saints. Our righteous Judge confronts us with what we are and have failed to be and do.

This contemporary excursion heightens our sensitivity of God's judgment on Israel. We can no longer smack our lips in consternation over the sins of God's people in Hosea's time. The feckless faith we have accepted, the culture-bound church we have accommodated, and the humanistic society we have tolerated should make the people of God today candidates for the name *Lo Ammi*. And our sensual, sex-centric, pornographically saturated culture might even make the priests of Baal blush!

Would God ever give up on us? Would He ever bypass the church to get His work done in the world? We dare not presume. Our hope is in God's faithfulness. His judgment is meant to restore us to a right relationship with Him. We fall on the knees of our hearts. It's the only spiritual posture in which we can fully appreciate the last passage of chapter 1 of Hosea.

RESTORATION AND NEW LIFE

Yet the number of the children of Israel shall be as the sand of the sea, which cannot be measured or numbered. And it shall come to pass in the place where it was said to them, "You are not My people," there it shall be said to them, "You are the sons of the living God." Then the children of Judah and the children of Israel shall be gathered together, and appoint for themselves one head; and they shall come up out of the land, for great will be the day of Jezreel! Say to your brethren, "My people," and to your sisters, "Mercy is shown." (Hos. 1:10-11)

The contrast of this passage with the previous verses of judgment could not be greater. Israel turned her back on the covenant with Yahweh. The negation of God's mercy and His call to be His people converged to portray Israel's doom. But here is a radically different picture of Israel restored to prosperity, peace, and harmony with Yahweh.

This passage should not be wrenched out of its context as a text for the preaching or teaching of grace and new beginnings. It can only be fully appreciated after a penetrating exposition of God's judgment in 1:3-9. The bracing news of God's judgment prepares the way to hear the good news of His restoration.

Hosea reaches back to the promises given to the patriarchs— Abraham, Isaac, and Jacob—to multiply their descendants beyond measure (Gen. 15:5; 22:17; 32:12). This appears to be a complete reversal of the decimation of the people and the land envisioned later in the book of Hosea in 4:3, 10; 9:12, 16; 13:16. Instead of being a contradiction, it is a vision of future hope beyond the time of destruction. In the future the people will suffer the consequences of rejecting Yahweh, but He will not give up on His people.

To emphasize the great restoration, Hosea prophesies that the same place the people heard that they were no longer God's people, there they shall be called *"sons of the living God"* (1:11). We might expect their new designation to be *My people*, as in 2:1, corresponding to the name *not My people*. But here the emphasis is on *the living God* who alone has the power and mercy to bring about the restoration.

23

The reference to Yahweh as *living God* also underlines the contrast between Him and the idols (Josh. 3:10; 1 Sam. 17:26; Pss. 42:2; 84:2). It highlights His role as the sole giver of life, an attribute Israel had forgotten in seeking hope of fertility from the Baal gods.

Most important, the power of Yahweh as life-giver is absolutely essential to the restoration of Israel after the radical judgment communicated by the previous verses and repeatedly throughout the rest of the book. Hosea had no other place to look than to Yahweh for new life after the judgment (Hos. 6:1–2). The juxtaposition of verses 9 and 10 serves to highlight the power of Yahweh to bring good out of evil, to reverse any situation; in essence, to bring resurrection out of death. What is impossible for us is possible with God (Mark 10:26–27).

And the propitiation goes further. Not only will the population expand, but the rift between the southern and northern kingdoms will be healed. They will appoint for themselves *one head,* which probably indicates a new king, as does the reference to David in 3:5.

The next promise, *"They shall come up out of the land"* (1:11) has been interpreted in various ways, from it being a reference to Israel's fruitfulness, to the return of the exiles, or to a foreshadowing of the resurrection. Wolff suggests that in keeping with the multiplication of people, reference to the "living God," and the meaning of Jezreel as "God sows," that this verse gives us another image for the fruitfulness of Israel, that is, they will sprout up.[7] A prevalent interpretation claims that Hosea uses Exodus imagery referring to a return from the exile he has prophesied. Andersen and Freedman propose that *come up out of the land* could mean raised from death, since land can be used as a term for the underworld. They say, "Recognizing Hosea's capacity for using language with more than one level of meaning, we suggest that the statement, 'And they shall come up from the land' has two senses, one historical (the Exodus), one eschatological (resurrection). . . .The emphasis on Yahweh as the living God thus continues."[8]

What is salient is that God will perform the miracle of regeneration and new life out of the death experience of judgment. What could have been the end is only part of a new beginning. *"The day of Jezreel"* intensifies this hope. This time, instead of referring to defeat and bloodshed (1:4–5), now its etymological meaning shines forth as "God sows."

As the name *Jezreel* now is given positive meaning, so, too, the names *Not My People* and *Not Pitied* are transformed. They appear in the plural, which indicates that Israel as a people is now the focus, not just Hosea's children. However, it should never be forgotten that Hosea's traumatic naming of his children at God's command provides the background for this passage. The reversal is complete—the three names signifying judgment now signify new life and harmony with Yahweh.

We can imagine the hope these promises provided for Israel amid the ruin of the northern kingdom in the eighth century and during the destruction of the southern kingdom in the sixth century. In the first century A.D., the apostles saw these promises in the light of Jesus Christ, the Savior of the world. Paul quoted them to focus God's calling not only on the Jews but Gentiles, who through faith in Christ are also called *My people* (Rom. 9:25–26). Another remarkable passage is in 1 Peter 2:10. Peter speaks of God's elect, the Christians scattered through the Dispersion (1:1), as *"a chosen generation, a royal priesthood, a holy nation . . . who once were not a people but are now the people of God, who had not obtained mercy but now have obtained mercy"* (1 Pet. 2:9–10).

As we look at this passage from Hosea with the refraction of the lens of Calvary and the perspective of the early church, we see not only what it meant to Hosea and both Israel and Judah, but what it teaches us about God's power to bring hope out of the ashes of human sin and rebellion. The theme reoccurs repeatedly throughout Hosea's prophecy.

It would be a neat homiletical package if we could say that the people of Israel repented as a result of being compared to a wife of harlotry or because of the shocking message-names given his children to confront them with their sin. But such is not the case. Hosea 1:10–2:1 is an expression of unmotivated grace, expressed simply because God could not give up on His people. The people could not say, "Aha, you see, we took God seriously and repented and in response He has made this grand promise to us!"

One of the deepest vestiges of our pride is that we think that we can manipulate God, even with our confession. Not so. God forgives before we ask. In fact, we confess not in order to be forgiven but because we already are. We plead for a chance of a new beginning not that God might devise one but because we know that God has always willed the rebirth and not the destruction of His people.

This is called prevenient grace, beforehand, unmotivated love at the heart of God's nature, offered not because we deserve it or even because we pray long and hard enough to earn it. This grace is not motivated into action because of how good or bad we are. That troubles some of us. We would like to think that God is gracious because of what we have achieved or because of our repentance for what we have failed to do or be. This passage, and so many others like it in Hosea, stand as a contradiction to this thinking.

And finally the Incarnation is the most convincing, undeniable evidence of God's prevenience. God came in Christ out of sheer grace. Christ went to the cross not because people asked for a sacrifice for their sins, but because God willed to redeem us. The disciples did not ask God for the resurrection of Jesus; God raised Him from the dead as a final victory over the power of death and evil. Pentecost was not God's answer to the pleas of Jesus' followers for power, but His sovereign unleashing of the Spirit through Christ whom He had appointed to reign over His new Israel, the church. At no time prior to the effusion of the Spirit do we hear the followers of Christ beg for regeneration; they were born again as an unsought for, free gift. And, after their regeneration, the interventions of the living Christ came as a surprise rather than a deserved blessing. The Lord was always out ahead of the early Christians leading the way. They soon found that prayer was to discover the mind of Christ for what He had planned rather than an effort to get Him to bless their own plans.

This puts into perspective God's mighty promise to restore His people in these concluding verses of chapter 1 and the opening of chapter 2 of Hosea. It would appear that God changed His mind, that He vacillated between wrath and grace. Some suggest that there are two sides to God's nature—judgment and mercy. I'd rather say that wrath and prevenient restoration are both expressions of grace, God's essential nature. He yearns and grieves over us. His confrontation and His conciliation are both meant to bring us back to Himself. One blasts at the ice jam in our hearts; the other melts the remaining chunks of ice that still block the flow of His Spirit in us.

It would be a distortion to say that if God's judgment doesn't alarm us, His love will woo us. The fact is He uses both — in all of us. He's never finished with any of us. So the preaching and teaching of the book of Hosea is for all our people: non-Christians, new believers, and seasoned saints. But our effectiveness as communicators in proclaiming both judgment and restoration as both alternate throughout Hosea will depend on the extent that we allow God to deal with our own need for His confrontive grace. Then our communication of Hosea will come flaming and burning out of our own experience and will have an irresistible ring of reality.

Is there any word from the Lord? Yes! A word of prevenient grace for what we are, expressed in severe judgment, and for what He elects to make us because He has chosen to be our God—a new beginning!

NOTES

1. Francis I. Andersen and David Noel Freedman, *Hosea*, vol. 24, *The Anchor Bible*, (Garden City, N.Y.: Doubleday and Company, Inc., 1980), 162.

2. Hans Walter Wolff, *Hosea: Hermeneia* (Philadelphia: Fortress Press, 1974), 14.

3. James Luther Mays, *Hosea, Old Testament Library Series* (Philadelphia: Westminster Press, 1969), 26.

4. Wolff, *Hosea*, 20.

5. Mays, *Hosea*, 27.

6. Andersen and Freedman, *Hosea*, 188.

7. Wolff, *Hosea*, 28.

8. Andersen and Freedman, *Hosea*, 209.

The Sin of Syncretism

Hosea 2:2–13

2:2 "Bring charges against your mother, bring charges; For she is not My wife, nor am I her Husband! Let her put away her harlotries from her sight, and her adulteries from between her breasts;

3 "Lest I strip her naked and expose her, as in the day she was born, and make her like a wilderness, and set her like a dry land, and slay her with thirst.

4 "I will not have mercy on her children, for they are the children of harlotry.

5 "For their mother has played the harlot; she who conceived them has behaved shamefully, for she said, 'I will go after my lovers, who give me my bread and my water, my wool and my linen, my oil and my drink.'

6 "Therefore, behold, I will hedge up your way with thorns, and wall her in, so that she cannot find her paths.

7 "She will chase her lovers, but not overtake them; yes, she will seek them, but not find them. Then she will say, 'I will go and return to my first husband, for then it was better for me than now.'

8 "For she did not know that I gave her grain, new wine, and oil, and multiplied her silver and gold— which they prepared for Baal.

9 "Therefore I will return and take away My grain in its time and My new wine in its season, and will take back My wool and My linen, given to cover her nakedness.

10 "Now I will uncover her lewdness in the sight of her lovers, and no one shall deliver her from My hand.

11 "I will also cause all her mirth to cease, her feast days, her New Moons, her Sabbaths — all her appointed feasts.

12 "And I will destroy her vines and her fig trees, of which she has said, These are my wages that my lovers have given me. So I will make them a forest, and the beasts of the field shall eat them.

13 "I will punish her for the days of the Baals to which she burned incense. She decked herself with her earrings and jewelry, and went after her lovers. But Me she forgot, says the Lord."

Hos. 2:2–13

We might like to linger on the safer shore of the mercy motif of Hosea 1:10–2:1. Instead, Hosea plunges us into deeper waters with even stronger currents of confrontive judgment before he offers a rescuing hand of further assurance of restoration. Where the first chapter focused on the call to marry a wife of harlotry and the message-names given the children, Hosea 2:2–13 concentrates on the failure of the marriage. The emphasis is primarily on the defection of Israel as the bride/wife of Yahweh.

We often hear and use the words *false gods*. In the first chapter, I spoke of the false gods of our own making and faking. The false gods of Israel were very real. They were the fertility gods of Baal. From the time of entering Canaan after the Exodus, Israel flirted with and then became devoted to Baal worship along with the belief in Yahweh. As we noted in the introduction, this is the sin of syncretism, the blending of loyalties to several gods. From her early times, Israel acknowledged Yahweh as the God of the patriarchs Abraham, Isaac, and Jacob and as the God of mighty acts of the Exodus and Sinai. But Israel seemed to have a clearer understanding of the role of Yahweh in the great events of the past than she did of His role in the constant supply of fertility and growth of crops and herds, particularly in the agrarian society of Canaan. She soon forgot that it was the promised land He had provided for her and that His first commandment forbade having other gods.

We can recall and empathize with how it happened. When the Israelites settled among the Canaanite people, they were inexperienced farmers. So they learned from the Canaanites. In adopting the Canaanite way of life, they observed that the people depended on their gods, particularly Baal, for the life-giving rains, produce of the earth, and reproduction in the herds. "What harm could be done by worshiping Baal along with Yahweh to ensure success and prosperity?" Israel wondered. So they, too, erected Baal shrines in their fields. (Remember that Gideon's father had them, and Gideon was called to tear them down as his first act of obedience to the Lord God.) Gradually the people of Israel were enticed into deeper mysteries of the sensual fertility cult with the hope that they could manipulate the gods for productivity. As the years went by, they depended more and more on Baal and less and less on Yahweh. The worship of the Canaanite gods along with Yahweh became firmly entrenched. Elijah did battle with this syncretism in his famous contest with the priests of Baal (1 Kings 17-18) and in his confrontation of Jezebel, who was a devotee of Baal worship. The problem of syncretism continued throughout Israel's history; Jeremiah took great pains to establish Yahweh's supremacy over the false gods to bring rain (Jer. 10:11-16; 14:22; cf. 44:17-19). Psalms 104, 147, and 148, among others, celebrate Yahweh's sovereignty over the natural world.

Chapter 2 of Hosea is one of the great prophetic passages stressing Yahweh's condemnation of Baal worship and stressing His power over the recurring and life-giving orders of nature in addition to His mighty acts in Israel's past. The Lord has the power to give and take away. In this passage the progression is that the Lord will first take away in judgment before He gives back His blessings.

An exposition of this passage is most penetrating when it is done in the context of the contemporary problem of syncretism in our lives and in the church. Each of us has beguiling false gods, and the church in our time has more than a few. A false god today that would correspond to Israel's syncretistic worship of Baal is whatever or whomever we give our allegiance and depend on for our meaning as persons—in addition to God. We can believe in God and at the same time worship at the shrine of power, prosperity, possessions, and position. It's possible to need people so much that we seek to draw from them the security and assurance only God can give us. And inordinate concern for our status, success, and the trophies of our accomplishments can also expose our competing gods.

The church is not exempt from the subtle and sometimes blatant sin of syncretism. We add to our worship of the Lord our devotion to heritage, traditions, numbers, buildings, programs, and popularity.

All these can be good things, but if they become our passion, they rob us of total dependence on God.

The essence of Baal worship was bartered devotion for desired provisions whether it was productivity, fertility, or prosperity. Our problem today is not just false gods but treating the Lord God in the same way Israel did by relating to the Baal gods. He becomes our means of accomplishing our ends. We barter for blessings while we maintain control over our own lives. In reality, we are the false gods of our own lives. Our wills stubbornly resist surrender; our own brand of spiritual adultery begins in our occluded hearts that refuse to be a throne for the reign of the Lord.

But whatever our false god, the Lord is a jealous God and with decisive judgment must expose the distorted allegiances that stand in the way of what the authors of the Westminster Shorter Catechism declared to be our chief end: To glorify God and to enjoy Him forever.

With that brief introduction about the historical and contemporary problem of syncretism, we are able to appreciate the severity of God's judgment of Israel's spiritual adultery in Hosea 2:2–13. Israel's primary relationship with God was at stake. If the passage seems harsh, we need only remember the depths of defection and degradation to which Israel had fallen. God's patience had been tried; His exasperation was acute. But He will not go back on His marriage vows to be Israel's God and to keep them as His bride/people. Again, the judgment is meant to lead to the desired reconciliation described in verses 14–23. Now let's first turn our attention to verses 2–13.

You will note that the name *Husband* in the New King James Version (NKJV) of Hosea 2:2–13 is capitalized as are the substituting pronouns. This is consistent with the understanding that this is God's word of judgment to Israel. The story line of the account of Hosea's marriage vows continues as the vehicle for the even greater pathos of God over Israel's spiritual adultery. Reading between the lines, Gomer has now left Hosea for other lovers. Eventually she becomes totally immersed in the cult prostitution of Baal worship. Hosea is left to raise the children alone. According to the Levitical Law, he would be justified in divorcing her and having her put to death. But it is his love and not the law that must somehow deal with Gomer. Now the prophet really feels his pounding heart beating at one with the righteousness and the loving-kindness of the heart of Yahweh. With the pain of his relationship with Gomer piercing his heart, the prophet speaks the word of the Lord to Israel.

Hosea 2:2–13 moves back and forth between Yahweh, the Husband's accusations against His unfaithful wife, Israel, and His threats in response to her behavior. Here we see how Israel has committed harlotry by departing from Yahweh (1:2). In these accusations and threats, some commentators have seen a legal process against the wife. But the overarching impact is less a clear legal proceeding and more an extended expression of the wounded heart of God: a mixture of grief, frustration, and anger mingled with yearning pain that reaches out to bring back the wayward wife, Israel. We find the goal of God/Husband in the hoped for repentance and return of the wife/Israel in 2:16.

The section begins with the call to the children to bring charges against their mother. The sense of the NKJV translation is better than the Revised Standard Version's *plead*, since the Hebrew verb always describes an accusation or confrontation, not just an appeal. The charges against the mother, here primarily Israel, are spelled out in the rest of the section.

The words, *"She is not My wife, nor am I her Husband"* (Hos. 2:2), have often been identified as a short divorce formula. In form this corresponds to the rupture of the covenant in 1:9 — *"You are not My people, and I will not be your God."*

While the wife/Israel may wish a divorce and the marriage is no longer functioning, the following statements show that God is not ready to renounce His claim on her. Divorce does not appear to be an option for Yahweh or for Hosea. We might have expected a completion of divorce or a call for the legal punishment, which would be death for adultery (Lev. 20:10; Deut. 22:22). Rather, the Husband admonishes the wife to change her behavior lest she be punished. God's and Hosea's goal clearly is not punishment but reconciliation with Israel and Gomer.

The call to *"put away . . . harlotries from her sight"* (or face) and *"adulteries from between her breasts"* probably indicates some physical marks of devotion to Baal or badges of her profession. These stand for the totality of her offense against her husband.

If the previous admonition is unsuccessful in turning the woman back to her husband, severe consequences will follow. She will be stripped naked in shame, no longer enjoying the husband's obligation to clothe her (Exod. 21:10), and will be left helpless, as at the time of her birth (Ezek. 16:4–8). She will then be subject to death, but not the traditional death by fire or stoning prescribed for adultery (Gen. 38:24; Lev. 21:9; Deut. 22:22–24). Rather she will die of thirst, which may indicate that Yahweh withholds life-giving rains, and the land becomes a desert.[1]

For a moment the spotlight falls on the children (2:4), recalling the children of harlotry and the removal of mercy in chapter 1. Here mother and children represent Israel in their guilt before Yahweh. The focus quickly shifts to the mother alone, whose guilt is established by her own rejection of Yahweh, her rightful Husband, for her lovers, later identified as Baal deities (2:8, 13).

Now we see her motive in pursuing these lovers—the gifts or harlot's wages she receives from them. This pay from her lovers includes the staples of life—food and clothing in the first two pairs, and oil for skin care. The last term translated "drink" is obscure but may refer to alcoholic beverages.[2]

The contrast between this statement of the wife/Israel and Yahweh's statements in 2:8–9 is very pointed, particularly with the repetition of the possessive pronoun throughout. Israel has committed two errors of judgment: first, she considered Baal, not Yahweh, to be the source of fertility and the staples of life (2:8); second, she failed to recognize Yahweh's ownership of everything (2:9), even when He provided it for her use and enjoyment.[3] This passage states one of the primary reasons Israel was tempted to worship Baal—the produce of earth and flock which sustained life. The people had lost the vision of Psalm 24 of God as the creator, sustainer, and source of life. "The earth is the Lord's and all its fullness, the world and those who dwell therein" (Ps. 24:1).

After quoting the wife's intention, the husband threatens to hamper her movement with barriers like those between fields so that she cannot contact her lovers (2:6–7). For Israel, this would mean blocking the way to the Canaanite shrines. The idea of restriction and discipline here is spelled out more fully in chapter 3, both for Hosea's wife (3:3) and for Israel (3:4).

The actions *seek* and *find* (2:7) have rich connotations in Hosea and elsewhere in Scripture. These are actions of lovers in Song of Solomon 3:1–4. Often they are used in the context of worship and petition. Here Israel seeks other gods in worship hoping to gain a favorable hearing and will not find them, that is, she will not gain a favorable hearing or any hearing at all. We find the same meaning in Hosea 5:6 where Yahweh says that the people will seek Him with flocks and herds (i.e., sacrifices of worship), but they will not find Him because He has withdrawn. The withdrawal of Yahweh here contrasts with His promise to the exiles in Babylon: "You will seek Me and find Me, when you search for Me with all your heart" (Jer. 29:13). In His teaching on prayer, Jesus encourages the disciples, "Seek, and you will find" (Luke 11:9).

The restriction of the wife's movement has one goal in mind: to bring her to her senses so that she returns to her husband (Hos. 2:7b). This expresses a hope, not an accomplished fact or even a certain outcome.

Here Hosea introduces the term *return*, which is sometimes translated "repent" and which plays a prominent role in the book. The people are called to return to Yahweh and are rebuked for their failure to return (i.e., renounce their disobedience and seek to follow Yahweh's word again; Hos. 6:1; 7:10, 16; 11:5; 14:1). Because of Israel's failure to *return*, Yahweh will *return* in judgment (2:9), threatening the people with a *return* to captivity in Egypt (8:13; 9:3; cf. 11:5). But beyond the discipline of judgment, there is hope that Israel will *return* (3:5).

Hosea's contemporary, Amos, presents a powerful series of condemnations of Israel when he describes her response to the discipline of Yahweh. After each hardship that fell on the people to try to turn them from their ways comes the refrain, "'Yet you have not returned to me,' says the Lord" (Amos 4:6–11). In that passage, in Hosea, and throughout the Scripture (e.g., Prov. 3:10–12; Heb. 12:5–11; Rev. 3:19), we see the discipline of God applied to try to turn people from their headlong plunge toward greater destruction.

The next verse (Hos. 2:8) is poignant with irony. Israel failed to acknowledge Yahweh as the true source of sustenance and instead used Yahweh's gifts for Baal worship. This irony is true of apostasy in any age or circumstance—we use the very gifts of God as tools of resistance against Him.

"She did not know." Here is no innocent ignorance, since it serves as an accusation that occasions the threat of the following verse. Rather, this is a willful turning from what Israel should have known.

Yahweh provided both the produce of the earth to sustain life and the riches that Israel enjoyed, the silver and gold in abundance, especially during the reign of Jeroboam II. The clause, *"which they prepared for Baal,"* could be translated "which they made into Baal."

The threat (Hos. 2:9) corresponds to the accusation—and the continuing theme—Israel had attributed Yahweh's gifts to the Baals; now

Yahweh threatens to withdraw the gifts. The repeated use of *My* emphasizes Yahweh's ownership in contrast with 2:5.

Hosea 2:10–13 amplifies the threat expressed in 2:9, the failure of the natural means of sustenance. This is no coincidental or accidental failure of a harvest. Yahweh appears as the active force in judgment over and over as the first person verbs continue through these verses.

In 2:10 the wife/Israel is threatened with exposure to shame, from which no one will be able to deliver her. The verb used here (*snatch, deliver*) is the same found in the previous verse when Yahweh takes back His wool. The use of the same word serves to contrast Yahweh's control and Baal's powerlessness before Him. In addition, the political implication may be included, that Israel's international allies will not be able to prevent the coming judgment.

Hosea 2:11 contains a series of three terms for cultic celebrations listed in ascending order of frequency, from annual festivals connected with the agricultural and pastoral year, to new moons, to weekly sabbaths. The beginning "mirth" and the closing *"assembly"* (translated "appointed feasts") refer to the whole series. This is not a critique of mirth or joy as such, since worship of Yahweh was to be characterized by joy. Rather, this is a rejection of the mirth or worship for other gods.[4]

The next verse indicates how Yahweh will end the festivals—by cutting off the harvest that the festivals celebrate. (Both figs and grapes matured in late summer, after which the great autumn festival was celebrated.) However, this is no brief interruption of a harvest of annually sown crops, but rather fruit trees ruined. The picture is of cultivated land returning to a wild state (forest) where the wild animals roam freely, a place of danger.

All this happens because of Israel's misplaced affections and worship—the festivals for the Baals, her lovers (Hos. 2:13). While Israel celebrates Baal festivals, adorning herself and actively pursuing her lovers. Yahweh stands forgotten. The final sentence communicates powerfully and briefly Yahweh's sad and wounded heart. In the Hebrew the object *Me* is placed first for emphasis. Moreover, *Me* immediately follows *lovers*, heightening the contrast. Forgetting Yahweh includes forgetting that He provides the gifts described in previous verses and failure to observe His word (Deut. 6:12; 8:11).

With that review of Hosea 2:2–13, we now are ready to reflect on the contemporary implications of what God has said to Israel and consider how we are to communicate this passage today.

THE TRAGIC TRANSITION

This passage provides us with a challenging confrontation of the tragic transition from adoration to apostasy, the abandonment of former loyalties. The stages are painfully clear.

The transition begins with the loss of praise to God as the source and sustenance of all. It is perilous to confuse what should be our basic conviction that all we have and are or ever hope to be or have is a gift from God. To begin to think we have achieved it ourselves is pride. And yet, how easy it is to use our gifts of intellect and think that our understanding is our accomplishment. We become proud of our talents as if we had acquired them ourselves. The same is true for our accumulation of the accoutrements of success, or our opportunities, or our privileges.

It is also misplaced praise to think of any person, group, or institution as the ultimate source of our blessings. An attitude of gratitude can be expressed to others, but it was God who provided these persons and decided to use them as His agents in our lives. When we say to a person, "Thank you for all you mean to me," the deeper implication should be, "I thank God for using you so effectively in my life."

In the same way we can be grateful for the church, our places of work, and our government as channels of God's provision, but never as the primary sources of our blessings. We are called to serve God in the church, our places of employment, or as responsible citizens, to be sure. And yet, no secondary channel is to be given our supreme loyalty as Lord of our lives.

Recently, I asked an outstanding Christian businessman what was the greatest difficulty he faced in living his faith. I expected he might answer that it was pressure, stress, or people problems. Instead, his answer was, "No question about it—my greatest difficulty is remembering that I could not breathe a breath, think a thought, envision a plan, earn a dollar, maintain strength, or remain faithful to what I believe if it were not for the moment-by-moment blessing of God. When I forget that, I'm in trouble."

When we lose our grip on that assurance, we begin to place our dependence on our own ability or on someone else's capacity to provide what we need. We make them diminutive gods. In an effort to assure a steady flow of provision from them, we forget God. Apostasy sets in. Even though it may be covered with the highly polished veneer of religiosity, at base, our time, devotion, energy, and commitment is given to a lesser god.

In preaching and teaching this section, I have often found it effective to begin at the end, with the poignant verse, *"'Then she forgot Me,' says the Lord"* (Hos. 2:13). That provides an excellent focus for four major points on contemporary syncretism: (1) How Israel forgot God as a result of losing the conviction that God is the source, sustainer, and sovereign of all; (2) how we can forget God today in our worship of false gods; (3) how God jogs us with judgment because He will not tolerate other gods before Him; and, (4) how to keep a vivid awareness that God is our ultimate strength and hope through consistent repentance and daily renewal.

It is the awesome realization of God's unwillingness to divorce His bride/Israel, the church, or any of us—even when we have committed spiritual adultery by syncretizing our commitment to Him with false gods—that draws us back to Him in repentance.

George Matheson, Scotland's preacher-poet of another generation, penned one of his greatest poems after he faced several false gods in his life. The encircling darkness of progressive blindness, he feared, would hamper effectiveness as a preacher. His fiancée broke off their engagement when she learned he was going blind. But he picked up his pen and wrote words of renewed commitment to God, which have been read and sung for decades:

> O Love that will not let me go,
> I rest my weary soul in Thee;
> I give Thee back the life I owe,
> That in Thine ocean depths its flow
> May richer, fuller be.

And Matheson went on to become one of Scotland's greatest scholars and preachers of the Word.

NOTES

1. Wolff, *Hosea*, 34.
2. Ibid., 35.
3. Andersen and Freedman, *Hosea*, 231–232.
4. Ibid., 250.

CHAPTER THREE

Singing in the Valley

Hosea 2:14–23

2:14 "Therefore, behold, I will allure her, will bring her into the wilderness, and speak comfort to her.

15 "I will give her her vineyards from there, and the Valley of Achor as a door of hope; she shall sing there, as in the days of her youth, as in the day when she came up from the land of Egypt.

16 "And it shall be, in that day," says the Lord, "That you will call Me 'My Husband,' and no longer call Me 'My Master,'

17 "For I will take from her mouth the names of the Baals, and they shall be remembered by their name no more.

18 "In that day I will make a covenant for them with the beasts of the field, with the birds of the air, and with the creeping things of the ground. Bow and sword of battle I will shatter from the earth, to make them lie down safely.

19 "I will betroth you to Me forever; yes, I will betroth you to Me in righteousness and justice, in lovingkindness and mercy;

20 "I will betroth you to Me in faithfulness, and you shall know the Lord.

21 "It shall come to pass in that day that I will answer," says the Lord; "I will answer the heavens, and they shall answer the earth.

22 "The earth shall answer with grain, with new wine, and with oil; they shall answer Jezreel.

23 "Then I will sow her for Myself in the earth, and I will have mercy on her who had not obtained mercy; then I will say to those who were not My people, 'You are My people!' And they shall say, 'You are my God!' "

Hosea 2:14–23

Life has its valleys. Dark, shadowy places of haunting memories of previous failures; narrow passes of self-condemnation and remorse. Our valleys block our vision of the future and close us in on the past. These spiritual valleys are surrounded by mountain peaks of promise we did not grasp and hope we could regain if only we could climb out of the lowlands of remembered sin.

Hosea 2:14–23 teaches us how to sing in these valleys of life. And the song we are taught is one of hope. The passage is bookended by the reference to two valleys—Achor and Jezreel—both filled with anguishing memories of Israel's past failures, moving metaphors of disobedience. God excavates the memories of both and expunges them with forgiveness and the promise of a new covenant and His betrothal of Israel as His bride forever. Wolff affirms that this passage gives the first outline to the new covenant and provides the basis for the New Testament concept of the church as the bride of Christ.[1]

The passage is filled with reversals of previous judgments, providential care, and covenant faithfulness—all parts of a new song of hope for our valley.

THE VALLEY OF ACHOR

With mercy and longing for things to be right again between Him and His people, God says of Israel, *"Therefore, behold, I will allure her, will bring her into the wilderness and speak comfort to her"* (Hos. 2:14). Remembering that the goal of the previous threats of 2:2–13 was not destruction, but restoration, the *therefore* signals a propitious transition to what God will do about His bride. Though she forgets Him (2:13), He will not forget her; though she is helplessly entangled, He will help her. Yahweh will allure Israel into the wilderness so that she will be alone with Him, free of the enticements of the Baals. The wilderness recalls Israel's youth, the time between the Exodus from Egypt and the entry into the promised land.

In the wilderness, Yahweh will *"speak comfort to her"* (Hos. 2:14). In Hebrew, the literal meaning is "speak to her heart." The expression is found in the context of courtship (Gen. 34:3; Judg. 19:3) as well as in other passages communicating comfort (Ruth 2:13; Isa. 40:2). The message Yahweh wanted the people of Israel to hear was one of new deliverance and hope. *"I will give her her vineyards from there, and the*

Valley of Achor as a door of hope; she shall sing there, as in the days of her youth, as in the day when she came up from the land of Egypt" (Hos. 2:15). The very vineyards which were to be destroyed in judgment (2:12) will be restored. Yahweh's goal is not to leave Israel in the wilderness of the exile to come, but to return her to the land and the vineyards of her own land.

The metaphor of the "door of hope" in the Valley of Achor, which is to be the motivation of a new song, needs to be explained. The Valley of Achor would have been the last place Israel would have expected a doorway to hope and joy.

For the people of Israel, the Valley of Achor was synonymous with failure. It was a kind of code name for defection. They knew well the story of how their ancestors under Joshua captured the city of Jericho. The instructions then had been made clear: all the spoils of the defeated city were sacred, and no one was to keep anything for himself.

But a man by the name of Achan refused to obey. He took a valuable robe, 200 shekels of silver, and a gold bar and hid them under his tent.

Meanwhile, not knowing about Achan's disobedience, Joshua led the army on to attack a place called Ai. That should have been an easy victory. Instead, Israel's forces were repulsed. Following on the heels of the spectacular victory over the formidable city of Jericho, it was a painful defeat for Joshua. He wondered why the Lord had not blessed him with victory. The commander knew something was amiss between the people of Israel and the Lord. Joshua put on sackcloth and ashes and prayed to the Lord to show him what was wrong.

It was then that Achan's sin was revealed, and Achan and his family were executed for their disobedience. This judgment took place in a valley that was subsequently named the Valley of Achor (Josh. 7). The word *"Achor"* was a technical term for the breaking of a taboo. "Therefore, the name of the place has been called the Valley of Achor to this day" (Josh. 7:26).

The Valley of Achor was seared into Israel's national mind as a dark page in her history. And the people who heard Hosea's prophecy knew exactly what the Valley of Achor meant. For them it meant a terrible failure. And it is in that context that they would have heard God's analysis of their own period. They were responsible for their eighth-century Valley of Achor because of their corruption, idolatry, and rejection of God.

But in spite of all that she had done in forgetting God, He was now saying that He would transform Israel's repetition of Achan's sin into a door of hope.

This promise has profound personal meaning to us and the people to whom we will communicate it. We all have our Valleys of Achor, memories of sin and failure. The liberating news is that the One who offered a door of hope to Israel came in Christ to be that door. With divine authority, Christ said, "I am the door. If anyone enters by Me, he will be saved . . . . I have come that they may have life, and that they may have it more abundantly" (John 10:9–10).

Paul describes a person who has passed through Christ, who is the door to the abundant life of redemption, as a new creation. "Therefore, if anyone is in Christ, he is a new creation; old things have passed away; behold, all things have become new. Now all things are of God, who has reconciled us to Himself through Jesus Christ . . ." (2 Cor. 5:17–18). The cross and the resurrection is our door of hope. We have been forgiven. When we accept Christ as our Savior and Lord, we go through the door to new life now and for eternity. And all through our lives the door to repeated forgiveness stands open.

So when we have done the things we promised ourselves we would never do or drifted into old patterns of resisting God, the door of repentance and renewal is open before us. There is great hope in the Apostle John's vision of the open door in heaven, "I looked, and behold, a door standing open in heaven" (Rev. 4:1). We do not have to stay in our Valley of Achor; there's a way out.

So why stay in the valley? A primary reason for our reluctance to go through the door of hope is that we get locked in a syndrome. We keep going round and round in the same circle. For lots of reasons, we fail—circumstances, mistakes, poor judgments, mishaps, taking on too much, other people's goofs. And, like the people of Israel, we syncretize our belief in God with our diminutive gods, or, like Achan, willfully do what we know is wrong. Whatever the cause, we've got the failure of our lives staring us in the face.

But that's not all we have: along with the memory of failure and sin, we have that strange mixture of self-condemnation and the desire to justify ourselves. Given time, we think, we can work our own way out of our valley. We want to sing, "I did it my way," rather than singing the Lord's song. And the marching song for leaving our valley behind and passing through the door of hope is a response to God's love and a commitment to His future for us. We don't have to search far for the words of that song. Great hymn writers have articulated it for us.

Here's a song with which to stand on our feet:

> Beneath the cross of Jesus I gladly take my stand
> The shadow of a mighty rock within a weary land,
> A home within the wilderness, a rest upon the way,
> From the burning of the noon-tide heat and the burden
> of the day.
> I take, O cross, thy shadow for my abiding place
> I ask no other sunshine than the sunshine of His face;
> Content to let the world go by, to know no gain or loss,
> My sinful self my only shame, my glory all the cross.[2]

And then a song to get moving with commitment through the door of hope.

> Were the whole realm of nature mine,
> That were a present far too small;
> Love so amazing, so divine,
> Demands my soul, my life, my all.[3]

AN ANSWER SONG

Our song is an answer to the Lord's offer of this amazing love. He longs to hear it from us, as He did from Israel. *"She shall sing there, as in the days of her youth, as in the day when she came up from the land of Egypt"* (Hos. 2:15b). The word translated "sing" can also mean "answer." In response to Yahweh's wooing, Israel's heart will be won over, and she will respond His love. The response will be more than words; it will be an answer of commitment.

The offer of love always demands an answer. So the metaphor of the door also extends to the door of our own hearts, which must be opened before we have the motivation and the will to go through the door of hope. Now, "I am" with us, the reigning Christ, seeks to rule from the throne of our hearts. "Behold, I stand at the door and knock. If anyone hears My voice and opens the door, I will come in to him and dine with him and he with Me" (Rev. 3:20). And we sing, "Your love is but my answer, Lord, to you."

In Hosea 2:15, Yahweh remembers the day of Israel's youth as a time of willing obedience. The reference is to the liberated, joyous, singing people coming out of the bondage of Egypt before the stubbornness and disobedience described in Exodus and Numbers set in, and especially before the people's later syncretism with the Baals.

After the judgment and restoration described in this passage of Hosea, Israel will sing a new answer-song. *"'And it shall be, in that day,' says the Lord, 'that you will call Me "My Husband," and no longer call Me, "My Master," for I will take from her mouth the names of the Baals, and they shall be remembered by their name no more'"* (2:16–17).

The punlike polemic against the Baal cult is stunning. Worship of Yahweh had disintegrated to the extent that the names of Yahweh and the Baal god were used interchangeably. The name of Yahweh reached its lowest syncretistic deprecation when Yahweh was worshiped as Baal! But Yahweh looks forward to a new day. It will be a day in which Israel will no longer call Yahweh, "My Master." The word for "Master," or "lord" is the same Hebrew word as the name of the Canaanite god, Baal. Instead of confusing Yahweh with Baal, and seeking the security and sustenance of life from Baal rather than from Him, Israel will call her God, *"My Husband."* The term carries both the endearment and the intimacy God's people had been elected to enjoy. But it implies the ownership and lordship that the people had erroneously squandered on the Baals.

Israel's new song of commitment will not include any duplicity with Baal. The Lord *"will take from her mouth the names of the Baals, and they shall be remembered by their name no more"* (Hos. 2:17). We know from experience that what's on our lips is first in our minds and hearts. So the implication here is a total transformation, a new creation, a new inner nature. Not only will pagan Baal shrines and worship be removed from the land but from the distracted devotion of Israel's heart.

Can this really happen? Can human nature be changed? Can we be liberated from false gods and make an unreserved commitment to God? Sadly, as we will learn from the later minor prophets, it did not happen. It took the transforming power of redemption—a Calvary, an empty tomb, and a living Savior—to create the "new man" Paul talks about in Ephesians. The mighty metamorphosis of human nature is nothing less than a miracle of God through Christ. He elects us, calls us, and gives us the gift of faith to accept His love and forgiveness, and fills us with His own Spirit. All that Paul prayed for the Ephesians in 3:14–19 can be the description of our transformation. It becomes a triumphant personal song when we change the pronouns from second person to first person. Then we can pray it again with deeper meaning in the original second person as our prayer to others:

> For this reason I bow my knees to the Father of our Lord Jesus Christ, from whom the whole family in heaven and earth is named, that He would grant *me*, according to the riches of His glory, to be strengthened with might through His Spirit in the inner man, that Christ may dwell in *my* heart through faith; that *I*, being rooted and grounded in love, may be able to comprehend with all the saints, what is the width and length and depth and height—to know the love of Christ which passes knowledge; that *I* may be filled with all the fullness of God.   (Eph. 3:14–19)

We are free to make that our prayer because God is more ready to answer than we are to ask. He at one time motivates it and mediates the answer. He is faithful to His covenant to be our God and consistently calls us back into relationship with Him.

COVENANT LOVE

Thus, in Hosea 2:18 the image changes from marriage to the covenant and what Yahweh will do to reverse His threat in 2:12 to destroy the animals of the field. He will not only preserve them, but He will end the enmity between humankind and wild animals. Added to this, Yahweh promises to remove the threat of war with other nations. Because of Yahweh's protection, and not the false security of other gods, Israel can *"lie down safely"* (Hos. 2:18; cf. Lev. 26:6).

The picture of peace focuses our minds on the greater safety and serenity offered us in the new covenant. Through reconciliation with God through Christ's blood, we experience lasting peace. It is the peace of forgiveness, profound trust, and the assurance that God will provide exactly what we need to face each hour. Peace is the gift that is given in the valley after we go through the door of hope. The enmity between us and God, between us and others, and between us and the natural world is over. Peace is knowing we belong to God forever.

This is the magnificent assurance of the next verses of the section of Hosea we are considering. Verses 19 and 20 reaffirm not only the length but the depth of God's covenant. *"I will betroth you to Me forever; Yes, I will betroth you to Me in righteousness and justice, in lovingkindness and mercy; I will betroth you to Me in faithfulness, and you shall know the Lord"* (Hos. 2:19).

THE BASIS OF HOPE

The text provides a moving basis for an entire sermon or class on the theme of the nature of God as the basis of hope. The key words offer a natural progression: righteousness, justice, lovingkindness, mercy, and faithfulness. All these qualities of God are the basis of our hope.

God's righteousness is the foundation on which we build our hope. It means that He is always consistent with His own nature and promises. He fulfills the covenants He has made.

Justice is often paired with righteousness (1 Kings 10:9; Ps. 89:14; Amos 5:24). Through His commandments and regulations, Yahweh has clearly defined how we are to live in relationship with Him and with one another in community. He is the judge of the whole earth (Gen. 18:25) and maintains order by His just decisions (Ps. 7:8; 9:8; 96:13).

The Bible celebrates Yahweh's lovingkindness. He acts kindly to maintain the relationship established by His covenants. He will remain steadfast and immovable to "hold fast My covenant" (Isa. 56:4,6). Yahweh keeps His covenant with His reliable love (Exod. 20:6; Deut. 5:10; 1 Kings 8:23; Ps. 89:28; 106:45).

You will remember the deeper meaning of mercy from our discussion of the term in chapter 1 of Hosea. We noted there that the word derives from the word *womb* and thus denoted parental love or sympathy, particularly for one who is weaker or in need. As with *"lovingkindness,"* mercy is demonstrated in Yahweh's actions. He forgives individuals or the nation (Deut. 13:17; Ps. 40:11; 51:1; 103:4), delivers from enemies (Ps. 25:6; 79:8; Isa. 30:18), and gives provision in the wilderness (Isa. 49:10).

The assurance of Yahweh's faithfulness is emphasized by placing the word last after the repetition of the promise, *"I will betroth you to Me."* The word *"faithfulness"* communicates Yahweh's constancy in character and deed toward His beloved Israel. It is set in direct contrast to the unfaithfulness of the wife/Israel in Hosea's prophecy.

Remember that these terms are Yahweh's own self-revelation through Hosea. The prophet did not think them up himself. It was Yahweh saying to His people, "This is what I am like and what you can always depend on Me to be to you." All the descriptive words are saturated with meaning from the way He dealt with Israel through history and her confessions in response. They communicate how Yahweh will be and act in any time or circumstance. We can stake our lives on them.

The capstone of all the attributes is given in a word that describes the relationship we can have with Yahweh when we respond to the attributes of His nature: "*You shall know the Lord.*" We might describe the attribute as the Lord is "knowable." We will focus on this in greater depth in our exposition of Hosea, chapter 4, but at this point it is vital to underline that the verb *know* connotes so much more than understanding information or theories or even personal acquaintance. Unlike the Greek word *to know*, *ginōskō*, to take in knowledge or to understand, the Hebrew verb implies intimate personal relationship. We often find it signifying the intimate sexual union between husband and wife: "Adam knew Eve his wife, and she conceived" (Gen. 4:1). While the sexual connotation is not intended here in Hosea, it certainly stands in the background of this passage which uses marriage imagery. And it helps us appreciate the depth of personal involvement Yahweh created us to experience with Him.

Knowing Yahweh includes the recapitulation of His nature in our character. A sure sign we "know" the Lord is that we express righteousness, justice, lovingkindness, mercy, and faithfulness to Him and in our relationships with others. That begins with personal acknowledgment of Yahweh's rule over all and devotion to Him without rival as He has revealed Himself to be (Hos. 2:8, 13; 13:4; Jer. 10:25). His sovereignty becomes profoundly personal in the "Thou-I" personal relationship He graciously initiates with us. However, knowing Yahweh is not fulfilled only in private or mystical experiences separated from community.

For example, righteousness with God comes to us through faith in Christ (Rom. 1:17), but our continuing right relationship is fulfilled in the demands of living in community — being to others what God has been to us, in care for those who don't know Him, the needy, those who are suffering, and in working to ensure justice in our society. Peace with God requires peace with others and active peacemaking. The breakdown of community that the prophets criticize is a failure of righteousness, a refusal to keep the covenant requirements of the law for community life. The righteous love God by loving their neighbors.

This was a basic thrust of the message of Jesus in His Magna Carta of righteousness in the Sermon on the Mount. The Beatitudes give us a challenging inventory of the extent to which our personal experience of the attributes of God have been reproduced in our character and relationships. He describes the qualities of the blessed—the truly joyous—those who know that they have been cherished and called to know God.

One of the most creative and challenging experiences we can have in our spiritual formation is to spend a month praying the Beatitudes morning and night of each day. We begin the day by confessing our poverty of spirit and our need to grow; our grief over our sins and our need for forgiveness; our desire to be leadable and our need to accept the bit and reins of the Lord; our longing to faithfully express righteousness in keeping the covenant and our need to be filled with strength to be obedient; our lack of mercy to those who are weak through failure and sin and our need to be as merciful to others as God has been to us; our desire to receive the lens implant of the Spirit to see God and His gifts in the natural world and in people and our need to be single-minded in willingness to do His will; our calling to be peacemakers and our need for peace in our own hearts; and our yearning to do what love demands and our need for courage even in rejection or persecution.

Then, in our prayers at the end of the day, we ask as we go back over the Beatitudes, "To what extent today have I lived out my commitment?" Each beatitude provides part of an incisive inventory of our application of our experience of this righteousness, justice, lovingkindness, mercy, and faithfulness of God. Few prayer disciplines will do more to help us realize how little we actually know God and how knowledge of Him needs to be expressed in our daily living.

THE DOOR OF OPPORTUNITY

Carrying through on the metaphor of the door with which we began, the door of hope leads to a door of opportunity. This door leads to people the Lord has prepared to receive His attributes through us. That was true for the Christians at Philadelphia to whom He spoke in His revelation to the Apostle John. "These things says He who is holy, He who is true, He who has the key of David, He who opens and no one shuts, and shuts and no one opens: 'I know your works. See, I have set before you an open door, and no one can shut it'" (Rev. 3:7–8). Philadelphia was located on one of the main trade routes in Asia Minor. The Christians needed to realize the strategic door the Lord had given them to share the gospel with the constantly changing procession of potential converts. And the bordering provinces were filled with potential converts to Christ if the Christians would become missionaries.

The same door of opportunity stands before you and me. Wherever the Lord has placed us is a strategic place to communicate the hope we have found in our Valley of Achor. Nothing is wasted, not even our disobedience and failures. They give us the healing knowledge of God, bring us to Him, give us empathy for people still on the other side of the door of hope. Most of the people around us are living in some valley of the memory of failure. They desperately need to see and hear the hope we have experienced through knowing God in the awesome attributes He revealed through Hosea.

John Masefield vividly portrays the adjoining doors of hope and opportunity,

> And God who gives beginning gives the end,
> A rest for broken things too broke to mend.
>
> ....
>
> The bolted door had broken in,
> I knew that I was done with sin.
> I knew that Christ had given me birth
> To brother all the souls on earth.[4]

One of the most moving accounts in history is of how Martin Luther ministered to Philip Melanchthon at a time when Melanchthon, a leading scholar of the German Reformation, was in a valley of spiritual despair. Luther wrote him, "From the bottom of my heart, I am against those worrying cares that are taking the heart out of you. Why make God a liar in not believing His wonderful promises, when He commands us to be of good cheer, and cast all of our care upon Him, for He will sustain us? . . . .Why then worry, seeing He is at the helm? He who has been our Father will also be the Father of our children. As for me (whether it proceeds from God's Spirit or from stupidity, the Lord knows), I do not torment myself about such matters."

But, in fact, years before that letter to Melanchthon, Luther *had* tormented himself. As a monk he had flagellated himself for his spiritual failures. His valley of Achor became a door of hope when studying Habakkuk 2:4, "But the just shall live by faith." He took up his pen and wrote "Sola!" (the Latin word for "alone") in the margin of the text. "The just shall live by faith alone" became the secret of knowing the righteousness of God for Luther personally and the battle cry for confronting the church and the complicated system of indulgences it had placed between people and God. Righteousness was a gift of God for Luther, but never a private one—it led him to a lifelong battle with the idolatry of the established church.

What Luther had experienced in his personal valley enabled him to encourage his friend Melanchthon. His letter may sound as if he had forgotten what he had been through himself. Actually, we are given a vivid picture of what life was like for Luther after he had gone through the door of hope in his valley. It is significant that Melanchthon's life verse became Romans 8:31, "If God is for us, who can be against us?" The words are inscribed in Latin over his study in his house in Wittenburg to this day. It is encouraging to know that our heroes and heroines of history also struggled to trust God's faithfulness and that renewed experiences of His lovingkindness refired their commitment to battle for righteousness in the church and society. They discovered that God was able not only to transform their valleys of Achor but valleys of worry and anxiety over the daily needs of life. The remaining verses of Hosea, chapter 2, help us to hope in the Lord in these valleys also.

THE VALLEYS OF NEED

"'It shall come to pass in that day that I will answer,' says the Lord; 'I will answer the heavens, and they shall answer the earth. The earth shall answer with grain, with new wine, and with oil; they shall answer Jezreel'" (Hos. 2:21–22).

Again, Yahweh clearly declares His supremacy as the source and sustainer of life. Jezreel, representing the nation, has obviously cried out for nourishment in the time of drought and agricultural privation predicted in Hosea 2:9. The valley of Jezreel, before an image of rebellion, will live up to the true meaning of the name, "God sows." Verses 21-22 are Yahweh's reaffirmation that He is creator and the sovereign over the interdependent aspects of the natural world for the production of the material needs of His people. They all belong to Him: the heavens with the sun and nourishing rain, the earth with its nutrients to enable germination and growth of the seed, and the plentiful harvest of grain, grapes, and oil. "My Father is the husband-man," Jesus had to remind Israel again in His day (John 15:1).

It is so easy to forget. Supermarkets are not usually the sanctuaries where we look at our basket full of food and while waiting for the checker to tabulate the cost exclaim, "The Lord provided all this and the money to pay for it as well!" Even those closest to the earth, farming its fields and tending its herds, are tempted to think it is their hard work that made it all possible or the refined methods of fertilization or mechanization that made it happen. Times of drought do shock us out of that daydream of self-aggrandizement. It's then that we are willing to call a prayer meeting. Even that may be a thing of the past with modern techniques of rainmaking.

Recently, in the late spring I was in Iowa to speak. A snowstorm covered the rich black earth with moisture that would later be the explanation for the plentiful wheat harvest. A farmer said to me, "Preacher, did you see the earth covered with God's manure?" Never thinking he meant the snowstorm, I said, "Well, no, what do you mean?" "What do I mean?" he replied with enthusiasm, "The snow of course. It's God's way of nourishing the winter wheat we've sown. He's behind every blessing you know! You people who live in the city sometimes forget that!"

The trip through the snowstorm to reach the Iowa town was worth the time and effort. My lexicon was improved by the simile. Now, sometimes when difficulties are blessings in disguise, I think, "Aha, God's manure!"

God is our provider. Even in our valleys of Jezreel, our resistance is not given deserved retribution but replenishment. We often think about what we deserve as we tabulate what God's quid should be for our quo. But what if we did get what we deserve in judgment? What if we had to pay for our sins and failures? Before our mind's eyes flash the scenes of the scenario of our lives, and we are overcome with wonder and praise for God's grace.

His goodness is no less stunning. Think of the times in the past He has stepped in to give us supernatural strength, insight, or courage. Our gratitude begins to soar when we think of the problems and the difficulties He has unraveled. God sows guidance as well as seeds that He might harvest His maximum plan for us.

There is no limit to what God is ready and able to do through us, around us, and in the people about whom we are concerned when we give Him the glory and leave the results to Him.

Worry in the valley of difficulty is rooted in lack of trust that God will provide. It becomes a habitual pattern. We get so used to being anxious that we would actually be uncomfortable without it. Like a narcotic, we become so addicted to fear that we cannot exercise our faith in God as our security.

It was this anxiety that led Israel to place her trust in Baal. The apostasy that resulted edged Yahweh and His righteousness out of first place in their lives. We can empathize: think of how important security and success become to us as individuals and to the church and what we are willing to compromise to assure a steady flow of them from others and our culture.

Sowing and Growing a People

The good news of the last verses of Hosea, chapter 2, is that Yahweh is relentless in His desire to have a people who will put Him and His righteousness above all lesser loyalties. He promises to sow and grow a people in the land who will produce the "fruits of righteousness" (Prov. 11:30) with stability and unswerving allegiance to Him.

Then I will sow her for Myself in the earth, and I will have mercy on her who had not obtained mercy; then I will say to those who were not My people, "You are My people!" And they shall say, "You are My God!" Hos. 2:23

After Yahweh's disciplining judgment, Israel receives mercy and communion with Him. Again the three names of Hosea's children are reversed. Instead of bloodshed, Jezreel will be a place where God sows. *No mercy* will be changed to *Mercy*, and *not My people* to *My people*.

The song of faith and obedience for the valley becomes the chant, *"You are my God."* It makes us the good ground that Jesus spoke about in the parable of the soils (Matt. 13:1–9). The seed of God's kingdom, His kingly reign and rule, "fell on good ground and yielded a crop; some a hundredfold, some sixty, some thirty" (v. 8). The seed may be small like the mustard seed (Matt. 13:31–32), but it will grow a stately person.

So the song in our valley is antiphonal. God sings, "You are My people!" and we respond, "You are my God!" The valley of failure becomes a door of hope, and the valley of furtive fear becomes the very place where God restores us. There's hope for you and me!

NOTES

1. Wolff, *Hosea*, 51–55.

2. Elizabeth C. Clephane, "Beneath the Cross of Jesus," *Hymns for the Family of God* (Nashville: Paragon Associates, Inc., 1976), 253.

3. Isaac Watts, "When I Survey the Wondrous Cross," *Hymns for the Family of God* (Nashville: Paragon Associates, Inc., 1976), 258.

4. John Masefield, *The Collected Poems of John Masefield* (London: William Heinemann Ltd., 1923) 125.

CHAPTER FOUR

Unbroken Love from a Broken Heart

Hosea 3:1–5

Get inside Hosea's skin. Feel the hurt and anguish. Sense the pain over the rejection of his love for Gomer. Identify with the dawning of the demeaning realization that she is caught in an addictive compulsion. Empathize with his desire to block his ears to the gossip about his wife's adultery. Allow your heart to be broken with his as he learns that she not only has other lovers, but that she has gone from flagrant promiscuity to cult prostitution to being sold into slavery. No longer a plaything of other men, no longer the sexual object of the sensual fertility rites, now she is the tool of the vicious sodomy of the slave traders. Give vent to the judgment, indignation, and the rage Hosea justifiably feels.

And the shame. Don't leave that out. A prophet's wife, an adulteress, a prostitute, a Baal worshiper, a sexual slave! Listen to your own voice chime with Hosea's pathetic cry of anguish, "If I never see that woman again, it will be too soon!"

Now try to imagine the consternation and utter astonishment Hosea must have felt when Yahweh commanded, "Go again, love this woman." The very idea sent shock waves through the prophet's heart. On the personal level, it meant vulnerability to be hurt again; on a religious level it meant the reversal of his justified condemnation of one who had become an anathema of all he believed as a prophet of Israel. How could Hosea do it?

The *how* was superseded by the motivation of the *why* of Yahweh's command. "*Go again, love a woman who is loved by a lover and is committing adultery, just like the love of the Lord for the children of Israel, who look to other gods and love the raisin cakes of the pagans*" (Hos. 3:1).

The source of the will and strength to follow the Lord's command would be the example *and power* of Yahweh's love for Israel. The choice Yahweh had made to love His people was the same choice Hosea had to make. He was to go to Gomer, who not only did not deserve reconciliation but had done every maligning thing she could do to scuttle his career and scathe his moral sensibilities.

There is a simplistic phrase that has often been used to describe Hosea: "A bad wife produced a great prophet." Half true. The call to love a compulsively rebellious wife led a faithful prophet to experience the greatness of God. The essence of that greatness is initiative love and reconciliation. We've spoken of the book of Hosea as a symphony of that grace. In chapter 3, the whole orchestra blends in a mighty crescendo of that prevenient, beforehand, undeserved favor.

Can we really empathize with Hosea? Few have had to endure the pain of a spouse like Gomer. But before we write off Gomer's psychological and character disorders as an extreme of what, thankfully, we have not had to face, we need to think of the pain and frustration we have experienced with loved ones and friends who have done us seemingly irreparable harm. Consider the people you have cut off because of what they have said or been. Now hear the call of God to "Go, love again!"

Most important of all, think of our own relationship to God. The full impact of this passage is experienced not just in Hosea's skin but in Gomer's. None of us naturally desires God. We are part of a fallen creation with a bent for willful independence from God's sovereign lordship of our lives. Because we find it humanly impossible to make Him Lord of our lives, He has had to be our Savior first. Our sins, though perhaps different than Gomer's, are no less serious. And the breathtaking wonder is what God came to earth in Christ to do for us on Calvary to atone for our sins and reconcile us to Himself.

Hosea, chapter 3, is that Gospel, that awesome Good News, in predated miniature. It is one of the clearest intimations of the Incarnation in the Old Testament. In it we find the limitless degree of God's love for humankind, for each of us personally, and what our attitude and action should be toward others who sin and those who have brought havoc to our lives as well as to their own.

But much as we try to personalize the message, we dare not miss that Gomer was a type of Israel and that God's reconciling love was for His wayward people. And the Incarnation Hosea 3 foreshadows is of an atonement that was cosmic, a once, never-to-be-repeated reconciliation of the world in time, on time, and for all time. It is beneath the cross that we move through an exposition of the verses of this spectacular chapter about God's unbroken love from His broken heart. We never really know how much a person loves us until we know how much he is willing to suffer for us; it is the suffering that measures the love. It is this quality of suffering love that is the focus of Hosea chapter 3.

"AGAINNESS" LOVE

The word *again* leaps off the page from verse 1. "Go *again*, love." The "againness" of God's repeated, indefatigable love for Israel is to be Hosea's purpose and passion (suffering love). "All human grace is but the reflex of the Divine."[1]

The word *love* is used four times in various forms in this first verse. It is used for the love of Yahweh for Israel, the love Hosea was to have for Gomer, the love she has received from her lover, and the love of Israel for the raisin cakes of the pagans. We might wish that contrasting words had been used. But the use of the same word highlights our own use of the word *love* for very different meanings. We speak of God's love, His love for us, our shallow affections, and our devotion to things. We say we love God and people but use the same word to express our love for places and things.

We have all seen the bumper stickers proclaiming love for everything from pets to places. The first person singular pronoun is followed by a heart shape and then the object. And so it goes: I love New York, Los Angeles, my dog, my cat, my car . . . and so on.

In Hosea 3:1 the use of the same term for *love* highlights the contrast between true and perverted love. The sensuality of adulterous love and love for Baal raisin cakes is set in bold distinction. Yet the use of the same word underlines the confusion of seeking true love in either the fleeting satisfactions of an adulterous affair or nutritionless raisin cakes of complicity with fake gods.

It is the againness of God's pursuing, persistent love in action Hosea is to emulate. Yahweh commands love that is no mere feeling but deliberate action. At this point Hosea probably was too wounded and hurt to feel love for Gomer. Yahweh knew that he would need a liberating reminder of His love for Israel to do what love demanded. It is only when we do what love demands that we have the feeling that love requires. If we wait to feel like it, we'll often put off the action required.

Over the years, I've counseled hundreds of people who faced the challenge of acting in love before they had a replenishment of the emotion of love. I think of one woman in particular. Her husband had broken their marriage vows repeatedly. The flickering embers of love for her husband were now turning to ashes. "What am I going to do?" she asked, tears streaming down her face. "I don't believe in divorce, and yet I can't go on with things the way they are."

Since she had decided to stay in the marriage regardless of her husband's behavior, I asked, "What would you *do* if you felt love?" She pondered the question for a long time and then gave me a list of things she would do to communicate love to her husband. After that, we talked about God's initiative love in Christ as the only source of instigative power to do what love demands. With a renewed experience of grace, she was willing to make a commitment to love her husband and trust the Lord for the rekindling of her feelings of love.

It worked. Acting in love brought the return of the emotions of love. The husband was so astounded by the love his wife expressed that after some time he came to see me. "Can't understand it!" he exclaimed. "After all I've done, my wife keeps on doing loving things for me. She tells me it's because of God's love for her and me. Guess I've drifted pretty far from Him myself. Will you help me?" Eventually, the man made a new commitment to Christ and got help with his compulsive sexual patterns. The couple is happily married today.

Nothing less than what this woman did is the challenge for all our relationships. We all experience people who have us on the ropes of exasperation. Our feelings of love seem long gone. The question isn't how we feel but what we are called to do to show love. We belong to God who never gives up on us and does not give us the luxury of giving up on others. We are Hosea's kin, part of a distinctly different people, God's people to express againness love.

At this point of an exposition of this passage, it's helpful to pause and ask, "Who is the Gomer of your life? To whom are you to go again and do what love demands?"

Hosea's love is to be like Yahweh's: deliberate caring for Gomer and commitment to her even while her affections are being given to another. Yahweh's love is not conditional on Israel's repentance. He loves His people even while they are looking to other gods, defying His command.

It is good to keep a finger in the Bible for ready cross-reference to Romans, chapter 5. We cannot deal with the radical demands of acting in love without consistent reference to the source of that quality of loving.

> The love of God has been poured out in our hearts by the Holy Spirit who was given to us. For when we were still without strength, in due time Christ died for the ungodly. For scarcely for a righteous man will one die; yet perhaps for a good man someone would even dare to die. But God demonstrates His own love toward us, in that while we were still sinners, Christ died for us.
>
> *Rom. 5:5b–8*

LOVE IN ACTION

Hosea's love for Gomer must begin by buying her from slavery. With first person intensity Hosea says, *"So I bought her for myself for fifteen shekels of silver, and one and one-half homers of barley"* (Hos. 3:2). This clearly identifies that Gomer had fallen into some kind of slavery. A homer was equal to about eleven bushels (Ezek. 45:11), and the going rate of a homer was about ten shekels. So in addition to the fifteen shekels, Hosea paid fifteen shekels worth of barley. The total price for Gomer's freedom was thirty shekels. According to Exodus 21:32, this was the amount of compensation paid to an owner for the killing of a slave, and it is generally concluded that this also became the price of a slave.

"So I bought her for myself . . . ." Such a simple statement of so profound an act! God's instructions were clear enough: "Go yet again. Love her. Bring her back home where she belongs even if you have to make yourself look like a fool to others." So, Hosea obeyed the call of God to incarnate God's kind of love for Israel. *"So I bought her for myself."*

The story has as much to do with what is not said in this verse as it does with the very clear meaning of Hosea's declaration. Obedience to his God's command required a loving heart as much as a loving act. Buying Gomer back would have meant nothing to God if Hosea's attitude was judgmental, arrogant, or resentful.

Here's the rub for us. We can do all kinds of good things for the wrong reasons and with the wrong spirit within. How much of our good works in the church are despised by our Lord because the heart is wrong?

Amos made that clear to us in his eighth century B.C. words to Israel: "I hate, I despise your feast days, and I do not savor your sacred assemblies. . . . Take away the noise of your songs, for I will not hear the melody of your stringed instruments. But let justice run down like water, and righteousness like a mighty stream" (Amos 5:21–24).

Flowing justice and streaming righteousness have to do with what the heart feels as much as what the hand does.

"Is this why our love often lacks redemptive power?" was the challenging question asked by Harold Cooke Phillips in his exposition of this passage.[2]

How to Discipline a Nation

In verses 3–5, God proclaims His plan for disciplining His disobedient people, and, again, Gomer images the nation Israel for us.

"You shall stay with me many days. . . ." Andersen and Freedman suggest that this is better translated "wait for me."[3] But the sense of the verse requires the presence of the one spurned and still caring. "Stay *with* me" is the way God does His healing. Yet, business is not to be as usual when Gomer returns home. It is not possible to pick up where things were before she ran off after her lovers. Nor was it possible for Israel to be restored to her place of blessing by the side of God as if nothing had ever happened. Too much pain has occurred, too much disobedience has been Gomer/Israel's response to the love of Hosea/Yahweh. Now must come a time for learning the lessons that must be learned, for working out what God is working in. Time is needed for the healing of the hearts of both Gomer and Israel.

A wife behaved badly toward her husband for some time. Over the years, her actions and attitude had all but destroyed the love and caring of her husband. Finally he had taken all that he could take and walked out on his shrewish wife. That desperate act was the needed shock therapy for his wife. She saw clearly what she had done, and she grieved for the pain she had caused. "I've learned my lesson. Come home and forgive me. Let's start over," was her plea.

In counseling with each of these two very dear people, both the raw wounds in his psyche and her regret were obvious. But space was needed now. Time needed to be given both for healing of his spirit but, perhaps more, for the "grooving in" of a new pattern of behavior on her part. If, indeed, new lessons had been learned, they needed now to be practiced until the sensitivity of her new way could overcome and replace the abrasiveness of the old. "Stay with me *many days*" (Hos. 3:3) because retraining old patterns will take that long!

For Gomer, sexual relations with both former lovers and faithful Hosea were denied her. For now, let there be a quieting and a healing of her tumultuous spirit.

And for Israel? "*For the children of Israel shall abide many days without king or prince, without sacrifice or sacred pillar, without ephod or teraphim*" (Hos. 3:4).

Notice again that the nation shall "abide many days" in a new style of life just as was required of Gomer. This chaste time for Gomer and this leaderless and celebrationless time for Israel were not to be the end of the story. They were the between time—between failure and restoration, between judgment and restoration, between weeping and rejoicing, between death and resurrection.

Notice that, as with Gomer, both legitimate and illegitimate relations are denied Israel. No king, no prince. There is to be neither holy sacrifice nor unholy pagan rite for Israel. For Gomer, there would only be the watchful, ministering presence of Hosea. For Israel, only the healing, patient, waiting presence of her God. And for both, for the time being, that would be quite sufficient!

Then, when the healing is accomplished, the restoration is completed. "*Afterward the children of Israel shall return, seek the Lord their God and David their king, and fear the Lord and His goodness in the latter days*" (Hos. 3:5). Do you hear the singing of chapter 40 of Isaiah? "The glory of the Lord shall be revealed, and all flesh shall see it together; for the mouth of the Lord has spoken" (Isa. 40:5).

We can have faith even in the midst of our suffering when we know the end of the story. When the doctor gives us the assurance that the pain of this present surgery will be finished in three days and I will be on my way home, I somehow quickly find the strength and patience to hang on. "Three days! I can handle that much!"

The excitement for us is that we do know the end of the story! Jesus' death was but a prelude to the resurrection. "All things work together for good to those who love God, to those who are called according to His purpose" (Rom. 8:28). And the end of the story of Gomer was restoration as the wife of Hosea and keeper of his household. The end of the story for Israel was that they would *"return, seek the Lord their God and David their king, and fear the Lord and His goodness in the latter days."*

Which picture most accurately portrays the church in our day? Are we Gomer/Israel caught in our sinfulness and disobedience and freshly judged as wanting by our Husband/Father/God? Or, are we in the between times, deprived of those things that were our former sources of security, both legitimate and illegitimate, having nothing and no one to lean upon in our healing time except the pervading presence of our loving God? Are we in the Saturday time between the Good Friday of our failure and disobedience and the Easter dawning of our total healing and renewed obedience? If so, we may well expect these to be chastening days for us, learning times for us, times for doing less and listening to our patient God more. But the best days are just ahead for us. *"Afterward the children of Israel shall return, seek the Lord . . . in the latter days."* Thank God we know the end of the story because it has been whispered to us by our Lord Jesus, by the Apostle Paul, and by this faithful prophet and husband of an unfaithful wife, the spirit of a wife and of a nation.

"You shall not play the harlot, nor shall you have a man; thus I will also be toward you" (Hos. 3:3).

NOTES

1. George Adam Smith, *The Book of the Twelve Prophets*, vol. 1 (New York and London: Harper and Brothers, 1928), 266.

2. Harold Cooke Phillips, *The Interpreter's Bible*, vol. 6 (Nashville: Abingdon Press, 1956), 597.

3. Andersen and Freedman, *Hosea*, 301.

CHAPTER FIVE

The Knowledge of God

Hosea 4:1–6

4:1 Hear the word of the Lord, you children of Israel, for the Lord brings a charge against the inhabitants of the land: "There is no truth or mercy or knowledge of God in the land.

2 "By swearing and lying, killing and stealing and committing adultery, they break all restraint, with bloodshed upon bloodshed.

3 "Therefore the land will mourn; and everyone who dwells there will waste away with the beasts of the field and the birds of the air; even the fish of the sea will be taken away.

4 "Now let no man contend, or reprove another; for your people are like those who contend with the priest.

5 "Therefore you shall stumble in the day; the prophet also shall stumble with you in the night; and I will destroy your mother.

6 "My people are destroyed for lack of knowledge. Because you have rejected knowledge, I will also reject you from being priest for Me; because you have forgotten the law of your God, I also will forget your children."

Hos. 4:1–6

There is nothing more important. With it life is sublime; without it there is constant stress. It is the secret of true success, the source of wisdom beyond our understanding, the strength to endure in hard times. It is our ultimate goal, life's greatest privilege, and our most urgent need.

This is a gift most of us have difficulty receiving. It is not just facts or theories or ideas or carefully worded theology. It cannot be earned, and yet it is the one thing that should demand our constant attention and the focus of our lives. It is of more value than power, positions, or portfolios. And yet, nothing is more needed in contemporary Christianity.

Hosea was called to prophesy to Israel because this quality of life was lacking. The sins of the nation and of individuals came from the absence of it. Truth and mercy were lost because it had been neglected. The people were being destroyed because they had rejected it.

What is it? Knowledge of God. Our purpose and passion is to know God. Many Christians admit that they do not really *know* God. For other believers, lack of knowledge of God is the cause of vacillating spirituality, inconsistency between the walk and talk of the faith, and ineffectiveness in prayer. For still others, inadequate knowledge of God accounts for the reluctant response to holy living and moral responsibility. Like the people of Israel to whom Hosea prophesied, truth and mercy (faithfulness and kindness), as well as social righteousness are missing because we do not know God.

What does it mean to know God and live with a knowledge of Him? It involves both intimacy and integrity. The intimacy of the Thou-I relationship we were created to experience with God requires the opening of our innermost being to Him just as He has revealed His innermost nature to us. The word *intimacy* means "proceeding from within, inward, internal." In the Hebrew, the word for "knowledge," as we have seen in our exposition of Hosea 2:20, has the same root as "to know." It also is used for the physical and spiritual oneness of a husband and wife. Knowledge of God is more than ideas about Him. Knowledge of God involves the total inner person: intellect, emotion, and will. God knows all about what is going on inside us — we cannot hide from Him. The beginning of our knowledge of God, our relationship with Him, is when we know that we are known. So the psalmist says, "O Lord, You have searched me and known me," (Ps. 139:1). The psalmist yields his inner being to God when he realizes he is known by Him, "Search me, O God, and know my heart; try me and know my anxieties; and see if there is any wicked way in me, and lead me in the way ever-lasting" (Ps. 139:23–24). Both our understanding and awareness of God are met in response to our being known absolutely and thoroughly by Him.

God has revealed Himself throughout history and sublimely in Jesus Christ. But until we yield our inner self to Him, we do not experience an intimate union with Him.

Knowledge of God also calls forth our integrity. The word means wholeness — undivided, unimpaired — completeness. Integrity is congruity of behavior, consistency between what we believe and what we do. Intimacy with God, knowing Him as He has revealed Himself, must be inseparably intertwined with His character and commandments. He has chosen to be our God and elected us to be His people. Knowing Him therefore requires integrity, congruity of a life of faithfulness. Obedience is the secret of a growing knowledge of God.

Hosea addresses the lack of both intimacy and integrity in Israel. What he said is salient for our time. Few Christians live in a daily intimate relationship of being searched and really known by God. Opening ourselves and daring to be real with God is difficult for us. Consequently, we lack integrity.

We move into our study of Hosea 4 keenly interested in an ancient prophet's words to an apostate people. Hosea speaks to our time! H.G. Wells said, "Civilization is in a race between education and catastrophe." Hosea would put it differently: We are in a race between knowledge of God and catastrophe.

Earlier in Hosea's prophecy God clearly stated His plan and His desire for His people to have both the intimacy and integrity of knowing Him.

> I will betroth you to Me forever;
> yes, I will betroth you to Me
> in righteousness and justice,
> in lovingkindness and mercy;
> I will betroth you to Me in faithfulness,
> and you shall know the Lord.
>
> *Hos. 2:19–20*

Now in chapter 4 the Lord confronts Israel with her denial of His purpose. *"There is no truth or mercy or knowledge of God in the land. . . . My people are destroyed for lack of knowledge"* (Hos. 4:1b, 6a).

Our understanding of 4:1–6 begins with a background exposition of verses 1–5 and then as a part of explaining verse 6, I will suggest an approach to preaching it and calling for a response. Throughout, I will frequently refer to intimacy and integrity as the essential ingredients of the knowledge of God.

WHEN KNOWLEDGE OF GOD IS LOST

Chapter 4 begins with a general address to all the people of Israel (Hos. 4:1–3) and then turns to priests and others singled out for judgment. This is an announcement of judgment against Israel with accusations (4:1–2) and a corresponding sentence (4:3). In its present context, it serves as a general introduction to the collection of prophetic speeches that follow.

Douglas Stuart suggests that this chapter is like the stating of a case in a court of law. He argues that 4:1–3 should be considered part of the unit 4:1–19, since the single lawsuit may progress from general (vv. 1–3) to specific (vv. 4–19) and because of the repetition of the words *rîb* (verb—"bring a charge, contend"; noun—"charge") and *ʾak* ("surely").[1]

The beginning of this collection of Hosea's sayings identifies the prophecy as the word of Yahweh, just as the introduction to the book in 1:1 does. "*For the Lord brings a charge against the inhabitants of the land*" (Hos. 4:1).

Charge is translated from *rîb*, the same root used in Hosea 2:2 where the children were called to "bring charges" against their mother. The language is that of legal dispute. Yahweh files a lawsuit against Israel, acting as both accuser and judge. The charge is that "*there is no truth or mercy or knowledge of God in the land*" (4:4).

Truth, translated from *ʾĕmet*, is sometimes rendered *faithfulness*, *integrity*, *stability*, or *trustworthiness*. It is from the same verbal root *ʾmn* (amen) as *ʾĕmûnâ*, the *faithfulness* of Hosea 2:20 (cf. Gen. 24:49; 47:29; Exod. 18:21; Josh. 2:12,14; 1 Sam. 12:24).

The other missing qualities are also closely linked with 2:19–20. *Mercy* is translated from *hesed*, the "lovingkindness" of 2:19. It "includes the essential ingredients of kindness and mercy; it transcends the formal requirements of a covenant, adding that basic requirement of generous and forgiving treatment that makes coexistence with other people possible and qualifies judgment with mercy, producing a blend of retribution and forgiveness which constitutes *mišpāṭ*, 'justice.'"[2] Israel did not reflect these qualities of Yahweh (Ex. 34:6; Ps. 89:14) in community life.

Knowledge uses the same root as *know* in Hosea 2:20. Mercy and the knowledge of God are also linked in the famous passage in Hosea 6:6: "*For I desire mercy and not sacrifice, and the knowledge of God more than burnt offerings.*"

In addition, the knowledge of God in Hosea 4:1 implies knowledge of and compliance with God's commands. The lack of knowledge is evidenced by actions in direct disobedience to prominent commands of God (4:2). Knowledge also is used in parallel with the law of God in 4:6. Wolff says this verse "characterizes Israel's guilt as an absence of faithful relationship among the members of God's people, which has its roots in contempt for God's will."[3] And Stuart notes how knowledge of God "represents the essence of the covenant relationship between God and His people. . . . Therefore, when there is *no* knowledge of God in the land, the covenant has obviously been abrogated."[4]

Lack of integrity resulted. The absence of inner character was manifested in *"swearing and lying, killing and stealing and committing adultery"* (Hos. 4:2).

The breakdown of community life indicates the lack of truth, mercy, and knowledge of God in the land. *Swearing* can mean "cursing" (Judg. 17:2) or *"taking an oath,"* as in Hosea 10:4. Hosea frequently uses the root for *lying* and *deceiving,* both as verb and noun (4:2; 7:3; 9:2; 10:13; 12:1), which could be connected with the command against bearing false witness in the Decalogue (Exod. 20:16).

The series *"killing and stealing and committing adultery"* uses the same roots as three of the Ten Commandments, which also occur in series, but in a different order (Exod. 20:13-15; cf. Jer. 7:9). Stealing and lying are both forbidden in Leviticus 19:11, using the same terms.

There is a mounting intensity as Hosea lists the charges. Without a knowledge of God, they break all restraint. Literally this means "they break out" or "they break through," with the idea of restraint or boundaries implied. The commandments of God defined boundaries or restraints against destructive tendencies of sinful humans. When the commandments were rejected (no knowledge of God), there was no longer any restraint. This causes *"bloodshed after bloodshed"* (Hos. 4:2).

Literally, this is "blood strikes (or touches) blood," the idea of continual violence. Recall the judgment against the dynasty of Jehu for the blood of Jezreel (Hos. 1:4). This also may allude to the frequent assassinations after Jeroboam II. However, it seems to be a more general indictment here, indicating the total breakdown in the community at large, of which the royal misdeeds were only a part.

Stuart suggests that this clause is actually "the idols touch the idols," referring to the multiplicity of idols. He proposes that *dāmîm* does not come from the root for *blood* but from the word for "resemble, be like" that is sometimes translated "image." Thus, the reference would be to breaking the second commandment (Exod. 20:4-6; Deut. 5:8-10).[5]

The Mourning of the Land

Although the picture of the land (including inhabitants) mourning is appropriate in the scene of death portrayed here, other commentators note that the word normally translated "mourn" can also mean "dry up."[6] The parallel with "waste away" here and with another word for "dry up" in other texts makes this a strong possibility (Jer.12:4; 23:10; Amos 1:2).

As with the short list of animals in Hosea 2:18, this similar list (4:3) recalls the summary of the animal kingdom in Genesis 1:26, 30; 9:2. Humans are to have dominion over the animals. When they forsake God and His word, not only does the human community suffer, but also the natural world—particularly the animals. While Yahweh does not punish the animals for human sin, Scripture views the whole world as interconnected and interdependent.

After the general introduction of Hosea 4:1–3, the accusations and announcements of judgment become more specific in the rest of the chapter. A priest, probably the chief priest, is the focus of judgment in 4:4–6. Verses 7–14 continue the accusations against the priest and the resulting destruction for the people caused by the apostasy of their cultic leaders. The focus turns to the whole nation in 4:15–19—the sorry state of those left alone in stubborn rebellion against Yahweh. Harlotry is a continuing theme. This section is probably from Hosea's early period during the reign of Jeroboam II while prosperity and complacence prevailed before the palace intrigues and the Assyrian threats broke the uneasy peace.

Verse 4 begins with what seems to be a quote of a rebuke from a priest or leader in Israel who objects to Hosea accusing Israel, "*Let no man contend, or reprove another.*" It is a shibboleth spoken in reaction to Hosea's penetrating exposure of the apostasy of Israel.

Hosea then presents the following speech as Yahweh's reply. "*For your people are like those who contend with the priest*" (4:4b). This is a close translation of the Hebrew Masoretic text as it now stands. However, many other versions and numerous scholars read the text differently, sometimes assuming scribal error in transmission of the text. Knight changes the sense very little, mainly changing the pointing of the last syllable of *kimrîbê* to get "But it is thy people who contend with me, O ye priests."[7]

The most popular reading is "With you is my contention, O priest." This is obtained by removing the *km* from *kimrîbê* and repointing the first two words. The *km* could have originally been a second plural ending on the first word *with you* that was changed during transmission to second singular with the *km* retained but attached to the following word.[8] Andersen and Freedman suggest that *km* is an emphatic particle (*indeed*) that became attached to the following word.[9] Their solution has the advantage of not altering the consonantal text. Another argument for this translation comes from the context — the following accusations are directed to the priest.

"Therefore you shall stumble in the day; the prophet also shall stumble with you in the night; and I will destroy your mother" (Hos. 4:5). Stumbling as a consequence of sin is found elsewhere in Hosea (5:5; 14:1) and in other prophets (Isa. 8:15; 28:13; 31:3; Jer. 6:21). While the priest will stumble in the day when one can see clearly (see John 11:9), the prophet will stumble at night, perhaps a reference to nocturnal revelations (cf. Mic. 3:6; Jer. 23:25–32; Zech. 1:8; 4:1).[10] The day/night combination does not necessarily indicate different times or types of punishment, but that the consequences will be continuous.[11]

We do not know if Hosea had a reason for singling out the priest's mother for judgment. Along with the reference to the children in 4:6, this probably emphasizes the gravity of the judgment on the priest, including his whole family. It may be that the priest's children deserved judgment themselves as did the sons of Eli in 1 Samuel.

Stuart proposes that the word usually translated "mother" should be repointed to read "terror" with an adverbial function. He translates the last part of verse 5 and the first part of 6: "You will perish in terror when My people perish from lack of knowledge."[12]

THE LACK OF KNOWLEDGE

We feel the acute anguish of God in verse six: *"My people are destroyed for lack of knowledge."* In applying this sentence to our own time, it is important to distinguish between secular learning and knowledge of God. We are not destroyed by a lack of education, but rather by a lack of in-depth study of the Scriptures, prayer, and living out the truth of God's revealed will in our lives. Consequently, our character is shaped by cultural values and not knowledge of God.

A businessman had served as a church officer for years before a profound experience of God's grace brought him to a renewed commitment of his life to Him. A part of that commitment was to take time each morning to read the Bible and pray. That awakened in him a hunger to go deeper into God's Word. He enrolled in an evening lay study course that took him through the Bible over a three-year period. When he was finished, he exclaimed, "I'm not only delighted by the chance to grow in the knowledge of God, but I'm astounded by what I didn't know. And to think I've raised a family, run a business, and helped lead a church all these years without really knowing God—you know what I mean—who He is, what He said, how to receive His guidance, how to do things His way. My deepest regret is all the decisions I made without prayer and a real biblical basis."

The man's statement reminds me of another man who resisted a new ministry to the poor in his church. "God helps those who help themselves," he said, implying biblical authority for this conviction. When he was told that the statement came from *Poor Richard's Almanac*, he replied, "Well, it's true anyway!"

Think back over the past three decades of the battles for social justice. It is no pleasure to remember that causes such as equal rights and racial integration had to climb over the stiff backs of good church people with an inadequate knowledge of God. Even more appalling were some clergy who refused to stand up and be counted by preaching the truth.

More importantly, though, church members who do not live out their faith are people who have little or no relationship with God. Thomas Torrence remarked that the great issue before the church in the 1990s is the evangelization of church members. I agree. We would be able to evangelize the world if we took that challenge seriously.

Recently while preaching through Hosea, this sixth verse of chapter 4 was my text. I began the message by saying, "I want you to ask yourself life's ultimate question. Reach way down into your inner being and get in touch with the real you. Be as honest as you can be in answering this most crucial of all questions. 'Do you know God?'"

I went on to say, "Notice that I didn't ask, 'Do you believe that He exists, or do you believe in Him?' Nor did I ask, 'Are you trying to live a good moral life?' What I did urge you to ask yourself is, 'Do you really know God?'

"Now if you said, 'Yes,' what evidence do you have that your answer is authentic? If you said, 'Well, I'm not sure,' what keeps you from that assurance? Or, if your response is, 'Is it truly possible to know God the creator, the sustainer of the universe?' then ask yourself about what grounds you base your doubt. And if you said, 'No, I can't honestly say I know God,' may I ask you another question, 'Would you like to know Him?'"

While that was sinking in, I used one of my favorite illustrations: One afternoon I watched a Japanese freighter being unloaded in the Los Angeles harbor. A gigantic crane lifted crates of merchandise out of the hull and lowered them down on the wharf. I noticed that each container had handling instructions stamped on the side in bold black letters in both Japanese and English. I suspected that something had been lost in the English translation. What was printed may have been ambiguous to the stevedores working with the cartons, but it was a clear message from the Lord to me: "If this side is up, this container is upside down."

I began to think about what that meant for my life and the people I love. "If this side is up, this life is upside down." How can we tell if our lives are right side up? What are the identifiable signs that we are realizing the purpose for which we were born? Or, what would be the undeniable marks of missing the reason we are alive?

God's diagnosis of Israel's spiritual illness was that because of the lack of clear teaching of the Torah, His people were being destroyed because of lack of knowledge of Him. That destruction is poignantly presented in Hosea's prophecy. But is it any less evident in our society? And what of the agnosticism inside and outside the church? Without a knowledge of God there is no inner peace, no cure for restlessness, no guidance for daily pressures, no absolutes for moral rectitude, no certainty in life or death. A kind of creeping destruction of ourselves and others results. But that is not what God intends.

We were created to know, to love, to glorify, and to serve God. Knowledge of God is our purpose. We were meant to experience intimacy with God, an intrinsic encounter, one that reveals and brings into union the essential nature and inner being of God and us. In that relationship His nature is recreated in us. From his recreation flows integrity, obedience to discover and do His will, to live His commandments, and to do the truth. We are destroyed without that knowledge. Our lives are wrong side up!

My introduction led into the main points of the message on how to really know God.

OUR DESIRE TO KNOW GOD IS BECAUSE HE KNOWS US
AND INITIATES IN US A DESIRE TO KNOW HIM.

God always makes the first move. As God said to Pascal, "Thou would not be searching for Me, had I not already found thee." Every discovery about God and His nature is but our response to His revelation. The people of Israel were being destroyed because of the lack of teaching by the priests about God, the Torah, and all that He had revealed of Himself to that point in history. Today our problem is not lack of information about God, but knowing Him as He has revealed Himself.

In Christ, God opened and revealed His intrinsic, essential, innermost heart. God dwelt bodily in the Messiah (Col. 1:19). The eternal God was revealed in time and space for all time and for all people. Nothing was left out or held back. Jesus said, "He who has seen Me, has seen the Father" (John 14:9). God came to His people who had been sucked into the seduction of the secondary rites and rituals about Him but did not know Him personally. Out of unreserved love He offered Himself in the person of Immanuel, God with us. "In Him was the life and the life was the light of man" (John 1:4). The Light of the world revealed both God and man. In that illumination, we see God as He is and ourselves in our need of Him. "The only begotten Son, who is in the bosom of the Father, He has declared Him" (John 1:18). Early manuscripts of that text have "only begotten God," *monogenēs Theos* rather than *monogenēs Huios*. It was God Himself who came to us in Christ, His Son, the Divine Logos, God's Word. He is the Redeemer, Reconciler, and Restorer of man to God.

So our knowledge, our relationship, with God begins and never ends in and through Christ. His word stands, "I am the way, the truth and the life, no man comes to the Father except through Me" (John 14:6). And "This is life eternal, that they might *know* You, the only true God, and Jesus Christ whom You have sent" (John 17:3).

Paul's life was wrong side up until he encountered the resurrected Christ. After his conversion and fourteen years of repatterning of his mind by Christ, Paul was called to preach. His purpose was, "That I may know Him and the power of His resurrection" (Phil. 3:10), and his priority, "For I determined not to know anything among you except Christ and Him crucified" (1 Cor. 2:2), and his passion, "I *know* whom I have believed and am persuaded that He is able to keep what I have committed to Him until that day" (1 Tim. 1:12).

THERE ARE VERY DIFFERENT LEVELS OF
KNOWING GOD THROUGH CHRIST.

J. Sidlow Baxter suggests four ways of knowing: historically, con-temporaneously, contactually, and familiarly.[13] We can know Christ as a great historical figure of the past, as we know about other historical persons. Or, we can know Christ is alive and present with us as our contemporary, but still without any more relationship than we might have with a current political leader in Washington, London, or Moscow. Then, we can know an acquaintance, but we do not really know the person in a profound relationship. Last, we can know very few people familiarly, mind to mind, heart to heart, spirit to spirit.

I have added to Baxter's four ways of knowing a fifth way, know-ing intimately. I believe that is the quality of relationship Paul knew, "I know whom I have believed" (2 Tim. 1:12). The Apostle did not say he knew *what* he believed, but *whom*.

To know the Lord intimately is to know Him experientially. We not only hear about God's grace in Christ offered to us, but we accept and experience being loved. Beyond studying theories of the atonement, we experience exoneration and regeneration. More than considering Christ's promise to abide in us, we invite Him to live in us; we enter the kingdom and experience Christ's reign and rule in us, in our relationships, and in all the responsibilities of life.

KNOWING GOD INTIMATELY IS AN EVER-DEEPENING EXPERIENCE.

This involves the personal disciplines of daily study of the Scrip-tures and profound prayer. Both require attentive listening to what the Lord has to say in His Word and in our quiet meditation times, then in acting on the marching orders He gives us. It also necessitates surrendering our problems and perplexities and expecting and ac-cepting His intervention.

KNOWING GOD IS OBEYING GOD.

G. Campbell Morgan once said, "People today know so much more than they did, with the result that they begin to question what they know." This has been a problem of religious people through the ages. We were created in the image of God and through Christ regenerated in the nature of God so that there might be in us a recapitulation of the character of God emulating His mercy and covenant love.

The opposite of knowing God, according to Hosea's prophecy in this stirring sixth verse of chapter 4 is *forgetting the laws of your God*. For us, that includes the Commandments, Christ's commandment to love, and all the undeniable admonitions for faith and practice in Scripture. Knowing God personalizes morality and makes obedience more than fulfilling a set of regulations and rules—the expression of gratitude for a love relationship. John Bunyan said, "There is knowledge and knowledge: knowledge that resteth in the bare speculations of things, and knowledge that is accompanied with the grace of faith and love, which puts a man upon doing the will of God from the heart."

I have given only a sketch of my outline of an approach to preaching Hosea 4:6. At the conclusion of the message I asked those who wanted to know God to come forward to the chancel for prayer with the pastors and elders. A great number responded, including church members. One man said, "I realize that I don't know God intimately. I have been closed, walled off from Him, resistant to a deep relationship with Him. And I'm the same way with others. I want to open myself to be known." A woman confessed, "My relationship with God has been one big 'No!' to some very clear guidance He's been giving me. The result is that I no longer feel I know Him. Now I want to say, 'Yes!'" And still another said to an elder, "I don't know God, but I want to know Him. Help me." Before praying with the man, the elder led him through the biblical plan of salvation and helped him become a Christian. People today long to know God.

They also need opportunities to make a renewed commitment. As I'm writing this, the fresh memories of last Sunday dance with delight in my mind. At the conclusion of the communion, we had a service for the reaffirmation of baptismal vows and the empowering of the Holy Spirit. People were invited to come forward for prayer and an anointing with oil, symbolic of their reaffirmation of the covenant, their commission to serve God and the empowering to be Christ's disciples and ministers. Literally hundreds of people responded at both services. Each was given a card to sign and keep in his or her Bible for a reminder.

The cards read:

> To the glory of God,
> I reaffirm my baptismal vows by:
>   Reclaiming my identity as God's person;
>   Reasserting my position in Jesus
>   Christ, His righteousness and His
>   authority over evil;
>   Receiving a fresh empowering of the
>   Holy Spirit; and,
>   Recommitting myself to be Christ's
>   disciple and minister in the world.
>   Signed on December 31, 1989, the Eve of
>   a New Year and a New Decade.
>   *Deo Volente. Carpe Diem.*

As I said in my preface to this volume, we are living in the most exciting days since Pentecost. Perhaps it is a God-entrusted gift for Christian leaders to think this way about their time in the unfolding drama of the kingdom. There's a spiritual hunger that cries out to be fed.

You and I have been given the privilege of preaching and teaching in this propitious time. Hosea's preaching about the priesthood in the eighth century is a sobering recall to our own holy calling. The apostasy of the priests and particularly the high priest was the direct cause of God's people being destroyed by lack of knowledge. The judgment of God is that because they have forgotten the law of God, He will forget their children. This means that He will remove His blessing from the family heirs of the priestly office.

We, too, will be accountable for what we preach and teach. The great need of the hour is for the exposition of Scripture for the deepest needs and most urgent questions of people today. We need the centered resoluteness of John Wesley, "O give me that book! At any price, give me the book of God. I have it; here is enough for me!" And he preached more than 800 sermons a year from the Bible, resulting in the conversion of hundreds of thousands and a social reform that swept across the British Isles. Nothing less is needed today.

NOTES

1. Douglas Stuart, *Hosea–Jonah,* vol. 31, *Word Biblical Commentary* (Waco, Tex.: Word Books, 1987), 73.

2. Andersen and Freedman, *Hosea,* 336.

3. Wolff, *Hosea,* 67.

4. Stuart, *Hosea–Jonah,* 75.

5. Ibid., 76.

6. Ibid., 72; Wolff, *Hosea,* 65; Andersen and Freedman, *Hosea,* 339–340.

7. Knight, *Hosea,* 67.

8. Wolff, *Hosea,* 70.

9. Andersen and Freedman, *Hosea,* 349–350.

10. Wolff, *Hosea,* 77.

11. Andersen and Freedman, *Hosea,* 350.

12. Stuart, *Hosea–Jonah,* 78.

13. J. Sidlow Baxter, *Going Deeper,* 14–15.

CHAPTER SIX

Like People Like Priest

Hosea 4:7–11

4:7 "The more they increased, the more they sinned against Me; I will change their glory into shame.

8 "They eat up the sin of My people; they set their heart on their iniquity.

9 "And it shall be: like people, like priest. So I will punish them for their ways, and reward them for their deeds.

10 "For they shall eat, but not have enough; they shall commit harlotry, but not increase; because they have ceased obeying the Lord.

11 "Harlotry, wine, and new wine enslave the heart."

Hos. 4:7–11

The awesome challenge of spiritual leaders is that people rise or sink to their level. We can lead people only so far as we have been willing to travel in our own spiritual pilgrimage. The finest gift a pastor or a teacher can give his or her people is to move deeper into the Scriptures, press on further in radical discipleship, and rise higher in vision of what God wants from His people in any period of history.

The idiom, *like people, like priest*, is a blunt reminder that people emulate their leaders. The Hebrew idiom can also be interpreted that priest and people will be judged. The construction does not indicate by itself who is being compared to whom. However, in the context, the focus is on the guilt of the priests who have misled God's people. The tragedy was that the people were willing to be led in the wrong direction. But without a consistent teaching of the Law, there was no objective standard by which they could discern right from wrong.

OPPORTUNISM OF THE CLERGY

Hosea 4:7-11 presents a picture of the opportunism of the priesthood. They judged success with size, lived sumptuous lives, and lacked purity of devotion to Yahweh.

During the reign of Jeroboam II and the ambience of political peace and economic prosperity, there was an expansion of religious activity (Hos. 8:11; 10:1; cf. Jer. 2:28). The priesthood grew in number, but instead of bringing greater devotion to Yahweh, it brought greater sin. "*The more they increased, the more they sinned against Me*" (4:7) is God's analysis of the "bigger is better" equivocation.

The verdict rendered is, "*I will change their glory into shame.*" The glory of the priests was that they occupied an awesome place of responsibility as representatives of Yahweh and as teachers of the Law. Some commentators follow the Targum and Syriac and here substitute the third person for the first person— "They exchanged their glory for shame."

The sin referred to, either directly or metaphorically, is the misappropriation of sin offerings or sacrifices that the people bring to worship for use in the sin offering. The priests were entitled to a portion (Lev. 6:17-23; 10:12-15). Hosea implied that the priests made a fat living off the offerings.

But look again at the eighth verse: "*They eat up the sin of My people; they set their heart on their iniquity.*" The word for sin here means to "miss the mark." The parallel with iniquity indicates that *sin* refers primarily to the people's offenses against God. The priests feed on and yearn for the people's sin and iniquity, which probably refers to sacrificial worship contrary to God's will. Wolff notes that *nepeš* here has its original sense of "throat," as in Proverbs 27:7; Micah 7:1; Is. 5:14; 29:8, and that *eat up*, "lift up the throat," graphically portrays the yearning greediness. Wolff comments incisively:

> The criticism of the cultic sacrifices is aimed at the selfish interests of the priests who in the sacrifices seek their own private gain. As in verse 6a, Yahweh, in the form of the messenger speech, again

sympathetically takes the side of Israel, calling them anew "My people!" With their sacrificial cult, the priests do not serve the people of God with the divine gifts entrusted to them; instead, at the people's expense they store up their own profit and advantage.[1]

Now the punishment is described: "*So I will punish them for their ways, and reward them for their deeds. For they shall eat, but not have enough; they shall commit harlotry, but not increase; because they have ceased obeying the Lord*" (Hos. 4:9–10). Though the priests eat their sacrificial portions, they will not be satisfied; though they "commit harlotry" (with worship of other gods or with sacral prostitutes), they will not increase (cf. Deut. 28:17–18; 32:24–28). The word for "increase" here is *pāras*, as in 4:2—*break all restraint*. Andersen and Freedman note, "The quasi-magical character of contemporary Israelite religion is apparent here. Ceremonial eating was intended to secure abundance of food, but it will have the opposite effect. Ritual intercourse was intended to secure fertility, but it won't succeed."[2]

The real punishment is because the priests have forsaken Yahweh for other gods. The end of verse 10 is difficult as it stands. Commonly the last word is combined with the first word in verse 11. Wolff translates, "They have forsaken Yahweh to devote themselves to fornication" (cf. Deut. 31:16), and Stuart renders it, "They have abandoned Yahweh to revere prostitution. Wine and the fruit of the vine dulls the minds of My people." The common object of *šāmar* ("to keep, hold to") would be the word or commandment of Yahweh, as in Deuteronomy 17:19. Instead, the priests have rejected that (4:6), turning to harlotry in the worship of other gods.

We pause to reflect on the contemporary application of this disturbing passage. We gain little comfort that it could reflect the corruption of leadership in many periods of Christian history. But it is particularly applicable to our time in which we are enduring the fallout crisis of credibility caused by the personal greed, moral pertinacity, and lack of financial integrity of some spiritual leaders. A Gallup poll in 1980 showed that 26 percent of the respondents said television evangelists were dishonest. By 1989, following the Jimmy Swaggart and Jim Bakker exposures, 70 percent of respondents said television evangelists were dishonest, with 79 percent believing the evangelists were not trustworthy with money. This has prompted the formation of FICOM, Federation of Financial Integrity in Communications, to be a watchdog of the books of those who voluntarily belong. Excellent as this is, it has not offset the mistrust created by the highly publicized scandals of the few. Giving to all ministries, including the local church, has been affected. Mistrust in the clergy abounds.

But let's move deeper than the obvious. The cult of "bigger is better" is still around. The size of our constituencies is deemed a measure of success even if at the cost of theological and biblical integrity. Rather than asking one another, "How large is your congregation?" we ought to ask, "Are people being converted, are lives being transformed, and are your members involved in personal evangelism and in mission where people suffer?"

Our challenge is to boldly, courageously preach and teach the word of God and raise up a laity to be distinctly different from our materialistic, success-oriented, sex-centric society that is drifting further and further from God.

We can't escape the truth that God has entrusted a glory, a special responsibility of high calling to leaders. Our people will move as fast and as far in discipleship as we dare to proclaim *and* live. Our leadership also includes the vulnerability of an honest, open life out of which we share what God is doing with our strengths and weaknesses. Our example should be what the Lord can do with a life immersed in His Word, engrossed in prayer, and liberated by trust in Him.

It is in the context of a congregation or a class fellowship that the Word of God is preached or taught with personal application. There, in relationship with our people, we can share our own struggles and victories in living out the truths we communicate. And with a ministry of attentive listening to what our people are facing in their discipleship, we can communicate with empathy. Our calling is not to superiority, but simply to making obedience to God and His word our priority.

NOTES

1. Wolff, *Hosea*, 81.
2. Andersen and Freedman, *Hosea*, 362.

CHAPTER SEVEN

When the Stubborn Stray

Hosea 4:12–19

4:12 "My people ask counsel from their wooden idols, and their staff informs them. For the spirit of harlotry has caused them to stray, and they have played the harlot against their God.

13 "They offer sacrifices on the mountaintops, and burn incense on the hills, under oaks, poplars, and terebinths, because their shade is good. Therefore your daughters commit harlotry, and your brides commit adultery.

14 "I will not punish your daughters when they commit harlotry, nor your brides when they commit adultery; for the men themselves go apart with harlots, and offer sacrifices with a ritual harlot. Therefore people who do not understand will be trampled.

15 "Though you, Israel, play the harlot, let not Judah offend. Do not come up to Gilgal, nor go up to Beth Aven, nor swear an oath, saying, 'As the Lord lives' —

16 "For Israel is stubborn like a stubborn calf; now the Lord will let them forage like a lamb in open country.

17 "Ephraim is joined to idols, let him alone.

18 "Their drink is rebellion, they commit harlotry continually. Her rulers dearly love dishonor.

19 "The wind has wrapped her up in its wings and they shall be ashamed because of their sacrifices."

Hos. 4:12–19

As communicators of Hosea, we may grow weary and tire our listeners by the prophet's seemingly repetitious confrontation of the same sins of harlotry and apostasy. Therefore, it is important to plumb the depths of each passage to find the deeper cause of the sins and relate that proclivity to our own spiritual and social problems today. There's usually a verse in a passage that provides the fulcrum for the focus of our exposition. Identifying that makes the verse by verse explanation of the text more unified and helpful to our people.

In Hosea 4:12–19 we see the problem of stubbornness and the frightening response of God to it. In verse 16, Israel is depicted as a stubborn calf. Although many of us have not lived on farms, we understand the image of an unteachable calf—willful, resistant, and petulant. And we identify with that calf. We all can say with the hymn writer, "Prone to wander, Lord, I feel it, prone to leave the God I love."[1]

We walk like a stubborn calf when we use a prayer to make our demands rather than listen for the Lord's instructions. And when His will is made undeniably clear, we confront the problem of answered prayer. Many times what we call unanswered prayer is really the problem of answered prayer. There are times when we concentrate so hard on asking for something that we are oblivious to the answer when it comes. Frequently, the answers to our prayers are more than we bargained for. Or, the answers arrive differently than we predicted. Then there are times when the answer presents us with a challenge to become part of the answer.

The theme of stubbornness and straying is consistent throughout Hosea 4:12–19. The "spirit of harlotry" leads God's people astray. It is as if an overwhelming force of evil came upon the people from beyond them, and they were prompted to stray. On the words "to stray" Wolff says, "The people now live as an animal gone astray (Exod. 23:4) or as a drunken person who loses his self-control and his way (Isa. 28:7)."[2] Consequently, the people turn to wooden idols and divination staffs for guidance. The people of God, who were to be enlightened by the living God, prayed to wooden objects and, as a device of divination, would throw sticks into the air at random then seriously consider the significance of where they fell. Currently, some Christians are not far from that when they check their horoscopes in the morning instead of praying for God's guidance.

The stubbornness of the people of Israel is further depicted by the way they "played the harlot against their God," or as Knight suggests, "from under their God, feeling emancipated from the restraint of the Law that was bound up with the Covenant."[3]

The people were intoxicated by a feeling of false freedom. They offered sacrifices on the mountaintops and incense on the hills, under the trees because the shade was good (v. 13).

In the twentieth century, we have our own set of idols that we stubbornly stray toward for worship. Money, security, pleasure, people, careers, and possessions are still idols that demand our loyalty. Again, our idols can be anything or anyone that threatens to occupy the throne of our hearts. God-substitutes can be very demanding of our time and money.

And our stubbornness is expressed in the most subtle ways. We juggle our idols while at the same time expressing our commitment to God. We set our priorities for our personal goals, our images, our families, and our future plans; then we not only ask God to bless them, but to help us achieve them. We try to keep the Lord in the idol-polishing and maintenance business!

But our stubborn self is the most dangerous diminutive god. While we say we are Christians, attend church, pray our prayers, and become involved in a few good works, we still control our lives. We only need God for Him to accomplish our predetermined plans and purposes.

Outwardly, we agree with the most forceful preaching and teaching about idols. We nod approvingly when a preacher takes on the diminutive gods. We affirm the exposure of the popular icons of the world. We wag our heads in consternation and look around smugly, enjoying the fact that the Gospel is being preached so relevantly *for other people*. Inwardly, though, our citadel of stubborn control is still intact.

Jesus' parable of the wicked vinedressers (Matt. 21:33–44) helps us understand our most dangerous idols. The owner of the vineyard rented out the vineyard, with its abundant vines, its many vine presses and vats, a protective wall, and a tower. All the vinedressers had to do was enjoy the vineyard and its profits, and at the end of five years pay the owner a third of the profits in affirmation that the vineyard belonged to him. That was the rub. The stubborn vinedressers began to believe and act as if the vineyard was theirs. They reasoned that they had worked it, fertilized it, pruned it, and harvested it.

"The vineyard is ours," they exclaimed. "What right does the owner have to claim any of the produce? It was our sweat and labor that developed the vineyard!"

When the delegation of servants came to collect, the stubborn vinedressers stoned them and cast them out of the vineyard. And when the owner's son came, they killed him, hoping to possess the inheritance as their own.

This parable of human stubbornness was told by Jesus during His last week in Jerusalem before He was crucified. It helps us to come to terms with what He believed to be His mission in Israel, the vineyards of God, and in our lives today. "You belong to Me!" He says, demanding our total lives. Yet, the transition from "His" to "mine" is never immediate but grows over a long time. We may invite the Lord into our vineyard and share the tithe of our efforts, but He is little more than an invited guest in *our* vineyard. We are convinced it belongs to us!

God does not want to be a guest. He will not take His place on our shelf of idols. He would not with Israel, and He will not with us.

Hosea 4:13b returns to Israel's stubborn, persistent obsession with the Baal fertility cults. In fact, verses 13b and 14 are a benchmark in biblical morality. The double standard for men and women is tossed away. Rather than castigating the daughters and the brides, Hosea points the finger at the fathers and the husbands who had been the examples of stubborn resistance to God's law. The prophet confronts the false idea that a man's sexual sins should be taken less seriously than a woman's. He says that the moral breakdown rested equally on the men and the women. The men should not be alarmed to find their wives or daughters off involved in the cult. They had set the example!

In verse 15, Hosea uses Judah as a foil to stir competitive consternation. *"Though you, Israel, play the harlot, let not Judah offend. Do not come up to Gilgal, nor go up to Beth Aven, nor swear an oath, saying, 'As the Lord lives.'"* In a way, Hosea is saying, "Though Israel plays the harlot, I pray Judah will not sink to this level." The prophet startled his listeners. They could have said, "Listen, Judah is as guilty as we are!" To which Hosea responded in effect, "Yes, you are guilty, aren't you?"

To avoid Judah's implied guilt, the people of Israel are admonished to discontinue their stubborn cultic pilgrimages to Gilgal (Josh. 5:2–9; Hos. 9:15; 12:11) and Beth Aven (house of wickedness), used here as a distorted name for Bethel (cf. Hos. 5:8; 10:5; 12:4; Amos' dispute at Bethel—Amos 7:10, 13). Beth Aven denotes a sanctuary that had become part of the Baal cult. The warning to avoid these sanctuaries echoes Amos 4:4; 5:5.

At these sanctuaries the people swear, "As Yahweh lives," and then enter the sanctuary to become part of the cultic worship. The name of

Yahweh was used with syncretistic deceit when the people knew very well that Baal was worshiped there (Jer. 4:2; 5:2).

There is an obdurate stubbornness that persists in spite of clear warnings or clear directions. Often we do what we know is not God's best for us, and we resist doing what we know He has guided. Each of us has his or her own brand of stubbornness. It's helpful to ask people to identify their own.

Often our problem with God's authority over us is the response of passive aggression. We would be the last to openly defy Him; we just do not do what we know He calls us to do. For example, often we do not pray, share our faith, forgive others, tithe our money, or become involved in mission. So God waits. He wants us to want what He wants for us.

"For Israel is stubborn like a stubborn calf; now the Lord will let them forage like a lamb in open country" (Hos. 4:16). This verse has had many different translations. The RSV renders it, "Like a stubborn heifer, Israel is stubborn; can the Lord now feed them like a lamb in a broad pasture?" This translation takes the second part of the sentence not as a promise but a question that anticipates the answer of "no." Wolff translates it, "Should Yahweh now feed them like lambs in a broad meadow?"[4] Our answer to that is, "Well, no and yes." For a shepherd to allow lambs to wander about eating in an open country is dangerous. They will nibble their way from the shepherd and get lost or be attacked by wolves. But isn't that an accurate picture of what Israel was doing? Wasn't Israel doing exactly what she wanted? Freedom from the Shepherd-God to find satisfaction where she wanted it? And, "Yes!" we say, if that is what Israel wanted, she should live with the consequences. Then we wonder — do we want the Shepherd to let us go? Do we deserve to be relinquished by God?

Verse 17 seems to suggest that there is such an anguished time of divine bereavement: *"Ephraim is joined to idols, let him alone."* We shudder at the possibility. The word play between "open country" of verse 16 and "joined" of verse 17 is more obvious in the Hebrew where the two words have the same root consonants. Because of Israel's heifer-like stubbornness, unyielding hardheartedness, the Lord for the time being allows the rebelliousness commitment to idol worship. *"Their drink is rebellion, they commit harlotry continually. Her rulers dearly love dishonor"* (Hos. 4:18). A more radical translation reveals the compulsive pattern of the people. Absolute infinitives in the

Hebrew emphasize this. The word translated "rebellion" in the NKJV could instead be "turn aside, cease," and so, essentially, the meaning is: When they cease drinking, or sober up, they constantly commit harlotry. Stubbornness can become a habitual compulsion. The spirit of harlotry has become like a wind that has swept up Israel and will finally carry her away into exile (v. 19).

A FINAL NOTE OF HOPE

But the second clause of the final verse of chapter 4, verse 19, flashes a ray of hope: *"And they shall be ashamed because of their sacrifices."* It took the judgment of the destruction of the northern kingdom and the exile to do that.

We wonder, what does it take today to break the bind of stubbornness? Sickness, broken relationships, tragedy sometimes wake us up. But only temporarily. God's grace in Christ is the only lasting cure. He knows that a stubborn spirit is one crying out for love. We are imperious in our control of the vineyard of our lives only because we have not had an adequate experience of being loved by the Son He sends to take charge of us.

An exposition of Hosea 4 sets in bold contrast the peace of knowledge of God and the loneliness of stubbornness. Does God ever say of us, "Let him alone"? No. He promised to never leave us or forsake us. When there is a feeling of distance between God and us, it is because we moved, not because He did. But sometimes He allows our lives to fall apart so that we can see what our stubbornness is doing to us. And He says, "Why are you rebelling against Me? I love you. Whatever I give or take away is only to draw you to Me. Give Me the broken pieces of your life and in exchange allow Me to give you My peace." And our only response to Him is in Andrew Reed's hymn:

> Holy Spirit, all divine,
> Dwell within this heart of mine;
> Cast down every idol throne,
> Reign supreme, and reign alone.[5]

NOTES

1. Robert Robinson, "Come, Thou Fount of Every Blessing," *Hymns for the Living Church* (Carol Stream, Ill.: Hope Publishing Co., 1974), 28.

2. Wolff, *Hosea*, 84.

3. Knight, *Hosea*, 70.

4. Wolff, *Hosea*, 72.

5. Andrew Reed, "Holy Spirit, Light Divine," *Hymns for the Living Church* (Carol Stream, Ill.: Hope Publishing Co., 1974), 194.

CHAPTER EIGHT

Redemptive Hand of Judgment

Hosea 5:1–15

Before proceeding with an exposition and commentary on Hosea, chapter 5, I think it is helpful to take an overview of the structure of Hosea 5:1–7:16.

Hosea 5:1–7 appears to be a unit at first analysis of the text. It begins with a summons to hear, then it presents charges and judgments to the priests and laity and to the leaders and people of both Israel and Judah. We have become accustomed to changes of style in Hosea. For instance, changes from direct address by Yahweh (5:1–2) to prophetic words about Yahweh and Israel in the third person (5:4–7) and then changes again from plural to singular and back to plural in reference to the hearers. Wolff accounts for the variations in the text by proposing that the audience replied before verses 3, 4, 5, and 6 — replies that trigger the change in theme and addressee. The unit continues the themes from chapter 4, regarding the leaders' misguidance of the people, their stubbornness, their stumbling as a consequence of sin, and the apostate cult. The continuities in vocabulary and subject matter between 4:4–19 and 5:1–7 suggest a similar setting for these passages.[1]

Then the imperative in Hosea 5:8 begins the next unit. Wolff calls it a "*kerygmatic* unit" of sayings all related to the disastrous days of 733 B.C. when the Assyrians attacked Israel and other Palestinian states following the appeal of Judah for Assyrian help against Israel and Syria (2 Kings 16; Isa. 7). Stuart also points to 735–732 B.C. as the time period for Hosea 5:8–7:1.

We will examine Hosea 5:1–7:19 knowing this background. Our exposition and commentary of chapter 5 will be divided into two parts: 5:1–7 and 5:8–15 with content subheads within each section, under the overall theme of the redemptive hand of judgment.

GOD DOES NOT PLAY FAVORITES

5:1 "Hear this, O priests! Take heed, O house of Israel!
Give ear, O house of the king! For yours is the judgment,
because you have been a snare to Mizpah and a net
spread on Tabor.
2 "The revolters are deeply involved in slaughter,
though I rebuke them all.
3 "I know Ephraim, and Israel is not hidden from
Me; for now, O Ephraim, you commit harlotry; Israel is
defiled.
4 "They do not direct their deeds toward turning to
their God, for the spirit of harlotry is in their midst,
and they do not know the Lord.
5 "The pride of Israel testifies to his face; therefore
Israel and Ephraim stumble in their iniquity; Judah
also stumbles with them.
6 "With their flocks and herds they shall go to seek
the Lord, but they will not find Him; He has withdrawn Himself from them.
7 "They have dealt treacherously with the Lord, for
they have begotten pagan children. Now a New Moon
shall devour them and their heritage.

Hos. 5:1-7

As we noted earlier in our discussion of the priesthood, leadership
is a privilege with great responsibilities.

Also, we are sobered when we realize that people evaluate Christ
and Christianity by what they see in us. I find it helpful to reflect:
"Who would want to become a Christian because of what he sees in
my relationship with Christ? Who would want to seek the Lord's help
with problems because of the way I deal with mine? And in a world of
anxiety, what kind of witness of the peace of Christ have I been? Or, in
a society filled with suffering, spiritual and physical, what have I
exemplified about the Christian's social responsibilities?"

We can be a snare for others because of the lack of God's authenticity in our lives — through our words and through our actions.

Emerson's words, "What you do speaks so loudly, I can't hear what
you say," remind all of us that our actions depict the intent of our
discipleship. A father told me how startled he was when his son said

proudly, "Dad, I want to be just like you." The man said, "Now I'd better take more seriously how I live my faith."

In my first parish I was affirmed but also awakened to my awesome responsibility when a baseball team of young lads named their team "the little Lloyds" and had the name printed on their uniforms. And every parent with grown children looks at them with a mixture of satisfaction and alarm to see his or her character strengths and hang-ups ingrained in the personalities of the next generation.

Hosea begins chapter 5 with a threefold summons for judgment to three groups: priests, house of Israel, and house of the king. Though the house of Israel probably refers to all the people, it is likely that the tribe chieftains of the northern kingdom are the target along with the priests and the kings and royal court.

The clause, *"For yours is the judgment"* (Hos. 5:1), can mean both "you are under judgment" and "you are responsible for justice." While the priests were responsible for teaching the Law, the chieftains had the duty for the local administration of justice, and the king and the royal court were to lead with integrity internally and externally with other nations. Hosea warns the leaders that God's judgment upon them for the dilution of justice and righteousness was impartial.

With the images of "snare" and "net" from the accouterments of the hunter, Hosea accuses the leaders of not having lived up to their responsibility for maintaining God's Law in the life of Israel. "Snare" is a trap for birds (Ps. 124:7; Prov. 7:23; Amos 3:5). A "net" may catch birds (Hos. 7:12), but also lions (Ezek. 19:8). The leaders are responsible for luring Israel away into apostasy. But so were the men, the fathers, and husbands.

The towns mentioned were sites of the syncretistic or Canaanite cult worship. Mizpah is probably the Mizpah of Benjamin nine miles north of Jerusalem. Excavations there have uncovered numerous Astarte statuettes from the eighth century B.C., showing that the fertility cult was active there. Tabor is a mountain on the northeastern edge of the Jezreel Valley, and was another cult site. Shittim is alluded to in verse two. The point is that cult worship had spread across the land.

Hosea's charge against the leaders continues in verse two: *"The revolters are deeply involved in slaughter, though I rebuke them all."* Andersen and Freedman suggest that this refers to the forbidden practice of child sacrifice (cf. Gen. 22:10; Ps. 106:36–39; Isa. 57:5; Ezek. 16:21; 23:39).[2]

The last half of Hosea 5:2 is literally "though/but I am chastise-ment/discipline to all of them", though it could be, following the Septuagint, "I am your chastiser/instructor." The root for *rebuke* or *chastise* connotes instruction by the father in the family. Yahweh, the Father of Israel, has established His rules for life among His people, and the purpose of chastisement is for new obedience (Deut. 4:36; 8:5–20; 21:18; Prov. 4:1–27; 19:18).[3]

Though the leaders deceive the people, the Lord is not deceived—He knows Ephraim/Israel (Hos. 5:3). The names are used interchangeably, a Hebraic repetition for emphasis. "*I know Ephraim, and Israel is not hidden from Me; for now, O Ephraim, you commit harlotry; Israel is defiled*" (Hos. 5:3). The New English Bible gives those words an affectionate tone, "I have cared for Ephraim and I have not neglected Israel." This affection heightens the chastisement as a soul-wrenching expression of unbroken care from a broken heart. An even more vivid contrast is that God knew all about Israel's unresponsiveness, and yet He continued to pursue her. Furthermore, God knew too well that Israel's apostasy defiled all the people, not just a handful of sinners. The *hiphil* stem of *zny* elsewhere has a causative sense ("cause to play the harlot" — Exod. 34:16; Lev. 19:29), but Hosea can use it in the same way as the *qal* ("commit harlotry" — Hos. 4:10, 18). Wolff takes the *hiphil* as causative here, "Because you, Ephraim, taught whoredom, Israel is defiled."[4]

To know that God knows and cares for us can be the motivation of a cleansing confession. Often after hearing a person relate a sorry tale of failure and sin, I'm led to say, "God knows and loves you, in spite of what you've done. He offers you forgiveness and a new begin-ning." Sometimes people are astonished that God knew all about them before they made their confession.

His omniscience and omnipresence jars them, as if what they had done had been beyond His all-seeing eyes. "How can He care for me knowing what I've done?" they often ask. "Because He is God!" is the only answer, coupled with an explanation of the magnificent way He was both the Just and the Justifier at Calvary.

Of greater concern are the people who will not come to God because of what they have done. The next section, Hosea 5:4–5 exposes that in a disturbing way.

DEEDS THAT DEBILITATE

"They do not direct their deeds toward turning to their God, for the spirit of harlotry is in their midst, and they do not know the Lord. The pride of Israel testifies to his face" (Hos. 5:4–5a).

Perhaps a better translation, found in the RSV, is, "Their deeds do not permit them to return to their God." The deeds were first an obstacle incompatible with God, and then an obsession that kept them from returning to God. Originally, the people wanted Yahweh and the Baals; ultimately they completely lost their desire for God. What they did was incompatible with their knowledge of God; inevitably they lost all yearning for knowledge of Him.

When the Israelites denied Yahweh's Lordship, they made themselves vulnerable to the spirit of harlotry, and obsession and compulsion set in. The evil spirits of rebellion, self-indulgence, and arrogance became ingrained in them and were sealed over with pride. This *"pride of Israel testifies to His face"* (Hos. 5:5). The people testified against themselves. They become proud of being proud!

It happened in the eighth century B.C., it happened during Jesus' ministry, and it happens now. The only way we can avoid this obstacle is through a consistent daily inventory of our conduct, habits, attitudes, possessions, or involvements. We need to see if any of these things are inconsistent with our obedience to God. This inventory must be followed by our confession and renunciation. When I recently preached on this portion of Hosea, a friend from the movie industry was in the congregation. He asked to see me. When we got together he said, "You were talking about me last Sunday. The pride membrane has not quite sealed me up—but almost. I used to know God, but I seem to have drifted away from Him. Something's wrong. Help me."

In response, I took him through this kind of inventory. I asked, "Is there any place in your life where you are resisting God's will in your life?" He replied, "How did you know?" So we wrote down the specific areas of his resistance. Then I asked, "Is there any area in your life where you need guidance and power?" He smiled, "You know me pretty well!" And we wrote down the challenges and responsibilities where life had him on the ropes. Then I asked, "Are there any broken relationships in which you need to express deeper love or forgiveness or caring?" He laughed, "Now you're meddling!" He talked honestly about a problem in his marriage and how he could make a difference by changing his priorities. Next I asked about the man's prayer life and what he was doing for spiritual nourishment. His response was that this too had drifted. Finally I questioned him about what he was doing to help with problems in the community. He threw up his hands, "Guilty as charged!" Looking at the long list we had compiled during our visit, he asked, "Now what do I do about all this?"

"My friend," I said, "you are very fortunate. God has given you the desire to know Him better before you got totally blocked by pride. You have taken the first step to begin walking in the light." I repeated 1 John 1:5-7, "This is the message . . . that God is light and in Him is no darkness at all. If we say that we have fellowship with Him, and walk in darkness, we lie and do not practice the truth. But if we walk in the light as He is in the light, we have fellowship with one another, and the blood of Jesus Christ His Son cleanses us from all sin." We then talked about what he had discovered about himself in that light. He saw the obstacles he had accumulated in attitude and actions. Then it was time to talk about grace, forgiveness, and a solid commitment to Christ and new priorities for his life. After prayer, the man grasped hold of the paper on which we had written what needed to be changed. "My new agenda!" he said as he left.

Reflecting on the conversation, I was thankful I had not left out of my preaching this portion of Hosea 5 about the danger of drifting so far away from God that we lose our desire to know Him. There are people in our congregations every Sunday who are teetering on the brink with unconfessed sins and failures that block the flow of God's power in their lives. Christians stumble today just as the Israelites in Hosea's time stumbled.

"*Therefore, Israel and Ephraim stumble in their iniquity; Judah also stumbles with them*" (Hos. 5:5). Both nations, with different brands of apostasy, stumbled. The northern kingdom with its Baal worship and the southern kingdom with its lack of justice and righteousness as Joel, Jeremiah, and Isaiah exposed with anguish. This verse provides an excellent basis for a message on spiritual stumbling when combined with Jude 24, "Now to Him who is able to keep you from stumbling, and to present you faultless before the presence of His glory with exceeding joy. . . ." Using the title "What to Do When You Stumble" opens the way for an outline something like this:

I.   Exposition — How Israel Stumbled

II.   Identification — How We Stumble Today

III. Application—Christ is Able!
    A. Able to pick us up when we have stumbled.
    B. Able to catch us before we stumble.
    C. Able to keep us from stumbling.
    D. Able to help us to walk in the light and see the obstacles on which we might stumble.

SEEK AND FIND

The scene in verse 6 is graphic in its irony and sadness: *"With their flocks and herds they shall go to seek the Lord, but they will not find Him."* Note that *Him* is italicized in the NKJV; and rightly so. They were looking in the wrong place. The "seek and find" motif was used in the cultic observances, particularly in the Baal myth of the absent divinity. Elijah spoofed that myth when he called for Yahweh to answer his prayer and God answered with fire on Mount Carmel (1 Kings 18:38).

What is clearly indicated in this sixth verse is that the people in Hosea's time were seeking Yahweh in the Baal shrines only to blend their worship of Him with the Baals. No wonder they did not find Him. *"He has withdrawn Himself from them"* (Hos. 5:6b). The word *withdraw* is normally transitive in the *qal* stem used here, often referring to the removal of clothing (Deut. 25:9–10; Isa. 20:2). Note the contrast—the spirit of harlotry is in their midst (5:4), while Yahweh has withdrawn from them, no longer in their midst.

It makes all the difference where and how we seek the Lord. He will not be found as one of our diminutive gods, and He will not be found when our loyalty and allegiance, even our worship, is given to anything or any person above Him. He has marked out the way, "You will seek Me and find Me, when you search for Me with all your heart" (Jer. 29:13, cf. Isa. 55:7). And Jesus Christ, the way to God, the truth about God, and the life of God, taught us in our prayers to, "Ask, and it will be given to you; seek, and you will find; knock, and it will be opened to you. For everyone who asks receives, and he who seeks finds, and to him who knocks it will be opened" (Luke 11:9–10).

Even Jesus has His own "seek and *not* find" challenges with the Pharisees who refused to believe that He was the Messiah. Indeed they could not find Jesus for they did not believe in Him or the resurrection He promised. But to those who did believe, He said, "And if

I go and prepare a place for you, I will come again and receive you to Myself; that where I am, there you may be also. And where I go you know, and the way you know" (John 14:3- 4). The sure way to seek and find God is through His Son, Christ our Lord. But He, too, will be strangely absent if we seek Him as anyone less than absolute Lord!

This first section of Hosea, chapter 5, closes with the frightening results of the spirit of harlotry. *"They have dealt treacherously with the Lord, for they have begotten pagan children. Now a New Moon shall devour them and their heritage"* (Hos. 5:7).

The terminology "dealt treacherously with the Lord" is repeated in 6:7 and connected there with breaking the covenant. It basically means "deception," such as the deception of an unfaithful husband. Andersen and Freedman conclude, "We are dealing with hypocritical Yahweh worship: the depravity that makes repentance impossible is not renunciation of Yahweh, but complacent religiosity."[5]

One specific offense is given: procreation of "pagan" (literally "foreign" or "strange") children through the sex rites of the fertility cults. No wonder Yahweh was absent from the Baal sites! Hosea 5:7b presents judgment coming on Israel for her offenses, but the meaning is not entirely clear. The difficulty is in connecting *"New Moon"* and *"devour."* Some scholars have suggested an agricultural catastrophe such as a drought, locust, or invasion. An even better possibility is that a corruption of the New Moon feast mixed with pagan worship will further devour the people's true loyalty to Yahweh. Isaiah 1:13-14 implies such an interpretation: "Bring no more futile sacrifices; incense is an abomination to Me. The New Moons, the Sabbaths, and the calling of assemblies—I cannot endure iniquity and the sacred meeting. Your New Moons and your appointed feasts My soul hates; they are a trouble to Me, I am weary of bearing them." This certainly fits with Yahweh's judgment on ritualism without renunciation of false gods.

AN OLD CONFLICT AND A DANGEROUS ALLY

> 5:8 "Blow the ram's horn in Gibeah, the trumpet in Ramah! Cry aloud at Beth Aven, 'Look behind you, O Benjamin!'
> 9 "Ephraim shall be desolate in the day of rebuke; among the tribes of Israel I make known what is sure.

10 "The princes of Judah are like those who remove a landmark; I will pour out my wrath on them like water.

11 "Ephraim is oppressed and broken in judgment, because he willingly walked by human precept.

12 "Therefore I will be to Ephraim like a moth, and to the house of Judah like rottenness.

13 "When Ephraim saw his sickness, and Judah saw his wound, then Ephraim went to Assyria and sent to King Jareb; yet he cannot cure you, nor heal you of your wound.

14 "For I will be like a lion to Ephraim, and like a young lion to the house of Judah. I, even I, will tear them and go away; I will take them away, and no one shall rescue.

15 "I will return again to My place till they acknowledge their offense. Then they will seek My face; in their affliction they will earnestly seek Me."

Hos. 5:8–15

The judgment of God on both Ephraim and Judah begins with a border war between the two nations, continues with an appeal for help from Assyria, and culminates with the fall of Ephraim to the dangerous ally. We see Yahweh as the Lord of all nations. Even though they did not recognize Him, He worked out measures of His judgment through their battles with each other. Eventually their self-seeking alliances backfired. The reality of divine justice is executed through the realities of military and political conflict between the nations.

Scholars have written countless pages discussing the question of whether Hosea 5:8–15 refers to the territorial aggrandizement of Judah along the border between the nations or the prediction of Assyria's invasion of the northern kingdom from the north penetrating as far south as the territory of Benjamin. I believe it is both. The princes of Judah had become the land grabbers *"like those who remove a landmark"* (Hos. 5:10). When Assyria attacked the northern kingdom, about 733 B.C., Judah apparently attacked the border cities of Israel. But Judah should be aware: *"Look behind you, O Benjamin!"* (5:8) or better, "Tremble, O Benjamin!" (RSV). Later, Assyria penetrated the northern kingdom as far as the borders of Benjamin. In 722 B.C., Israel fell to Assyria, and in 701 B.C. Jerusalem was brought under siege.

Both Israel and Judah appealed for help from Assyria in the conflicts with each other, but eventually Assyria was used in Yahweh's judgment on both nations. He will be like a moth eating the weakened fabric of Ephraim's military strength and like dry rot decay in Judah's pride. Palliative appeals to Assyria by both nations would not heal Ephraim's sickness or Judah's wound (v. 13). Yahweh will use Assyria like a lion to crush Ephraim and a young lion to track Judah down to Jerusalem where the city would survive by a hair's breadth at the midnight hour, only to be sacked 115 years later by Babylonia. Continuing the lion imagery, Yahweh states that He *"will tear them and go away"* (5:14) — the people of the northern kingdom will be carried away into Assyrian captivity, and eventually the people of the southern kingdom will be exiled in Babylonia.

Two versions of history capture the full impact of this section of Hosea. First, we see the aggression and greed of nations in war, destruction, occupation, and the displacement of captive people as t he spoils of warfare. Second, we see Yahweh punishing His arrogant people who will not renounce apostasy or pride. But in it all, His intention is not just punishment, but repentance and a return of His people to Him.

Verse 15 portrays this redemptive purpose of punishment: *"I will return again to My place till they acknowledge their offense. Then they will seek My face; in their affliction they will earnestly seek Me."* Again we feel the pulse beat of God's grace-pounding heart. God will not give up on His people, but out of grace He expresses His wrath while simultaneously He patiently persists, waiting for His people to repent and seek His face, His presence, Himself.

The inescapable truth for us today, as nations, as the church, and as individuals is the bracing truth that God does use both people and adversities to break our pride. All with the purpose that we will return to Him and trust Him as our Lord.

NOTES

1. Wolff, *Hosea*, 96.
2. Andersen and Freedman, *Hosea*, 386–388.
3. Wolff, *Hosea*, 99.
4. Wolff, *Hosea*, 94.
5. Andersen and Freedman, *Hosea*, 395.

CHAPTER NINE

Repentance That's Real

Hosea 6:1–7:3

> 6:1 "Come, and let us return to the Lord; for He has torn, but He will heal us; He has stricken, but He will bind us up.
>
> 2 "After two days He will revive us; on the third day He will raise us up, that we may live in His sight.
>
> 3 "Let us know, let us pursue the knowledge of the Lord. His going forth is established as the morning; He will come to us like the rain, like the latter and former rain to the earth."
>
> *Hos. 6:1–3*

It is important to define our interpretation of Hosea 6:1–3 as either a further appeal from the prophet for a return of the people to the Lord or a response of the people to the prophet's preaching. If it is the former, Hosea takes for granted the need for authentic repentance and reconciliation. But if it is the latter, the response lacks the radical dimension of true contrition. If this is a record of the response of the people to the prophet's word from the Lord, then it is too glib and accounts for the Lord's exasperated, "O Ephraim, what shall I do to you?" in the opening of the second section of the chapter in verse 4. If verses 1–3 were Hosea's appeal, then the people did not heed it; if it was the people's response, then it was lacking in both depth and length.

I have raised this question because Hosea 6:1–3 is a favorite, familiar passage for preaching and teaching. It is used as a call for people to return to God. But we need to be careful not to offer our people marked-down grace. We can avoid this by interpreting the word *return* in the context of the entire book of Hosea.

In our preaching and teaching, consistently we need to invite people to renounce the ways of sin, the compulsive, repetitive patterns of resisting God, and the power of evil that seeks to influence us to worship false gods. Sometimes a brief responsive reading in which people respond to the question, "Do you renounce the ways of sin?" and can say flatly, "I renounce them!" underlines the importance of renunciation in repentance.

One man told me after a service in which we had such a reading, "I usually have the back door of my mind open for a quick escape after the prayer of confession. Actually saying that I renounce the deeper causes of what I might need to confess, really slams that door shut and bolts it!"

Often we all want to escape when we are called to authentically confess and renounce our old addictions to sin. Sometimes we try to get by with beautiful but vague phrases such as, "Forgive me for not doing what I should have done and doing what I should not have done." Other times our confession means to us little more than Catherine the Great's flippant expression: *"Le bon Dieu pardonnera; c'est son metier"* (The good Lord will pardon; that's His trade).

In the deeper context of authentic repentance *and* renuniciation, we must say, *"Come, and let us return to the Lord; for He has torn, but He will heal us? He has stricken, but He will bind us up"* (Hos. 6:1). The word *return*, in the light of Hosea's prophecy, either means reassociation or repentance and reconciliation. True repentance not only involves acknowledging that the Lord has torn, but why He has had to take such drastic action. Getting well spiritually or psychologically involves recognizing the underlying causes of our sickness. God does not bind us up with Band-aids; rather, He wants to heal us. His healing necessitates praise for His love that forces us to see ourselves as we are.

In the post-resurrection, post-Pentecost age in which we are living, the ministry of healing is assigned by the Father to Christ, the reigning Lord. He doesn't just give healing, He is the healing Spirit. He dredges up memories that need to be healed. He guides our confession, *homologia*, freeing us to say after Him the things He discerns we need to repent of and renounce. He has the authority to say, "Your sins are forgiven; go and sin no more." He pronounces that absolution with the power of His own death on the cross.

In an even more profound way, we read verse 2 in the light of Christ's resurrection and the recapitulation of death and resurrection as the essence of regeneration and as the key to continuing spiritual power. *"After two days He will revive us; on the third day He will raise us up"* (6:2). This death and resurrection description reminds us of Ezekiel 37:11–14 in which Israel confesses, "Our bones are dry, our hope is lost, and we ourselves are cut off!" (v. 11b), and the Lord responds, "I will put My Spirit in you, and you shall live, and I will place you in your own land. Then you shall know that I, the Lord, have spoken it and performed it" (v. 14).

Hosea 6:2 strikes the same note. Nothing less than resurrection is needed for Israel. The words *the third day* would have meant "very soon" to the people in Hosea's day. But to us, along with the New Testament church, the verse has Messianic overtones and along with the sign of Jonah foreshadows the death and resurrection of Christ. It also emphasizes that our true repentance and confession of faith in Christ must be a death to self and a resurrection to new life. Paul details this cycle of recapitulation in Romans 6:4–5, "Therefore we were buried with Him through baptism into death, that just as Christ was raised from the dead by the glory of the Father, even so we also should walk in newness of life. For if we have been united together in the likeness of His death, certainly we also shall be in the likeness of His resurrection."

The cycle of death and resurrection continues after our initial regeneration. In fact, it is the key that unlocks growth in Christ and the abundant life. The more we die to our tenacious control, the more He is able to resurrect His best for us. When we surrender our failures, He raises out of the ashes a new start; when we cry out for help in our problems, He gives us insight and direction we would not have dreamed were possible; when we have challenges that are beyond us, He gives us supernatural strength and wisdom. Likewise, the more we let go of our worry over the future, the clearer His guidance becomes. The secret of fullness of life is dying to the arrogant willful self. With each diminutive death it is a step forward in knowing the Lord.

"Let us know, let us pursue the knowledge of the Lord" (v. 3), becomes our motto for daily living. Any day lived without a new discovery of an aspect of God's nature is a wasted day. If we do not know Him better this week than last week, we are settling for sameness. And if we can't say we have grown in knowing God, then we are backsliding into the future. A pastor of a large church complained that he had the largest cradle roll in his denomination—most of his members.

There's a great difference between being childlike in trusting God and childish in never going beyond the infant steps of knowing God. As a young pastor, C.H. Spurgeon opened a sermon with a statement about the purpose of life, one that he pursued all through his ministry:

> It has been said by someone that the proper study of mankind is man. I will not oppose the idea, but I believe it is equally true that the proper study of God's elect is God. . . . The highest science, the loftiest speculation, the mightiest philosophy, which can ever engage the attention of a child of God, is the name, the nature, the person, the work, the doings, and the existence of the great God whom he calls Father.
>
> There is something exceedingly improving to the mind in a contemplation of the Divinity. It is a subject so vast, that our thoughts are lost in its immensity; so deep, that our pride is drowned in its infinity. Other subjects we can compare and grapple with; in them we feel a kind of self-content, and we go our way with the thought, "Behold, I am wise."

No subject of contemplation will tend more to humble the mind, than thoughts of God. Spurgeon goes on:

> But while the subject *humbles* the mind, it also *expands* it. He who often thinks of God will have a larger mind than the man who simply plods around this narrow globe. The most excellent study for expanding the soul, is the science of Christ and Him crucified, and the knowledge of the Godhead in the glorious Trinity. Nothing will so enlarge the intellect, nothing so magnify the whole soul of man, as a devout, earnest, continued investigation of the great subject of the Deity.

All that we learn about God helps us to worship Him more joyfully and serve Him more obediently. We are motivated to grapple with soul-sized issues and press on in doing His will. The more magnificently we think about God, the more reverently we will accept the gift of a personal relationship with Him.

Hosea 6:3 keeps us focused on the faithfulness and grace of God who is infinite, eternal, and unchangeable in His being, wisdom, power, holiness, goodness, and truth. *"His going forth is established as the morning; He will come to us like the rain, like the latter and former rain to the earth."* The One who divided night and day is as sure as the sun that rises at His command, and His mercy replenishes our souls as the rainfall and spring replenishes the earth. He does this so we can return to Him daily, hourly, as the only reliable certainty of life. But we must return with renunciation of anything that denies His absolute sovereignty, not just over the sun and the rain, but our total lives.

Apparently Israel was not ready to give everything to God. And so, from the summit of the bright hope of Hosea 6:1–3, we go back into the dark valley of her willful transgression of God's covenant. The people did not heed Hosea's call to return. Their response thus far lacked the honesty of true repentance.

WHAT GOD REALLY WANTS

In Hosea 6:4–6, as before in the prophet's declaration of the word of God, we are led into the heart of God, witnessing the struggle of God within Himself over His fickle people. God wanted renunciation of the past evidenced by *hesed*, or loyalty, translated "faithfulness" in 6:4 and "mercy" in 6:6. *"For Your faithfulness is like a morning cloud . . . for I desire mercy and not sacrifice, and the knowledge of God more than burnt offerings."*

Israel's loyalty is unsteady, fleeting and changeable as the morning mist, a ground fog, that disappears as the sun rises. God's faithfulness was affirmed in verse 3 by the constancy of morning. In verse 4 we encounter the image of a morning fog that disappears in the presence of the sun. Could God be suggesting that His people do not really want His presence? Certainly the short-lived presence of the fog would be metaphorical for Israel's efforts to escape God's holiness and righteousness and light. *"And your judgments"* (margin note in NKJV—"the judgments on you") *"are like light that goes forth."* Israel was committed to the deeds of darkness and not the light. Even though Yahweh had cut them asunder with the words of the prophets and slew their apostasy with His own words spoken through the prophets, Israel did not return to *hesed* faithfulness and loyalty to Him and the covenant.

Verse 6 clearly states what God wants: *"For I desire mercy and not sacrifice, and the knowledge of God more than burnt offerings."* The sacrifices cited here were the legitimate sacrifices of Israel's religion, not the Baal cult. Yahweh wanted something more than a legalistic, ritualistic return to the traditional worship of Him. These sacrifices, efficacious as they were, would be only substitutes for knowledge of God. *Hesed* and *daʿat³ ĕlōhîm* were to be inseparably related. Wolff comments incisively:

> The parallel concept *daʿat* shows that this relationship to God—indeed this communion with the God who is active, who gives and speaks—is the foundation of everything. This cognitive idea in the phrase 'knowledge of God' makes clear that God's covenant loyalty can be 'known' from the revelation of His word (4:1f,6) and His work (11:1–3; 2:10; 13:4). Since it is the knowledge of Him who is the continually efficacious God of Israel, it creates a relationship between Israel and her God. To know Him is to experience Him and to live in communion with Him in trust and obedience. For Hebrew thought, these existential components are inseparably bound to the cognitive functions, all of them in turn belonging to the structure of *daʿat*. . . . In the kind of worship He desires, Yahweh is not satisfied with pious rituals. In genuine worship God's relationship to His people is experienced, for there His deeds in history and His instructions for life are "represented." Such worship—entirely different from the ritual of sacrifice and penitence cited here—would have an effect on Israel's political relationships with foreign powers and with her brother Judah.[1]

God does not want us to placate Him in self-justifying rituals but in praise of a sanctified relationship. For us, sacrifices instead of knowledge would include all that we do to justify ourselves rather than submitting to a relationship marked by those two powerful ingredients we have talked about previously—intimacy and integrity. What we should do because of God's *hesed* to us sometimes becomes our effort to earn it. Subtly, it soon becomes a substitute for knowledge of God, within a responsive relationship with Him. Essentially though, often we cannot be bothered with God. We want to do His basic requirements, then get on with our agendas. Our sacrifices can include dutiful prayer, attendance at worship, church work, service, and good works. What is to be done in intimate communion *with* God we do *for* God, and eventually we do it *without* God. All these responsibilities are crucial for authentic discipleship. But the danger is that we can become so preoccupied with working for the Lord in our self-justifying effort, that our personal relationship with Him becomes perfunctory rather than primary.

Jesus tells us that God is seeking true worshipers who will worship Him in spirit and truth (John 4:23–24). He referred to Hosea 6:6 in both Matthew 9:13 and 12:7 in rebuking the Pharisees for ritual observances without knowledge of God. And when a scribe quoted Hosea 6:6 to Him, Jesus said, "You are not far from the kingdom of God," (Mark 12:32–34). After His "Well, then do it" intensity, no one dared question Jesus further, but they did not change. Nor did Israel take seriously Yahweh's call for faithfulness and knowledge.

THE OFFENSES OF THOSE WITHOUT FAITHFULNESS AND KNOWLEDGE

> 6:7 "But like men they transgressed the covenant; there they dealt treacherously with Me.
> 8 "Gilead is a city of evildoers, and defiled with blood.
> 9 "As bands of robbers lie in wait for a man, so the company of priests murder on the way to Shechem; surely they commit lewdness.
> 10 "I have seen a horrible thing in the house of Israel; there is the harlotry of Ephraim; Israel is defiled.
> 11 "Also, O Judah, a harvest is appointed for you, when I return the captives of My people.
> 7:1 "When I would have healed Israel, then the iniquity of Ephraim was uncovered, and the wickedness of Samaria. For they have committed fraud; a thief comes in; a band of robbers takes spoils outside.
> 2 "They do not consider in their hearts that I remember all their wickedness; now their own deeds have surrounded them; they are before My face.
> 3 "They make a king glad with their wickedness, and princes with their lies."
>
> *Hos. 6:7–7:3*

In contrast with Yahweh's desires in 6:6, this section begins, "but . . . they," and goes on to list a series of offenses against Him because they resisted obedience and knowledge. Continuing previous themes, they defraud or ignore Yahweh, even though He knows them and their deeds. Their wickedness (compulsive sin) has continued to the point that "their own deeds have surrounded them" (7:2), with the implication that they no longer break out of the siege of apostasy and strife.

The beginning phrase, *"But like men,"* in the NKJV is one possible translation of the Hebrew text. Alternatives are "As at Adam," in keeping with the text, or "in Adam," changing the preposition. Usually ʾādām is taken as a place name to supply the antecedent for *there* in the following clause. A prime candidate is the Adam in the Jordan River above the place where the Israelites crossed at the time of the conquest (Josh. 3:16). While this may be a reference to some apostasy at that time, Wolff suggests that this probably refers to a more recent offense.[2] As in 4:2 and 5:2, bloodshed among the people is a prominent part of the offense.

Andersen and Freedman propose that verses 7-9 point to a particularly heinous crime of murder that occurred at Adam in the district of Gilead (6:8) on the road to Shechem (6:9).[3]

The contrast of what Yahweh desires in verse 6 and the behavior described in 6:7-7:3 is emphasized by the beginning emphatic pronoun with the conjunction (*but they*). The second clause, *"they dealt treacherously with Me,"* shows that the covenant of the first clause is the covenant Yahweh established with Israel, not some treaty with another nation.[4] The covenant was to be characterized by *hesed* (6:6).

In 6:8 the inhabitants of Gilead, east of the Jordan, are accused of unspecified evil connected with bloodshed. The construction translated "defiled with blood" is quite difficult. Andersen and Freedman see ʾāqubbâ as an adjective, *deceitful*, modifying *city* and *middām* meaning "because of bloodshed." Thus, they translate "a deceitful city, because of bloodshed."[5]

Though the beginning of 6:9 is not quite clear, the murderous deeds of the priests are compared to the assaults of robbers. The deeds are characterized as lewd and take place on the way to Shechem.

Verse 10 serves as a summary of the accusations of verses 7-9. Wolff notes that the word translated "horrible thing" suggests cultic more than political offenses, along with the connection of verses 7-10a with verse 6 and the mention of the priests in verse 9.[6] Again the offenses are characterized as harlotry, echoing closely the expression of 5:3.

Hosea 6:11b is normally attached to the following clauses. Yahweh refers to His past restoration and healing of people, encompassing Israel and Judah as a whole. The terminology used "denotes the restoration of the people's wounded body (cf. 5:13; 6:1)."[7] Although the terms can refer to returning exiles, a more general sense of reversing fortunes is possible (cf. Job 42:10). After this restoration, new transgression broke out in Israel. "Earlier as well as now (6:7,10a), whenever Yahweh has mercy on His people, their pious outward appearances are not followed by appropriate deeds; rather there is theft and robbery within and without."[8]

Ignoring Yahweh's keen perception (Hos. 5:3; 6:10), the people act as if Yahweh is ignorant or forgetful of their deeds (7:2). The refusal to repent and renounce the past sin led to a captivity from which Israel no longer seeks freedom. The king and princes are glad because that, too, is their spiritual condition (7:3).

Richard Baxter had placed on his pulpit the words, "I preach as a dying man to dying men and women as if never to preach again." May God give us that centered focus as we warn people of the rigors of spiritual and moral death that causes death long before our pulse ceases and with boldness and clarity share the secret of renunciation for resurrection *now*!

NOTES

1. Wolff, *Hosea*, 120–121.
2. Ibid., 121.
3. Andersen and Freedman, *Hosea*, 436.
4. Wolff, *Hosea*, 121.
5. Andersen and Freedman, *Hosea*, 432, 440.
6. Wolff, *Hosea*, 123.
7. Ibid., 123.
8. Ibid., 124.

CHAPTER TEN

Epigrams of Exacerbation

Hosea 7:4–16

Hosea's prophecy makes use of pithy epigrams to describe Ephraim's spiritual, moral, and political condition. We have encountered two of them thus far: she is like a stubborn calf and like a morning cloud or fog. Hosea 7:4–16 contains four more: the nation is like an overheated oven, like a cake unturned, like a silly dove without sense, and like a faulty bow. These have to do with both domestic and international political problems dealt with in this section. And yet, they are all epigrams of the exacerbation of Ephraim's essential spiritual problem of refusing to turn to Yahweh and receive knowledge of Him. We cannot imagine that things got worse, but they did.

Like Jesus' use of parables, Hosea's similitude epigrams paint pictures. They give us, "Aha, now I see what you mean" insight. They provide the preacher or teacher of Hosea an opportunity to vary his or her method.

A HOT OVEN

7:4 "They are all adulterers. Like an oven heated by a baker—he ceases stirring the fire after kneading the dough, until it is leavened.

5 "In the day of our king princes have made him sick, inflamed with wine; he stretched out his hand with scoffers.

6 "They prepare their heart like an oven, while they lie in wait; their baker sleeps all night; in the morning it burns like a flaming fire.

7 "They are all hot, like an oven, and have devoured their judges; all their kings have fallen. None among them calls upon Me."

Hos. 7:4–7

In Hosea's day an oven was about three feet in length, cylindrical in form, with the walls sloping to an open aperture at the top. Fire was set in the oven early in the morning, and the flames would leap up through the top. Later, when the walls were thoroughly hot, the fire would be removed and the flat cakes of kneaded dough would be slapped on the inside walls of the oven.

Yahweh says His people are like that red hot oven in the morning when the fire is at its height of intensity. The metaphor presents a startling picture of flames and smoke leaping out of the oven top. The comparison is to Israel's passions. *"They are all adulterers"* (Hos. 7:4). This refers to the people's immorality and their involvement in Baal worship. It also involves the inflamed domestic political scene that followed the Assyrian invasion. Douglas Stuart comments, "The passion of the king, his court officials, and the influential nobility is likened to a baker's oven so hot that the baker need not tend the fire during the entire baking process. The heat of their treachery and transgression drives them to take matters into their own hands, ignoring Yahweh in their maneuverings."[1]

The leaders abandoned their security in Yahweh and flamed with passionate lust for power in the political confusion before and after 733 B.C. The throne was grasped by one assassin after another. After Jeroboam's death, consecutive kings took the throne by bloodshed. Zechariah ruled for six months, Shallum for one month, Manahem eight years, and Pekahiah two years. Hoshea, the last of Israel's kings, with the help of Tiglath-Pileser of Assyria, conspired against Pekah, slew him, and ascended to the throne (2 Kings 15:30) and reigned for nine years. Shalmaneser V was not as willing to conspire with Hoshea. He attacked Israel, sending Hoshea scurrying for help from Egypt. Falsely secure in Egypt's help, Hoshea refused to pay the Assyrians their annual tribute. Shalmaneser laid siege to Samaria and took Hoshea into captivity.

Verse 5 gives the account of an orgy on the anniversary of one of their short-lived monarchies. We are not told which one. The important thing is that the conspirators got the king drunk, and *"he stretched out his hand with scoffers,"* probably toasting Baal or some foreign god. But the conspirators *"lie in wait"* (v. 6), and when their passions are *"all hot, like an oven"* (v. 7), they murder the royal court as well as the king. Hosea suggests that it was a common occurrence (four of Israel's last kings were assassinated), and none among them trusted in the Lord. Kings and courts, leaders and people all turned from Him.

"There is none among them who calls upon Me" (v. 7). George Adam Smith caught the depth of the depravity, "A king surrounded by loose, unscrupulous nobles: every man striking for himself; none appealing in truth to God."[2]

Without knowledge of God, without a relationship with Him, our passions do flame like a flaming oven. And not just sexual passion. Add to that more obvious passion—flaming anger, uncontrolled emotions, and competitiveness.

It is fascinating how many of our expressions about our thoughts, emotions, wills, and bodies use the simile of fire. We talk about getting fired up about some idea, or a burning desire, or being aflame with passion, or being burned up with anger. Like physical fire, the potential of fire in our human nature can destroy or create. The fire of conviction can be a driving power, a heart filled with love can express warmth, and a passion for service can motivate our discipleship.

Hosea 7:3–7 is an example of uncontrolled, unchanneled fire that destroys. It vividly depicts why Christ had to come to transform us. The raging fires of our natures have to be transformed. Regeneration by Christ into a new creature does that. The fire of His Spirit burns out the chaff and sets us ablaze with radiance, a will to do His will, emotions that are channels of His love and compassion, and minds aflame with His truth. We are called to be "on fire" Christians. Now our human nature becomes fuel for the flame of the Spirit. Amy Carmichael put it well:

> Let me not sink to be a clod:
> Make me Thy fuel, Flame of God.

THE PROBLEM OF BEING HALF-BAKED

7:8 "Ephraim has mixed himself among the peoples; Ephraim is a cake unturned.

9 "Aliens have devoured his strength, but he does not know it; yes, gray hairs are here and there on him, yet he does not know it.

10 "And the pride of Israel testifies to his face, but they do not return to the Lord their God, nor seek Him for all of this."

Hos. 7:8–10

The baking motif continues in this next epigramic simile about Ephraim being half-baked. In its context, the simile tells us that Israel's dependence on other nations makes her something other than she was created to be. The cake's problem begins with its flour. It is mixed. In Hebrew the word *mixed* is a liturgical term from Exodus 29:2. A meal offering that was mixed had oil added to it until every particle of the flour was saturated with the oil. Now we can understand the words, "*Ephraim has mixed himself among the peoples*" (7:8). The flour is mingled not with the oil of the Spirit but with the dependence on human strength from other nations. The dough for the cake is polluted.

The next thing that is wrong is the way the dough is baked. It is baked only on one side. One side is burned black and the other is a gooey, sticky, soggy, unappetizing, unnourishing mess. If you had a pancake served to you for breakfast that was only fried on one side, you might say, "What a nauseating sight. That makes me sick!" And that's exactly what Yahweh was saying to Ephraim. "You are a cake *unturned*. Your putrefied dough—half-baked before Me—nauseates Me!"

I can remember thinking of this simile when I saw a woman baking thin cakes of bread on stones in a Palestinian camp during my first visit to the Middle East years ago. The women had built fires of red hot coals with flat rocks around them as the cooking surface. When the stones were fully heated, oil was placed on the surface which sizzled and crackled. Then they dropped the flattened dough in the sizzling oil. At that moment, one woman was distracted by another woman who engaged her in a conversation. By the time she returned to the fire, the cake was charred black on one side, but the side facing up was soggy. She swore, took the half-baked cakes, and threw them into the fire. As I stood watching, the words *Ephraim is a cake unturned* hit me with new force.

It makes little difference whether this was the kind of baking alluded to in Hosea or the larger oven that we described in connection with the simile of the hot oven where the bread was placed on the hot sides of the wall. The point is that in either method, the bread (cakes) had to be turned. If not, they are useless and must be thrown away.

Israel was charred on the side of her false hope in other nations but soggy toward Yahweh. She paid more allegiance to the Baals than to Him. And we cannot evade the impact of the simile today. We can be half-baked Christians with a soggy side.

We have to admit that we are overcooked on the side of depending on human resources but are often soggy on the side of trusting God.

Our soggy side exposes our anxieties, worries, and fears. In times of need, we singe dark on the side of consulting people but uncooked in prolonged prayer.

When we consider the quality of our faith, we confess that we tend to be one-sided. We may be orthodox on one side but be raw dough when it comes to "orthopractics," that is, living our carefully worded doctrine. Rather than seeking a balance between piety and social action, we are satisfied with one without the other. Our creeds may be in order, but we may care little for evangelism and mission. Or, our problem might be that we are totally focused on revelation and in trouble with our relationships.

We were created for four basic relationships — with God, ourselves, others, and the world. And God is to be Lord of all four. When I became a Christian, I became totally engrossed in Bible study and prayer. A few years later God showed me how soggy my relational side was. When that tended to get overdone, He put me through a third conversion to become involved in evangelism and mission. Most importantly, though, I must constantly be sure that the flour of my soul is saturated with the oil of the Holy Spirit and not *mixed* with false dependence on people, popularity, or positions.

A SILLY DOVE

7:11 "Ephraim also is like a silly dove, without sense — they call to Egypt, they go to Assyria.

12 "Wherever they go, I will spread My net on them; I will bring them down like birds of the air; I will chastise them according to what their congregation has heard.

13 "Woe to them, for they have fled from Me! Destruction to them, because they have transgressed against Me. Though I redeemed them, yet they have spoken lies against Me.

14 "They did not cry out to Me with their heart when they wailed upon their beds. They assemble together for grain and new wine, they rebel against Me;

15 "though I disciplined and strengthened their arms, yet they devise evil against Me."

Hos. 7:11–15

Ephraim is portrayed as a fluttery, simpleminded, silly dove, inconsistent in its ways, flitting about from place to place. *"Without sense"* (Hos. 7:11), is literally "without heart." Andersen and Freedman call it the "culpable ignorance" of the people who have "abandoned covenant knowledge and thereby perverted their knowledge of other reality."[3] What is lacking is not intelligence but discernment.

Israel places false hope on the great international powers between which it lay — Egypt and Assyria. Instead of turning to God, the leaders of Israel flitted back and forth calling for help. But because of their apostasy, it is the Lord who will catch the flittering bird in the net of judgment. *"Woe to them, for they have fled from Me!"* (Hos. 7:13). Fleeing from Yahweh, soon they will be homeless in captivity.

Verse 14 depicts the pitiful state of Israel's lack of knowledge of God. *"They did not cry out to Me with their heart when they wailed upon their beds."* Not even in their anguish did they return to the Lord. I like to compare that with what the psalmist did under similar outward circumstances: "Commune with your own hearts on your beds, and be silent. Offer right sacrifices, and put your trust in the Lord" (Ps. 4:4–5). The psalmist also lived in a time of pressure and strain. That drove him to prayer to cry out to God. In the middle of his prayer, he was driven inward. His admonition to others was a reminder to himself: Be honest about your spiritual condition; look, examine your heart with God. Offer the sacrifice of a broken and contrite heart, but most of all, put your complete trust in the Lord — and only in Him!

Long before the inner crisis of separation from God and the outward threat of Assyrian invasion, Israel had little by little closed her heart to the overtures of Yahweh's love and correction. Finally, they no longer even cried out to God; they just wailed upon their beds. John Steinbeck's Ethan was right: "Men don't get knocked out, for I mean they can fight back against big things. What kills men is erosion: they get nudged into failure." But sometimes that nudging over the years renders us incapable of handling the big things. And in the crisis we are so unacquainted with God that we wail rather than pray. That is when we flit about like a silly dove going from place to place, person to person looking for quick remedies. The middle of a crisis is not a good time to get ready for the crisis.

But, on the positive side, if we were to stop racing about and did indeed meditate on our relationship with God, how would He guide that meditation? He begins with a word of grace. "You are Mine! I love and accept you. I know all about you." Then He leads us down all the memories of past hurts and failures and offers healing forgiveness. Then He reviews with us those things that keep us from Him. "I cannot be your God if you persist in trying to be your own god and running your own life."

Now that our personality structure is dissected under His careful penetration, showing us ourselves as we are, He then gives us a picture of what we could be by His power. He shows us patterns we have developed that contradict His best for us. He helps us examine our beliefs, values, presuppositions, and prejudices in the light of His Word. We are confronted with the inconsistencies. He flashes before us our commitments as He affirms our strengths and exposes the areas where we need to grow.

"But what about the future?" we ask anxiously. Then He takes us through His promises and assures us. "I will give you enough guidance for each day; I will guide you in each decision. You will have enough wisdom, discernment, clarity, and strength for each situation. But come back here in the quiet with Me each day, and I will show you the next steps, how to act and react, what to say and how to decide. I will give the day and show the way."

Communing with the Lord in this in-depth way leads to what is the psalmist's admonition to himself: "Offer right sacrifices, and put your trust in the Lord." Once we have communed with our Lord in silence, we know what to confess and are open to receive grace. Contriteness replaces contrariness. Arrogant self-determination, mixed motives, distorted relationships, grandiose purposes are all tempered, melted, and recast in the mold of His plans for us. All He wants from us is the sacrifice of our hearts—an inner person completely under His control and an outer life lived in obedience. That is hardly too much to ask. Especially in the light that He alone knows what is best for us, will guide us, and will give us power in life's pressures. Instead of having to be caught in a net to bring us down, we will be able to rest in the nest of His care and then fly with freedom according to His flight plan and destination in formation with others who also have been transformed from being silly doves to soaring eagles.

This process of creative communion with God is just the opposite of what Israel had done prior to the crisis facing her in the last decade before the kingdom fell. Instead, she treated God like the enemy. She didn't have the honesty of a soldier in Konstantine Simonou's story of the Battle of Stalingrad, called *Days and Nights*. A fellow soldier said, "They don't give us any date when they will take Stalingrad. . . .what is the reason?" And he replied, "We are the reason." The people of Israel were not honest enough to say, "We are the reason for all this. We have seen the enemy and it is us."

A FAULTY BOW

> 7:16 "They return but not to the Most High; They are like a treacherous bow. Their princes shall fall by the sword for the cursings of their tongue. This shall be their derision in the land of Egypt.
>
> *Hosea 7:16*

Israel has become a faulty bow, a slack bow unable to propel an arrow to its target. They are totally ineffective in battle. The reason is that they did not turn to Yahweh. Instead, they curse both Hosea and God. Their cursing will be scoffed at in Egypt where they will be the laughing stock because they turn from Egyptian help to Assyria only to be invaded by the armies of Assyria. But the real reason God's people were the butt of raucous ridicule was that they no longer had strength and courage—that had been eroded through the years because of leaving the source of supernatural power in their God. Prior to the depleting defection from Yahweh, the Israelites' courage and military prowess had been a continual amazement to the major powers; now they were ridiculous!

Individuals, churches, and movements can become a defective, slackened bow. It happens when we forget that the reason we are able to do what we do is because of the Lord's Spirit. Once we try to compete on a human level with only human resources, the bow is slackened and no longer can we send the arrow. We are to be astounding miracles of what God can do with a person totally committed to Him. Our challenge is to point away from ourselves to Him, giving Him the glory. When we take the credit ourselves, we are left to operate on our own very limited resources. The bow is limp; the arrow falls short of the mark. And to miss the mark, remember, is sin—to miss the goal of a God-empowered life for which there can be no other explanation than that we belong to Him.

NOTES

1. Stuart, *Hosea-Jonah*, 119.
2. Smith, *The Twelve Prophets*, vol. 1, 287–288.
3. Andersen and Freedman, *Hosea*, 468.

CHAPTER ELEVEN

The Misplaced God

Hosea 8:1–14

8:1 "Set the trumpet to your mouth! He shall come like an eagle against the house of the Lord, because they have transgressed My covenant and rebelled against My law.

2 "Israel will cry to Me, 'My God, we know You!'

3 "Israel has rejected the good; the enemy will pursue him.

4 "They set up kings, but not by Me; they made princes, but I did not acknowledge them. From their silver and gold they made idols for themselves—that they might be cut off.

5 "Your calf is rejected, O Samaria! My anger is aroused against them. How long until they attain to innocence?

6 "For from Israel is even this: A workman made it, and it is not God; but the calf of Samaria shall be broken to pieces.

7 "They sow the wind, and reap the whirlwind. The stalk has no bud; it shall never produce meal. If it should produce, aliens would swallow it up.

8 "Israel is swallowed up; now they are among the Gentiles like a vessel in which there is no pleasure.

9 "For they have gone up to Assyria, like a wild donkey alone by itself; Ephraim has hired lovers.

10 "Yes, though they have hired among the nations, now will I gather them; and they shall sorrow a little, because of the burden of the king of princes.

11 "Because Ephraim has made many altars for sin, they have become for him altars for sinning.

12 "I have written for him the great things of My law, but they were considered a strange thing.

13 "For the sacrifices of My offerings they sacrifice flesh and eat it, but the Lord does not accept them. Now He will remember their iniquity and punish their sins. They shall return to Egypt.

14 "For Israel has forgotten his Maker, and has built temples; Judah also has multiplied fortified cities; but I will send fire upon his cities, and it shall devour his palaces."

Hos. 8:1–14

The last verse of Hosea 8 not only summarizes the whole chapter but serves as a fulcrum for the levers of truth throughout the whole chapter. When we take verse 14 as the text for a message, we have a basic theme for the exposition of the main points throughout the chapter. *"For Israel has forgotten his Maker"* (Hos. 8:14).

Years ago, Allan Redpath wrote incisively, "Do we understand what it means to forget God? I'm not sure we do. It does not mean that God was put into the realm of oblivion. You cannot forget God like that! Even in denying God you are remembering Him. Intellectually we do not forget God. The word "forgot" here means, 'Israel hath mislaid his Maker.' If you forget something, it is out of your memory altogether. If you mislay something you are completely aware of its existence, but as far as you are concerned, it is out of use, out of circulation."[1]

When we shelve, file, or misplace things, they become "out of sight and out of mind." Soon we cannot remember where we put them—we know they still exist, but they have no current importance in our lives.

We sometimes do that with God—we file Him away and forget where we put Him. Finally, we lose any conscious awareness of the presence of God. He did not remove Himself from us, rather we removed ourselves from Him. He has ordained that we should grow in Him through knowledge of and obedience to His Word. Discerning and doing His will is the secret of a deepening relationship with Him. We cannot know Him intimately if we give our allegiance to false gods. If we place our ultimate security in people, and not in Him, the flow of His power is lost. Soon, God is misplaced among the multiplicity of altars to false gods in our lives. The same can happen to a church and to a nation.

Few of us set out to extricate God from our lives. We simply neglect to do what keeps alive a vital relationship with Him. That is when we

114

need a trumpet blast to sound the reveille of revival and renewal. Preaching or teaching Hosea 8 can be that awakening call to a new day for our listeners and our churches. As preachers and teachers of this passage, we accept the assignment to *"set the trumpet to your mouth"* (v. 1). Chapter 8 provides an excellent basis for a renewal retreat, a sermon on how we misplace our God, or, perhaps, a message for church officers or pastors about how renewal must begin with us if we are to sound the call to a new beginning among our people.

To aid us in our exposition of chapter 8, I will divide our progression into the four ways Israel neglected, misplaced, and eventually forgot God. Our headings will focus the contemporary application: (1) misplaced authority; (2) misappropriated autonomy; (3) misdevoted adoration; and, (4) miscalculated assurance.

Misplaced Authority

God is, in H. H. Farmer's memorable phrase, "absolute demand and ultimate succor."[2] We are accustomed to hearing more about the succor, God's gracious love, than about the absolute demand of His holiness, righteousness, and judgment. We need a return to the absolute authority of God in our lives and in our churches. Revivals and renewal have taken place in history because the people of God submitted to the authority and discipline of the Father. Then the preaching and experience of His grace in Jesus Christ and His power in the Holy Spirit are truly Good News. Lasting renewal does not just come from ecclesiology or charismology or missiology, but from Patrology. The *first steps* of renewal today are not accomplished by restructuring the church, or by new commitment to Christ, or by a fresh infilling of Holy Spirit power, or even by trying to find ourselves by getting into mission. Rather, we need the Father's authority, a forthright proclamation of His sovereignty over our lives. Then the faith, grace, and power we have heard so much about will make sense as the only way to live under the Father's authority.

I know that from my own experience. The most moving times of renewal for me have come when God the Father forced me to see myself as I truly was. He did not just deal with surface problems but penetrated to the citadel of my soul. The absolute demands of His commandments could not be equivocated. All the things that were blocking His total command of my life were exposed and had to be confessed. My emptiness had to be admitted, my lack of power acknowledged. My pride and willfulness lanced at the core. And the Father did it out of unqualified, healing love. He is the Refiner of the gold, the Purifier of the silver, the Potter of the clay, the Surgeon of the soul.

I can never escape Jesus' bracing challenge and promise, "Therefore you shall be perfect, just as your Father in heaven is perfect" (Matt. 5:48). I am called not to perfectionism on my own strength but to my basic purpose, which can be accomplished only by the Father's power. The Greek word for "perfect" is *teleioi*, referring to us, and *teleios*, for God. Both come from *telos*, meaning "purpose, end, goal." The awesome promise is that I am to accomplish my purpose even as the Father accomplishes His. And His purpose is to enable me to accomplish my ultimate purpose—a family likeness of my Father, emulating His justice by living the commandments, being transformed into the image of His Son. I believe that a reaffirmation of the Father's authority is a prelude to a rediscovery of my need for Calvary and Pentecost.

A new commitment to the Father's authority makes it possible to preach and teach Hosea 8:1–3 with deeper empathy with Christians today who have evaded the absolute demand of our Holy God, whom Thomas A. Smail calls, "The Forgotten Father."[3]

Israel had forgotten her Maker by transgressing the covenant and rebelling against God's Law. The people asserted that they knew God and yet were devoid of obedience to His authority.

The passage begins with a command to sound the trumpet. The blast of the trumpet is to alert the people to danger. An enemy is about to "*come like an eagle against the house of the Lord.*" Wolff translates *eagle* as a "vulture" and observes, "the vulture is a metaphor for swiftness, for dangerous voracity and majestic superiority"[4] (Exod. 19:4; Deut. 32:11; 2 Sam. 1:23; Job 9:26; Prov. 30:17; Jer. 4:13; Lam. 4:19; Ezek. 17:3; Hab. 1:8). The vulture's attack is on Yahweh's house, probably implying the people and the land of Israel rather than the temple.

The reason for this attack is clearly stated: Israel transgressed Yahweh's covenant (1 Kings 19:10, 14) and rebelled against His Law. In the covenant Yahweh elected Israel to be His people and chose to be their God. The Law was given as a gracious gift to guide the people in the covenant relationship with Yahweh. His absolute authority

116

over His people was established and maintained by both the covenant and the Law. For God's people to transgress the covenant was to step over the demarcation line drawn by the call for ultimate obedience to Yahweh and give that obedience to another god. The Israelites' rebellion (*pešaᶜ*) against the Law was faithlessness to all Yahweh had disclosed about His will for His people. The Torah was more than instruction by the priests, it represented Yahweh's written commandments, promises, and statutes. To go against them was to rebel against Yahweh Himself.

For us today, the Father's authority is clearly established in both the old and new covenants. We are adopted daughters and sons of the Father and have been made part of His eternal family. Our absolutes for holy living come from Sinai, the Mount of Beatitude and Calvary. We are not exempt from the *Shema* but are given the power and new nature of the new covenant to love the Lord our God with all our heart, soul, and might, and as Jesus added, with all our mind (Mark 12:29–31). Love is at the center of God's authority over us. Our motivation for our faithfulness and obedience to Him comes from our reciprocal love for Him.

A sure sign we are living in the covenant of the Father's love is when we realize how difficult it is for us to love Him, others, and ourselves as deeply as He loves us. We are humbled when we honestly admit our humanity.

Israel lacked both humility and honesty. Their proud, defensive response to the charge that they transgressed the covenant and rebelled against the Law is "My God, we know You!" (Hos. 8:2). However, as we have examined the concept of knowledge in Hosea, we know that true knowledge means singlehearted loyalty to God and consistent righteousness in the covenant community. Israel's resistance to Yahweh's authority over her had gone so far that the people could not respond to His clear word of judgment. They refused to accept God's word through Hosea. Their spirits were the opposite of David's when he accepted God's confrontation through Nathan. They would not say, "I have sinned against the Lord" (2 Sam. 12:13).

We see the insidious nature of sin. It perverts our perception of our need and blocks the desire for reconciliation. We would suppose that the more Israel sinned the more they would know about sin. The opposite was true. The further the people sank into apostasy, the less they could recognize it as sin. Andersen and Freedman comment,

"The claim of the people to know Yahweh is doubtless sincere, that is, they believe it. . . . But in fact, they do not know Him at all. . . . This is not hypocrisy—although that ingredient may be present as well—but sublime arrogant self-deception, invincible self-delusion. As long as they continue in that state, no hope for recognition of the true state of affairs or genuine repentance remains."[5]

Misplacing God's authority over our lives results in this kind of blindness and insensitivity to God. His commandments no longer disturb us or challenge us. We no longer evaluate our lives on the basis of His goals for us.

James S. Stewart drives home that application.

> Every time any of us sins, we are making it not more but less possible, for ourselves to appreciate what sin is; and therefore not more but less likely that we shall feel that there is anything to be forgiven. Every time I indulge in pride, selfishness, or censorious-ness, I am reducing my power to realize how essentially hateful and unChristlike pride, selfishness, and censoriousness are. Every time I reject some voice in conscience, I am making it certain that next time that voice is going to speak not more, but less, imperi-ously and convincingly. Until we have grasped this, we have not begun to glimpse the terrible nature of the problem God had upon His hands when He faced the task of man's redemption.[6]

This problem is vividly portrayed for us in Israel's response to judgment, "My God, we know You!" They claimed to have what they had lost. In so doing they blocked the possibility of receiving what they needed most. Verse 3 portrays the sad result: *"Israel has rejected the good; the enemy will pursue him."* The word *good* is a comprehensive word that includes knowledge of God, the gifts of the covenant, the commandments, the promises of God's provision and protection, and a future filled with hope. Israel has made a choice. She rejected not only the good, but the Good One (as some translators render it) and consequently received the enemy in judgment for her obstinate stub-bornness.

We see why the Incarnation and the cross was necessary. Only the cross could break this cycle of pride and sin. Humankind could not save itself. God had to do it in His Son. He broke our armor of human conceit and revealed His forgiving love. And those who accepted His grace became a new breed of people who manifested a new quality of humility willing to submit to the authority of the Father, exercised in the present reigning power of the resurrected, abiding Christ.

But today we may have more in common with eighth-century B.C. Israel than with the early church. As D. M. Baillie put it:

> In our Christian religion we talk a great deal about contrition and repentance and forgiveness and new beginnings; but very often we don't give ourselves to these experiences. We are too proud. We don't want to be rebuked. We are not going to have ourselves continually upset. As we go about this world we would receive a good many hard knocks, and often find ourselves in the wrong, and frequently be made ashamed and have to acknowledge our shortcomings—if we were to allow ourselves to be touched and wounded in that way. But very often we won't. We are too proud. We encase ourselves in the armour of pride—we will see our neighbor's faults but not our own. That saves us the pains of penitence. But it is at a terrible cost. For it keeps us time after time from making a new start. It keeps us from turning our back on the past and becoming better men and women. It is not a good thing to keep ourselves safely encased in the armour of conceit.[7]

We, too, have seen the danger of wearing that "armour" too long. It can become so familiar that we no longer realize that it has kept us from receiving the Father's authority and correction. What will motivate us to take off that armor? Grace.

The succor H. H. Farmer talked about is always combined with the Father's absolute demand. When we submit to His authority with even the least bit of willingness, we begin to experience what Paul described so vividly in Galatians 4. As God's adopted children, we are given the power of the indwelling Christ. "And because you are sons [and daughters], God has sent forth the Spirit of His Son into your hearts, crying out, 'Abba, Father!'" (Gal. 4:6).

Christ in us guides our perception of what happens to and around us, motivates our prayers of confession, and assures us of forgiveness.

MISAPPROPRIATED AUTONOMY

The second way Israel misplaced Yahweh was in misappropriated autonomy. They moved from being a theocracy to an independence from Yahweh in the affairs of the nation as was manifested in the way power was grasped by a succession of kings during the last years before the fall of the northern kingdom. Ever since the day of Samuel, the people of God lived as a theocratic monarchy. Kings were selected and anointed by Yahweh through the prophets. Kings were responsible first to Yahweh. They called on His help in government and battles with enemies. Over the years, this balance of power was tipped and men usurped the monarchy without the call of Yahweh or any accountability to Him. Verse 4 expresses Yahweh's indignation over this: *"They set up kings, but not by Me; they made princes, but I did not acknowledge them."*

We reviewed the condition of the monarchy in the northern kingdom in our discussion of Hosea 7:7. We saw the treachery and the assassinations that haunted the halls of human power. In Hosea 8:4 we see the rebellious consequence—a people who had declared, in essence, a complete autonomy, a self-governing refusal to bow to Yahweh as divine ruler of His people. Israel had forgotten her Maker. They had misappropriated His authority and claimed it for themselves.

The crucial problem was that Israel no longer sought the guidance of God. This was a decisive step away from Him in the downward spiral of forgetting Him. He was no longer the source of wisdom for large or small decisions, but shelved as an anachronism.

The same thing can happen to us as individuals, families, the church, or parachurch movements. Our lives and any unified enterprise we attempt is to be envisioned as a diminutive kingdom with God through the reigning Christ as King.

Bryan Jeffrey Leech's contemporary hymn provides a dynamic confession of faith as well as a stirring song:

> Let God be God in this our present moment
> Let God be Master holding in control
> All parts of life as gifts of His bestowment
> For making men now broken whole
> Let God, be God, let Christ be king!
>
> Let God, be God, or we shall never finish
> The task to which He calls us every day
> Lest, erring, we in unbelief diminish
> The force He wishes to display
> Let God be God, let Christ be King![8]

The opposite of forgetting God is to receive His sovereign control and guidance in every moment, choice, and decision. He will accept no vice-regency in our lives. Nor will He serve as our advisor while we reign on the throne of our little kingdom.

MISDEVOTED ADORATION

When God is deposed as Lord of our lives and no longer has our ultimate commitment, our unmet needs will drive us to lesser gods whom we think we can control and manipulate for our purposes. When we forget God, our endowed capability for adoration is misdevoted to our idols. We are back to a familiar, oft-repeated theme of the book of Hosea. However, the proclivity to idolatry in human nature is focused in the context of being a direct result of no longer seeking God's guidance. We simply cannot live without a god. If we drift from the Lord God, the adoration-shaped void in us will be filled by some person, project, plan, or possession. We simply cannot avoid our need to worship whether the focus of our devotion is ourselves, someone else, or some idol of our own making.

Through Hosea, Yahweh condemns the many forms of misdevoted adoration in Israel. He speaks of idols in the plural (see also 4:17; 13:2; 14:8). Added to the calf idols in Dan and Bethel, there were cultic idols scattered throughout the region of the northern kingdom as well as statuettes and plaques for private worship. *"From their silver and gold they made idols for themselves"* (8:4). Yahweh's gift of natural resources of gold and silver were used to make substitute objects of adoration.

The result? *"That they might be cut off."* *That* or *so that* (*lĕmaʿan*) introduces a result clause and a purpose clause, "So that they will be cut off." The use of the precious metals to fashion idols will result in destruction of the people. Wolff comments,

> Of concern here are the factual results. Israel should know that all worship of idols is doomed for destruction. According to the divine law, destruction from Yahweh comes above all upon the idolaters themselves. This explains the early conjecture *"they* will be cut off"*. . . . But the singular form is part of the sentence's irony: the use of precious metal in disobedience against Yahweh results in its destruction.[9]

In addition to condemnation of idols of silver and gold, Yahweh expresses His anger over the worship of Baal. "*Your calf is rejected, O Samaria! My anger is aroused against them*" (Hos. 8:5). The same verb, "throw off, reject," is used in 8:3a. The calf could mean a calf idol in the city of Samaria or the royal sanctuary at Bethel. Jereboam I erected calf images at Bethel and identified them not only as gods but confused them with Yahweh.

> Therefore the king took counsel and made two calves of gold, and said to the people, "It is too much for you to go up to Jerusalem. Here are your gods, O Israel, which brought you up from the land of Egypt!" And he set up one in Bethel, and the other he put in Dan. Now this thing became a sin, for the people went to worship before the one as far as Dan.
>
> 1 Kings 12:28–30

Baal or El was represented as a bull or calf in the Canaanite cults. By Hosea's time the calf of Samaria exemplified the degradation of the apostasy of the whole nation.

This idolatry over the years brings Yahweh's anger and lament. "*My anger is aroused against them. How long will it be until they attain to innocence* [become clean]?" (Hos. 8:5). Again we feel the struggle in Yahweh's heart: a combination of indignation and grieving. Also shock. Perhaps verse 6a, "*For from Israel is even this*," belongs with verse 5, for it expresses the consternation that this idol worship could happen in Israel. Another interpretation is to keep verse 6 as it stands in the NKJV text with 6a expressing amazement that in Israel there could be such an equivocation as, "*A workman made it, and it is not God.*" The meaning would be that the people explained away the manmade idols, saying that they really know they are not God but participate in worshiping at the Baal shrines anyway. "It's not all that serious—we can worship Yahweh and for good measure add the idols."

The more traditional interpretation is that verse 6 represents the judgment from Israel's prophet that the idols are not God because they have been made with human hands. Because they have been made, they can be destroyed. This will be the final proof that the calf of Samaria is not a god. Other prophetic texts deride idol worship in this manner (Isa. 2:8, 20; 40:19–20; cf. Ps. 115:3–8; Isa. 44:9–20; 46:1–7; Jer. 10:1–16). The idols are not just inconsequential aids but false gods in competition for Israel's adoration and will be broken to pieces.

All three of the above interpretations of verses 5 and 6 are applicable to our problem with idols and false gods today. We need to feel the anguish of God over our divided loyalties and hear His pathos, "How long will it be before Christians and the church attain to innocence? Even among My people is a lack of trust and dependence on Me only! Where is the clean holiness, the loyalty, the single-minded adoration I require?"

Too often we could be counted among equivocators of Israel as we would be the first to say that those things that attain idol status in our lives are not God. Even as good, pious Christians we say, "A workman made it, and it is not God," as we point to our houses, cars, achievements, or material accomplishments. But we are the workman, and our pride of ownership often displaces our praise to God. All this—and heaven too! Syncretism tightens its grip when at the same time we berate idols and maintain them.

So it is with God's voice and not our fulsome equivocation we need to hear—every day. Either we break the hold of our idols, or God must break them to pieces. This includes all of the fine things that creep into first place status in our lives and displace God as Lord of our lives. When what we think we do for God becomes more important than God, it is an idol. This might even be our ministries, causes, churches, or polished self-images.

Our biggest problem in facing our idols is that we try to use God to prop them up. When difficulties, reversals, or failures hit what would threaten our idols, we expect a quick fix from God. In a way, we try to get help from God to keep from facing the inadequacy of our false gods. Sometimes God blesses us with what we call unanswered prayer until we want Him more than anything or any one else. If we will not face and confess a false god, He will destroy it. Whatever He gives or withholds is to bring us to Him as the only God of our lives.

MISCALCULATED ASSUMPTIONS

The rest of chapter 8 deals with the miscalculated assumptions of Israel. The people assumed that the fertility rites of Baal worship would produce good crops, that alliances with foreign powers would bring security and safety, and that they could evade the Lord's punishment by vain sacrifices. The whole passage underlines the undeniable truth we can never escape: without the Lord, nothing works right.

"They sow the wind, and reap the whirlwind" (Hos. 8:7). The agricultural proverb establishes the irrevocable connection between present actions and future judgment.

Wolff interprets each aspect of the proverb in this light.

> The order God has established in the world can be demonstrated to Israel's farmers by using the harvest as an example (v. 7a). The deed is the seed that sprouts up in abundance for harvest. Here, *rûah*, a gentle breeze, is a catchword used in Wisdom for unstable, helpless vanity (Eccl. 1:14, 17; Prov. 11:29; Job 7:7). Trust in cultic and political maneuvers thus leads to self-deception (cf. 12:2). Just as surely as the calf of Samaria will be shattered. *Sûpâ* is a destructive whirlwind which, like the harvest, grows out of the seed of a gentle breeze. . . . With the wind and vanity of their idol worship, Israel brings upon itself a whirlwind of disaster.[10]

On the other hand, Andersen and Freedman translate the proverb, "They will sow when it is windy. They will reap in a whirlwind," and comment:

> The purpose of idol-making was to secure good harvests, among other benefits, and it is likely that the king himself was a sacral person in the performance of the necessary rites. A fit punishment for such contempt toward Yahweh would be the removal of the kings, destruction of the idol (v.6), and ruination of agriculture.... The farmer is to be frustrated at each major stage of his work. Sowing in the wind, he loses much of the grain at the start. Harvesting in a gale, he loses most of the yield at the end.[11]

Stuart underlines the futility of the fertility cult in bringing abundance.

> Verse 7 contains three brief futility curses, in which expectations are thwarted before they can be realized (. . . cf. Deut. 28:30–42). In ancient times sowers would throw their seed with a gentle wind, which helped scatter it evenly on a tilled field; *rûah* has thus an adverbial sense, i.e., 'with a wind' without symbolic overtones. The disaster which brings to naught the planning and effort of the sower is seen in the storm disintegrating and scattering the heads of grain before they can be harvested.[12]

However, Stuart also allows that the interpretation of Wolff may be valid as well and that the saying is a double entendre with the sense that "what you sow you will reap many times over," with *rûaḥ* standing for worthlessness.

Under the arresting heading of "The Ersatz God is Effete," Knight interprets *wind* as "the way of passion and of disloyalty" and *whirlwind* as "the tornado of destruction." The coming storm will destroy Israel's crops (i.e., her policies).[13] Indeed, the ersatz, substitute, god of Baal was effete, incapable of production, barren.

To sow with the wind, then, was to sow with a false expectation of Baal's fertility. The consequences would be Yahweh's judgment in the destruction of the crop. As a result, "*The stalk has no bud; it shall never produce meal*" (8:7). In the Hebrew, this is expressed in rhyme. Wolff's translation clearly reads, "Grain with no head yields no bread."[14] He comments:

> A dry stalk of grain yields no meal. Likewise, Israel waits in vain for dead cultic objects to provide it with life. The second saying appears to state metaphorically the interpretation of the matter which Hosea goes on to develop in what follows. . . . The grain standing in the fields is irretrievably poor. If it should nevertheless yield a harvest, the attacking enemy will devour it.[15]

"*If it should produce, aliens would swallow it up. Israel is swallowed up; now they are among the Gentiles like a vessel in which there is no pleasure*" (vv. 7b–8). As a further evidence that nothing works without the Lord, the pitiful remains of the whirlwind will be swallowed up, just as the nation will be swallowed up in 733 B.C. with the Assyrian invasion of Galilee and Gilead. Israel will lose its distinctive quality as she is mixed among the Gentiles. The nation is like a vessel that has lost its beauty and shine. The supernatural blessing and providential advantage as the people of God are gone. Nothing precious, notable, or desirous is left.

Knight points out that the use of *now* in verse 8 "is an instance of the so-called 'prophetic perfect.' So sure is the prophet, speaking as he is from God, that what he says will eventuate, that he can declare, '*Now,* they have become among the Gentiles, *now,* they are no longer a vessel, an object, of pleasure to anyone.'"[16] Or, as J. B. Phillips puts it, "A crock that no one wants."

The contemporary application of verses 7 and 8 is neither difficult nor pleasant. When Christians squander their devotion on false gods, eventually the Lord must withdraw His glory and power. Our distinctive quality is that we belong first and only to Him. We have been chosen, called, redeemed, and set apart to be vessels of the Spirit of Christ. When we depend on our understanding rather than the spiritual gifts of wisdom and knowledge, when our security is rooted in our abilities and not the Spirit's power, when we put our trust in our ingenuity rather than divine intervention, we have our own idols in the fields as we sow the wind and will reap the whirlwind. The first signs of judgment are in the bland, lackluster of our vessels and in the absence of any dynamic or impelling witness.

Hosea 8:9-10 continues the exposure of Israel's misguided assumptions. Added to Israel's dependence on Baal fertility, the nation cast about for alliances to avert a catastrophe. "*For they have gone up to Assyria*" (v. 9). As we observed in 7:11, Israel was constantly changing sides between Egypt and Assyria. Gambling on the influential friendship of Assyria eventually proved disastrous.

Another of the pithy epigrammatic similes of the book of Hosea describes Israel: "*like a wild donkey alone by itself*" (v. 9). The donkey image uses a pun on the word *donkey* with the name Ephraim. Instead of remaining with the herd, the wild donkey goes off to seek its mate. "*Ephraim has hired lovers.*" The image shifts. The people are like a whore who has sunk so low that she must pay her lovers and cannot even earn a whore's wage. Then a further shift of image: The metaphor changes from the prostitute to the nation's vacillating foreign policy. "*Yes, though they have hired among the nations, now I will gather them; and they shall sorrow a little, because of the burden of the king of princes*" (v. 10).

The figure of *gather* is one of judgment, as in Hosea 9:6, Joel 3:2, Micah 4:12-5:1, and Ezekiel 16:37 and 22:20. Israel will be gathered like ripe fruit placed in a container, there to waste away under the rule of the Assyrian "king of princes" or mighty king.

The reason for the judgment is explained again in Hosea 8:11-13. "*Because Ephraim has made many altars for sin, they have become for him altars for sinning*" (v. 11). The NIV renders it "altars for sin offerings . . . have become altars for sinning." Sin offerings were traditionally for the expiation of sins committed in ignorance or what might be called "unwitting sins." The ritual prescribed is detailed in Leviticus 4:1-5:13. Hosea's prophecy is against the multiplicity of altars at which the people went through the ritual for unwitting sins while at the same time wittingly sinking deeper into pagan worship and syncretism with the Baals. The very altars prescribed for Yahweh worship were used for sacrifices contrary to the Torah and in violation of Yahweh's covenant. *"I have written for him the great things of My law, but they were considered a strange thing"* (v. 12). Stuart observes, "The 'laws' mentioned are surely the Mosaic laws. The problem for Israel was not that they lacked the Sinai code, but that they flagrantly disregarded it."[17] The priests were negligent in teaching the Law, and it became a strange or foreign thing to them. Therefore, they offered sacrifices for sin as unrepentant people. This was the arrogance of the people against Yahweh.

Verse 13 reveals the extent of the distortion of the sacrifice. *"For the sacrifices of My offerings they sacrifice flesh and eat it, but the Lord does not accept them."* The very sacrificial animals offered to Yahweh were then eaten in a common meal by the participants in the cult. The love of eating the flesh superseded the love for the Lord. This shows us how far the worship of God can be divided from obedience to God. When our worship is not in keeping with what God desires from us, it degenerates into a worship of ourselves.

The people forgot their God, but He would remember their sin. *"Now He will remember their iniquity and punish their sins. They shall return to Egypt"* (Hos. 8:13b). Here Egypt can stand as a metonym for captivity or exile, though when the northern kingdom began to crumble, a few, like Hanun, the Philistine prince of Gaza, did escape to Egypt.

As in Hosea 2:13b, verse 14 of chapter 8 asserts the basic cause of Israel's plight. *"For Israel has forgotten his Maker."* This is the reason for the misplaced authority, the misappropriated autonomy, the misdirected adoration, and the miscalculated assumptions. In this final verse of chapter 8, both Israel and Judah are assured of the fateful loss of conscious accountability and consistent attention to their Creator, Sustainer, and absolute sovereign Lord. Israel *"has built temples; Judah also has multiplied fortified cities; but I will send fire upon his cities, and it shall devour his palaces."* The problem was that these buildings were built to the people's glory and not to God's. Judah's misplaced trust was focused in forty-six fortified cities, including the refortification of Jerusalem. 2 Kings 18:13 shows the extent of the misplaced trust,

"And in the fourteenth year of King Hezekiah, Sennacherib king of Assyria came up against all the fortified cities of Judah and took them." Jerusalem itself endured a long siege and escaped destruction through an intervention of the Lord in 701 B.C. But the final devastation by Babylonia was only 115 years away after that. The destruction of palaces and cities in both kingdoms would come at the hands of human enemies, but they would be agents of Yahweh's judgment. What He *allowed* was the direct result of what both Israel and Judah had *disavowed*.

Something I have hinted at throughout this exposition of chapter 8 must now be confronted directly. We have touched on it previously and will have to deal with it repeatedly all through the Minor Prophets. When we forget God and misplace our loyalty, by the very nature of our covenant relationship with Him, He must use whatever means necessary to get our attention and bring us back into a vital relationship with Him. The only alternative to heartbreaking measure is a heart that is obedient to Him and sensitive to His guidance. Unless we consistently face the reemergence of old and new false gods, the Lord will force us to see them for what they are.

Wolff summarizes the impact of chapter 8 and underlines its importance for us.

> This chapter represents a high point in the prophet's struggle against pagan worship. But in significant contrast to 4:4–19 and 5:1–7, chapter 8 is at the same time concerned with Israel's political attempts to create security for herself, which is also a rejection of God's covenant with His people. This reminds us of Paul's anathema against those who proclaimed a "different gospel" (Gal. 1:6ff). Whenever Christianity "having begun with the Spirit," is tempted "to end with the flesh" (Gal. 3:3), the prophets can render special help. Especially this chapter discloses the wrong path taken by God's New Testament people whenever they place false authority over themselves, whenever they succumb to the idolatry of their own accomplishments, whenever they seek help in their own works, whenever they give in to unbelief, whenever they take delight in their "worship services" instead of hearing and obeying the will of God, whenever they delude themselves with self-glorification and a false self-confidence, instead of placing their future in the hands of their Creator.[18]

NOTES

1. Alan Redpath, *Learning to Live* (Grand Rapids, Mich.: Wm. B. Eerdmans Publishing Company, 1961).

2. H. H. Farmer, *The World and God* (Nisbet, 1935) 25.

3. Thomas A. Smail, *The Forgotten Father* (Grand Rapids, Mich.: Wm. B. Eerdmans Publishing Co., 1980). This provides excellent background reading about the missing emphasis on the Father in some evangelical and charismatic circles today.

4. Wolff, *Hosea*, 137.

5. Andersen and Freedman, *Hosea*, 490.

6. James Stewart, *The Strong Name* (Edinburgh: T.& T. Clark, 1964), 14.

7. Donald M. Baillie, *Out of Nazareth* (New York: Charles Scribner's Sons, 1958), 58.

8. Bryan Jeffrey Leech, "Let God Be God" c 1972, Fred Bock Music Co., All rights reserved. Used by permission.

9. Wolff, *Hosea*, 139.

10. Wolff, *Hosea*, 142.

11. Andersen and Freedman, *Hosea*, 497.

12. Stuart, *Hosea – Jonah*, 133.

13. Knight, *Hosea*, 90.

14. Wolff, *Hosea*, 132. However, Stuart claims that the rhyme works only in Hebrew with medieval pointing and that in the eighth Century B.C. the initial vowel sounds would be different. (Stuart, *Hosea – Jonah*, 134.)

15. Wolff, *Hosea*, 142.

16. Knight, *Hosea*, 91.

17. Stuart, *Hosea – Jonah*, 136.

18. Wolff, *Hosea*, 147–148.

CHAPTER TWELVE

Threefold Judgment

Hosea 9, 10

The ninth and tenth chapters of Hosea focus a threefold judgment on Israel. Hosea 9:1–9 deals with the judgment of dispersion, 9:10–17 with the judgment of barrenness, and chapter 10 with the judgment of destruction.

THE JUDGMENT OF DISPERSION

9:1 "Do not rejoice, O Israel, with joy like other peoples, for you have played the harlot against your God. You made love for hire on every threshing floor.

2 "The threshing floor and the winepress shall not feed them, and the new wine shall fail in her.

3 "They shall not dwell in the Lord's land, but Ephraim shall return to Egypt, and shall eat unclean things in Assyria.

4 "They shall not offer wine offerings to the Lord, nor shall their sacrifices be pleasing to Him. It shall be like bread of mourners to them; all who eat it shall be defiled. For their bread shall be for their own life; it shall not come into the house of the Lord.

5 "What will you do in the appointed day, and in the day of the feast of the Lord?

6 "For indeed they are gone because of destruction. Egypt shall gather them up; Memphis shall bury them. Nettles shall possess their valuables of silver; thorns shall be in their tents.

7 "The days of punishment have come; the days of recompense have come. Israel knows! The prophet is a fool, the spiritual man is insane, because of the greatness of your iniquity and great enmity.

8 "The watchman of Ephraim is with my God; but the prophet is a fowler's snare in all his ways—enmity in the house of his God.

9 "They are deeply corrupted, as in the days of Gibeah. He will remember their iniquity; He will punish their sins."

Hos. 9:1-9

This judgment of hypocrisy probably took place at the harvest festival. Hosea marches into the celebration with a flaming word of judgment, "No more festivals!" The festival, which should have been a time of thanksgiving to Yahweh, the true source of the harvest, had degenerated into orgies in worship of Baal. The prohibition, *"Do not rejoice, O Israel, with joy like other peoples"* (Hos. 9:1), contains cult words identified with Baal worship. *Rejoice* and *joy* were connected with calf worship (10:5).

But most serious is the fact that the festivals were occasions for harlotry. The Israelites made love for a harlot's fee—in this case the grain of the harvest. Verse 2 begins the announcement of coming disaster. The harvest may have been plentiful, but it is deceptive. It is likely that the people shouted out their objections to Hosea's condemnation of their festivals and touted the plenteous harvest as a sign of blessing. But not for long, Hosea responds. Because the people denied the real Provider, soon the threshing floors and the winepresses will not be available to the people. Prosperity has deceived them. The word *fail* in "the new wine shall *fail* in her," can also mean "deceive."

Nothing fails like success—if we attribute our success to anything or anyone other than God. Prosperity is not always a sign of His approval. Recently I met a man who wore a badge with the words, "Prosperity—Our Divine Right." But I wonder, does that mean that a person who is not presently prosperous is unblessed? Or does it imply that prosperity is always a sure sign of God's blessing? If so, has a prosperous person no need to examine his or her relationship with God? Just because things are going well at a particular point in our lives does not necessarily mean we are right with God. In fact, our success may have come as a result of complicity with some very beguiling false gods.

Jesus' parable of the rich fool (Luke 12:13–21) shocked His listeners who thought prosperity was an undeniable mark of true success. A rich man's productive farm yielded fine crops. His barns were full to overflowing. What to do? The man exclaimed, "I'll tear down my barns and build new ones! Then I'll have room for further expansion. I'll be able to sit back and relax with enough stored away for years to come. I can take it easy—eat, drink, and be merry!" Success? He had missed the purpose of life. His voice of assurance came from within himself, an echo of his frenzied accumulation. The pronouns the rich fool used explore the wrong kind of success. *I* is used six times; *my* is used five times, with a self-gratifying *you*, referring to himself, thrown in for good measure. The man's whole life was inverted onto himself. He reasoned with himself. He talked with the wrong person.

The voice of God interrupted his self-accolade. "Fool! Tonight you will die. Now who will get all you have acquired?" Jesus adds His commentary to the startling story: "So is he who lays up treasure for himself, and is not rich toward God" (Luke 12:21).

The deception of prosperity among the people to whom Hosea spoke would soon be exposed. The threat of losing food and wine in their threshing floors and winepresses is explained in verse three. The people will not enjoy the produce of the land because they will no longer dwell there. Their salvation history will be reversed. Some of the people will be exiled in Egypt. They will be punished by being sent back to the bondage from which the people of God had escaped in the historic exodus centuries before. Others will be carried off to exile in Assyria, where they will eat food offered to other gods. This is an ironic twist for the Israelites. They had worshiped false gods in their own land; now they would be forced to eat food that was taboo. They would have to stomach their own apostasy!

Further, because the people resisted worshiping Yahweh in their own land, they will not be able to worship Him in customary ways in the dispersion. Verse four plays on the irony. Thank offerings had been misdirected to false gods in their home land; now the wine offering, the drink offering, which should express gratitude to Yahweh, would not be permitted in captivity. Sacrifices that should have been made for sin and the assurance of atonement before, now will not be pleasing to Yahweh. The words, "Nor shall their sacrifices be pleasing to Him" (9:4), may also be rendered, "They shall not offer their sacrifices to Him." The reason will be that traditional altar sacrifices to Yahweh will not be allowed. All food in the foreign lands will be ritually unclean and unfit for offering to Yahweh. At home the Israelites had substituted physical for spiritual satisfaction. In captivity they would have only physical satisfaction.

These sacrifices "*shall be like bread of mourners to them*" (Hos. 9:4). Numbers 19:14–15 help us understand the meaning of "mourner's bread." This is the law when a man dies in a tent: "All who come into the tent and all who are in the tent shall be unclean seven days; and every open vessel, which has no cover fastened on it, is unclean." The point Hosea makes then is that the offerings in the Assyrian exile would be unclean like the bread from a mourner's house. It shall be bread that only satisfied the gullet (*nepeš*), physical life, but not suitable for the satisfaction of spiritual needs because it was unclean for the sacrifice. "*It shall not come into the house of the Lord*" (9:4). If this reference is the Temple, it is a later addition from Judah; if it is an authentic saying of Hosea, it means Yahweh's land. The impact is the same, however. What the people neglected will now be taken from them.

Verses 5–7a carry on this implication of judgment. Though they now rejoice at the festival, the question is posed: What will they do on these festival days when they are deported? "Appointed day" is synonymous with "feast of the Lord" (cf. 2:11), probably the autumn festival, established around 930 B.C. by Jereboam I as a counterpart in the northern kingdom to the festival celebration in the southern kingdom. In Hosea's day it had become an occasion for harlotry instead of thanksgiving. Now in the destruction the feast will only be a memory for the Israelites. Egypt will gather some of them up. A complete destruction of the festivals of Israel's religion will take place there as well as in the Assyrian exile. Memphis, famous for its great graveyard and burial pyramids, will bury them—the festivals and the people themselves.

Hosea further illustrates the judgment. Nettles, plants covered with stinging hairs, "*shall possess their valuables of silver; thorns shall be in their tents*" (v. 6). The image is of abhorred nettles growing up around the people's silver valuables and homes. Picture abandoned Samarian houses, valuables left behind, now overgrown with thorny vines and weeds. Verse 7a concludes, "*The days of punishment have come; the days of recompense have come.*" The root of the Hebrew word for recompense implies completeness. The fulfillment of the result of Israel's adultery with other gods is at hand. Note that the word is a pun on the name of Shallum, a king who usurped the throne by assassination (2 Kings 15:10).

I suggest that 7b, beginning with "Israel knows," begins a quote of Hosea's opponents. The Septuagint translation of this text suggests that the original Hebrew may be "Israel cries out," rather than "Israel knows." The words that follow are usually taken as the retort of the prophet's antagonists, accusing him of being a fool and insane. (On the rejection of other northern kingdom prophets, see 2 Kings 2:23; 9:11; Amos 7:12-13, 16).

The connection of the final phrase of 7b is disputed. Andersen and Freedman see this as a continuation of the opponent's words, accusing Hosea of insanity because of his incisive confrontation of Israel.[1] Others have proposed moving the clause. Wolff understands this to mean that their great guilt has led to their monumental hostility.[2] This view also is held by Stuart.[3]

Verse 8 is rendered either as a continuation of the opponents' accusations or as Hosea's response. *"The watchman of Ephraim is with my God; but the prophet is a fowler's snare in all his ways – enmity in the house of his God."* If this is the antagonist's cry against Hosea, it would mean, "The true prophet (watchman) of Ephraim is with God, but this prophet causes the people to trip and produces enmity in God's land."

A stronger case can be made for this verse being Hosea's response. It means that he is a prophet, a true watchman of Yahweh, setting a trap on Ephraim's path of apostasy and causing hostility because of his exposure of the worship of false gods. Stuart revocalizes *ᶜim* to *ᶜam* and follows the Septuagint reading for *God*: "Is Ephraim a watchman? Is God's people a prophet? A fowler's snare is on all his paths, hostility in the house of his God?"[4]

This intriguing translation involves minor changes and can fit well in the context. Stuart comments,

> Hosea turns the tables on the people's cynical derision of the prophets. Their mockery assumes that they know more than the inspired prophet(s), so Hosea asks ironically, "Is Ephraim a watchman? Is God's people a prophet?" The answer, obviously is "No!" "Watchman". . . a lookout from an early-warning outpost, is applied metaphorically to prophets several times in the Old Testament (Isa. 56:10; Jer. 6:17; Ezek. 3:17; 33:2, 6, 7), emphasizing their role in warning of approaching danger (cf. Ezek. 33:7-20). In

the synonymous parallelism of the first couplet of v.8 it is thus paired with *nābî* "prophet." So Hosea, in effect, mocks the people who mocked him. If Ephraim really is a watchman, a prophet, he ought to be able to see the severity of his plight: snares every-where he turns, hostility in his own country. . . . Ephraim, the arrogant, complacent rejecter of prophets cannot see what the prophets see: danger and divine hostility. . . . Their land is Yahweh's "house" and He is preparing to eject them from it.[5]

My own view is that Hosea identifies himself as the true prophet, a watchman of Ephraim, and that in the exercise of his calling he did indeed become a fowler's snare and caused enmity in Yahweh's land among the apostate people.

Nothing less is sure to happen when we exercise our prophetic office in our time. Jesus' warning haunts us, "Woe to you when *all* men speak well of you, for so did their fathers to the false prophets" (Luke 6:26, emphasis added).

We long for everyone to like us and speak well of us. We are troubled when people object to disturbing truth. Sometime ago, I preached a very pointed message. After the service I greeted the congregation exiting from the sanctuary. Hundreds of people ex-pressed gratitude for my forthrightness. Several people were angry and told me so. One man said, "That was the worst sermon you've ever preached. Keep off those social issues and stick to the Gospel!"

Later in the day, my wife Mary Jane asked me how people had reacted to my message. You guessed it—instead of telling her about the hundreds who appreciated the bracing truth, I told her about the few who objected and the man who said it was my worst sermon. Until she pressed me for the bigger picture, all I could remember were the critics and the crank!

A prophetic communicator must face the cocker spaniel part of his or her nature that likes to be liked. The Gospel is an offense, a snare, a fowler to the proud and the irrelevantly pious. When we spend time in the prophet's watchtower (Hab. 2:1) and accept our calling to be a watchman-prophet of the whole counsel of God in His Word, we will be given challenging, disturbing truth to speak. When we encounter resistance, we can empathize with the prophets of old, the apostles, and Christians through the ages who spoke the truth with tough love.

Hosea's concluding confrontation in this section on the judgment of dispersion is given in verse 9. The deep corruption of the nation is compared to that in the days of Gibeah. Gibeah was Saul's home (1 Sam. 10:26; 11:4), though this is probably not the point of contact, but rather Judges 19–21, which relates the crime committed against a Levite by Benjamites in Gibeah. Like Hosea and the prophets of his time, the Levite was given brutal treatment.

The latter half of verse 9 recalls clauses in 8:13, almost word for word. The verbatim verdict reasserts that Yahweh will remember Israel's iniquity and will punish His people with the exile. (Note our previous comments on Hosea 8:13 in chapter 11.)

But God remembers not only Israel's iniquity, but also wistfully remembers when He initially called His people. The next section of chapter 9 begins with God's yearning recall of how He found Israel and His gracious plan and purpose for His beloved people. Then the memory is clouded again by the dark memory of Israel's apostasy. The previous section (9:1–9) was marked by alternation of second and third person references to those accused and threatened with punishment. The divine speech in the first person picks up in verse 10. The theme of Yahweh's words again is Israel's sin and the judgment of barrenness.

THE JUDGMENT OF BARRENNESS

9:10 "I found Israel like grapes in the wilderness; I saw your fathers as the firstfruits on the fig tree in its first season. But they went to Baal Peor, and separated themselves to that shame; they became an abomination like the thing they loved.

11 "As for Ephraim, their glory shall fly away like a bird—no birth, no pregnancy, and no conception!

12 "Though they bring up their children, yet I will bereave them to the last man. Yes, woe to them when I depart from them!

13 "Just as I saw Ephraim like Tyre, planted in a pleasant place, so Ephraim will bring out his children to the murderer.

14 "Give them, O Lord—what will You give? Give them a miscarrying womb and dry breasts!

15 "All their wickedness is in Gilgal, for there I hated them. Because of the evil of their deeds I will drive them from My house; I will love them no more. All their princes are rebellious.

16 "Ephraim is stricken, their root is dried up; they
shall bear no fruit. Yes, were they to bear children, I
would kill the darlings of their womb.
17 "My God will cast them away, because they did
not obey Him; and they shall be wanderers among the
nations"

Hos. 9:10–17

The tone of this section changes dramatically to historical retro-
spect. Yahweh's speech is more reflective, but no less anguished. The
two divine speeches, verses 10–13 and verses 15–16, are followed by
two prayers by Hosea for the deserved punishment of the people,
verse 14 and verse 17. This alternation of divine speech and prophetic
prayer is like the accounts of prophetic visions and responses in Isaiah
6:8–11 and Amos 7:1–6. Wolff proposes that this section of Hosea
comes from a time shortly after the address of 9:1–9 when Hosea
could no longer speak publicly because of the opposition, but spoke
to an inner circle of those with like convictions.[6] Stuart suggests a time
in the "mid-720s, very close to or at the beginning of the fall of the
North."[7]

Verse 10 causes our hearts again to be pressed to the broken heart
of God over His people. A joyous memory is mingled with pain. He
remembers when He found *Israel like grapes in the wilderness; I saw your
fathers as the firstfruits on the fig tree in its first season.* The allegories of
the vine and the fig tree are used for Israel throughout the Scriptures.
The psalmist and the prophets had etched those images into the Hebrew
consciousness. Psalm 80:8–11, 14–16 is an apt summary:

You have brought a vine out of Egypt; you have cast out the nations,
and planted it. You prepared room for it, and caused it to take deep
root, and it filled the land. The hills were covered with its shadow,
and the mighty cedars with its boughs. She sent out her boughs to
the Sea, and her branches to the River . . . Return, we beseech You,
O God of hosts; look down from heaven and see, and visit this
vine and the vineyard which Your right hand has planted, and the
branch that You made strong for Yourself. It is burned with fire, it
is cut down; they perish at the rebuke of Your countenance.

Isaiah focused the dual images of vine and fig tree even more sharply:
"For the vineyard of the Lord of hosts is the house of Israel, and the

men of Judah are His pleasant plant. He looked for justice, but behold, oppression; for righteousness, but behold, oppression" (Isa. 5:7).

In Hosea 9:10, God says that finding His beloved bride was like one who comes across grapes in a hot and thirsty desert and is delighted. The first fruits of the fig tree carry the same joyful discovery when at the end of May they are very tender and juicy. The word for "firstfruits" or "first ripe" is from the same root translated "firstborn." The pun would be familiar to the Hebrew listeners.

The key for the interpretation of this verse is to remember that the name *Ephraim* was closely connected to the word *fruitful*. And this is exactly what the chosen vine and fig tree of Ephraim eventually proved not to be. Not in the wilderness, not in Hosea's time, and not in response to the Messiah. It is helpful to compare God's delight of discovery of the grapes of the vine and the succulent figs with Jesus' parable of the fig tree (Mark 11:12–14, 19–22; Luke 13:1–9). Note the difference between the fig-laden tree God found in the wilderness and the fig tree Jesus cursed because it had leaves but no figs.

Mark says Jesus "found nothing but leaves" (Mark 11:13). That is more than a horticultural observation. Leaves on a fig tree never precede the fruitage of figs. They sometimes accompany, but usually follow, the fruit. Jesus, seeing the leaves, would expect to find figs. As we have noted, the time for the fruitage of the first figs was May; Jesus spoke the parable of the fig tree and cursed the figless tree during Passover week, sometime between the last of March and the middle of April. It was most unusual for a fig tree to be in the leaf stage at that time of the year. The issue is the leaves but no fruit. All the life of the tree had run to the leaf. That is why Jesus cursed the fig tree: it was like Israel, a leaf without any fruit of righteousness.

When the disciples passed by the fig tree the next morning, they saw it withered to the roots. Peter expressed the astonishment of the rest of the disciples, "Rabbi, look! The fig tree which You cursed has withered away." Jesus' response is startling. No explanation; just the admonition, "Have faith in God" (Mark 11:21–22). The quality lacking in Israel was faith in God. The outward forms of Israel's religion in Jesus' day signified the knowledge and experience of God, but Jesus only found the leaves of pretension. Rites, rules, regulations, and restrictions had become more important than the fruit of personal faith. Jesus was concerned about weightier matters of the law—righteousness, justice, and love (see Matt. 23:23).

At the end of the Sermon on the Mount, Jesus said,

> Beware of false prophets, who come to you in sheep's clothing,
> but inwardly they are ravenous wolves. You will know them by
> their fruits. Do men gather grapes from thornbushes or figs from
> thistles? Even so, every good tree bears good fruit, but a bad tree
> bears bad fruit. A good tree cannot bear bad fruit, nor can a bad
> tree bear good fruit. Every tree that does not bear good fruit is cut
> down and thrown into the fire. Therefore by their fruits you will
> know them.
>
> Matt. 7:15-20

Jesus called His disciples to fruitfulness. His judgment on the Israel
of His day was that the tree of God produced leaves of religion but not
the fruit of righteousness in individuals and the nation as a whole. Com-
bining a discussion of this parable with Hosea 9:10 reveals the fruitfulness
that delights God and the fruitlessness that disappoints him.[8]

Yahweh's disappointment with Israel in the wilderness was that
the people *"went to Baal Peor, and separated themselves to that shame; they
became an abomination like the thing they loved"* (9:10). Numbers 25:1-3
recounts the event: "Then Israel remained in Acacia Grove, and the
people began to commit harlotry with the women of Moab. They
invited the people to the sacrifices of their gods, and the people ate
and bowed down to their gods. So Israel was joined to Baal of Peor,
and the anger of the Lord was aroused against Israel." Mount Peor,
probably about twelve miles east of the northern end of the Dead Sea,
was the site of apostasy mirrored in Hosea's time—the worship of
Baal combined with fertility rites denounced as harlotry.

The statement that they *"separated themselves to that shame"* is ironic.
The verb is *nāzar*, the same root as *Nazirite*, one who abstained from
certain things in devotion to Yahweh (Num. 6:2-21; 5f; Judg. 13:5, 7;
16:17; Amos 2:11-12). Instead of devotion to Yahweh, the people
devoted themselves to shame, probably a reference to the Canaanite
worship including the fertility rites. *Shame* (*bōšet*) sometimes is a derogatory term used for the name of Baal (Ishbosheth, Mephibosheth,
etc.). By loving an abomination, a word used for heathen idols, they
became abominable themselves.

Verse 11 points up the eighth-century B.C. application. *"As for
Ephraim, their glory shall fly away like a bird."* Because the people had
perpetuated the same sins as Israel in the wilderness, the glory of

God's election and the glory of His presence will depart. Like Ichabod they will be inglorious because of the absence of God's glory. This glory had been manifested in a large number of offspring. Now conception, pregnancy, and birth will be denied. In verse 12 the threat continues: even these children who have been born, before or escaping the previous judgment of barrenness, will die, making their parents childless in the end (v. 14). But an even greater woe than childlessness will be Yahweh's withdrawal from them (cf. 5:6, 15; 7:13).

Wolff calls Hosea's prayer in verse 14 an "inconspicuous intercession." What might seem to be a harsh petition is really an alternative to total destruction. "The way Hosea intercedes for His people," says Wolff, "though it is entirely bound up with the proclamation of God's will, shows that he cannot relinquish his struggle for God's mercy."[9] Hosea chooses a lesser punishment. Miscarrying wombs and dry breasts would be in direct contradiction to the false prayers for fertility offered in the Baal rites. Hosea in essence asks for punishment to fit the crime of harlotry, but not annihilation.

Verse 15 picks up Yahweh's continued confrontation of Israel's sin. What has happened at Gilgal is particularly excruciating. In the very place in Canaan where His people had worshiped Him (Josh. 4:20), they were committing bigamy against Him. The judgment is strong: *"For there I hated them. Because of the evil of their deeds I will drive them from My house; I will love them no more."*

The word *hate* in verse 15 sticks in our craw. But there it stands. It is expressive of the intensity of the wrath of God against both sin and sinners. The primal sin of pride pervades and pollutes our whole being. That puts the awesome atonement of the cross in perspective. God did not just forgive our sin and leave us with an old nature. He has made us new creatures in the new creation of Christ. All because "He made Him who knew no sin to be sin for us, that we might become the righteousness of God in Him" (2 Cor. 5:21). That flashes with brightness against the dark backdrop of Hosea 9. It makes all the difference on which side of Calvary we are living.

When we see the just recompense of Israel's barrenness of verse 16 as a result of false prayers for fecundity that were prayed to Baal and not to Yahweh, we sense the degradation of both sin and sinners. It makes us cry out for Calvary.

> Down beneath the shame and loss
> Sinks the plummet of the Cross
> Never yet abyss was found
> Deeper than His love could sound.

Hosea's second prayer in verse 17 was the best the prophet could hope for from his perspective of God's justice. Again, as in the prayer of verse 14, the intercession was for a punishment far less than Israel deserved and far better than the people would have expected. *"My God will cast them away, because they did not obey Him; and they shall be wanderers among the nations"* (9:17). This much can be said with a note of hope. One cast-off can be embraced again and a wanderer can be found and returned home. And that, as we know, is what God did in His mercy at a later time.

THE JUDGMENT OF DESTRUCTION

10:1 Israel empties his vine; he brings forth fruit for himself. According to the multitude of his fruit he has increased the altars; according to the bounty of his land they have embellished his sacred pillars.

2 Their heart is divided; now they are held guilty. He will break down their altars; he will ruin their sacred pillars

3 For now they say, "We have no king, because we did not fear the Lord. And as for a king, what would he do for us?"

4 They have spoken words, swearing falsely in making a covenant. Thus judgment springs up like hemlock in the furrows of the field.

5 The inhabitants of Samaria fear because of the calf of Beth Aven. For its people mourn for it, and its priests shriek for it—because its glory has departed from it.

6 The idol also shall be carried to Assyria as a present for King Jareb. Ephraim shall receive shame, and Israel shall be ashamed of his own counsel.

7 As for Samaria, her king is cut off like a twig on the water.

8 Also the high places of Aven, the sin of Israel, shall be destroyed. The thorn and thistle shall grow on their altars; they shall say to the mountains, "Cover us!" and to the hills, "Fall on us!"

Hos. 10:1–8

WHAT GOD HATES MOST

More than seventy years ago, the great Scots preacher Arthur John Gossip entitled one of his most moving sermons, "What Christ Hates Most." It was based on Moffatt's translation of the psalmist's words in Psalm 119:113, "I hate men who are half and half," and on Jesus' condemnation of the lukewarmness of the Laodician church. "I know your works, that you are neither cold nor hot. I could wish you were cold or hot. So then, because you are lukewarm, and neither cold nor hot, I will vomit you out of My mouth" (Rev. 3:15–16).

Gossip said that the call for wholeheartedness is like a haunting theme in some intricate piece of music that keeps recurring over and over in Scripture, almost on every page. "So Christ claims you," Gossip urged, "to work for Him, live for Him, die for Him, the whole of you. To offer to go shares with Him, to grant Him some place in your life is to insult Him. To Him faith means a passion, an enthusiasm, a consuming zeal that eats up all one's life. It is a love that keeps back nothing. And yet, how half-hearted we are."[10]

Guilty as charged! The call for wholeheartedness has a pertinent timeliness for us today. Like the psalmist, we abhor people who are half and half—especially when we realize that one of those people lives in our own skin.

A delivery truck had a bold promise painted on its side. "You can *always* count on us!" Someone expressed his disbelief, or at least his doubt, with spray-can paint: "Oh really?!" was spelled out in crudely shaped letters.

The same question might be asked when we boldly sing,

Take my life and let it be
Consecrated, Lord, to Thee. . . .
Take my silver and my gold,
Not a mite would I withhold.[11]

So often we sing beyond where we are willing to live. And the "Oh really?!" question might be applied to our own egregious prayers of loyalty to God while our hearts are consistently in hot pursuit of our own plans and purposes. We fear losing control of our lives—even to God—and develop the art of religious posturing and pretending while our commitment is carefully conditioned. Sometimes there are brash contradictions between our beliefs and our morals, between our ethics and our shifty follow through, between our prayers and how we treat others.

An exposition of Hosea 10:1–8 helps us confront the fatal spiritual disease of split loyalties. A rendition of Gossip's title could well be the focus—what God hates most. One phase from verse 2 dilates that focus into sharp perspective. *"Their heart is divided."*

This is Hosea's answer to a question he seems to be asking himself and his inner circle of confidants. Hosea 10:1–8 is obviously a continuation of the prophet's address in 9:10–17. During an interlude in Hosea's public ministry, he grapples with the question, "How did Israel get to this stage of apostasy?" The prophet reflectively discusses the nations petulant persistence down the path of rebellion and anticipates God's judgment of destruction. Now he sees more clearly the real root of Israel's sickness.

The problem is a divided heart. Depending on the vocalization of the text, there are two possible renderings of the Hebrew: "Their heart is false (ḥālaq RSV)," or, "Their heart is divided (ḥullaq)." Both strike at the essential spiritual malady: falseness in turning from God to false gods and a divided heart by giving loyalty to both. ḥālaq also means "deceitful," literally "smooth." Applied to the heart, this would mean a slippery loyalty. God wanted wholehearted devotion and intentional commitment to Him and the covenant. He abhorred the double-minded, half and half, divided heart of His people that made them false and slippery in their commitment. He demanded from His people what His heart had consistently expressed to them: faithfulness (ʾĕmet), trustworthiness (ʾĕmûnâ), and loyalty (ḥesed). God required an undivided heart (šālēm).[12]

Now we are ready to note the manifestations of Israel's divided heart in Hosea 10:1–8. These divisions are not limited to the eighth century B.C. They have persisted in God's people in every period. Ours is no exception.

DIVISION BETWEEN LOVE AND LOYALTY

The essential division in Israel's heart was that love for God was divided from singular loyalty to Him. The people cherished their self-image as the vine of God but misused the blessings in self-serving ways. *"Israel empties his vine; he brings forth fruit for himself. According to the multitude of his fruit he has increased the altars; according to the bounty of his land they have embellished his sacred pillars"* (v. 1).

Before spelling out the implications of this verse, we need to look carefully at its meaning. The word *empties* (*bôqēq*) can also mean "be luxuriant." The idea is that Israel is a luxuriant vine that yields abundant fruit. Israel had been blessed with abundant prosperity, but instead of responding with grateful loyalty to Yahweh, the people misused their privileges. The nation's blessings became a bane. The more prosperity the Lord poured on His people, the more they poured it into the construction of pagan altars and pillars.

The pronouns in the NKJV rendering of this verse require particular attention. Note: "He has increased the altars; according to the bounty of his land they have embellished his sacred pillars." Some commentators have raised the question of whether it is the Lord or Israel referred to with the possessive pronoun *his*. Some reason that the altars and sacred shrines were for Yahweh worship and were desecrated with Baal worship. Others suggest that Israel built altars to Baal and blended worship of Yahweh at these cultic shrines. In either case, disloyalty of syncretism had been practiced.

The implications for us today as Christians is that prosperity often leads us away from God rather than closer to Him. We are better at trusting Him in tough times than in good times. Sometimes we invest the proceeds of His providential care in possessions and projects that eventually become false gods. Self becomes the real contender for the throne that belongs to God. And we use His blessings as a further fortification of our egos, drifting further from the One who blesses us. We do not stop believing in Him or being religious or even praying, but our hearts are divided. The Blesser and the blessings are separated. Eventually, pride takes a death grip, and we begin to think we created the blessings. We talk about loving God, but our love lacks loyalty. We give Him obeisance but not single-hearted obedience. Soon we worship God in and around the primary shrines of our squandered loyalty — our houses, cars, jobs, portfolios, people.

Loyalty is what God offers to us and demands from us. Once love for Him is coupled with loyalty, then our ministry to others is reliable and strong. We serve God by serving people rather than making them false gods. Self-centered pride and grandiosity are cut at the core.

The judgment of Israel's divided heart between Yahweh and false gods would be the destruction of the altars and pillars that had become the focus of the people's misplaced loyalty. Now they are held guilty. He will break down their altars; He will ruin their sacred pillars. The Hebrew of "break down" really means "break the neck of."

DIVISION BETWEEN WORDS AND ACTIONS

Hosea 10:3-6 shows that Israel's divided heart was manifested in a drastic dichotomy between words and actions. In verses 3 and 4 the people confess that they have not feared the Lord; in verses 5 and 6 they mourn over the loss of a calf image of Baal worship. Their divided, false hearts were slippery indeed! The encroaching catastrophe will awaken the people to a surface repentance, but their behavior will not be changed.

Verse 3 presents a thin ray of hope. The people will realize their king, Hoshea, is really no king at all, but the puppet of Assyria. They will acknowledge that he was placed on the throne not by the Lord in response to the people seeking His will but by the enemy Tiglath-Pileser III. With fulsome glibness the people say, "Ah, if men have no reverence for the Eternal, what good of a king?" (v. 3b; Moffatt). With oily solicitousness the people admit that they did not trust in the Lord in the selection and anointing of their kings in those declining years. They see that their kings have sworn falsely, have uttered empty vows, and have made compromising, placating political agreements (v. 4). What is implied is that covenants with Assyria were probably consummated with rites and sacrifices dedicated to the chief god of the Assyrians. Royal justice became polluted. The empty oaths and treaties were like poisonous weeds planted in the furrows of the field. By trying to barter with an implacable enemy, the monarchy had sown poison seeds that would eventually destroy the nation.

But in the time of national calamity, instead of returning to Yahweh, the people intensify their worship of Baal. Words of repentance did not bring reformation of old patterns. The inhabitants of Samaria fear because of the calf of Beth Aven. The word *fear*, here *gûr* ("to be afraid of"), is a word for cultic worship. Beth Aven was a derogatory term for the shrine at Bethel (cf. Hos. 4:15). The people would continue worshiping at the shrine, but the calf would be gone. This explains the mourning and shrieking. *"For its people mourn for it, and its priests shriek for it — because its glory has departed from it"* (10:5). The calf idol had been carried off as a trophy and tribute and then presented to King Jareb *melek yārēb* (those two words are usually revocalized to read, "the great king," the title of the Assyrian monarch). As we noted earlier, Israel would be the laughing stock of the nations. Trying to barter with the Assyrians only brought Israel closer to complete domination and eventual destruction. The people ended up with a broken relationship with Yahweh and no calf idol in the shrine of Bethel — the sorry results of a divided heart.

The hard truth for us is that words are not enough. When there is no congruity between what we say and do, soon our words become empty religiosity. The test of what we say is what we do to remove our false gods and how we put words into actions in living our faith.

Division of Present Behavior from Future Consequences

A divided heart loses a sense of the inseparable relationship of present behavior from future consequences. When we refuse to give God undivided loyalty, He must dislodge our false securities and topple our diminutive gods. Often He allows a problem that alerts us to the fact that our hearts may have become fragmented.

In a severe way God removed both Israel's king and destroyed the pagan altars that had festered syncretism. Another of Hosea's apt similies pictures what will be the helpless plight of Israel's puppet king. As for Samaria, her king is cut off like a twig on the water. The image is pitiful — a twig caught in the currents with no control of its destiny or destination.

What is worse, the temple at Bethel will be destroyed. In Hosea 4:15, we noted how Hosea called Bethel "Beth-Aven," the "house of iniquity." Bethel was meant to be the place where Israel was to meet God and receive His forgiveness. Instead, it had become a place of sacrifice to Baal and, consequently, a place of God's judgment. *"Also the high places of Aven, the sin of Israel, shall be destroyed. The thorn and the thistle shall grow on their altars"* (Hos. 10:8). The verb *shall grow on* is also the verb used by the cult to offer up sacrifices. Rather than sacrifices to Yahweh, which had been supplanted by Baal sacrifices, now thorns and thistles would be the only things on the altar. Hosea is obviously referring to Genesis 3:18 in which thorns and thistles are a sign of judgment of Adam's rebellion against God. The meaning is that the altar, which had been a place of forgiveness before the intrusion of syncretistic sacrifice, will now be a place of judgment and condemnation. The people would not have the false comfort of Baal worship or the true assurance of forgiveness. After the destruction, the abandoned altars will be overgrown with thorns and thistles like a long uninhabited ghost town.

Those who survive the Assyrian rape of the land and find no refuge in the destroyed sanctuaries will cry out for death. Their cry will be for the very mountains and hills, which had been a metaphor of God's protection, to fall on them. Instead of crying out for forgiveness and returning to the Lord, they will beg to die. The narcissism of a divided heart, if it can not get its own way, turns to masochism. (Note the commentary on Jonah.) The people extend their impervious control even to their own punishment rather than repenting. They say, "We'd rather die than change or admit our shame."

This unit of Hosea calls us to face any evidence of a divided, false, or slippery heart in our own lives and our churches. A divided heart begins so subtly and ends so tragically. Our task is to preach and teach these verses with boldness so that our people can take an inventory of what is competing with God for first place in their hearts.

Elected to Serve

> 10:9 "O Israel, you have sinned from the days of Gibeah; there they stood. The battle in Gibeah against the children of iniquity did not overtake them.
>
> 10 "When it is My desire, I will chasten them. Peoples shall be gathered against them when I bind them for their two transgressions.
>
> 11 "Ephraim is a trained heifer that loves to thresh grain; but I harnessed her fair neck, I will make Ephraim pull a plow. Judah shall plow; Jacob shall break his clods.

12 "Sow for yourselves righteousness; reap in mercy; break up your fallow ground, for it is time to seek the Lord, till He comes and rains righteousness on you.

13 "You have plowed wickedness; you have reaped iniquity. You have eaten the fruit of lies, because you trusted in your own way, in the multitude of your mighty men.

14 "Therefore tumult shall arise among your people, and all your fortresses shall be plundered as Shalman plundered Beth Arbel in the day of battle—a mother dashed in pieces upon her children.

15 "Thus it shall be done to you, O Bethel, because of your great wickedness. At dawn the king of Israel shall be cut off utterly

Hos. 10:9–15

This unit of chapter 10 appears to be a resumption of Hosea's public prophetic ministry. You will remember that Hosea 9:10–10:8 was spoken to the prophet's inner circle. Now Hosea once again speaks the word of the Lord publicly, probably in the presence of the royal court at Samaria. The date would likely have been around 725 B.C., during the period when Israel was recovering from the crises of 733 B.C. and trying to rebuild its military strength. The relative calm was only a lull before the storm in 722 B.C. when Samaria would fall. There are three sections in Hosea 10:9–15. Verses 9–10 cite Israel's continued sin and the consequence of war; 11–13a is Yahweh's wistful reflection on what He had elected His people to be, and 13b–15 pronounces the forthcoming doom because of Israel's denial of that election. We will review briefly all three sections and focus particular attention on the middle section and the theme of election.

Hosea 10:9–10 again recalls the atrocities committed in Gibeah against the Levite and his concubine by a group of Benjaminites and the ensuing punishment of the tribe of Benjamin by the tribe of Israel (see Judg. 19–20). Gibeah has been referred to twice before by Hosea in 5:8 and 9:9. The name *Gibeah* became tantamount to the depravity of the people throughout the generations. The words,"*There they stood,*" mean that the people persisted in the same attitude, remained unchanged. Thus the Lord will punish His people. As the tribes of Israel had sought to punish the tribe of Benjamin, now the Lord will gather the nations to execute His judgment on all His people for their two transgressions. This double iniquity implies the former and continued sin, which must be chastised by the inevitability of war.

The second section, verses 11–13a, is a vignette of the election of Ephraim to be a chosen people with purpose. The agricultural metaphors point up that the people were called to be useful heifers, trained for threshing and pulling a plow rather than simply grazing in the field. Their purpose was to have been plowing the field, sowing the seed of righteousness, and depending only on the Lord for productivity and fruitfulness.

Verses 13b –15 return to the theme of judgment because of Israel's resistance to being called and chosen. The tumult of the war will ensue, and her fortresses will be destroyed. Hosea refers to a current event to describe the tumult, "*As Shalman plundered Beth Arbel in the day of battle*" (v. 14). Although the event must have been meaningful to Hosea's audience, it is difficult to identify it with any known event. What is salient is that in Hosea's mind it was but a foretaste of the terrible things to come. The picture of mothers and children being dashed in pieces underscores the completeness and horror of the forthcoming destruction. Verse 15 drives home the point. Wolff follows the Septuagint readings in his translation, "Exactly thus shall I do to you, O house of Israel, because of your great wickedness. At dawn shall be utterly silenced the king of Israel."[13] He comments,

> Israel's God prepares exactly this kind of disaster for those who depend upon their own power instead of His covenant, for this is their "great wickedness" (cf. vv. 12f). Even the king of Israel will be silenced once and for all, i.e., he shall perish "at dawn," the very beginning of the day of battle. In point of fact Hoshea ben Elah was to be taken captive by Shalmaneser V before the siege of Samaria began (II Kings 17:4; cf. Hos. 10:7).[14]

The major preaching and teaching value of Hosea 10:9–15 is in the second section of the unit (vv. 11–13a). It provides an excellent basis for a discussion of election. Israel was chosen, called, and cherished. She was given special status to serve the Lord and be an agent of blessing in the world (Exod. 19:5–6). Israel's election was not to be a grazing cow but a working heifer. Her purpose was to plow the field, plant righteousness, and reap mercy.

This is a central theme in the Scriptures. As members of the new Israel—the church—we are the saints of God, His holy people, set apart to serve Him and be His servants in serving others.

Christ is both the example and source of power of our servanthood. He revealed the servant heart of God, was faithful to serve a rebellious, haughty humanity, and called into being a new breed of servants to whom He could entrust the power of His own Spirit. He said, "For even the Son of Man did not come to be served but to serve, and to give His life a ransom for many" (Mark 10:45).

Christ's own identification of His nature was that He was "meek and lowly" (Matt. 11:29 KJV). The word *meek* means "leadable and receptive." It was used to describe an animal brought under the control of the bit and reins of its master; *lowly* means "teachable." In His humanity, the divine Son was subservient and obedient to the Father. As the Suffering Servant, He was obedient even to death on the cross for our redemption.

As our risen Lord, He calls us to be servants. He frequently reminded the disciples that a servant is not higher than his master. "Remember the word that I said to you, 'A servant is not greater than his master'" (John 15:20). Then He called the disciples to emulate Him in servanthood. "It is enough for a disciple that he be like his teacher and a servant like his master" (Matt. 10:25).

We are called to be servants of Christ. Each day we report in for duty as servants. Our hourly question is, "Lord, how can I serve you by serving others?" The Lord releases His power to those who realize that they have been elected to serve.

The Christian life is one of struggle, strain, and stress until we accept our calling to servanthood as the key to experiencing authentic power. We will be troubled by the lust for power and the lack of power until we do. And what is worse—until we understand the vital link between servanthood and power, we will limp on in our inadequate facsimiles of power.

Recently, I had the privilege of spending an hour with one of the great thinkers and theologians of our time. I had read and admired his benchmark writings for years. After the pleasantry of greetings, this giant of wisdom and knowledge looked at me intently with his warm brown eyes and said, "Now, how may I serve you?" He had no need to impress or wield the power of his intellect. The purpose of his scholarship and concern for people is simply to serve.

After the visit, I thought a lot about the question, "How may I serve you?" That question is really the antidote to false power, competitiveness, and self-centered ambition. It is a question to ask at the beginning of every day and one for every relationship and situation. How can we serve?

In our marriages, with our friends, in our jobs, in our communities — our purpose is to serve and not expect to be served. Our concern is not what we get, but what we can give.

What a difference it would make in our marriages if we thought of what we could do to serve our mates rather than keep a scrupulous account of what he or she had done for us lately. This means listening, bearing burdens, doing the practical (and sometimes gloriously impractical) things that communicate that we care. Our calling is to express initiative affection, simply giving ourselves away unselfishly, and forgiving unqualifiedly. A tall order? Yes. But there is no true power without it.

What about serving our friends? When we serve our friends, we earn the right to share our faith, introduce them to Christ, and experience the profound joy of a creatively powerful relationship.

And on the job, there are few things more liberating than serving the people for whom we work, who work for us, or who work around us. But we must surrender our worries about future advancement to the Lord. We do not need to jockey for position or use other people as rungs on the ladder to success. Our territorial defensiveness about our own power is supplanted by a commitment to serve. Then the Lord will make it abundantly clear where He wants us. And if we are given greater advancement, recognition, or the accouterments of success, this will be to serve the Lord by serving in greater opportunities.

In the communities in which we live, there are manifold opportunities to be a servant. The power of our Servant-Master is released when we serve the poor, the homeless, the sick, the disadvantaged, the hungry. We are called into ministry. The very word *ministry* means servant. So does the word *deacon*. And Christ, our Eternal Deacon, calls us to serve in His name.

NOTES

1. Andersen and Freedman, *Hosea*, 533.

2. Wolff, *Hosea*, 157.

3. Stuart, *Hosea–Jonah*, 146.

4. Ibid., 139–140.

5. Ibid., 146.

6. Wolff, *Hosea*, 163.

7. Stuart, *Hosea–Jonah*, 150.

8. See my full treatment of the parable of the fig tree in Chapter 23 of *The Autobiography of God*, (Ventura, Calif.: Regal Books, 1981), 242–251.

9. Wolff, *Hosea*, 167.

10. Arthur John Gossip, *The Hero in Thy Soul*, (Edinburgh: T & T Clark, 1928), 182.

11. Frances R. Havergal, "Take My Life and Let It Be," *Hymns for the Living Church* (Carol Stream, Ill.: Hope Publishing Co., 1974), 385.

12. Wolff, *Hosea*, 174.

13. Ibid., 181.

14. Ibid., 188.

CHAPTER THIRTEEN

THE LONELINESS OF GOD

Hosea 11:1–11

11:1 "When Israel was a child, I loved him, and out of Egypt I called My son.

2 "As they called them, so they went from them; they sacrificed to the Baals, and burned incense to carved images.

3 "I taught Ephraim to walk, taking them by their arms; but they did not know that I healed them.

4 "I drew them with gentle cords, with bands of love, and I was to them as those who take the yoke from their neck. I stooped and fed them.

5 "He shall not return to the land of Egypt; but the Assyrian shall be his king, because they refused to repent.

6 "And the sword shall slash in his cities, devour his districts, and consume them, because of their own counsels.

7 "My people are bent on backsliding from Me. Though they call to the Most High, none at all exalt Him.

8 "How can I give you up, Ephraim? How can I hand you over, Israel? How can I make you like Admah? How can I set you like Zeboiim? My heart churns within Me; my sympathy is stirred.

9 "I will not execute the fierceness of My anger; I will not again destroy Ephraim. For I am God, and not man, the Holy One in your midst; and I will not come with terror.

10 "They shall walk after the Lord. He will roar like a lion. When He roars, then His sons shall come trembling from the west;

11 "they shall come trembling like a bird from
Egypt, like a dove from the land of Assyria. And I will
let them dwell in their houses," says the Lord.

Hos. 11:1-11

The eleventh chapter of Hosea presses our hearts next to the lonely
heart of God. It is a profound quality of loneliness, much deeper than
our usual understanding of loneliness.

Loneliness. What images are conjured up in your mind by the word? A
homeless person wandering through the city streets? A person away
from home in a strange land? Someone enduring the absence of loved
ones? A grief-stricken survivor of the death of a loved one?

Yet, there is a kind of loneliness that has little to do with the absence
or presence of people or familiar surroundings. We can be lonely in a
crowd, in a marriage, surrounded by friends, and in the midst of a
busy life. The deepest level of loneliness is the anguish of unrelatedness, the disturbing realization of separation and estrangement. It
is the pathos of longing to love a person and having your love resisted
or rejected.

Broken or estranged relationships cause the most distressing loneliness. It is being with a person but out of communication, the ache of
separateness, the yearning for intimacy again. Our hearts overflow
with caring and concern for someone, but he or she refuses to accept
what we desire to express. Our loneliness becomes especially acute in
those times when others are in trouble, have failed, or are on a crash
course with self-destructive patterns. We want to step in and reverse
their course, but our efforts are rebuffed. There is no loneliness as
painful as enduring unrequited love.

A woman expressed this depth of loneliness over her son who had
been into heavy drugs for thirteen of his twenty-nine years. "I've tried
everything!" she said. "I can't affirm his life-style or his values, and I
anguish over what he's becoming. I'm trapped. He won't accept either my love or my help. I feel a terrible kind of loneliness."

A man whose wife found it difficult to love herself or accept his
affirmations said, "I'm lonely in my marriage. I love my wife and
have no intention of leaving her, but she won't let me inside the shell
she's built around herself. Her critical, negative attitude spills over on
her friends. I try to get her to talk about it, but she won't. She simply
won't let me or anyone else love her."

And a young man expressed feelings we have all experienced about people who reject our efforts to share God's grace with them. "I see the emptiness of people's lives and want to help, but they don't seem to want to listen. When they mess up their lives, it's awfully hard not to step in and give them advice they haven't asked me to give. It's difficult to wait until people are ready and receptive. It's like being with somebody but not really being together."

Many people feel lonely in their churches, not because of a lack of comradery and activities, but because their vision for the people of God is way beyond what institutional Christianity offers. Their loneliness is rooted in their inability to get through to people who seem to be satisfied with the bland traditionalism of playing church.

I meet pastors and church officers all over the country suffering from this kind of loneliness. Few people in their churches seem to share their hope that the church will be the biblical, Christ-centered, Spirit-empowered fellowship of the burning heart. Those leaders long to see lives changed, on fire for Christ. They are impatient with the lack of both evangelism and mission. And they are embarrassed by how little impact their churches are having on the suffering in our society.

A pastor and his wife expressed their loneliness. "We lead a congregation of nice church people, but they resist any changes. They are threatened by our challenge to press on with dynamic discipleship. There's no acrimony, just passive resistance. We pray, preach, share our hearts out, but it's as if we were speaking in a foreign language."

Behind this benign balk is a struggle for power. Resistance to vision is often the desire to keep control. Parishes remain in dead center not just because of differences of theology, but because of an old guard that remains very guarded about their turf. And their leaders experience the loneliness of feeling misunderstood and misinterpreted.

When we get in touch with the frustration we feel over people we want to love, care for, and encourage, we are able to empathize with God's anguish over us. We think back to how we rebuffed His love before we first accepted our salvation. And even more distressing— we realize how often we still turn away from Him and try to run our own lives. We edge Him out of first place in our lives, resist His guidance, and, for periods of time, close off the flow of His healing love. Prayer becomes strained, then perfunctory, and eventually ineffective. Finally, when life's problems and pressures pile up, we feel a homesickness for God. It is really a reverberation of the loneliness of

God for us. We often hear about God's grandeur and glory, His majesty and might. Don't miss His loneliness. It is one of His greatest attributes. True love is inseparably linked to vulnerability. When God created us to receive His love and to love Him, He became vulnerable to our rejection.

It is awesome to contemplate. Almighty God, lonely. Lonely for the rapture of our reconciliation with Him. The intimacy for which we were created—His heart and our heart made one again. He is lonely for those who pretend He does not exist, those who deny their family likeness with independence and pride, and those who say they belong to Him but resist trusting Him completely. You and I.

The startling realization of what we do which causes loneliness in God's heart prepares us to consider Hosea 11 with more than an aloof exposition. It is one of the most moving, tender chapters in the Bible. We are given an opportunity to feel the pulse beat of God's yearning heart over His people. And once we have, we are ready to preach or teach this chapter in a way that introduces people to the loneliness of God and calls them home to Him. We never outgrow needing the assurance or the continuing challenge of being a child of God.

Once again in our study of Hosea, we are given a sweeping review of the history of the people of God. This time we see the past, present, and future of Ephraim as God's child from the vantage point of the divine Parent who remembers with joy, anguishes with grief, suffers with loneliness, and looks forward with hope.

THE LONELINESS OF VULNERABLE LOVE

"When Israel was a child, I loved him, and out of Egypt I called My son" (Hos. 11:1).

There you have it . . . vulnerable love . . . love freely given with the possibility of it being rejected. From the perspective of the omniscience of God the Parent, it was love given with the knowledge of what Israel might become as a rebellious child. Nevertheless, He lavishly poured out His grace.

This first verse could be reworded with personal and contemporary application. "When I was called out of bondage, to claim my election as a child of God, and was reborn and began a new life, God loved me." We all remember the ecstasy of our first experience of being loved by God. Our minds were flooded by the amazement that God would choose us, the joy of knowing we were forgiven, the wonderment over His care for us, the delight with the sublime surprises of His interventions.

And yet, mingled with those memories are the remembrances of times, so soon after our rebirth as a child of God, in which we rebelled and threw tantrums of independence. Obedience to God became hard for many of us. Now, faithfulness continues to be difficult. And God remembers, too, our willfulness that became a habitual pattern, our sins we never confessed, our estrangement never healed.

Like Israel, after we hear the call of God, there soon come other calls that jam with static the channel to our hearts. "As they called them, so they went from them; they sacrificed to the Baals, and burned incense to carved images" (Hos. 11:2). Both Stuart and Wolff, along with the RSV, follow the Septuagint reading here, "The more I called them, the more they went from me." The final word of the sentence, *mippĕnêhem* ("from them"), should be divided into *mippānay* ("from me") and *hēm* ("they"), which goes with the following clause.[1]

God graciously loved His son Israel and helped him leave Egypt. Israel responded with rebellion, chose new gods (Josh. 24:15; Judg. 5:8) and broke the basic rule of the covenant, "You shall have no other gods before Me" (Exod. 20:3).

The close connection between the thought of verses 2 and 3 stressed how soon Ephraim turned and ran to other gods after God had taught His child to walk.

"I taught Ephraim to walk, taking them by their arms" (Hos. 11:3a). Do not miss the innocence of the Parent and the child, the delight of both over the first steps. I think of the shared joy I saw on the faces of my son and my youngest granddaughter as she took her first steps recently with her hand held by her daddy. Our first steps of learning to walk with God were equally exciting. With our hand firmly held by our Father and confident of His strength, we put one step in front of the other. Then, aware of His presence close at hand, we walked with freedom. All of life is meant to be a faithful walk with God. Throughout the Scriptures, walking with God is synonymous with trust and obedience.

Yahweh has called Ephraim to emulate Enoch, Noah, and the patriarchs, Abraham, Isaac, and Jacob who walked with God. But the people quickly forgot who taught them to walk. *"But they did not know that I healed them"* (11:3b; *rĕpāʾtîm*, meaning "I restored them to health"). A vital part of teaching the people to walk was to bring them back to health after the bondage of Egypt. How quickly they forgot.

But Yahweh remembered. *"I drew them with gentle cords, with bands of love, and I was to them as those who take the yoke from their neck. I stooped and fed them"* (11:4). The text is difficult to translate from the Hebrew. The metaphor seems to shift from sonship to animal husbandry. If this is the intent, then the image is of Yahweh lifting the yoke of bondage and leading Ephraim with a compassionate guiding hand and a band of love rather than a bit. He stooped to their needs and fed them, as with the manna in the wilderness (Exod. 16:4–35; Num. 11:4–34).

While acknowledging the use of animal imagery for Israel elsewhere in Hosea (4:16; 10:11), Wolff prefers to see the family imagery continuing here in verse 4. He suggests that the word *yoke* is not correct here, reading ʿûl ("suckling, suckling child") rather than ʿōl, which yields, "And I was to them as those who lift a small child to their cheek, and I bent down to him and fed him."[2] This rendition seems to fit with the context and the thrust of the passage. It provides a vivid image that continues the flow of thought of Yahweh teaching His child Ephraim to walk, healing him, and holding him with tender parental love like a father or a mother. We can sense the delight of lifting a child and pressing our cheek to his or her cheek, with warm, affirming affection. Or, we think of Zephaniah 3:17, "The Lord your God in your midst, the Mighty One, will save; He will rejoice over you with gladness, He will quiet you in His love, He will rejoice over you with singing." Anyone who has held a sobbing child or a distressed adult until his or her anguish is quieted can identify.

But whether the image is graciously lifting a burden from a beast of burden and guiding its movements with gentle care or tenderly lifting a child in an embrace of love, the impact of this verse is the same. Yahweh gave Ephraim compassionate attention and provision. And as He reflected on the past, the heart of God was stirred with loneliness. It could not be otherwise. To love that deeply and have that love rejected is loneliness with an aching sob in it.

The heartrending memories of Ephraim's early years could not deny the reality of what the grown child had become. Verses 5–7 deal with the painful necessity of punishment and judgment. With verse 5 the mood shifts suddenly. The metaphors of the past stop momentarily and the reality of the consequences of sin are declared. *"He shall not return to the land of Egypt; but the Assyrian shall be his king, because they refused to repent."*

Both Wolff and Stuart follow the Septuagint in reading *him* rather than *not* in verse 5, connecting it to the previous verse ("and fed him").[3] The sense is that Yahweh stooped and fed His son but now must return him to Egypt. As we have observed, Egypt stands as a metonymy for reentry into bondage. Because of Ephraim's disloyalty to the covenant, he will be returned to the slavery from which Yahweh had delivered him in the historic exodus. Wolff reasons that the "return to Egypt" means Ephraim appealed for help instead of trusting Yahweh.[4] In either case, Assyria will be Ephraim's king. And the cause of judgment is not just the sins of apostasy and rebellion, but the persistent refusal to repent. The people would not turn from their habitual patterns and return to the Lord. The repentance God longed for was more than an outward contrition, but a reorientation of life and personality and obedience to the ethical and moral requirements of the covenant.

Repentance is not a once done art but the continuing daily, hourly response to the grace of God. As Spurgeon put it, "Repentance is not a thing of days and weeks . . . to be got over as fast as possible. No, it is the grace of a lifetime, like faith itself. . . ." Our initial act of repentance must be followed by constantly returning to the Lord. A *metanoia*, a change of mind, is required from pride to praise, from self-sufficiency to self-surrender, from willfulness to willingness.

Recently, after I had completed a message on repentance at a conference, a man said, "Dr. Ogilvie, I did that as a teenager when I became a Christian. Now, do you have anything to say to—how shall I put it—'advanced Christians?'"

I responded, "Yes, I do have a word for advanced Christians, 'You must repent!' We never outgrow that need. In every situation, relationship, challenge there is a constant need to *return* to the Lord for guidance and power."

The man's question brought to mind a woman who disliked printed prayers of repentance in the worship bulletin. "Repentance is for evangelistic services, not for believers. It's for sinners. The prayer you had us pray today is like stirring up the dust on the sawdust trail. What do you have to say to that?"

"You need to repent!" I replied.

"Of what?" the woman asked.

"Self-righteousness and pride," I said, going on to tell the woman that repentance, returning to the Lord, is not only the key to beginning the Christian life but the secret of receiving daily strength and courage. We drift from the Lord, so easily add false gods to our worship of Him, and repeatedly require a change of mind about our self-reliance and a fresh renewal of our relationship.

Israel had not heeded Hosea's call, "Come and let us return to the Lord" (Hos. 6:1), even though the Lord had returned again and again to renew His covenant with His people and plead that they put Him first in their lives. Now He had to allow their judgment expressed in the destruction brought about by their enemies. We see the inevitable unfolding of the course of events. But we also see something else. The picture of the lonely figure of their God standing with hands clasped behind His back, biting His lips in self-imposed restraint, refusing to invade their recalcitrance with a hasty intervention that would deny His people the opportunity to grow up through facing the consequences of their rebellion and sin.

There is only sadness in Yahweh's description of the forthcoming doom and destruction. *"And the sword shall slash in his cities, devour his districts, and consume them, because of their own counsels"* (Hos. 11:6). The warfare would not only be fought in the field, but Assyria would invade the cities. The walled cities would provide no refuge for their residents or for the people who would run from the countryside in hope of safety. The Assyrians would breach the fortifications, invade cities, and slaughter the people with slashing swords.

Israel had foolishly listened to "their own counsels" about the future. The word translated "his districts" in the NKJV (*baddāyw*) can also refer to false prophets (Isa. 44:25; Jer. 50:36). The false prophets were diviners of the future who predicted happy things for Israel instead of the destruction that was really at hand. Sadly, Hoshea's naive complicity with Shalmaneser V was supported by such divination from the *baddîm*.[5]

Verse 7 explains the real cause of the judgment at hand. *"My people are bent on backsliding from Me. Though they call to the Most High, none at all exalt Him."* This verse, particularly the second half, is difficult. Stuart translates, "My people are stubborn in turning away from me—it is Baal on whom they call, all together they exalt him."[6] Wolff follows a similar course except for the last clause: "But My people are bent on apostasy from Me, to Baal they call, but he by no means raises them up."[7]

The opposite of the repentance the Lord desired was backsliding. Instead of returning, the people turned away. In exalting Baal rather than Yahweh, they were not exalted by claiming their true destiny.

We exalt God when we praise Him. Praise is our response to God in the dialogue we call prayer. Our praises act like a thermostat opening our minds and hearts to the Spirit of God. They are our way of telling God that we love Him. And He is pleased. But when we squander our endowed ability to exalt Him on ourselves in pride or on false gods, He is lonely. It is like being a parent who taught his child to talk, but the adult child refuses to talk to him. Or, a lover whose beloved persists in a petulant silence.

God longs to hear our voices. Over and over again the Scriptures call us to praise the Lord. He inhabits the praises of His people — draws nigh, is present to bless. We are encouraged to give thanks in all things. "Rejoice always, pray without ceasing, in everything give thanks, for this is the will of God in Christ Jesus for you. Do not quench the Spirit" (1 Thess. 5:16–19).

God desires our exalting praise so much that He has made it the turning point in our deepest problems and perplexities. When we praise God, we acknowledge that He can use even the most painful things life has dished out. If we can praise God for frustrating relationships, we see people in a new perspective, and He gives us the insight and power we need to express His love. Often the key to unlocking complicated problems comes after we have praised God for trusting us to be His agents in solving our problems.

Praying prayers of praise without ceasing is our cumulative friendship with God. It saves us from exalting ourselves, others, our culture, or an impersonal fate. All of life becomes a conversation with a Friend who wants to give us His best in all of life. Moment by moment, we check in with the Lord to thank Him and to receive His direction. We become life affirmers who believe that it is not the number of breaths we breathe but the number of breath-taking experiences each day offers. Open to life's serendipities, we pray, "Alright, Lord, what are You going to do with this problem or potential? I believe You work all things together for good and Your glory. Now what's next on Your agenda for me in this?" This quality of prayer keeps us open channels for what the Lord wants to accomplish in every situation. Instead of being thrown by changes, we can throw ourselves into making changes according to His guidance. Authentic communion with God

161

comes from this consistent companionship with God. Ambrose of Milan said, "No duty is more urgent than that of returning thanks." Praise opens us to further blessings and more praise. Andrew Murray knew this, "To be thankful for what we have received, and for what my Lord has prepared, is the surest way to receive more." Sin is ingratitude. Refusing to exalt the Lord follows. John Henry Jowett was on target: "Every virtue divorced from thankfulness is maimed and limps along the road." But when we exalt the Lord, we are liberated from false pride and from imperious self-control. A thankful heart is the parent of authentic exaltation. We can enjoy our talents, the people around us, the opportunities that come our way, and the wonder of life much as we do the natural world, knowing that we did nothing to earn or deserve any of them.

When we take the credit ourselves and break off prayers of exaltation of God, His heart is broken by our silence and, as with Israel His son, He endures the loneliness.

THE GLORY OF GOD'S GRACE

The glory of God's grace is that He does not give up on us. Our hope is based on the faithfulness of God regardless of our unfaithfulness to Him. Verse 8 suddenly shifts from Israel's lack of exaltation to an expression of the pent-up grace in God's heart. The words knit together the strands of His unqualified favor into a bond that slips around our wandering hearts. What is our God like? Behold Him in His relentless love. Lonely, *leal* love that will not let us go!

> How can I give you up, Ephraim?
> How can I hand you over, Israel?
> How can I make you like Admah?
> How can I set you like Zeboiim?
> My heart churns within Me;
> My sympathy is stirred.
>
> *Hos. 11:8*

God must judge and punish His people, but He can never finally "give up" on them or "hand them over" to total destruction. He would not do to Ephraim/Israel what He had done to Admah and Zeboiim, cities that had been destroyed along with Sodom and

Gomorrah (cf. Gen. 10:19; 14:2–8). Divine wrath had been exercised on the sin-saturated cities in which not one faithful person could be found. These cities had been paradigms for what could happen to Israel if the people continued to break the covenant with apostasy. Now, instead, is a momentous conversion, a change of mind from God. Israel will be punished with the exile, but God has decided not to obliterate His people; rather, reaching out beyond His judgment is His desire to win His people back to Himself. We are reminded of the poet's words to his beloved.

> I will not let you go
>   I hold you with too many bands
> you say farewell and lo!
>   I have you by the hands,
> and will not let you go.[8]

Still, no human poetry or expression can come near plumbing the depth of God's lonely heart. It churns, is turned over from condemnation to compassion. His sympathy is stirred. Verse 9 communicates the bond of love He has with Ephraim/Israel, *"I will not execute the fierceness of My anger; I will not again destroy Ephraim."*

The people will not receive the obliteration they deserved. After the destruction of the land by the Assyrians, the Lord will begin the process of restoration of His people. His nature includes grace as well as wrath. *"For I am God, and not man, the Holy One in your midst; and I will not come with terror"* (Hos. 11:9b).

God is not vindictive. He is righteous in His judgments, remedial in His punishments, and indefatigable in His forgiving grace. His purpose and plan is for reconciliation. He would use the course of historical events of the Assyrian invasion, He would utilize the exile, He would persist in love for His people even in the exile, and He will bring His people back to the land.

All because God is the Holy One and not restricted by the quid pro quo of human nature. Wolff comments on this reference to the glory of God's grace as the Holy One.

> The motive clause states that God proves Himself to be God and the Holy One in Israel in that He, unlike men, is independent of His partner's actions. Remaining completely sovereign over His own actions, He is not compelled to react. . . . It is important to

note that the concept of Yahweh's holiness, appearing only once in Hosea, provides the foundation not for His judging will but for His saving will, to which He had committed Himself from the very beginning of Israel's saving history.[9]

THE NORM OF THE FUTURE

The future is God's norm for His present gift of grace. He sees what our future can be and sets us free of the past so we can grasp what He has prepared for us. Our God wants to give us a future and a hope (Jer. 29:11). We can prioritize the present when we focus on His future goals for us. Some of us make the past the norm for the present. Others hold the present as the norm for the future. God wants us to allow His vision for the future to invade our present so we can begin now to realize His promise.

A few years ago Alvin Toffler wrote a book entitled *Future Shock*. His thesis was that the future has invaded the present with alarming anxiety. My thesis is that God's people can live with *future hope*. God is always more concerned about what we can become than what we have been.

In verses 10 and 11 of Hosea 11, we feel the lonely heart of God reaching out to the future. He envisions a time when His people will live in an obedient, trusting, faithful relationship with Him. He is the Lord of the future, the God of new beginnings, who longs to make all things new, the Father of the thousandth chance, the Spirit of the fresh start. In these verses we sense His pulsating *boulēma* will that requires Israel's willing cooperation to be realized.

What the Lord longed for from His people then, He desires from us now. After repentance, He seeks our reconciliation. Only this will fill the daughter/son void in His lonely heart. And so He wistfully looks into the future when His people will express what He called and cherished them to be able to give to Him: faithful obedience, awe and wonder, and grateful acceptance of His providential care. Put together all three spell the quality of intimacy that alone can be the antidote for both His loneliness for us and ours for Him.

God looks into the bright future after the necessary judgment and punishment of Israel is past. When the exile is completed, *"they shall walk after the Lord"* (Hos. 11:10a) With swaggering arrogance, they walked ahead of Him and then without Him. In the blessed future, they will follow Him as devoted disciples and not as deviant defectors from the covenant. Once again they would depend on Him as of old — as a pillar of cloud by day and of fire by night. He alone would be their God, and they would be His people.

For us, a new commitment to *walk after the Lord* is a viable, vital norm for our future that radically changes our present. It is our purpose, calling, vocation (note the exposition of Amos 3:3). Amos asked, "Can two walk together, unless they are agreed?" The meaning of *agreed* is "met." Can two walk together, unless they have met and decided to walk together? But once two meet, they must move together toward a set destination. In our walk of faith, God must set the direction, pace, goal. God looks forward to the time when Israel's willful disobedience will be replaced by faithful obedience.

This will be expressed with renewed awe and wonder. Yahweh *"will roar like a lion. When He roars, then His sons shall come trembling from the west; they shall come trembling like a bird from Egypt, like a dove from the land of Assyria"* (Hos. 11:10-11a). This is an amazing affirmation in contrast to Hosea 7:11, "Ephraim also is like a silly dove, without sense." The chastened and renewed people will come back to the land at God's invitation and timing. The creative fear of the Lord (Deut. 6:2) will fill their hearts with trembling adoration instead of trifling apostasy. They will know that "the fear of the Lord is the beginning of knowledge" (Prov. 1:7), and "is clean, enduring forever; the judgments of the Lord are true and righteous altogether" (Ps. 19:9). God's vision is that His people would no longer pare life down to the size of false gods. His majesty and righteousness, His holiness and justice were to be the absolute basis of ethics and holy living.

A sense of the glory of God fills us with the amazement of true awe and wonder. We are constantly startled by the fact that He has chosen to be our God and to call us back into intimate communion with Him. Reverence for the awesome greatness of God produces grateful praise for the amazing grace of God. Terror about life grips us when we lose our fear of God, awe, and wonder. Without this one creative fear, we have no defense against all our destructive, diminutive fears. The fear of the Lord is not cringing anguish before an imperious tyrant God, but adoration, praise, and obedience. We come to know God as our Redeemer and Friend when we also know Him as our Judge and

Lord. Kierkegaard's idea of "fear and trembling" must be a prelude to assurance and comfort, when humble reverence deepens our intimacy with God. He seeks people who are overcome by the sheer privilege of loving and obeying Him.

He also is lonely for people who will make His future promises the norm of the present. The third thing Yahweh envisioned for His people is that they would claim their future return from exile as a blessing of the covenant and not as their just desserts. The land was His land and theirs only because of their election to be His people. A sense of privilege must replace pride. Don't miss the aroma of grace in the assurance, *"And I will let them dwell in their houses"* (Hos 11:11b). God's faithfulness to the covenant would make it so. The people could endure the suffering of the exile with the promises of God to sustain them.

Salient for us is the assurance that God believes in our future more than our past. He has plans for us. When our repentance returns us to relationship with Him, He begins to unfold possibilities we never dared imagine. He moves us off the dead center of rumination over our past sins and failures onto the realization of our potential.

A woman sat alone in the balcony of my church. Her polished exterior betrayed the fact that inside she suffered the excruciating pain of loneliness. Friends, a successful career, and a busy life had not filled the empty pit of the aloneness she felt. Over months of consistent attendance, she heard about God's grace and felt it communicated by a loving congregation. As a gift of His Spirit, it dawned on her that she was really lonely for God. But the clincher came when she heard the startling, awesome truth that God was lonely for her. After she accepted the gift of faith, she exclaimed, "Just imagine! There's an empty place in God's heart only I can fill. Experiencing His grace has liberated me from the guilt that kept me from Him and feeling worthy of deep relationships with others. Now I'm free to get on with life—His life for me. For the first time ever, I'm excited about the future!"

This woman put her own name to God's question "How can I give you up? How can I hand you over?" And it was the good news of what God had done in Christ to reach her lonely heart that brought her home to His heart.

The shadow of the lonely God incarnate in Immanuel falls over this eleventh chapter of Hosea. In Christ's life, message, death, and resurrection, we see the extent God was willing to go because He would not give us up or turn us over. Christ is the word of God saying, "I will not let you go." He is the Mediator between our lonely hearts and God's lonely heart— ". . . God our Savior, who desires all men to be saved and to come to the knowledge of the truth. For there is one God and one Mediator between God and men, the Man Christ Jesus, who gave Himself a ransom for all, to be testified in due time" (1 Tim. 2:3-6).

You and I preach and teach as part of that propitious due time, the era of grace. Christ the God-Man knew both the loneliness of God and the loneliness of humankind. As the heart of God with us, He came to seek and to save the lost. He pictured for us the lonely Father heart of God running to meet His son. He characterized the shepherd heart of God going out to find the lost sheep. He boldly taught the startling truth of the initiative, seeking heart of God in quest of true worshipers who "will worship the Father in spirit and truth; for the Father is seeking such to worship Him" (John 4:23). And at the center of His divinity was the awesome purpose of His incarnation. God had sent Him because, by His sovereign choice, He had chosen not to condemn the world but to save the world (John 3:16). Grace. "How can I give you up, humankind?"

From the human side of the mysterious hypostatic union of the divine and human in His nature, Jesus knew the excruciating pain of human loneliness. The loneliness of unrelatedness, of longing to love, to bless, to heal, and to care while meeting resistance and rejection from those who most needed their loneliness healed. He took no one for granted; broken, wretched people as well as scribes, pharisees, and kings had the common problem of a masked loneliness for God. And though He knew no sin, with profound empathy He identified the cause. Sin, pride, willfulness, self-justification—all manifestations of estrangement from God.

Sue Rainey, contemporary singer and composer, asks in her winsome song, "Was He Ever Lonely?" Sue is a member of my congregation, and when she sings that song there is a hushed silence from the congregation. We all intrepidly reach out to a Savior who knows our deepest need. As Sue sings, we picture the lonely Jesus, misunderstood, misquoted, misrepresented, misused. We feel the rejection and resistance He endured.

Surely that is why Christ constantly slipped away to be alone with the Father. He knew the cure for loneliness. No cheering crowd could satisfy the need for communion with the One who had sent Him. And in the defection of His disciples and the degradation of the leaders of Israel, the Savior was sustained by the oneness He knew with the Father. His dominant desire was that all women and men know that oneness. That required a substitutionary sacrifice for the sins of the world. The Father had to be the Just and the Justifier through Him. Atonement had to be made—Calvary!

> Jesus walked this lonesome valley,
> He had to walk it by Himself;
> O nobody else could walk it for Him,
> He had to walk it by Himself.

It was during the last, dark hours of the crucifixion that Jesus knew the ultimate pain of loneliness. When the full weight of the sin of the world, past, present, and future, was placed upon Him, He endured for us the just judgment of the wrath of God. Writhing in inexplicable pain, He became sin, though He knew no sin (2 Cor. 5:21). For us Christ endured the ultimate loneliness of forsakenness. Totally identifying with the estrangement of humankind, He repeated the words of Psalm 22 that expressed the depths of bereftness and clearly predicted what He would go through as the suffering Savior, "My God, My god, why have You forsaken Me?" (Matt. 27:46). Martin Luther confronted the mystery. "God forsaken by God? How can this be?" And yet, as the reformer went on to conclude, it had to be. Christ suffered those hours of forsakenness that through Him and His cross we might claim the promise, "You shall no longer be termed Forsaken" (Isa. 62:4). We have been forgiven, reconciled, restored once and for all time.

When those dark hours between noon and three in the afternoon were completed, Jesus, reassured by the Father, commended His Spirit to the Father's hands and cried, "It is finished." And the Father's vindication of His finished salvation was to raise Him from the dead, glorify Him, and loose Him on the world to spread His finished salvation abroad through the centuries.

As communicators of His cross, we can be sure that He will be present when we share the good news that our listeners are loved and forgiven. He is the Glorifier of the Father in our midst, the risen Mediator bringing our lonely hearts to the lonely heart of God. He alone has the power and authority to whisper in our souls, "Come home, come home!" Then we can sing,

> As we walk our lonesome valley
> We do not walk it by ourselves
> For God *sends* His Son to walk it with us
> We do not walk it by ourselves.

Through Christ we can know the same oneness with the Father He lived throughout His ministry and went to the cross to provide for us. He is commissioned by the Father to assure us, "I will never let you go!"

NOTES

1. Stuart, *Hosea – Jonah*, 175; Wolff, *Hosea*, 191.
2. Wolff, *Hosea*, 191.
3. Stuart, *Hosea – Jonah*, 174–175; Wolff, *Hosea*, 191–192.
4. Wolff, *Hosea*, 200.
5. Stuart, *Hosea – Jonah*, 180.
6. Ibid., 174.
7. Wolff, *Hosea*, 192.
8. Robert Bridges, "I Will Not Let Thee Go."
9. Wolff, *Hosea*, 202.

CHAPTER FOURTEEN

The Jabbok Encounter

Hosea 11:12–12:14

In any prolonged series of sermons or classes on Hosea, it is effective to shift gears at this point and use a different approach. After chapter 11, people will tend to feel that nothing more need be said. There is a natural reluctance to move off the mountain peak of grace we climbed. A squint into the valley of further judgment in 11:12–13:16 makes us wonder whether we want to descend for a further repetition of charges against Ephraim's apostasy and idolatry. We would like to leap to the next peak found in chapter 14, but the route to get there is clearly marked through the valley of chapters 12 and 13.

The story of Jacob is used by Hosea to communicate what Hosea wants to have happen to his people. First, he identifies the deceit and willfulness of Jacob before Jabbok. The prophet's biographical strokes are brief, but the story line can be traced through the passage. Allow me to suggest a method that will help our listeners journey on with us.

A creative approach to this passage is with a character study of Jacob. I will sketch some of the details to dramatize the before and after Jabbok picture of Jacob. This will help us to deal with the Hosea text with greater insight. The key verse for the whole passage is Hosea 12:6, *"So you, by the help of your God, return; observe mercy and justice, and wait on your God continually."*

> 11:12 "Ephraim has encircled Me with lies, and the house of Israel with deceit; but Judah still walks with God, even with the Holy One who is faithful.
> 12:1 "Ephraim feeds on the wind, and pursues the east wind; he daily increases lies and desolation. Also they make a covenant with the Assyrians, and oil is carried to Egypt.

12:2 "The Lord also brings a charge against Judah, and will punish Jacob according to his ways; according to his deeds He will recompense him.

3 "He took his brother by the heel in the womb, and in his strength he struggled with God.

4 "Yes, he struggled with the Angel and prevailed; he wept, and sought favor from Him. He found Him in Bethel, and there He spoke to us —

5 "that is, the Lord God of hosts. The Lord is His memorable name.

6 "So you, by the help of your God, return; observe mercy and justice, and wait on your God continually.

7 "A cunning Canaanite! Deceitful scales are in his hand; he loves to oppress.

8 "And Ephraim said, 'Surely I have become rich, I have found wealth for myself; in all my labors they shall find in me no iniquity that is sin.'

9 "But I am the Lord your God, ever since the land of Egypt; I will again make you dwell in tents, as in the days of the appointed feast.

10 "I have also spoken by the prophets, and have multiplied visions; I have given symbols through the witness of the prophets.

11 "Though Gilead has idols — surely they are vanity — though they sacrifice bulls in Gilgal, indeed their altars shall be heaps in the furrows of the field.

12 "Jacob fled to the country of Syria; Israel served for a spouse, and for a wife he tended sheep.

13 "By a prophet the Lord brought Israel out of Egypt, and by a prophet he was preserved.

14 "Ephraim provoked Him to anger most bitterly; therefore his Lord will leave the guilt of his bloodshed upon him, and return his reproach upon him."

Hos. 11:12–12:14

THE JACOB SYNDROME

Sooner or later, we must have a Jabbok encounter. For some, it happens when they become Christians; for others, it comes later. Our Jabbok encounters occur at the time when we come to the end of trying to manipulate life, others, and God. Especially God. Our Jabbok is when we are completely honest with God. We give up our patterns of duplicity and dissembling, posturing and pretending. Our real self meets the true God. And we go to the mat for a wrestling match over who will run our lives. The first Jabbok encounter took place between Jacob and God. Jacob the manipulator met God the mansmith. Some background is helpful to understand what happened at Jabbok.

From the moment of birth to manhood, Jacob had been a crafty conniver. Before he came out of Rebekah's womb, he tried to cheat his twin, Esau. He was born with his hand clutching Esau's heel. His birth-name means "he-is-at-the-heel," though the root really means "to deceive." He lived down to his name in stealing his brother's birthright and in manipulating Isaac for the blessing. Enmity between Jacob and Esau ensued. Fearing for his life, Jacob left home and headed for Paddan-Aram to live with his uncle, Laban.

On his way to Paddan-Aram, one night Jacob had a dream about a ladder set on earth but reaching up to heaven with angels ascending and descending on it. He was lifted up into the presence of God. In the dream, God assured him of a greater birthright than he had manipulated Isaac to get.

> And behold, the Lord stood above it and said, "I am the Lord God of Abraham your father and the God of Isaac; the land on which you lie I will give to you and your descendants. Also your descendants shall be as the dust of the earth; you shall spread abroad to the west and the east, to the north and the south; and in you and in your seed all the families of the earth shall be blessed. Behold, I am with you and will keep you wherever you go, and will bring you back to this land; for I will not leave you until I have done what I have spoken to you.
>
> *Gen: 28:13–15*

When Jacob awoke he said, "Surely the Lord is in this place, and I did not know it. . . . How awesome is this place. This is none other than the house of God, and this is the gate of heaven!" (Gen. 28:16–17). He had not expected to meet God under the stars there at Luz. Note that he was not searching for God and certainly had done nothing to deserve a revelation from God. What it did for Jacob was to confirm Isaac's blessing. Jacob was deeply moved by his dream and built an altar calling it Bethel, meaning "house of God," and made a vow to tithe a tenth of all the Lord would give him. Jacob the manipulator was confronted with the majesty of God, who was getting him ready for what would happen at Jabbok twenty years later.

At Paddan-Aram Jacob almost met his match in his uncle Laban, a rogue of rogues. When Jacob fell in love with Laban's daughter Rachel, he struck a bargain with Laban. He offered to work for seven years for Rachel's hand. Laban agreed, but with a trick up his sleeve. When the seven years were up, Jacob demanded his beloved Rachel. Laban gave a wedding feast and late at night sent Leah, his older daughter, to Jacob's tent as his wife instead of Rachel. The feast must have had more than enough libation to dull Jacob's perception, for he did not know until morning that it was Leah and not Rachel with whom he had consummated the marriage. Strange irony—reminiscent of the deed of deception he accomplished when he falsified his identity with his near-blind father for the birthright. Life does have costly boomerang for the deceptive!

Laban had outmaneuvered Jacob the manipulator. He persuaded Jacob to work another week before he could marry Rachel, work another seven years to keep her, and six years beyond that. These thirteen years were prosperous and productive, but not without conflict between the women in Jacob's life. Rachel and Leah had a continuing battle over Jacob's affections. Leah bore him six sons and a daughter. This prompted Rachel, who was barren through the first years of marriage, to have two children vicariously through her maid, whom she gave to Jacob. Not to be outdone, Leah, at a time when she had temporarily stopped bearing, gave Jacob her maid for two more sons. That made ten sons. Finally, Joseph was born to Rachel, and she died giving birth to her second son, Benjamin.

When the twenty years were completed at long last, Jacob was restless, for there was unfinished business in his soul. He could not forget what he had done to Esau, and he longed to return home. After a further doublecross from Laban, and Jacob had rebuilt his herd, he secretly left Laban's land with great prosperity and strength. When Laban caught up with him, a negotiated truce between them was possible only because of an intervention of the Lord. Laban was warned by God to deal fairly with Jacob and let him go. It was not Jacob's wit or will that won the battle. The repeated phrase, "The Lord was with Jacob," repeatedly punctuates the account.

Indeed, the Lord was with Jacob. God was getting Jacob ready for a very decisive encounter, not just with Esau, but with Himself. Jacob would not have been ready for what God had in store for him on his journey home if he had not endured the trials and had been forced to realize that the Lord—not his grit, his guts, or his guile—made possible his triumphs and prosperity.

Free of Laban, Jacob could now get on with the task at hand, one that he dreaded. The panic he felt at the thought of meeting Esau was prompted by the memories of what he had done to his brother. The old manipulator rose to the surface again. Momentarily he fell back on his old ways rather than claiming that God was with him. Jacob sent messengers ahead to assure Esau that he had great flocks and herds to share.

Spiritual transformation is slow in any of us. There was both an old person and a new person battling within Jacob. The elaborate lengths he went to in preparing a spectacular gift for Esau indicate that Jacob was still dependent on manipulation rather than on God. Jacob carefully briefed his peace envoys, instructing them to tell Esau, "Behold, your *servant* Jacob is behind us." His strategy was calculated, "I will appease him with the present that goes before me, and afterward I will see his face; perhaps he will *accept* me" (Gen. 32:20).

Jacob longed for acceptance. He had never really experienced it from Isaac and had little right to expect it from Esau. What Jacob did not realize was that only God could give that precious gift. When we accept God's gift of acceptance, we finally have a chance of getting free of manipulating people to assure its flow. And that is exactly what happened to Jacob during the night before he met Esau.

Genesis 32:24–32 records vividly the battle for Jacob's soul. The Scripture says that a "man" wrestled with Jacob all night long at the Jabbok ford. Jacob's own testimony and the name he gave to the place of his wrestling match gives us the real truth. He called the place Peniel, which means "the face of God," and he said, "I have seen God face to face, and my life is preserved" (Gen. 32:30). In reality, now life was just beginning.

As the crucial night of encounter ended, Jacob was crippled in the socket of his thigh. G. Campbell Morgan has succinctly entitled the experience, "Crippled to Crown," an apt description. Jacob would not let the Lord go until He blessed him. This was Jacob's deepest need, and the lack of it was the real cause of his deceptive, manipulative life. Reading between the lines, we discern that Jacob had to face the man he had been and had to relinquish the control of his life to God. He persisted in his struggle that must have included soul-searching honesty and confession.

As a result of the Jabbok encounter, Jacob was given a new name. No longer Jacob, the supplanter and deceitful one, but now Israel, meaning "God strives." This became the issue for the new man emerging in the old Jacob. God had and would always strive with, for, and on behalf of him and his descendants.

God gave the blessing that Jacob longed because it is His nature to bless. The patriarch did nothing to earn or deserve it. Now he had a limp that would remind him that God touched not only the socket of his thigh but the secret places of his heart.

When morning came, it was the beginning of new life. We meet a totally new Jacob, now called Israel. After that night, his new name reminded him that God had striven with him and would strive for him. The deceitful, willful manipulator had become willing to be molded by God. From that time on, we feel compassion, gentleness, and receptivity in Israel.

As Israel awoke, he looked up and saw Esau coming. No panic this time. The wrestling with God had accomplished a transformation. Israel was free from needing to manipulate. It was a tender scene as Esau ran to him and fell on Israel's neck. Then Israel expressed his new blessed heart, "I have seen your face as though I had seen the face of God, and you were pleased with me. Please, take my blessing that is brought to you, because God has dealt graciously with me. . . ." (Gen. 33:10–11)[1]

The transformation of Jacob/Israel is exactly what Hosea sees is needed in both the northern and southern kingdoms. The kingdom of Israel had descended down the slippery, spiraling path of deceit and lies. Judah was not far behind. Hosea 11:12–12:2a shows that both nations share a common plight. The Hebrew text is far less lenient on Judah than the Septuagint, on which both the RSV and the NKJV apparently are based. The NIV and the NEB follow more closely the Hebrew text. The NIV renders the second couplet of 11:12, "And Judah is unruly against God, even the faithful Holy One." The Hebrew *rād* is from the root *rûd* used in Jeremiah 2:31 to express being truant, running wild. So both nations are acting as Jacob did before his Jabbok encounter.

The condition of Ephraim is described with vivid images. *"Ephraim feeds on the wind, and pursues the east wind"* (Hos. 12:1a). The wind of apostasy is not a very nourishing diet. It makes for a windbag religion of false idols and the malnutrition of the soul of the people. The "east wind" is the hot, scorching, destructive wind from the desert. This is an apt description of the destruction resulting from lack of honesty with God, growing moral decay, hedonism, and seeking the security of manipulated alliances with Assyria and Egypt. And Judah was on its way to the same plight (12:2a).

Both nations are included in the comparison to the eponymous ancestor Jacob. They are like him in his deceit before Jabbok and unlike him in seeking the blessing of God in their own Jabbok encounter. Hosea combines both the Bethel and Jabbok experiences in his couplets in 12:3–4. Our review of these events helps us interpret these verses and prepares us for verses 5 and 6. The purpose Hosea had in retelling Jacob's encounters with God was to remind the people of their sacred election through Jacob and to call them to a contemporary recapitulation of the patriarch's metamorphosis. *"So you, by the help of your God, return; observe mercy and justice, and wait on your God continually"* (12:6). In other words, "Your name is Israel, therefore Yahweh is your God. Therefore emulate your namesake after Jabbok and not before!

We are reminded of Alexander the Great's words to his cowardly son who bore the great general's name. "Change your character, or change your name!" Hosea's challenge was, "Claim your name. Live it with mercy and justice rather than lies and deceit. Return to God. Stop wrestling against Him, and let Him strive for you. Wait for your God to bless you. You will find your true identity, purpose, hope, and survival only in your God."

Derek Kidner puts Hosea's meaning in a graphic way.

> "So you return" — for your name is not Jacob/Israel for nothing! If you are more "Jacob" than "Israel," so was he when the call came, in the far country, with the words, "Return to the land of your fathers . . . And I will be with you." And if he received a new name when he insisted, "I will not let You go, unless you bless me," so you are to be equally in earnest: to "hold fast" to His will, and "wait continually" for His presence.[2]

CONTEMPORARY APPLICATION

We are left with a question about our own Jabbok encounter. On which side of the Jabbok encounter are we living? Are we still Jacob, persistently striving against God, or like Israel, allowing God to strive for us? The issue is the will. Willfulness is a distortion of our volitional gift. It is demanding our way, manipulating others to get it, becoming intractable. Willful people must be in charge. They become competitive and combative. The name of our power games is "control." We must be in charge at all costs. And the price is high. We miss the blessing of God, His guidance, His peace.

The opposite of willfulness with its particular blend of false self-sufficiency and posturing is meekness. Jesus lived this quality of true greatness. "Take My yoke upon you and learn of Me, for I am meek and lowly in heart and you will find rest for your souls" (Matt. 11:29). The Master made meekness one of the sure signs that we have accepted our blessedness — being chosen, called, cherished. "Blessed are the meek, for they shall inherit the earth" (Matt. 5:5). Surely He had Psalm 37:9 in mind when He listed meekness as one of the essential ingredients of greatness according to God's measurements of greatness. "But those who wait on the Lord, they shall inherit the earth."

There are seven verbal imperatives that precede this promise in the 37th Psalm. I think Jesus had all of them in mind when He spoke of the blessedness of the meek:

1. "Do not fret because of evildoers, nor be envious of the workers of iniquity. For they shall soon be cut down like grass . . . " (vv. 1, 2).

2. "Trust in the Lord, and do good; dwell in the land, and feed on His faithfulness" (v. 3).

3. "Delight yourself also in the Lord, and He shall give you the desires of your heart" (v. 4).

4. "Commit your way to the Lord . . ." (v. 5a).

5. "Trust also in Him, and He shall bring it to pass" (v. 5b).

6. "Rest in the Lord, and wait patiently for Him" (v. 7a).

7. "Cease from anger, and forsake wrath; do not fret — it only causes harm" (v. 8).

These are the character traits of the ʿānāw, the God-molded, Jesus had in mind when He affirmed meekness as essential for life in the kingdom of God.

Meekness is the greatness of being free of covetous comparisons and envy. We claim our uniqueness as a cherished work of the Potter's hand. We pray with Isaiah, "But now, O Lord, you are our Father; we are the clay, and You our potter; and all we are the work of Your hand" (Isa. 64:8). God's promise is our security, "Look, as the

177

clay is in the potter's hand, so are you in My hand" (Jer. 18:6). Meekness is trusting the Lord's faithfulness. We seek to know His will and do it. His intervention and provision delight us. In response we commit our way to Him and are set free of tension and worry; we rest patiently in the Lord, willing to live on His timing. That cures our tendency to fret. Our anger and wrath are replaced by His peace. The outer manifestation of meekness is freedom from destructive, smoldering animosity and destructive condemnation.

The theme of the week is expressed in the old familiar hymn,

> Have Thine own way, Lord! Have Thine own way!
> Thou art the Potter, I am the clay.
> Mold me and make me after Thy will,
> While I am waiting yielded and still.[3]

Often when speaking of a stellar personality we say, "The Lord threw away the mold after He made him!" But God's true mold for human personality has not been thrown away. It is Christ. He has been delegated by the Father to be both the pattern and the Potter's hand. Meekness is the result of yielding to His molding. "Our wills are ours, we know not how. Our wills are ours to make them Thine."[4] So the first step to true meekness is to be Christ-molded.

The second step is to discover the joy of being Christ-led. The Greek word for meekness is *praus*, a word used in animal husbandry for a horse or ox that had been tamed and could submit to the bit and reins of its master. Meekness in the kingdom is accepting the reins of the reign of Christ. He graciously places His reins on our hearts and leads the way.

Or shifting metaphors slightly, He calls us to put our lives in the training yoke. A training yoke had two sides, one was smaller for the ox being trained, and the other was larger for the stronger ox who carried the weight, set the pace, and kept the furrow straight. Now we can catch the full impact of Jesus' invitation to receive His training in meekness. "Take My yoke upon you and learn from Me, for I am gentle and lowly in heart, and you will find rest for your souls" (Matt. 11:29). Christ helps us carry our burdens, He is the pace-setter, and He leads the way. Our challenge is to put our lives in His training yoke.

That is not all. The third step to meekness is being Christ-centered. The Greek word for meekness has a further meaning. It was used for

178

the mean between extremes. Meekness means being centered. The meek do not go off in opposite directions but are centered in an equipoise balance in Christ. It means being focused on Him and inspired by Him. There is a perfect inflow of power for the outgo of strength for our daily challenges.

Finally, the fourth step to meekness is being Christ-confident. It is the antidote to the Jacob syndrome. Because we are sure of Christ's presence and power, we can be nonmanipulative, noncoercive, nonpretentious. The French translation of the third Beatitude captures the attractive charisma of the meek. *Heureux les debonaries* —joyous, happy are the debonair. They are confident because they know, "All things are yours . . . the world or life or death, or things presents or things to come—all are yours. And you are Christ's, and Christ is God's" (1 Cor. 3:21–23). The meek inherit and enjoy all that Christ has done and does for us. The cross, Pentecost, His indwelling Spirit, the fruit of the Spirit as His character transplant in us, the gift of the Spirit for supernatural living, liberation from daily tension, and assurance of eternal life. Indeed, all things, all that really counts, are ours. We are blessed.

It takes a Jabbok encounter of wrestling with the Lord until our pride, willfulness, and arrogance is crippled and we can be crowned with the assurance that we are His blessed person.

Some time ago, I was part of a prayer and Bible study group that set as its goal a study and application of what it means to experience the blessing of God. Though the group was made up of successful people, most of them felt unblessed. They had not been blessed by their parents and had clawed their way to the top of the ladder in their professional life in an effort to establish their worth. Eventually, as part of our Bible study of characters like Jacob, we discovered the only lasting, satisfying security of being blessed by God. When we finished the Old Testament, we turned to Jesus' description of blessedness in the Beatitudes. The group took one Beatitude a week and tried to live it with faithfulness and obedience. You probably are not surprised that we found this third Beatitude the most difficult. In fact, we stayed with it for more than a month, grappling with its meaning and trying to live it in a culture that contradicted it in every way.

As with each of the Beatitudes, we developed a daily morning motto and an evening evaluation of our application of this third Beatitude.

Our morning commitment went like this: Seven days without meekness, makes one w-e-a-k. Therefore, today I will live the true meaning of meekness by seeking to be Christ-molded, Christ-led, Christ-confident person who submits to His leading and guidance. I commit this day to discover and do what He desires in my relationships and responsibilities. I will claim my spiritual inheritance as His disciple and will live joyously and expectantly in the flow of His love, power, and hope.

Our evening evaluation was: Was I an open, leadable, responsive disciple today? For what positive evidence can I give thanks? In what ways did I balk at Christ's guidance or blunder on in my own insight without asking for His direction? I accept forgiveness for any willful independence so tomorrow can be different. I rest this night in complete trust and peace knowing that as I am given a new day, Christ will show the way.

You can imagine what the impact of living this Beatitude with that kind of intentionality had on all of us. One man said, "I never realized what a willful character I am. All the talk about surrendering my will to Christ never made sense to me until I spent a week trying to let Him mold, lead, and center me. I've been running off in all directions doing my own thing. I really thought I could earn the blessing. Accepting the fact that I'm already blessed by Christ and trying to live with meekness has sure turned my life upside down."

Being absolutely honest with the Lord about our patterns of willfulness is not easy. Somewhere we got the idea that we can hide from Him what we are. But He knows when we return to Him with confession and receive forgiveness we can begin to live with openness and honesty in all our relationships. We, too, are Israel, a part of the new Israel, new creatures in the new creation, called to claim our name.

THE ETHICS OF THE BLESSED

For Hosea, a renewed Jabbok for the nation of Israel would be a return to God and new covenant mercy and justice. Waiting on God was not just passive meditation but active covenant loyalty and righteousness in daily living. The ethics of the blessed are rooted in the holy nature of God and His commandments. Life on the right side of Jabbok is expressed in obedience. We are blessed to be a blessing by living out mercy and justice. Waiting on God continually (*tāmîd*) is the opposite of the flighty nature of Ephraim in Hosea's time.

For Hosea, practicing mercy and justice and waiting on God continually out of necessity should produce a counterculture vigilance. His people had become just the opposite. He gives them a tongue-in-cheek kind of tribal blessing. *"A cunning Canaanite! Deceitful scales are in his hand; he loves to oppress"* (Hos. 12:7). Disloyalty to God had produced dishonesty in daily life. The people of God had taken on the values and idols of the land of Canaan. The prophet shocks them with the most derogatory names for Ephraim, "A cunning Canaanite!" It was a very derogatory double entendre. Stuart comments,

> "Canaanite" would mean not only an inhabitant of the promised land, ("Canaan" derives originally from the name of the Phoenician coast) but also a "trader" or merchant (cf. Prov. 31:24; Ezek. 17:4; Zeph. 1:11) as the Phoenicians were associated with long distance commercial trade. By this metaphor, Hosea declares Ephraim to be a greedy merchant, and at the same time no better than the Canaanites whose immoral culture deserved extinction (cf. Gen. 15:16).[5]

"Deceitful scales" were a dishonest merchant's fraudulent tools for cheating their customers. (Note how often dishonest scales are symbolic in the Old Testament of unethical behavior—Deut. 25:13; Prov. 11:1; 20:23; Mic. 6:11). And Hosea accuses Ephraim of being no better than the unscrupulous Canaanites. As a part of their culture they, too, oppressed the poor. Emulating the false values of their culture, they kept the downtrodden and poor in their place. This was in direct denial of the Law, "You shall not defraud your neighbor" (Lev. 19:13).

The response of Ephraim in verse 8 prompts us to say, "Surely you protest too much!" The words sound a bit like Jacob on his way to meet Esau before Jabbok. He hoped to manipulate his brother with his gifts. Ephraim falsely identified wealth as a sign of God's blessing. *"Surely I have become rich, I have found wealth for myself; in all my labors they shall find in me no iniquity that is sin* (v. 8). Wealth does have an insulating force. It makes one foolishly think that he can control his environment and destiny, as well as people and groups. Here Ephraim places itself above reproach and any accountability to God in the use of wealth. Wolff translates the Hebrew text, "All my gains bring me no guilt that would be sin." This is in blatant denial of

Hosea's charge. Their wealth had been gained dishonestly and had not been used to lift the burden of the oppressed.

Honesty with God requires constant vigilance about what we earn, save, and spend. Money so easily becomes an extension of our souls. We begin to think it is ours because we worked to earn it. The money membrane grows around our souls. We forget that it is a sacred trust to be used not as a sign of our value as persons, but to glorify God, extend the work of the kingdom, and alleviate suffering. I always worry about people who protest their impeccability with money. Like Ephraim's arrogant response, it usually is a cover-up for what is not said or revealed.

A friend of mine who is a wealthy entrepreneur confided, "The power of money is intoxicating. It will get you anything you want from people except real love and will get you into any place except heaven. The more you have, the closer you have to stay to God. The minute you think you've got what you have in your own strength, you've got an idol, and the day you spend or give or invest without gratefully asking for guidance, you're on the way to using money to manipulate. And when you think you're perfect in the way you handle money, trouble is on the way."

No Self-Made Nation

Yahweh's response to Ephraim's pride in wealth and sinlessness is direct and pointed. In verses 9 and 10, He reminds the people who their real God is. He alone was their benefactor, and all that they received had come from His gracious goodness. *"But I am the Lord your God, ever since the land of Egypt"* (v. 9a). He is Yahweh, the God who makes things happen. He is also the God who gave clear instructions for the conduct of nations. These were denied. Like a self-made man who worships his maker, the people had lost the attitude of gratitude and praise of obedience. Therefore God says, *"I will again make you dwell in tents, as in the days of the appointed feast"* (v. 9b). The rich nation will be forced to live in nomad tents as in the wilderness during the exodus. In the forthcoming exile the people will be brought to a new sense of loyalty and gratitude such as they had when the appointed feast, the Feast of the Tabernacles, was a time of praise to God as their provider.

The people have no excuse. In verse 10 Yahweh reminds the people that He had spoken to His people through the prophets. From Moses onward, he had spoken (*dābar*) through the prophets, given revelations to reveal His plan (*ḥāzôn*) and had inspired parables (*dāmâ*). Hosea makes a case for the calling of the prophet and for his own prophetic ministry. But the people had not listened to him or to previous prophets who called them back to covenant loyalty. The fate of the heedless nation is spelled out in verse 11. By this time Gilead had probably been destroyed by Tiglath-Pileser. The meaning is that just as Gilead had been made worthless, Gilgal would be destroyed.

The key word of verses 12 and 13 is *šāmar*, "keep, preserve, or tend." Reference is again made to Jacob, a keeper of sheep. Then Moses is mentioned as the keeper of the nation, during the exodus. "*Jacob fled to the country of Syria; Israel served for a spouse, and for a wife he tended sheep. By a prophet the Lord brought Israel out of Egypt, and by a prophet he was preserved*" (12:12–13). Stuart suggests the deeper meaning of the use of *šāmar*.

> Hosea's implication is clear: the sheep have strayed from their shepherd's keeping (cf. Isa. 53:6). The person, Israel, kept (*šmr*) sheep. The nation Israel was kept (*šmr*) by the prophet Moses who remains their keeper through the covenant he mediated. On the basis of this catchword Hosea builds not a syllogism but a simple reminder: Israel disobeyed the keeper by not keeping the covenant. . . . Inasmuch as *šmr* is the verb most associated with keeping the commandments/covenant of Yahweh in the Old Testament, occurring scores of times in that sense, the mere mention of *šmr* as what Moses did for Israel—on the analogy of what Jacob did for sheep—must have been intended as a subtle reminder of Israel's central task.[6]

Because of the nation's persistent refusal to accept its calling, the sentence of the divine law court is rendered in verse 14: "*Ephraim provoked Him to anger most bitterly; therefore his Lord will leave the guilt of his bloodshed upon him, and return his reproach upon him.*" Blood guilt is a term used for a crime that requires capital punishment. The nation would not return to the Lord and continued in reproach, contempt, for Him. The same contempt the people expressed for the divine law will be the contempt they will experience. They behaved as if they did not want God or His covenant. Now God would give them what they wanted. They would be bereft and left to the devouring invasion of their enemies.

It is an awesome, frightening, thought. So often we act as if we wish God would leave us alone. Willfully, we want to run our own lives. Then, graciously, God gives us a picture of what life would be without His sovereign care of the universe and His personal providence. We are stabbed awake to what our actions and attitudes say to God. What if for one hour He related to us as we relate to Him? Our stubbornness deserves a blood guilt sentence as far as our eternal life is concerned. And yet, God sent Christ to take the blood guilt sentence and cleanse it with His blood. This sentence has been pardoned! And that sends us to our Jabbok not to wrestle with God until He blesses us, but to surrender our wills and accept His blessing offered freely because of another place—Golgatha.

NOTES

1. Some of these thoughts about Jacob are also expressed in my book, *The Lord of the Impossible*, (Nashville, Tenn.: Abingdon Press, 1984).

2. Derek Kidner, *The Message of Hosea: Love to the Loveless*, (Leicester, England; Downers Grove, Ill.: InterVarsity Press, 1981), 109.

3. Adelaide A. Pollard, "Have thine Own Way, Lord," *Hymns for the Living Church* (Carol Stream, Ill.: Hope Publishing Co., 1974), 372.

4. Tennyson, *In Memoriam*.

5. Stuart, 192.

6. Ibid., 195.

CHAPTER FIFTEEN

The Rejected Helper

Hosea 13:1–16

13:1 When Ephraim spoke, trembling, he exalted himself in Israel; but when he offended through Baal worship, he died.

2 Now they sin more and more, and have made for themselves molded images, idols of their silver, according to their skill; all of it is the work of craftsmen. They say of them, "Let the men who sacrifice kiss the calves!"

3 Therefore they shall be like the morning cloud and like the early dew that passes away, like chaff blown off from a threshing floor and like smoke from a chimney.

4 "Yet I am the Lord your God ever since the land of Egypt, and you shall know no God but Me; for there is no savior besides Me.

5 "I knew you in the wilderness, in the land of great drought.

6 "When they had pasture, they were filled; they were filled and their heart was exalted; therefore they forgot Me.

7 "So I will be to them like a lion; like a leopard by the road I will lurk;

8 "I will meet them like a bear deprived of her cubs; I will tear open their rib cage, and there I will devour them like a lion. The wild beast shall tear them.

9 "O Israel, you are destroyed, but your help is from Me.

10 "I will be your King; where is any other, that he may save you in all your cities? And your judges to whom you said, Give me a king and princes?

11 "I gave you a king in My anger, and took him away in My wrath.

12 "The iniquity of Ephraim is bound up; his sin is stored up.

13 "The sorrows of a woman in childbirth shall come upon him. He is an unwise son, for he should not stay long where children are born.

14 "I will ransom them from the power of the grave; I will redeem them from death. O Death, I will be your plagues! O Grave, I will be your destruction? Pity is hidden from My eyes."

15 Though he is fruitful among his brethren, an east wind shall come; the wind of the Lord shall come up from the wilderness. Then his spring shall become dry, and his fountain shall be dried up. He shall plunder the treasury of every desirable prize.

16 Samaria is held guilty, for she has rebelled against her God. They shall fall by the sword, their infants shall be dashed in pieces, and their women with child ripped open.

Hos. 13:1-16

THE HELPLESS AND THE HELPER

The final stage of the sin of pride and arrogance is to be helpless yet unwilling to cry out for God's help. Throughout Israel's history God identified Himself as the Helper. The patriarchs, prophets, priests, and psalmists discovered that He was the only reliable help in trouble. Adversity was a constant recall to trust the Helper and say with the psalmist, "Behold, God is my helper" (Ps. 54:4). Israel's darkest day came, however, when the people sank to the lowest levels of willful independence in which they no longer could admit their helplessness or call on God as their Helper. Life tumbled in, destruction was imminent, human helpers had failed. And yet, the people were helpless to confess their helplessness. The persistent refusal of God's help became a habitual pattern. They could no longer say and live the assurance that, "God is our refuge and strength, a very present help in trouble . . . " (Ps. 46:1).

Hosea 13 captures the plight of the helpless people of the northern kingdom and the final pleas of the rejected Helper of Israel. The end had almost come during the years of 724 and 723 B.C. Hosea's prophetic ministry was drawing to a close. What he had predicted was happening. The people had not heeded his message. The repeated opportunities to realize their helplessness without God did not break their bonds of self-sufficiency, but tightened them. Their arrogance was reinforced with each escape from calamity. Their survival led to further sin rather than to God.

Meanwhile the Helper waited to help. In this chapter of Hosea, we feel His pain and anguish over a helpless people addicted to independence from Him. For me, the key verse of this chapter is verse 9, *"O Israel, you are destroyed, but your help is from Me."*

An exposition of this chapter in the context of a helplessness made more helpless by an inability to cry for help enables us to deal with our contemporary manifestations of this malady. Many of our listeners are on the edge of addiction to self-help. Some have resisted God's help so long that they have fallen into the greatest need of all — of not knowing they have a need. Those who are not yet at this point may still be open to realize the drift into the addiction. And surely we all know people whose helplessness has reached the stage of refusing to ask for God's help.

For all of us, some inventory questions expose where we might be. Have our experiences of God as a very present help in trouble led us to seek His help daily? Can we remember times when we blundered on without asking for help? Have we ever known a long period in which we lived on our own strength and running our own lives became a pattern? Have we persisted in some habit or activity we knew was wrong and refused to ask for God's help because we feared what He might do to change us? Do we fear losing control of our lives by seeking God's help? Can we admit our addiction to trying to appear adequate? Are we willing to allow others to know that we are utterly helpless without the help of God? On whom or what do we often depend for help instead of God?

ADDICTION TO SUBSTITUTE HELPERS

The first three verses of Hosea 13 review the progressive dependence on substitute help rather than Yahweh that led into an addiction to independence from Him.

"When Ephraim spoke, trembling, he exalted himself in Israel; but when he offended in Baal, he died" (13:1). There in a sentence is the shift from the Lord to Baal. When Ephraim, the largest tribe, had trembled before the Lord, they expressed praise and dependence on Him. But then, as we have seen in our previous exposition of Hosea, Ephraim turned away from the Lord as their only source of strength, security, and success and turned to Baal. The syncretism of worshiping the Lord and Baal eventually descended into a singular loyalty to Baal. Ephraim became helpless to extricate themselves from dependence on the cult. The people no longer called for help from the Lord.[1]

Instead, *"now they sin more and more"* (v. 2a). Caught in the whirlpool of defection and idolatry, they doggedly persisted in breaking the first commandment. Breaking the second followed: *"And [they] have made for themselves molded images, idols of their silver, according to their skill; all of it is the work of craftsmen"* (v. 2b). God-given talents of craftsmanship were being used to manufacture substitutes for God Himself. When we are separated from our true Help, we produce facsimiles to worship. We chop trees and build houses, shape metal and make cars, mine ore and fashion weapons, split the atom and create bombs. We place our security in them rather than our Maker. We speak glibly of our love for our possessions as if they were animate and able to satisfy our deepest needs.

Sometimes our worship of the accouterments of power is as unconstrained as the Baal worship orgies. The worship of Baal often simulated a copulation with the bull image. *"Let the men who sacrifice kiss the calves!* (v. 2a). The people sacrificed to the craftsmen's golden bulls and kissed them as an evidence of their fervent devotion to them. Wolff and Andersen and Freedman go further to suggest that human sacrifice is meant. Wolff translates, "Those who sacrifice men kiss bulls."[2] He follows the Hebrew text closely and notes that the Greek and Latin translations have *men* as the object of *sacrifice*. Stuart, on the other hand, divides the clauses differently, seeing men *ʾādām* as the subject of *kiss* and revocalizing the text to read "sacrifice lambs."[3]

Our problem today is that we tend to worship what gives us security. We put our trust in people and things. They become our idols when we seek from them what only God can provide. We were created to trust God, love people, and use things. When trust in God as our help diminishes, we usually use people and love things. And what gets sacrificed is our true selves! When we deny the Lord's help, we deny our full potential. It is impossible to become all that we were meant to become without the Lord's help.

NOT WANTING GOD'S HELP

Hosea 13:3 describes the fate of those who reach the final stage of helplessness of not wanting the Lord's help. Four similes are used to describe their fate. Those who refuse to put their ultimate trust in the Lord will be like mist, dew, chaff, and smoke. We might call these the similes of disappearance. They all describe the forthcoming disappearance of Israel. The nation of Israel will vanish as a national entity, and the people will disappear from the promised land. They shall be like a morning mist and dew that vanished with the heat of the sun, like chaff blown away by the wind, and like smoke that is seen coming out of a chimney only to be absorbed into the atmosphere.

The stark reality is that those who persistently refuse the Lord's help are given what they wanted: no help. As I noted earlier about the unforgivable sin—we can say "no" for so long that we no longer want to say "yes."

YET! YAHWEH . . .

The *yet* at the beginning of verse 4 has the same conjunctional force that *But God* expresses in Ephesians 2:4, *"But God,* who is rich in mercy, because of His great love with which He loved us. . . ." Here in Hosea 13:4, the "Yet, Yahweh" is a first person statement of hope.

In spite of all that Israel had done, yet I AM, Yahweh, was their God. What follows is an expression of the quality of *leal* love communicated in chapter 11. The Helper was rejected, but He still longs to help. He remembers the call and commissioning of Israel with the covenant. *". . . ever since the land of Egypt, and you shall know no God but Me; for there is no savior besides Me; I knew you in the wilderness, in the land of great drought. When they had pasture, they were filled"* (Hos. 13:4-6a).

Don't miss the emphasis on *"savior."* In this context it means "deliverer, provider, protector." This is exactly what the people of Israel denied in their search for saviors among the Baals, human strength, and other nations.

The "Yet Yahweh" and the "But God" emphases of Scripture punctuate the descriptions of what life is like with false saviors and prepare the way for an affirmation of the faithfulness of God. And so, it is really never too late to see ourselves in our helplessness and sob, "My help comes from the Lord, who made heaven and earth" (Ps. 121:2).

We wonder what might have happened if before 723 B.C. the people of Israel had heard God's incisive diagnosis of their spiritual illness and the prognosis of His judgment along with His reminders of His help as their only savior in the past. What if repentance had swept across the land? What if their arrogant self-help, Baal-help, rebellious hearts had been broken open to the Lord? What if, indeed. . . .

Each week following our worship services in the Hollywood Presbyterian Church, the elders and pastors pray with people who have been brought to an abject realization of their helplessness. Some are church members, and many others are visitors. Life has brought them to the end of their confidence in their own ability to help themselves or in other human resources. Over and over again I hear three words expressed in lots of different ways "God help me!" And He does. Authentic conversion and transformed lives result. New power, fresh guidance, supernatural strength are given.

The secret of the effectiveness of that prayer ministry is that the pastors and elders are on their knees prior to those services praying the same "God help us!" prayer. We know that we cannot preach or pray to meet the unrealized needs of those addicted to self-help without constantly confessing our own helplessness. The Lord has stretched us beyond our human talents and training. We have learned that it is not skilled techniques or manipulative methods, but the Lord's grace convincing people of their helplessness and His very present help that brings repentance, response, or results.

Repeatedly as church officers we are brought to a renewed sense of helplessness. Budgets, buildings, and programs can easily distract us. Pride over past effectiveness can dull our vision for the future. Then the Lord breaks through with a new call to repent and trust Him as our only help. And that repentance has always been the prelude to an even greater outpouring of power.

Over the years I have discovered that it is not just problems but a realization of the potential of what God wants done that brings us to authentic confession of our helplessness and a new trust in Him.

But each step of the way we face the danger of taking the credit ourselves or in seeking the approval and accolades of people or in human measurements of success. Whatever causes us to forget that God is our only help and hope must consistently be recognized as a false idol and torn from its throne.

What happened to Hosea's Israel is not limited to the eighth century B.C. It is the persistent problem of Christians in this century. *"They were filled and their heart was exalted; therefore they forgot Me"* (Hos. 13:6b). (Note exposition on Hos. 2:13 on pages 36–37).

Before the Battle of Edge Hill, Lord Ashley prayed, "O Lord, Thou knowest how busy I must be this day. If I forget Thee, do not forget me." He was wide of the mark in both of his petitions. We do not have to ask the Lord to remember us. We are never off His mind. And because that is true we can pray, "Lord, you know how busy I must be this day. Help me never to forget You and that I belong to You and that my only help is from You!"

Israel not only forgot that her help comes from the Lord; she rejected His help. Verse 7 and 8 detail in three couplets what God's response will be. In the first couplet in verse 7, He says He will be like a prowling lion and a leopard watching their prey pass along the road. The second couplet pictures Him as a ferocious bear whose cubs have been taken from her. The images reach a crescendo of judgment in the third couplet: The Lord will be like a devouring lion and a wild beast that tears the flesh of its captive.

This, of course, is an apt description of what was about to happen with the Assyrian invasion. Presently the enemy was prowling about, circling the prey of Israel. Soon the attack would come and the people and their land would be devoured. Through the confluence of national affairs and the conquering might of the Assyrian enemy, God would execute His judgment on His people.

The reason is set forth clearly in the pivotal verse 9. *"O Israel, you are destroyed, but your help is from Me."* The text of this verse is difficult. Both Stuart[4] and Wolff[5] follow the common suggestions to vocalize the first word ("He destroyed you") as first person rather than third person and to revise 13:9b according to the Septuagint, which yields a question. Stuart translates, "I will destroy you Israel. Who then will be your helper?"[6] The verse reflects the assertion in verse 4 that *"there is no savior besides Me."* This is God's own answer to His question in verse 9. "No one" is the obvious response. The covenant promise to

Israel in Deuteronomy was that God would help (*ʿāzar*) His people, especially providing help against their enemies (Deut. 33:7, 26, 29). This covenant promise was broken when Israel sought her help other than in Yahweh. The covenant curse (Deut. 32:28–42) replaces the covenant promise.

Where Is Your Help?

The question, "Where is your help?" is expanded in verse 10. The Lord presses the point: "Without Me, who will save you in your cities? Where are the judges from whom you demanded a king? And where is the king I gave you?"

For more than three centuries from 1031 B.C. to 725 B.C. the people demanded a king to rule over them. From Saul to Hoshea ben Elah there had been twenty-three kings The people had wanted kings to be like other nations, but often the people put their trust in human rulers rather than Yahweh as divine Sovereign of His people. Now Hoshea had been removed from the throne. But even in that calamity, the people did not turn to Yahweh for help.

A Self-Made Prison Its Consequences

Verse 12 tells us why. *"The iniquity of Ephraim is bound up; his sin is stored up."* The people have entered the self-made prison of their own sin. They have come to a state of immobility, of catatonic inability to cry out to God for help. The result of years of sowing rebellion, apostasy, and polytheism had reaped a national character of people totally incapable of repentance.

The mixed but moving metaphor of childbirth in verse 13 spells out the tragic consequences of not wanting God's help. The people will miss the possibility of a new birth of hope, a new beginning. *"The sorrows of a woman in childbirth shall come upon him. He is an unwise son, for he should not stay long where children are born."* Ephraim is pictured as a breech unborn child in the womb of the nation. The malpositioned fetus was dead. The mother will also die unless the dead fetus is turned and presented properly so as to pass through the cervix. A grim metaphor indeed! The application is even more so. The tribe of Ephraim, including the leaders of Samaria, caused the death of the whole nation.

Verse 14 is another of the sudden shifts of tone from judgment to hope that we have experienced often in the prophecy of Hosea. It comes as a piercing ray of light in the darkness. The eyes of our souls squint at the radiance, redilating to register its promise. All may not be lost.

Hope for the Hopeless

"I will ransom them from the power of the grave; I will redeem them from death. O Death, I will be your plagues! O Grave, I will be your destruction! Pity is hidden from My eyes" (Hos. 13:14). Note that the Septuagint renders *"I will be your plagues"* as "Where is your punishment?" and *"I will be your destruction"* as "Where is your sting?"

Depending on how we translate this verse, we either have a further condemnation or a statement of great hope that God will conquer the last enemy of death. Let's look at the alternatives.

If our interpretation is governed by the fifth clause, *"Pity is hidden from My eyes,"* then the first four clauses might best be rendered as questions. "Shall I ransom them from Sheol? Shall I redeem them from death? Where are your plagues, death? Where is your scourge, Sheol? Pity is hidden from Me!" This rendering suggests that the statement is a forceful negative declaration of ultimate punishment.

However, we need to note that the Hebrew of 14a does not use the interrogative prefix but has the form of a direct statement. There are times when the context of a statement seems to imply an interrogative inflection.

The Septuagint takes this verse as a great affirmation. The NIV is a close English translation of the Septuagint, "I will ransom them from the power of the grave; I will redeem them from death. Where, O death, are your plagues? Where O grave, is your destruction?" A space is made between these four clauses and the fifth, "I will have no compassion," thus connecting it to the thought of verse 15. The Septuagint obviously carries the perspective of later history. And the Apostle Paul, using the Septuagint and writing on this side of the resurrection of Christ, claims the Hosea verse was fulfilled in the Messiah's victory over death, "O death, where is your sting? O Hades where is your victory?" (1 Cor. 15:55).

THE ESSENTIAL TEST

The essential test of the meaning is in answer to the question, "What did God intend when He inspired these words to be spoken through the prophet Hosea?" I take verse 14 to be another of those startling flashes of hope following the grim reality of judgment we have observed throughout Hosea's prophecy (as in Hos. 11:8 – "How can I give you up, Ephraim?") In the case of the nation of Israel, God promises life beyond the death of the Assyrian invasion and destruction, the exile, and suffering. God has plans for His people. There will be a new beginning beyond their deserved death and grave.

But added to that, I sense God serving notice on death as the last enemy. The astounding promise has the ring of a prophetic Messianic hope. And, indeed, from our perspective, it has been fulfilled in Christ's defeat of death and His victorious resurrection.

Whatever approach we take to the interpretation in the Hebrew of Hosea 13:14, it must be done in the context of what this verse meant to the Apostle Paul who wrote his Corinthian letter under the guidance of the Holy Spirit. Along with the early church, we claim that the tyrants of death and the grave have been divested of their power. We live in the assurance of Revelation 20:14: "Then Death and Hades were cast into the lake of fire." God our Helper has freed us to live this life as a brief part of our eternal life.

MEANWHILE BACK TO SAMARIA

And so we return to Yahweh's further judgment on Ephraim and Samaria with the sense that though verses 15 and 16 are harsh words, as we will see in chapter 14, they were not His last words.

Ephraim is addressed first and then Samaria in particular: *"Though he is fruitful among his brethren, an east wind shall come; the wind of the Lord shall come up from the wilderness. Then his spring shall become dry, and his fountain shall be dried up. He shall plunder the treasury of every desirable prize."*

The word *fruitful*, really *flourish*, is a play on the name Ephraim, that has the same sound. *Brethren* should be *reeds* from *ʾāhû* Ephraim flourished like a reed plant. The image implied is that the land was fertile and the people had known great prosperity. As we have seen, this led to pride and not to praise, to greed and not to goodness. The east wind off the desert, a metaphorical reference to Assyria, will come as the Lord's judgment. He will use the enemy. Assyria will be the wind of the Lord. Ephraim will become like a land that has suffered drought, and the storehouse of treasures will be denuded.

Samaria, once so influential as the rump of power, will be the focus of the Assyrian assault. *"Samaria is held guilty"* (v. 16a). The Septuagint reads, "Samaria will be desolated," rendering the verb as *tēšam* from *šāmam* rather than the Masoretic text *teʾšam*. Wolff stays with the Masoretic text and translates, "Samaria must bear her guilt."[7]

The poignant verdict is rendered as a pointed summary of Hosea's prophecy, *"For she has rebelled against her God."* The city, and eventually all of the northern kingdom will *"fall by the sword, their infants shall be dashed in pieces, and their women with child ripped open"* (v. 16). Wolff comments incisively, "In the conclusion Hosea returns to the theme of childlessness and extermination (4:10; 9:11–16). Baal, the Canaanite god of fertility, brings Israel ultimately to her death (cf. 13:1)."[8]

Reference to 2 Kings 17:5 and to the annals of Sargon II help us to picture the fulfillment of Hosea's prophecy. The siege of Samaria lasted three years. When the siege ended, the capital city was decimated and 27,290 of the Israelites still alive were taken captive by Sargon II, who came to power as the siege was coming to an end. The death of the nation was complete, and the exile had begun. As the ravage of the land continued, we wonder if any remembered the Lord's words through Hosea, *"For there is no savior besides Me"* (13:4).

The impact of chapter 13 lingers in our souls. We have seen the obdurate obstinacy of helpless people unable to return to God their Helper. Frightening? Yes! Persistent, willful independence can bring people to the state of not being able to cry out for God's help.

Whenever I finish a study of this alarming chapter, I am reminded of Isaac Watts's hymn of trust in God the Helper. It should be a daily prayer for all of us and a declaration of dependence for any church and nation.

195

> O God, our help in ages past,
> Our hope for years to come,
> . . . .
> Be Thou our guide while life shall last,
> And our eternal home!

NOTES

1. It should be noted that some scholars have placed this first verse of chapter 13 as the concluding verse of the previous unit, 11:12–13:1, and translate it with Yahweh as the understood subject and with the *b* before Israel doing double duty with Ephraim as well. Stuart, for example, translates, "Truly He has spoken terror against Ephraim, He has raised His voice against Israel: 'Because he has incurred guilt with Baal he must die.' (*Hosea–Jonah*, 186.)

2. Wolff, *Hosea*, 219.

3. Stuart, *Hosea–Jonah*, 198–199.

4. Ibid., 200.

5. Wolff, *Hosea*, 220–221.

6. Stuart, *Hosea–Jonah*, 199.

7. Wolff, *Hosea*, 222.

8. Ibid., 229.

CHAPTER SIXTEEN

How to Return to the Lord

Hosea 14:1-9

Hosea is eminently the prophet of God's grace and the need for human repentance. Both themes reach a triumphant crescendo in the final chapter of his prophecy. We are shown how to repent and are given the divine promise of restoration.

Throughout our study of Hosea, we have tried to stand with one foot in eighth-century B.C. Israel and the other foot in our own time. Furthermore, we have sought to listen with two ears: one tuned to what God was saying to the northern kingdom in its final decades, and the other alert to hear what He is saying to us as individuals and as the church today. Both this solid stance and unimpaired listening are required as we approach chapter 14.

Hosea's call to repentance and the assurance of God's restoration provides us with a magnificent guide for sounding our clarion call for people to return to the Lord today and receive His grace. We must be faithful to our commitment to take no one for granted. We will find that in every class we teach there are numbers of people who are in need of finding a way home to God. And when we are honest with ourselves, we know what it is like to wander away from God. It has happened to all of us — whether through busyness, neglect, or brasher sins. We cannot read Hosea chapter 14 without feeling a tug in our souls. Whenever we lead worship or teach, there is a longing to return to the Lord in a new way. When we are open about our own wanderings, we gain the precious quality of empathy we have talked about often in this *Communicator's Commentary*. So again — nothing can happen through us that is not happening to us. To really communicate this final chapter of Hosea, we need to take people's hands and join with them as we all return to the Lord.

There is nothing explicit in this passage that gives us an exact date of when Hosea delivered it. We surmise that it was spoken during the last days of the siege of Samaria or soon after. There is no vindictive "I told you so!" but rather a message of lasting hope that God would not abandon His people. Even in the exile, they could return to Him. He was going to restore His people. Hosea outlines the steps of returning to Him.

> 14:1 O Israel, return to the Lord your God, for you have stumbled because of your iniquity;
>
> 2 take words with you, and return to the Lord. Say to Him, "Take away all iniquity; receive us graciously, for we will offer the sacrifices of our lips.
>
> 3 Assyria shall not save us, we will not ride on horses, nor will we say anymore to the work of our hands, 'You are our gods.' For in You the fatherless finds mercy."
>
> 4 "I will heal their backsliding, I will love them freely, for My anger has turned away from him.
>
> 5 "I will be like the dew to Israel; he shall grow like the lily, and lengthen his roots like Lebanon.
>
> 6 "His branches shall spread; his beauty shall be like an olive tree, and his fragrance like Lebanon.
>
> 7 "Those who dwell under his shadow shall return; they shall be revived like grain, and grow like the vine. Their scent shall be like the wine of Lebanon.
>
> 8 "Ephraim shall say, What have I to do anymore with idols? I have heard and observed him. I am like a green cypress tree; your fruit is found in Me."
>
> 9 Who is wise? Let him understand these things. Who is prudent? Let him know them. For the ways of the Lord are right; the righteous walk in them, but transgressors stumble in them.
>
> *Hos. 14:1–9*

THE FIRST STEP

The first step in returning to God is to accept responsibility for departing from Him. When we have stumbled and are flat on our faces, we tend to blame others and circumstances for tripping us.

Hosea is very direct in confronting Israel with the undeniable truth, "You have stumbled because of your iniquity." Persistent sin, ʿāwōn, that became habitual caused the nation to stumble, kāšal. God's repeated overtures of love, guidance, and blessings were consistently denied.

We all know what it is like to sense a growing distance between us and the Lord. Prayer becomes strained, life becomes increasingly stressful, and our heart becomes restless. Sometimes the cause is unconfessed sin or resistance to what God has clearly guided us to do. The danger is that we settle for this kind of spiritual mediocrity. We feel the emptiness but seek to forget it by filling our lives with distractions. Then when life crumbles or a crisis strikes, we are brought face to face with the person we have become. We stumble because we wandered away from a trusting relationship with God.

THE SECOND STEP

The second step home to God is to make an honest confession to Him. Hosea calls the people to *"take words with you, and return to the Lord"* (14:2a). They are to have an encounter with the Lord, not with sacrifice offerings, formal rites, and rituals, but with words that expose their true condition before the Lord. The people had tried to substitute sacrifices. *"With their flocks and herds they shall go to seek the Lord, but they will not find Him"* (5:6). No impersonal ritual will do— the people must *"take words"* that express their deepest selves.

It is an awesome experience to tell God what we have done to cause us to drift apart from Him. We cannot hide from God what we have tried to hide from others, even ourselves. When we verbally express what we are, this prepares us for an incisive encounter with Him.

The prayer Hosea calls the people to pray is a confession acknowledging that what God told them through the prophet about them is true. Then, the people acknowledge God. *"Take away all iniquity; receive us graciously"* (v. 2b). In other words, "We confess our iniquity; we believe You are gracious." G. A. F. Knight suggests the wording, "Receive us, O Good One." We cannot confess our sin until we know that God is merciful. The Gospel initially is bad news about our condition before it is good news about God's forgiving love in Christ. In the words of the old hymn, we sing, "Nothing in my hand I bring, simply to the cross I cling."

When we have nothing to offer God but our stuttered confession from a broken heart we *"offer the sacrifices of our lips"* (v. 2c). There is nothing else to offer. We cannot barter our good works to justify ourselves. We simply trust that because of His graciousness, God will not despise a broken and contrite heart (Ps. 51:17).

For us, on this side of Calvary, the sacrifice of our lips that follows our confession of our sin is to express our faith in Christ. "If you confess with your mouth the Lord Jesus and believe in your heart that God has raised Him from the dead, you will be saved. For with the heart one believes to righteousness, and with the mouth of confession is made to salvation" (Rom. 10:9–10). Even after we have received the grace of God in Christ and have drifted away, the only way back is through a heartfelt offering of faith on our lips.

THE THIRD STEP

Turning from old ways of living that led us away from God is the third crucial step back to Him. Hosea calls the people to tell God they heard His judgment of their false and futile beliefs and practices. Each of the things that lured them away from God had to be relinquished in a specific prayer of commitment. As we noted in our exposition of chapter 6, repentance without relinquishment does not change us. So, the people of Israel must tell God that they now know what He had told them repeatedly — that *"Assyria shall not save us."* Indeed not. Assyria destroyed them. No longer could they trust in their own military might: *"We will not ride on horses."* The idols of Baal had to be discarded forever along with the syncretistic worship of idols they made. They had to say farewell to idolatry and say to the Lord, *"Nor will we say anymore to the work of our hands, 'You are our gods.'"* (v. 3). All the previous objects of trust had to be disavowed. A dramatic return to a covenant trust in Yahweh had to be made by saying, *"For in You the fatherless finds mercy."* This assurance in the covenant with Yahweh is often expressed in the penitential psalms.

The application for us comes with an honest analysis of what lures us away from an intimate, trusting relationship with God. As we have asked repeatedly throughout this commentary on Hosea, "Who or what has the potential of becoming our false god? What in our lives do we use to draw security and assurance that only God should provide?" The way back to God is to be as specific about confessing our false gods as Hosea challenged the people of Israel to be.

Recently I talked at length with a man who confessed, "I've lost the relationship I once had with God. Please help me find my way back to Him." After reassuring the man that his desire to return to God was because God had instigated the desire, we talked specifically about what took God's central place in his life. We went back to when he thought the drift away from God had begun. Then we focused on what he thought had become his false gods. When we finished this painful searching, I said, "Telling me is not enough. You must tell God what you've told me. He loves you and wants to forgive you." We got on our knees, and the man poured out the *"sacrifice of . . . lips,"* words of deep confession. It was a profound time of prayer that changed the man's life. Currently, he is in a fellowship group with other young executives who are tempted by the same gods of money, power, sex, and control of their own lives. Weekly they share the battle and keep each other honest before God.

THE FOURTH STEP

The fourth step of returning to God and remaining in fellowship with Him is to claim His promises for the future. Repentance must be followed by restoration. We need to know that God has accepted our broken hearts and now wants to give us a new life.

The hope of the restoration of Israel is the focus of the rest of chapter 14. It is teeming with *hesed*, unqualified and undeserved mercy and grace. As God called for specific repentance, He responds with specific promises of restoration.

"I will heal their backsliding, I will love them freely, for My anger has turned away from him" (v. 4). The poetry is full of promise. The breach of the covenant that brought about Israel's punishment will be healed. The covenant terms are used for generous love, *ʾāhab*, including loyalty and faithfulness, and *nĕdābâ*, for generously, freely, voluntarily given. The anger of God, *ʾap*, also a covenant term, will be turned away and punishment will cease.

This same redeeming love was fully poured out in the life, death, and resurrection of Christ. In Him we have been loved freely. The Mediator took the penalty for our sins and reconciled us to God. We know the ultimate fulfillment of this promise in Hosea 14:4. "Therefore, if anyone is in Christ, he is a new creation; old things have passed away; behold, all things have become new . . . . For He [God] made Him who knew no sin to be sin for us, that we might become the righteousness of God in Him" (2 Cor. 5:17, 20). And so, we read the words, *"I will love them freely"* (Hos. 14:4), with the full knowledge of what that meant on Calvary.

In Hosea 14:5–6 the blessings to the restored Israel are graciously described in magnificent imagery drawn from nature. God promises to be the source of new and abundant fruitfulness. *"I will be like the dew to Israel"* (v. 5a). The picture is of the dew or mist that rolls off the Mediterranean at night (night mist) and moistens the vegetation. God will come to His people like that, to refresh, to give life. Israel *"shall grow like the lily."* The abundant future splendor of Israel will be like the rapidly growing lily because of the nourishment of God. But, unlike the shallow rooted lily, Israel will *"lengthen his roots like Lebanon."* The image of the cedars of Lebanon is suggested, with their roots anchored deep underground. Further covenant blessings for Israel's future will be like the beauty of the olive tree and the scent of the cedars of Lebanon. It is a lovely picture of God's gracious presence bringing to Israel abundance, beauty, growth, firm rootedness, and the fragrance of holiness.

Verse 7 is a clear promise of return from the exile. *"Those who dwell under his shadow shall return; they shall be revived like grain, and grow like the vine. Their scent shall be like the wine of Lebanon."* The return of the people to Yahweh will assure their return to the land after the exile. Those who remain faithful to the Lord and under the shade of the covenant during the exile will, when they return, enjoy rebirth like a germinated seed of grain and will grow like a verdant vine. Israel will once again be God's vine in the vineyard of the promised land.

The response to these abundant promises is given in verse 8. Stuart's translation, following the Septuagint closely, provides clarity. "What will Ephraim have to do any more with idols? I will have responded and I will bless him. I am like a luxuriant fir tree, on Me your fruit is found."[1] Perhaps these closing words of this great and profound prophecy should be read antiphonally to capture the sense of intimacy now possible between God and Israel. It is as if the ending of the story needs to be sung rather than spoken. Do you hear it?

"Ephraim shall say, 'What have I to do anymore with idols?'"

To which God responds: *"I have heard and observed him."* Do you sense the delight in those words?

Ephraim lays claim to God's renewal: *"I am like a green cypress tree."* What a surprise in light of God's judgment pronounced in 13:15!

And God closes the duet with the truth Hosea (and Jesus) proclaims: *"Your fruit is found in Me!"*

This is an expression of the commitment of Israel to renounce all previous dependence on Baal for fruitfulness and trust only in the Lord for sustenance, prosperity, and strength. To make complete the step of renunciation of the past, there must be total dependence on the propitious promise of God to provide for our future.

THE FIFTH STEP

The epilogue of verse 9 serves as a conclusion to the whole prophecy of Hosea but also provides us with the final step of returning to and remaining in fellowship with God. The wise and prudent and righteous person has discovered that *"the ways of the Lord are right."* There are only two ways to live—to walk in the ways of the Lord or to stumble over them. And the only way to walk in the way of the Lord is to surrender our will to Him. When we trust Him each step of the way, He will reveal His will and give us the courage to obey.

We began this commentary on Hosea with the question: "Is there any word from the Lord?" We have heard His Word through the prophet. God will not let us go. His unbroken love from His broken heart will reach us in our sin, separation, and idolatry. He will topple our false gods and break our pride. He will melt our cold hearts and woo us with His love. But the one thing He will never do is give up on us. And when He has pressed our hearts to His, He will recall us to love others who desperately need His grace through us.

NOTES

1. Stuart, *Hosea — Jonah*, 211.

Introduction to the Book of Joel

The Situation of Joel

As many of the other Old Testament prophets, Joel spoke to his people at a moment of crisis. The immediate crisis was an extraordinarily severe locust plague combined with drought, which destroyed most of the crops on which their food supply depended. It was so serious that it affected the harvest of more than one year. The very survival of God's people in Jerusalem and Judah was in question.

In the locust invasion Joel saw an even greater danger prefigured — the approach of the day of the Lord, when God would lead a fearsome army in judgment on His wayward people. They remained outwardly religious, but their hearts strayed from Him.

Joel spoke to wake up his people, so that they would realize the grave danger in which they were living. Then he exhorted them to come before the Lord sincerely, to return to the Lord with all their hearts, and to pray that the Lord would spare them. Finally Joel spoke God's words of encouragement to His threatened, but now repentant, people.

Since the book of Joel is located between Hosea and Amos in the Hebrew Bible, we might be tempted to locate Joel's ministry in the eighth century B.C. with those prophets. However, the books appear in a different order in the Greek Old Testament. The location of Joel before Amos in the Hebrew canon seems to be based more on links of content (Joel 3:16 with Amos 1:2; Joel 3:4, 19 with Amos 1:6–12) than on historical situation.

The book of Joel contains no explicit references that allow us to date the locust plague or the writing of the book with confidence. There is no list of contemporary kings, such as in Hosea or Amos. Scholars have suggested dates ranging from the ninth century B.C. to the

Maccabean period. Many have gravitated to the period of Persian rule after the Babylonian exile. However, there is no certainty.

This uncertainty of date does not hinder our interpretation of the book of Joel. Perhaps it is just as well, since the message of Joel has timeless significance. The people of God continue be faced with crises and tough times. The book of Joel speaks across the centuries to all of God's people in trying times.

THE STRUCTURE OF JOEL

Joel 1:1 serves as a title for the whole book. It is a simple superscription, like those of other prophetic books, asserting this to be *"the word of the Lord that came to Joel."*

After the title, the book divides into two major sections. Joel 1:2–2:17 contains a series of exhortations, warnings, and appeals to Joel's fellow citizens. In the face of their current agricultural disaster and the threat of greater future dangers, Joel calls the people to "return to the Lord" and earnestly petition Him to spare His people. The rest of the book, Joel 2:18–3:21 contains assurances that God will answer the people's prayer. God promises to restore their food supply, to protect them from the great future dangers, to vindicate them against the nations who have oppressed them, and to be vitally present with them. The prophet paints vivid pictures of the restored land and community of God.

An Outline of Joel

CHAPTER ONE

The Vital Connection

Joel 1:1–20

Seven words. We have heard them said with a sigh of hopeless resignation or with a cry of anguished grief. We hear them in hospital rooms, in deep conversations with friends, in times of calamity and adversity. The seven words expressing the loneliness of suffering are: "I just don't know where to turn!"

We have all said these words. We get to the end of our endurance and do not know what to do. We face seemingly impossible problems that stretch us beyond our understanding and our ability to find solutions. All of the alternatives seem equally unacceptable and un-workable.

Sometimes physical suffering brings us to the place where we do not know where to turn. Emotional pain can be just as excruciating. Failures, broken relationships, anxiety, and fear can paint us into a lonely corner.

Then there are times when these seven words take on a third person intensity or shared dilemmas. In a marriage in tension, a family facing a crisis, or a church that needs renewal, we cry out, "*We* just don't know where to turn!"

Also, these words are drenched with dismay when we confront the monumental problems of our society or allow ourselves to empathize with the suffering of the disadvantaged, the poor, and the hungry. And we wring our hands over the lack of morality and integrity around us.

Added to all this are the natural disasters that hit us or someone we know. The emergency makes us wonder where to turn.

For many people, times when we do not know where to turn expose that we have been living life on two separate tracks that seldom meet. One track is our relationship with God that often lacks vitality and power because of either benign neglect, willful independence, or unconfessed sin. On the other track is the reality of daily life with its mixture of routines, pressures, and busyness pursued with little thought of God. Sometimes this track gets littered with disappointments, frustrations, and conflicts.

It is in times of great distress that these two tracks have an opportunity to come together in a profound way. In those times, the vital connection is made between what is happening to or around us and our supreme need for God. Then we can discover the prescription for perplexity: "When you don't know where to turn, return to the Lord."

This is the central theme of the prophet Joel. He is the prophet of the vital connection. At a time of a national catastrophe in Judah, Joel called the people to return to God. Their only hope was in Him. He helped them connect what was happening and what God wanted to have happen in His people.

Preaching and teaching from Joel gives us an opportunity of being communicators of the vital connection. There is a tendency in our day to think that being a Christian should put us on a route bypassing the distresses of life. But shallow triumphalism does not help in the depths of difficulties. If God is only for the up, successful, hurrah times of life, He is excluded from three-fourths of our lives. Joel helps us stand at the intersection of the two tracks of life when painful, heartbreaking things happen. It is then that people exclaim, "What can I say?" and we enable them to ask a much more crucial question, "What is God saying in this?" There is a place to turn. Tough times are the times to return to God. He has something to say to us.

THE WORD OF THE LORD TO JOEL

"The word of the Lord that came to Joel the son of Pethuel" (Joel 1:1).

The book of Joel begins with a simple superscription like so many other prophetic books. We receive only the slightest information about the prophet: his name and his father's name. Joel is a contracted form meaning "Yahweh is God." This was a common name in Israel, but appropriate for the bearer of this word, who would announce the day of Yahweh with forcefulness and who would point to the uniqueness and power of Yahweh as God (2:27; 3:17).

The word of Yahweh came not merely to communicate information, but as a word of power, an agent to accomplish the purpose of God in difficult times. The word came "*to*" Joel, but was not to stop there. It was a word for Joel's generation and beyond (1:3), continuing to accomplish God's purpose long after Joel had left the scene. This is the quality of all of God's word given to us in the Bible (2 Tim 3:16–17), but seldom is it so explicit as in the opening verses of Joel.

Listen and Tell of the Extraordinary

1:2 Hear this, you elders, and give ear, all you inhabitants of the land! Has anything like this happened in your days, or even in the days of your fathers?
3 Tell your children about it, let your children tell their children, and their children another generation.
4 What the chewing locust left, the swarming locust has eaten; what the swarming locust left, the crawling locust has eaten; and what the crawling locust left, the consuming locust has eaten.

Joel 1:2–4

Joel begins his communication of the Lord's word with an impassioned call to attention. The call to hear and give ear marks the message to follow as especially crucial, worthy of undivided attention. First Joel addresses the elders, the leaders of the community. He wants to make sure that they understand God's word for their position of responsibility and influence in the community. But Joel does not rely upon them alone to communicate the message. He also addresses all the inhabitants of the land. This is a message for all the people of Judah and Jerusalem. A vital connection needed to be made between something that happened and what the Lord wanted to say to His people.

Joel draws his listeners into the communication of the Lord's word with a question: "*Has anything like this happened in your days, or even in the days of your fathers?*" (Joel 1:2b). He challenges them to analyze the present situation and compare it with past events, and thus to recognize the extraordinary quality of what was happening to them. This recalls some of the descriptions of the extraordinary events during the exodus (Exod. 10:6, 14; Deut. 4:32–35).

But Joel speaks not merely to entertain his people with the extraordinary, nor just to help them analyze the present situation and stop there. They are to pass what they learned on to their children, so that the word continues throughout the generations. This reminds us of other exhortations to pass on the truth of God's word: "You shall teach them diligently to your children" (Deut. 6:7); "And the things that you have heard from me among many witnesses, commit these to faithful men who will be able to teach others also" (2 Tim. 2:2).

God's word does come to each of us to meet our needs and speak to us in our own difficulties, but it does not stop there. It comes to us so that as we interact with the truth of what God says, we are changed by it and pass it on. This is our calling as communicators. The truth of Scripture is most effective when it comes clothed in the live authenticity of a disciple who is being shaped by that truth in the crucible of life's challenges, and who can tell of experiences where that truth is making a difference in his or her life. Joel did that powerfully in his prophecy to Judah.

The extraordinary event to which Joel called attention was an especially severe locust plague that ruined the crops of the land. Locust infestations are mentioned in a number of biblical texts. The extraordinary severity and the fact that locusts devour leftovers recall the locust plague in Egypt (Exod. 10:4–6, 14–15). Locusts were also one of the Deuteronomic curses for disobedience (Deut. 28:38). Amos's visions of God's judgment on Israel include locusts (Amos 7:1) as well as judgment by fire or drought, which Joel 1 also portrays (Joel 1:10, 12, 19–20). In Amos as well as other passages, locust plagues are occasions for repentance and return to God (Amos 4:9; 1 Kings 8:37).

Scholars have suggested that the terms used for locusts here indicate different developmental stages of locusts or distinctions between local and outside locust populations, which combined to wreak terrible havoc on the vegetation.[1] Whatever the exact meaning of the terms for locusts, verse 4 emphasizes the horrible extent of the destruction by repeating a construction three times: what one wave of locusts left, the next wave devoured. The destruction likely stretched over a period of several months, so that the crops of more than one year were affected (2:25).

Devastation caused by locusts was not in itself a unique event—severe infestations still occur once or twice a century in that region. A report in the December 1915 *National Geographic* gives us a further picture of the devastation of a locust attack when Jerusalem, Palestine, and Syria were subjected to terrible devastation as a consequence of an influx of locusts.

> At the end of February, great clouds of locusts began flying into the land from a northeasterly direction, so that "attention was drawn to them by the sudden darkening of the bright sunshine." They came in enormous numbers, settling on the fields and hillsides. There they laid their eggs in vast numbers (it was calculated that some 60,000 could come from the eggs planted in 39 square inches of soil, and that figure involved a 30 percent loss rate!). Once hatched, the new broods started crawling across the ground, at a rate of 400 to 600 feet per day, devouring every scrap of vegetation in their path.[2]

It was the *degree* of the destruction that made the locust attack in Joel's time an extraordinary event. Yet Joel's main burden was not to have his people pass on the report of a locust infestation. It was primarily what the locust plague exposed about the people's relationship to God. They had drifted from Him and were ill-prepared to face the crisis. The significance of this extraordinary event is developed in the rest of the word of the Lord to Joel.

An Impassioned Call to Lament

> 5 Awake, you drunkards, and weep; and wail, all you drinkers of wine, because of the new wine, for it has been cut off from your mouth.
> 6 For a nation has come up against My land, strong, and without number; his teeth are the teeth of a lion, and he has the fangs of a fierce lion.
> 7 He has laid waste My vine, and ruined My fig tree; he has stripped it bare and thrown it away; its branches are made white.
> 8 Lament like a virgin girded with sackcloth for the husband of her youth.

9 The grain offering and the drink offering have been cut off from the house of the Lord; the priests mourn, who minister to the Lord.

10 The field is wasted, the land mourns; for the grain is ruined, the new wine is dried up, the oil fails.

11 Be ashamed, you farmers, wail, you vinedressers, for the wheat and the barley; because the harvest of the field has perished.

12 The vine has dried up, and the fig tree has withered; the pomegranate tree, the palm tree also, and the apple tree—all the trees of the field are withered; surely joy has withered away from the sons of men.

13 Gird yourselves and lament, you priests; wail, you who minister before the altar; come, lie all night in sackcloth, you who minister to my God; for the grain offering and the drink offering are withheld from the house of your God.

14 Consecrate a fast, call a sacred assembly; gather the elders and all the inhabitants of the land into the house of the Lord your God, and cry out to the Lord.

Joel 1:5–14

After the initial call to the elders and people and a brief description of the destruction, Joel goes on to address specific groups of people as he portrays the distress in more detail. This section consists of four calls to lament (vv. 5–7; 8–10; 11–12; 13–14) followed by the reason for lamentation—the details of the agricultural devastation. The first three calls to lament are brief and followed by an extended portrayal of the reasons for lament. The final call reverses the pattern, majoring on the imperatives and only briefly stating the cause. This final call leads up to the lamentation statements given in the next section (1:15–20).

Surprisingly, Joel first addresses the drunkards, calling them to awake. This group may be blind to the present distress because of their intoxication, but they will be wide awake when their supply of wine is exhausted without any to replenish it. Not only drunkards, but all drinkers of wine are called to wail in lament, because the *"new wine"* is cut off. This refers to the juice just taken from the winepress, before it has turned to wine. The locust plague has denuded the vine and blocked its production.

Perhaps Joel addresses this group first because they represent a larger portion of his people—unaware of the real implications of the present situation, whether they are drunk or not.

In verse 6 the locusts are portrayed as an invading army. The military metaphor is found also in Proverbs 30:27, where the locusts "advance in ranks" even though they have no king. This language prepares us for the more detailed description of the invading army in chapter 2. That the locusts are *without number* recalls the locust plague in Egypt (Ps. 105:34).

With the destructive power of a lion's teeth, the locusts have ruined vine and fig tree. They stripped the trees of bark, leaving the branches white.

In the text of verse 8 as we have it, no specific group is named, as in verses 5, 11, and 13. The addressee is exhorted to *lament like a virgin girded with sackcloth for the husband of her youth* (1:8). Sackcloth was a course garment made of goat or camel hair, which was often worn as a sign of mourning. A virgin mourning for her husband seems to us a contradiction in terms. Scholars have generally agreed that this points to a time of death after engagement but before the wedding.[3] The extreme sorrow of a woman in that bitter moment indicates the intensity of the lament to which Joel calls his people in their present distress.

Joel again expands on the reasons for the anguish: the absence of grain and drink offerings in the temple. Israel received the agricultural produce as a gift from the Lord (Ps. 104:14-15; cf. Hos. 2:8-9) and offered a portion of that produce to the Lord in thanksgiving. The grain offering consisted of flour and oil, while the drink offering was wine (Lev. 23:13, 18), all products which were cut off by the locust plague. In contrast to the normal joy in serving the Lord in the temple, the priests now mourn. They grieve over the loss of produce, which was at the same time a sign of God's blessing on the people, the material used in their offerings, and their own food supply (Lev. 2:3, 10).

Joel then turns from the scene in the temple to the land itself in verse 10. Grain, wine, and olive oil appear together in the Bible as a summation of the land's produce (Deut. 28:51; Hos. 2:8). The source of the food supply and the offerings has been dramatically destroyed.

Now Joel turns to the agricultural workers themselves, described as farmers and vinedressers (cf. 2 Chron. 26:10; Isa. 61:5). He calls them not only to wail in mourning, as is customary, but to be ashamed in their failure to produce. Joel uses a play on words here between "be ashamed," *hōbîšû*, and the word for "dried up" or "withered" in verses 10 and 12, *hōbîš*. The prominence of this terminology, which is normally connected with drought, probably indicates that the devastation of the locusts was compounded by a severe drought (cf. 1:20).

In this section addressed to the farmers, Joel adds new crops to the list of produce destroyed. He specifies wheat and barley as the primary types of grain (v. 11). To the grape vine and fig tree mentioned previously, he adds the pomegranate, palm, and apple trees. He concludes with a summary statement indicating the extent of the devastation: "*all the trees of the field are withered*" (v. 12). As the fruits have withered away from these trees, so the fruit of joy has withered away from the people. Joy was expected at the harvest (Isa. 9:3); the present situation calls for mourning instead.

In verses 13-14 Joel turns to address the priests directly. He introduced their distress in verse 9. Now he offers a series of exhortations that they lead the people to seek God in the midst of their trouble.

"*Gird yourselves*" implies that they wear sackcloth, the garment of mourning, in contrast to their magnificent priestly garments. Along with poems and songs composed to eulogize the dead and express the tragedy of the person's death (2 Sam. 1:17-27), lamentation in that culture included striking oneself and wailing aloud.

Joel reiterates the reason for the lament, the lack of produce for grain and drink offerings, and then calls the priests to involve the rest of the people. They are to call the people to several related cultic acts: to fast, to assemble at the temple, and to cry out to God.

Fasting was customary when urgently seeking divine aid in the face of a calamity (Judg. 20:26; 1 Sam. 14:24; Ezra 8:21-23) and in times of mourning (2 Sam. 1:12; 12:16-23). It could also be part of the expression of repentance (1 Sam. 7:6). The term *sacred assembly* often refers to one of the regular festivals, when the people ceased from their labors and gathered in the sanctuary for special worship (Lev. 23:36; Deut. 16:8; Neh. 8:18). The prophets criticize the empty formalism of Israel's sacred assemblies when they were divorced from a life of righteousness (Isa. 1:13; Amos 5:21).

Fasting, ceasing from work, and gathering at the temple set the stage for the final exhortation, to cry out to the Lord. Here Joel's call to lament reaches its zenith—the call to bring the situation before the Lord as a united community. The content of the prayer to God is the subject of the next section and also of parts of chapter 2.

The prophet identifies a current predicament as warranting the full attention of the community. Even though the danger should be obvious, he has to call some people to wake up. He exhorts the religious and civil leaders to gather the people to cry out to God as a united body.

We can examine ourselves, our churches, and our community in the light of Joel's call to lament. At this point in our exposition we need to get in touch with the often unexpressed pain people feel about their lives. What do we need to ask God to heal, to change, to transform? But we cannot stop there. What about the church, our local congregations, denominations, the cause of Christ in the world? There is reason to lament for the bland ineffectiveness, the divisions, the lack of power. And our communities are reason for genuine lamentation. God has put the pain of Hollywood on my church's heart. At our prayer gatherings we list the specific needs and cry out to God for His intervention to save our city. We lament for the plight of the hungry, the street people, the addicted, the men, women, and child prostitutes, the fact that so much pornographic literature emanates from our community. And as the communications capital, we lament over what is communicated in the movies and television we produce. But the lamentation is not an end in itself—it is a call to prayer and action in the very problems that confront us.

A FORETASTE OF THE DAY OF THE LORD

15 Alas for the day! For the day of the Lord is at hand; it shall come as destruction from the Almighty.

16 Is not the food cut off before our eyes, joy and gladness from the house of our God?

17 The seed shrivels under the clods, storehouses are in shambles; barns are broken down, for the grain has withered.

18 How the animals groan! The herds of cattle are restless, because they have no pasture; even the flocks of sheep suffer punishment.

19 O Lord, to You I cry out; for fire has devoured the open pastures, and a flame has burned all the trees of the field.

20 The beasts of the field also cry out to You, for the water brooks are dried up, and fire has devoured the open pastures.

Joel 1:15-20

The truncated nature of this prayer indicates that it is not Joel's primary purpose here to give a model of the prayer to be offered in the face of the locust plague. Moreover, Joel introduces a new theme that is central to the rest of the book: "*the day of the Lord.*" He begins with an exclamation of horror at the prospect of this day — "alas" or "woe" for the day — and then states that the day of the Lord is near. With forceful alliteration between the words "destruction" (*šōd*) and "Almighty" (*šadday*), Joel characterizes the coming day of the Lord as one of destruction.

Thus, we see that the urgency of Joel's appeals throughout verses 2-14 are based not only upon the severe locust plague, but more on the perception that the agricultural devastation was a forerunner and foretaste of the day of the Lord, which Joel identifies as near. The people hardly needed someone to tell them of the awful destruction of the locusts and the drought. That was plain to see and was keenly felt by all but the continually intoxicated. It was to be expected that the community would turn to God in mourning, repentance, and petition for relief from the famine (1 Kings 8:35-40). Joel's special burden is to lift the gaze of his people from their present distress to the more awesome destruction that it foreshadows and to lead them to a proper response.

The day of the Lord (day of Yahweh) was a concept familiar in Israel's traditions. Frequently it was portrayed as a day of God's wrath. The chief difference among the various biblical texts is the object of that wrath. Many scholars have seen the origin of the concept in Israel's holy war traditions where Yahweh comes to fight for his people and defeats Israel's enemies.[4] This was probably the concept popular in Israel at Amos's time. The people were eagerly awaiting the day of the Lord, but Amos turns it around and portrays it as a time of terror and darkness for Israel (Amos 5:18-20; 8:9-14).

Zephaniah 1:7-2:3 paints a dreadful picture of the day of the Lord as a time of God's wrath on all inhabitants of the earth. As in Joel, the day of the Lord in Zephaniah is connected with an appeal to assemble and to seek God. The oracle against Babylon in Isaiah 13 contains descriptions of the day very close to those in Joel (Isa. 13:6, 9–10). Except for the beginning of the verses, Joel 1:15 and Isaiah 13:6 are almost identical. The cry of "woe" or "alas" at the beginning of Joel 1:15 is closely parallel to Ezekiel 30:2. In Ezekiel 30 the day of the Lord is a time of wrath against Egypt and her allies.

Joel contains more references to the day of the Lord than any other book in the Bible. It is a day of wrath against Israel in 1:15, 2:1, 11 and against the nations in 2:31 and 3:14. As in Joel, the day of the Lord in Zechariah 14 is first a day of judgment upon God's people and then upon the other nations.

In 1:16 Joel returns to portraying the present distress. Again he involves his hearers with a question, asking them to concur with his observations. Food is scarce, and the temple service is thereby disrupted. Joy and gladness normally characterized the offerings of the temple as the people thanked God for His provisions, but now there was little to celebrate.

Joel then turns from the temple service to the farms. The seed is not producing because of the continuing drought. Since there is no harvest, no one bothers to repair storehouses and barns. Cattle and sheep are also in distress for lack of food. Not only the cultivated crops of grain and fruit trees fail, but the grass of the pasture is gone, devoured to the roots by locusts and prevented from growing again by drought.

In verse 19 the prophet addresses God directly for the first time. It is not yet petition or penitence. With "*to You*" in emphatic first position, Joel emphasizes that he seeks Yahweh above all in his cry. In this calamity, as in all of life, the people must ultimately deal with God.

The imagery of fire and heat prevails in verses 19–20. This probably indicates drought in the current situation but also recalls the judgment of God by fire (cf. 2:3; Gen. 19:24; Deut. 4:24; 32:22; Josh. 7:15; Amos 7:4) and descriptions of God's coming (Gen. 15:17; Exod. 3:2; 13:21–22; 19:18; 1 Kings 18:24, 38). The continuing drought has dried up the vegetation and the water supply together. The animals join the people in crying out to God in their distress.

A DIMINUTIVE DAY OF THE LORD

Just as the locust plague was a foretaste of the day of the Lord for Judah, so, too, the major crises that invade our lives serve as a diminutive day of the Lord for us. We are reminded that there will be an ultimate day of the Lord, a final day of judgment when He will judge the nations, the church, and each person. In a sense, the end of our lives will be a day of the Lord for us, an accounting of our righteousness through Christ. In the meantime, God does use what we go through to remind us that we are accountable to Him and to call us to return to Him.

Think of God's control and guidance of our lives as a gentle bit and reins placed on a thoroughbred. The reins are loosely held as the owner rides. The slightest tap on the reins are responded to by the steed. But when it refuses the owners directions, goes off in its own direction, the owner must pull up the reins and tighten the bit to remind the horse that it belongs to its master. It is "brought up short."

Our failures, life's distresses, and the calamities around us can have the same effect on us. They wake us up to the fact that we may be heading off in the wrong direction away from God's best for us. As a friend of mine exclaimed after going through a tough time, "When I reached the darkest point, I realized that I had no place to go but back to God. I wouldn't want to go through it again, but I wouldn't trade what I learned for anything in the world!"

NOTES

1. Hans Walter Wolff, *Joel and Amos*, Hermeneia (Philadelphia: Fortress Press, 1977), 27.
2. Peter C. Craigie, *Twelve Prophets: Volume 1*, The Daily Study Bible (Philadelphia: Westminster Press, 1984), 86.
3. Wolff, *Joel and Amos*, 30–31; Stuart, *Hosea-Jonah*, 243.
4. Wolff, *Joel and Amos*, 34.

CHAPTER TWO

Sound the Alarm

Joel 2:1–11

Sometimes the cartoons in the *New Yorker* magazine give us more than a laugh. Occasionally they poke us in our pretentious religious ribs. One was of a beautiful cathedral with people streaming out carrying their priest on their shoulders with his surplice flapping in the breeze. Two men are standing off to the side watching the amazing sight.

"What happened?" one asked.

The other replied, "Oh, he just said sin doesn't matter anymore."

Chances are slim that we will be carried out on the shoulders of our listeners for faithfully teaching and preaching the book of Joel. But then, we are not trying to win a popularity contest. What we are doing is trying to help people and the church as a whole hear what God may be saying when difficulties snap them to attention.

Sin does matter. Not just the little things but the persistent, progressive drift away from God. When the heartbreaking events of life bring people to realize that they have been missing the mark, we dare not interrupt the Refiner's process. Not all trouble is brought on by sin, but often trouble brings a person to realize his sin.

When I begin worship with the words, "The living God is here," I am filled with awe and wonder over the different ways He wants to deal with His people and with me. Sometimes we need comfort and assurance, but not without confrontation about our lives. We often pronounce people healed before they have admitted their illness. Only a sinner needs a Savior, and only those who are honest about their lives can hear what He has to say.

A call to worship or preparation for the prayer of confession might well be taken from this next section of Joel. "Sound the alarm, God is coming!" He alone can give us perspective on what is happening to us in our needs and what they alert us to about our far greater need to return to Him. Joel 2:1–11 confronts us with the realization that it is the Lord Himself who we must deal with day by day and in that ultimate day of the Lord. Our challenge is to live as if it were today. That will change all the rest of our days.

BLOW THE TRUMPET

2:1 Blow the trumpet in Zion, and sound an alarm in My holy mountain! Let all the inhabitants of the land tremble; for the day of the Lord is coming, for it is at hand:

2 a day of darkness and gloominess, a day of clouds and thick darkness, like the morning clouds spread over the mountains. A people come, great and strong, the like of whom has never been; nor will there ever be any such after them, even for many successive generations.

3 A fire devours before them, and behind them a flame burns; the land is like the Garden of Eden before them, and behind them a desolate wilderness; surely nothing shall escape them.

4 Their appearance is like the appearance of horses; and like swift steeds, so they run.

5 With a noise like chariots over mountaintops they leap, like the noise of a flaming fire that devours the stubble, like a strong people set in battle array.

6 Before them the people writhe in pain; all faces are drained of color.

7 They run like mighty men, they climb the wall like men of war; every one marches in formation, and they do not break ranks.

8 They do not push one another; every one marches in his own column. And when they lunge between the weapons, they are not cut down.

9 They run to and fro in the city, they run on the wall; they climb into the houses, they enter at the windows like a thief.

10 The earth quakes before them, the heavens tremble; the sun and moon grow dark, and the stars diminish their brightness.

11 The Lord gives voice before His army, for His camp is very great; for the strong is the One who executes His word. For the day of the Lord is great and very terrible; who can endure it?

Joel 2:1-11

From the scenes of agricultural collapse, Joel turns to a vision of an invading army in 2:1-11. The vision starts with a call to sound an alarm and then proceeds to describe the fearsome army in detail as they approach and then enter Jerusalem. References to the day of the Lord enclose the vision (verses 1, 11), while the vision itself shares many elements of other texts on the day of the Lord: horn-blasting and alarm (Zeph. 1:14-16); a day of darkness and clouds (Amos 5:18-20; Zeph. 1:15); a description of the invading army (Isa. 13:2-5); pain and anguished faces (Isa. 13:8); and cosmic upheaval (Isa. 13:10, 13). The vision reaches its climax in Joel 2:11, where we learn that this is none other than the Lord's army. This vision then prompts a call to repentance in verses 12-17, the subject of the next section.

Penetrating the normal noise of life in Jerusalem comes the call to *"blow the trumpet"* and *"sound an alarm."* The word translated "trumpet" here actually designates a ram's horn made into a wind instrument. It could be used in religious ceremonies (Num. 10:10), but was also a warning signal that danger was near (Jer. 4:5; 6:1; Hos. 5:8; 8:1). Each city normally had watchmen whose job it was to warn of impending danger (Ezek. 33:2-4).

The danger is identified as the approaching day of the Lord, a fearful prospect that should have all the populace trembling. The introductory elements of this section in verses 1-2 take on additional significance when seen in the light of other biblical texts. Israel's encounter with Yahweh at Sinai included similar elements: blasting horns, fire, clouds and darkness, and trembling people (Exod. 19:16, 18, 19; 20:18; cf. Ps. 97:2-3). Zephaniah 1:14-16 portrays the day of the Lord as a day of horn-blasting and darkness as the wrath of God descends upon Jerusalem. These associations add to the sense of the dread before the approaching army, whose identity is finally confirmed in verse 11. This is not the army of some local potentate, but the army of Yahweh Himself. The Lord is in charge from beginning to end, both outside and inside the city: He not only brings the army but is also the One who calls the watchmen to *"sound an alarm in My holy mountain."*

Other images from the biblical tradition combine to enhance the power of the vision. The devouring fire and flame (Joel 2:3; cf. 1:19–20) recall other texts about the Lord's judgment by fire (Gen. 19:24; Deut. 4:24; 32:22; Josh. 7:15; Amos 7:4). In contrast to the promises of Isaiah 51:3 and Ezekiel 36:35, where the desert would become like the Garden of Eden, here the land, which was like the Garden of Eden before the invaders, is left as a *"desolate wilderness"* (2:3). This account shares a number of features with other prophetic descriptions of armies threatening God's people: the powerful and swift horses, the relentless advance, the uniformly well-equipped and strong ranks without obvious weak point, the destruction and terror they cause (e.g., Isa. 5:26–30; Jer. 5:15–17; 6:22–23; Hab. 1:6–11).

Certain descriptions of the situation and the invading army recall elements of the locust invasion in chapter 1. The locusts were described as *"a nation . . . strong, and without number"* in 1:6. Here *"a people come, great* [or numerous] *and strong"* (2:3). The devastation of the land in 2:3, the noise, leaping, and simile of devouring stubble in 2:5, marching in ranks (2:7–8; cf. Prov. 30:27), climbing the walls (2:7), entering houses and windows (2:9), and the resulting darkness (2:2, 10) all would be appropriate portrayals of the locust infestation. In fact many of these same elements occured in the locust plague in Egypt (Exod. 10:4–6; 14–16). But Joel's concern is beyond the current situation of the agricultural ruin.

Joel uses images from the locust plague, certainly connecting with his audience's situation, to communicate the much greater danger of the approaching day of the Lord. Here is more than an army of hungry locusts or the army of another monarch bent on conquest. Note that the descriptions of the invading army (2:4–7) use simile and metaphor repeatedly as if to say that this army bears some resemblance to armies that the people would recognize, but that it is really outside the realm of the people's experience. The final phrases of verse 2 underscore the uniqueness of the event—there is nothing like this army in the past nor will it be found in the future (*"even for many successive generations"* is a fairly mild translation; the RSV "through the years of all generations" catches the implication better). This is an even stronger statement of uniqueness than the one found in Joel 1:2, which introduces the extraordinarily severe locust plague. Moreover, the descriptive language of chapter 1 never moved beyond the level of the agricultural disaster that cut off the food supply of man and beast alike. Yet the coming of the day of the Lord described in chapter 2 results in a cosmic upheaval described in 2:10. This is more than the effect of locusts or even a powerful human army. The language here is reminiscent especially of various theophany texts (Judg. 5:4–5; Ps. 18:7–15; 68:8; 97:2–5) and also of other day of the Lord passages (Isa. 13:10, 13).

The above attempt to show the connections of this text with other biblical passages is not merely an exercise in locating cross references, nor is the meaning exhausted by pointing out the interconnected nature of the Word of God. Rather, it draws attention to an important quality of effective communication. Joel's vision draws upon vivid and powerful images that would have been familiar to his hearers/readers.

Finally in verse 11 Joel reveals the identity of the army — this is Yahweh's own army. Yahweh issues the commands to the army, which has established a great military encampment, recalling the description of the great and strong people of verse 2. The prophet describes Yahweh as strong, One who executes His word — carrying out His commands and ready to fulfill previous prophecies about the day of the Lord.

Joel concludes with a focus on the day of the Lord. It is *"great and very terrible,"* that is inspiring fear and dread. These descriptions are found also in verse 31 and in Zephaniah 1:14 and Malachi 4:5.

If this section were to stand on its own, we might take the final statement, "Who can endure it?" simply as a rhetorical question with the obvious answer, "No one." Joel has already stated that there is no prospect of escape from the invading horde (2:3). Yet in the context of Joel's previous and following appeals, where he holds out hope, it becomes a profound question: Who can endure the day of the Lord? or, How does one endure the day of the Lord? No one can without the One who also marched into Jerusalem, purged the temple and went to the cross. Not a different Yahweh, but I AM incarnate to atone for sin so that those who repent and believe might live now and forever.

CHAPTER THREE

Return to Yahweh

Joel 2:12–17

12 "Now, therefore," says the Lord, "Turn to Me with all your heart, with fasting, with weeping, and with mourning."

13 So rend your heart, and not your garments; return to the Lord your God, for He is gracious and merciful, slow to anger, and of great kindness; and He relents from doing harm.

14 Who knows if He will turn and relent, and leave a blessing behind Him—a grain offering and a drink offering for the Lord your God?

15 Blow the trumpet in Zion, consecrate a fast, call a sacred assembly; gather the people, sanctify the congregation, assemble the elders,

16 gather the children and nursing babes; let the bridegroom go out from his chamber, and the bride from her dressing room.

17 Let the priests, who minister to the Lord, weep between the porch and the altar; let them say, "Spare Your people, O Lord, and do not give Your heritage to reproach, that the nations should rule over them. Why should they say among the peoples, 'Where is their God?'"

Joel 2:12–17

Joel now turns from the vivid description of the threatening army to the response God wants from His people. Verses 12–14 contain a call to repentance with supporting reasons. Verses 15–17 take up a call to a community lament, with parallels especially to 1:13–14 with its exhortation for the religious leaders to gather the people. Let's take a close look at these verses and then spell out the application to our lives today.

The beginning of verse 12 stands in contrast to what has gone before and should be seen as more of a surprising development than a consequence or result of the previous vision. The RSV translation, "Yet even now," seems more appropriate than the NKJV, *"Now, therefore,"* in this regard. *Now* implies that the situation has progressed to the point where rescue could hardly be imagined. Unexpectedly, Yahweh, the One who assembled the invincible army against Jerusalem, breaks into the situation with an appeal for repentance. When the judgment of God is ready to break, the only escape lies with God Himself.

The prophet quotes an appeal of God to His people: "Turn [or return] to Me with all your heart." The word translated "turn" (šûb), sometimes translated "return" or "repent," is used both of the people's proper response in verses 12 and 13 and of Yahweh's turning from His course of judgment in verse 14. The call to return to God with all the heart would be pregnant with meaning for Joel's hearers, since it has a strong place in the instruction of Deuteronomy (4:29-31; 30:2) and in the prophets (Jer. 3:10, 12; 4:1; 24:7; Hos. 3:5; 14:1; Amos 4:6-11).

One moving experience of reading the Bible in Hebrew is to see the word *repent* used both of people and of God and to realize that this word is used more often of God's response to people than of people's response to God. The word implies a complete change of direction or change of mind. When we turn from disobedience and return to the Lord, He changes His mind and direction from judgment to blessing. In this sense, the will of God is not immutable. He has given us the awesome responsibility of choice, and He takes our choices seriously, responding accordingly. "'Return to Me, and I will return to you,' says the Lord of hosts" (Mal. 3:7).

Joel does not identify specific practices of disobedience or apostasy from which the people are to turn, as do several of the prophets. This is not to say that the people are without fault. The turn that God expects is first and foremost a turn of the heart. *Heart* in the Old Testament corresponds more closely to what we would call *mind* today, the faculty of thought and will which provides direction to our lives. This turn, then, is to remake our thought and will, to turn from self-centered to God-centered thinking, to will to obey God rather than to follow our self-interest alone. This reconstruction of thought and will should issue in a new lifestyle, since a tree is known by its fruits.

The change of the heart takes priority over any ritual demonstrations of penitence, such as rending the garments (cf. Jer. 4:4). That Joel does not dismiss ritual or outward signs of repentance as useless is shown in verse 12, where the people are encouraged to return to God *"with fasting, with weeping, and with mourning."* Yet the priority is clear: outward religiosity without a change of heart is worthless.

Joel calls the people to a change of heart, to return to God. He then portrays the heart of God with ancient confessional language as the basis and motivation for such a return. We have noted at other points in Joel the images of Israel's encounter with Yahweh in the exodus. The confessional formula given here has its roots in those texts (Exod. 34:6–7; Num. 14:18). It was reiterated in various forms (Neh. 9:17; Ps. 86:15; 103:8; 145:8; Jon. 4:2; Nah. 1:3) as a foundational expression of Israel's understanding of Yahweh, which continued to have profound implications for her thought and action.

The adjective "gracious" (*ḥannûn*) is used only as an attribute of God in the Hebrew Bible. It comes from a root which means "to show favor" (*ḥānan*). The picture is one of a person in authority granting a favor out of his or her own good will. Here is no compulsion or coercion but a free act of kindness (to the poor—Prov. 14:31; to conquered peoples—Deut. 7:2; God's provision of prosperity—Gen. 33:11; God's favor to spare the lives of His people—Amos 5:15).

The word *merciful (raḥûm)* is often combined with the word *gracious* in these confessions about Yahweh's character. *Merciful* is related to the noun *womb (reḥem)*, so it has often been described as a motherly love or compassion for the helpless or needy, or the familial love among those from the same womb. God's mercy is active for the people with whom He established a familial relationship in His covenant. In His mercy He provides for their needs (Isa. 49:10), forgives them (Isa. 55:7; Hos. 1:6), and delivers them from their enemies (Neh. 9:27–28).

The Old Testament is filled with references to the anger of God and the anger of people. The ability to control anger, to be slow to anger, is commended in both God (Num. 14:18; Neh. 9:17) and people (Prov. 14:29; 15:18; 16:32; cf. James 1:19). Proverbs 22:24 warns against friendship with "an angry man." The people of Israel knew that God's anger was kindled or burned hot (Exod. 4:14; 32:10–11) against their wrongdoing. However, they could trust in the basic assurance that God was slow to anger, that He provided ample warning and sought to turn them from the folly of their ways, that He would not blast them with a short-fused temper as people so often do.

Kindness (*ḥesed*), also translated "lovingkindness" or "steadfast love," is one of the key words of the Old Testament, often used to characterize Yahweh. It connotes the loyal love or kindness characteristic of a covenant relationship (Deut. 7:12; 1 Sam. 20:8), and is sometimes translated "loyalty." Hosea rebukes Israel for lacking this kindness or loyalty that knits the community together (Hos. 4:1). Yahweh finds more pleasure in kindness than in sacrifices (Hos. 6:6; cf. Mic. 6:8).

The Bible celebrates Yahweh's kindness throughout. His kind actions operate to maintain the relationship established by His covenants. Often *kindness* is found in parallel with *covenant:* Yahweh keeps covenant and kindness (Exod. 20:6; Deut. 5:10; 1 Kings 8:23; Ps. 89:28; 106:45). Yahweh's covenant love is faithful and steadfast, often associated with the word *faithfulness* (Hos. 2:19–20) or described as enduring forever (Ps. 136).

The final sentence in the confession about Yahweh is, *"He relents from doing harm"* (Joel 2:13), or "repents of evil" (RSV). Yahweh's announcements of judgment are not irrevocable. His judgment comes not just as tit-for-tat punishment for wrongdoing but to turn the wrongdoer from his evil. "'As I live,' says the Lord God, 'I have no pleasure in the death of the wicked, but that the wicked turn from his way and live'" (Ezek. 33:11). When people repent in the face of threatened judgment, God repents and does not carry out the threat of harm.

This last trait is especially relevant for Joel's audience. They had experienced the ruin of the locust plague and drought, and now they were faced with the threat of destruction before the apocalyptic army. If they would repent, then there was hope that God would repent from fulfilling the threatened disaster.

Joel concludes the call to repentance in verses 12–14 with a question (*"Who knows?"*), which humbly recognizes the freedom of God (cf. 2 Sam. 12:22; Jon. 3:9). God's people can trust Him to remain *"gracious and merciful"* (2:13), but they cannot dictate what His grace will perform in their present situation of distress, even when they obediently *"return."* Joel says that it may be possible that God will *"turn and relent"* (2:14), that is *"relent from doing harm"* (2:13). In turning from harm, God may *"leave a blessing behind Him"* (2:14) instead of the scorched earth and desolation of 2:3, supplying the produce of the land to make possible again the offerings in the temple.

After issuing the call to repentance, Joel directs the priests to take the lead in gathering the people to express their turn to God and to pray for His mercy (2:15-17). The first exhortation, to blow the ram's horn, recalls 2:1, where the ram's horn is the warning signal of the approach of Yahweh's army. Here it functions as a call to assembly. The next several exhortations are nearly identical to those in 1:14. In addition to the call to assemble the elders and all the people and to sanctify them, Joel specifies that the gathering should include even young children and the bride and bridegroom who are enjoying the privacy of their wedding night. That is to say, this assembly and turning to God is of such vital importance to the community that no one should be excused from joining.

Once these preparations are made, the priests who serve the Lord in the temple are to lead the people in prayer. Their manner of prayer before the altar of burnt offering in the temple is characterized as weeping, an attitude of mourning reflecting the gravity of the crisis.

A Petition with Motivation

Finally, Joel presents the prayer that the priests are to offer, a petition with motivation. The prayer reminds God that these people enjoy a special relationship with Him: they are His people and His possession (better than the translation "heritage" NKJV or "inheritance" NIV Joel 2:17). The petition consists of two requests, that God spare or take pity on His people and that He not hand them over to reproach or shame. The prayer then turns to the motivation for God to fulfill the petition, basically that God consider His reputation before the peoples of the world. The people of God in Jerusalem would be subject to shame when other nations rule over them. Moreover, in that situation, other peoples would consider the Lord an ineffective or absent deity. Thus, the petition is not merely a selfish request to be spared from destruction or shame, but a request that the honor of God's name be upheld.

At this point we should put this request within the greater context of Scripture. Certainly there are numerous texts that talk about Israel's life and freedom from foreign domination being a witness to the power and special care of God. But when this position is taken to extreme without other balancing perspectives, it gives rise to the dangerous presumption that being the chosen people of God makes them immune from His judgment. They were tempted to think that since they were the Lord's people and fulfilled the ritual demands of devotion to the Lord, the character of their lives did not matter. This was the presumption against which Amos, Hosea, Isaiah, and Jeremiah prophesied (e.g., Jer. 7:9-10; Amos 5:21-24). The presumption is not just of historical interest but continues to be a danger among God's chosen people in the church to this day.

The common view in antiquity was that the gods of the conquerors were more powerful than the gods of the defeated. Thus, the gods of the defeated people were subject to shame. This is the cultural background of the petition and motivation of the prayer in Joel 2:17. However, other texts credit the peoples of the world with a more informed response to disaster in Israel and Judah: other nations would recognize that the Lord was judging His people for their apostasy and stubborn disobedience (1 Kings 9:8-9; Jer. 22:8-9). This perspective permeates the history of Israel in the books of Judges, Samuel, and Kings. The Lord hands over Israel and Judah to conquerors when they go after other gods and disobey His commands, but He has pity on them and delivers them when they earnestly repent and pray for deliverance (Judg. 2:11-23; 2 Kings 17:7-23).

Taken by itself, the prayer in Joel 2:17 could be seen as an attempt to save one's own skin by blackmailing God, in effect saying to God, "If I go under, so does Your name, since Your reputation is linked to mine." However, the prayer should be seen in the context of the whole call to repentance in 2:12-17 and in the wider context of Scripture that we discussed above. The prayer for pity rests on sincere repentance in which the people turn to the Lord with all their hearts, combined with the heart of God, who by nature is gracious and merciful. This sort of return to the Lord is exactly what Hosea, Amos, Isaiah, and Jeremiah desired to see. The sincere repentance and humility before God expressed in 2:13 is evidence that this prayer is not presuming on the Lord's kindness. This *"return to the Lord"* is the indispensable foundation for the petition that the Lord spare His people.

How God Calls Us to Repent

Sometimes God may use the tough times to correct our ways, to refine and purify us. Other times He may use the tough times as a way to lead us to a deeper relationship with Him or to equip us better to serve others. In the midst of the agony of the moment, we may not know the reason for the distress. In any case, our proper response to the hardship is not, "God, how do I get out of this?" but rather, "God, what do You want me to get out of this?"

Today there is a lot of nonbiblical thinking that being a Christian should exempt us from hardships and give us a trouble-free life. The prophets of the Old Testament and the apostles of the New Testament knew better.

Israel fell into a similar trap. Since they were God's chosen people, too often they concluded that they were not subject to disaster or the judgment of God. When their lives got too far out of congruence with their profession of faith in Yahweh, He sent prophets, such as Hosea, Amos, Isaiah, and Jeremiah, to warn them. When the prophets' words did not get the people's attention, God allowed disaster to come upon them. This is what Joel saw happening in the plague of locusts.

God may choose to turn aside the disaster or to let His people go through it. Either way, their only hope is in Him. When the Assyrians besieged Jerusalem during the time of Isaiah, God answered the prayers of King Hezekiah for deliverance, and the city was spared. Several generations later, the Lord told Jeremiah that the city was doomed. The Babylonians destroyed Jerusalem and took the people into exile. Jeremiah wrote to the first group of exiles (Jer. 29:4–14) to encourage them to continue to trust in God, that God still had plans for their good. Their deliverance was not from the disaster of exile, but *through* it to receive a future and a hope from God.

We might think that the disaster of judgment was reserved for the Old Testament. But this is to miss a significant part of the New Testament teaching, not only for unbelievers, but also for the church. Whatever we believe about election and eternal security, it is clear that the judgment of God does come on the church for ungodliness. The letters to the seven churches in Revelation chapters 2 and 3 are in part threats of disaster against the churches for disobedience to God.

There are times when we have to look no farther than our individual or corporate disobedience, selfishness, or greed for the explanation of our distress. But we cannot simply assume that sin is the cause of all imminent or actual disaster, especially on an individual level. Jesus rebuked His disciples for this kind of assumption when they asked Him about the blind man, "Rabbi, who sinned, this man or his parents, that he was born blind?" (John 9:2).

This simplistic logic was also the fault of Job's friends. In harmony with the prevailing wisdom of their day, they thought that sin caused suffering and, therefore, if someone was suffering, he or she must have sinned. God rebukes them at the end of the story for their "folly" (Job 42:7–9). Not that Job was without fault, but their simplistic formula did not fit his situation, and it continues to do harm in the community of faith to this day when applied rigidly.

Job starts out humbly, accepting the disaster from the Lord. However, with the repeated blows from his friends, Job speaks long about the injustice of life and demands an opportunity to vindicate himself before God. When given the audience with God that he desired, Job finds not an explanation for his suffering or for injustice in the world, but a fresh encounter with the living and powerful Creator of all, an encounter that leaves him humble and repentant (Job 40:3–5; 42:2–6). Through the disaster Job came to a deeper relationship with God: "I have heard of You by the hearing of the ear, but now my eye sees You" (Job 42:5). Just as there is a special quality of human friendship among those who have suffered together, often our relationship with God grows in certain ways only by going through tough times with Him.

And as our relationship with God grows through suffering, so our ability to serve others grows during those times. Simply put, if we never suffer, it is difficult, if not impossible, for us to empathize or to speak with authenticity to those who do. The Lord Jesus is our prime example here: "For we do not have a High Priest who cannot sympathize with our weaknesses, but was in all points tempted as we are, yet without sin" (Heb. 4:15). "Let this mind be in you which was also in Christ Jesus, who, being in the form of God, did not consider it robbery to be equal with God, but made Himself of no reputation, taking the form of a servant, and coming in the likeness of men. And being found in appearance as a man, He humbled Himself and became obedient to the point of death, even the death of the cross" (Phil. 2:5–8).

The Apostle Paul assumes that suffering and affliction, far from being abnormal, are the lot of the believer. Suffering in the form of persecution or abuse from others is to be expected when the church opposes the prevalent and corrupt structures of its society. These are the wounds from spiritual warfare. In fact, Paul could rejoice in suffering (Rom 5:3–5). Not that Paul was a masochist, but he could see the results of suffering in those who were yielded to God: endurance, character, hope. In suffering we receive the comfort of God "that we may be able to comfort those who are in any trouble" (2 Cor. 1:4).

When we are tempted to throw in the towel and turn from God because of disaster, it may help to look again at the Lord Jesus for several reasons. First, in the cross, God bore the ultimate disaster. "Who can endure the day of the Lord?" says Joel, as Jerusalem was threatened with ruin. Across the centuries comes the answer: God has already endured the wrath of the day of the Lord for us. The judgment on sin, which we each deserved, He took upon Himself in the person of His Son so that none of us need to know the ultimate disaster, separation from God for eternity. This reminds us that God is not some unsympathetic or unmoved supervisor of the universe, indifferent to the pain of our suffering. It should also remind us of how valuable we are to God and how committed He is to each of us: "He who did not spare His own Son, but delivered Him up for us all, how shall He not with Him also freely give us all things?" (Rom 8:32).

Moreover, as we look at Jesus, we are reminded that not even the Son of God looked forward to suffering with delight or bore it only in stoic silence. In the Garden of Gethsemane, Jesus prayed that God might spare Him from the cross (Matt. 26:42). On the cross, He cried out in anguish as He bore the sin of the world, "My God, my God, why have You forsaken me?" (Matt. 27:46). We need not demand more of ourselves or others as we endure suffering.

When you do not know where to turn, return to the Lord. Why? Because He is not some cosmic policeman or sadistic headmaster who delights in our suffering, but is *"gracious and merciful, slow to anger, and of great kindness"* (Joel 2:13). We see these qualities of God through the pages of the Old Testament and in the book of Joel which we are considering, but nowhere do we see them more clearly than in Jesus, the Son of God and the Word of God to us.

CHAPTER FOUR

Promises of Prosperity and Freedom

Joel 2:18–27

18 Then the Lord will be zealous for His land, and pity His people.

19 The Lord will answer and say to His people, "Behold, I will send you grain and new wine and oil, and you will be satisfied by them; I will no longer make you a reproach among the nations.

20 "But I will remove far from you the northern army, and will drive him away into a barren and desolate land, with his face toward the eastern sea and his back toward the western sea; his stench will come up, and his foul odor will rise, because he has done monstrous things."

21 Fear not, O land; be glad and rejoice, for the Lord has done marvelous things!

22 Do not be afraid, you beasts of the field; for the open pastures are springing up, and the tree bears its fruit; the fig tree and the vine yield their strength.

23 Be glad then, you children of Zion, and rejoice in the Lord your God; for He has given you the former rain faithfully, and He will cause the rain to come down for you — the former rain, and the latter rain in the first month.

24 The threshing floors shall be full of wheat, and the vats shall overflow with new wine and oil.

25 "So I will restore to you the years that the swarming locust has eaten, the crawling locust, the consuming locust, and the chewing locust, My great army which I sent among you.

26 "You shall eat in plenty and be satisfied, and praise the name of the Lord your God, Who has dealt

234

wondrously with you; and My people shall never be
put to shame.

27 "Then you shall know that I am in the midst of
Israel: I am the Lord your God and there is no other.
My people shall never be put to shame."

Joel 2:18-27

The book of Joel divides into two halves at this point. In 1:2-2:17 the
burden has been to communicate the significance of the present and
future distress of the day of the Lord and to call the people to repentance and prayer. From 2:18 to the end of the book we find promises
of prosperity and restoration for God's people and judgment upon
their enemies. We might suppose that the assembly for which Joel
called has occurred and that the promises are addressed to the people
who have returned to the Lord and prayed as Joel directed.

Joel 2:18-27 has been characterized as an oracle of assurance, a
promise that the petition offered has been heard and will be answered. The pattern of assurance after petition is found in a number
of lament Psalms (Ps. 60; 85). It also fits the pattern of restoration
promises in Deuteronomy (Deut. 4:29-31; 30:1-10) and in other prophetic books where disaster is announced and then restoration is
promised beyond the disaster along with judgment on enemy nations
(e.g., Jer. 30-33; 46-51).

Joel 2:18-27 contain primarily promises of restoring the agricultural and economic prosperity of the land after the severe locust
plague and drought described in chapter 1. As in other prophetic
books, many of the promises here appear in the perfect or completed
tense, sometimes called the prophetic perfect in these contexts. This
lends further assurance to the promises, a sense communicated by the
RSV in translating these verbs with past tense: "Then the Lord became
jealous for his land, and had pity on his people" (2:18).

Verse 18 provides a general statement about the action of God to
which specific details are added in the following verses. He intervenes in the situation for his possessions — *"His land,"* against which
the locusts came (1:6), and *"His people,"* who offered the prayer, *"Spare
Your people"* (2:17).

God is *"zealous"* or jealous for His land. The word is from the same
root used to describe Yahweh as a "jealous God" in the explanation of
the second commandment (Exod. 20:5; Deut. 5:9) and in God's response to His people worshiping other gods (Deut. 32:16, 21; Ps. 78:58;

Ezek. 16:38, 42). Using the same construction "to be zealous/jealous for" something, other texts describe God as jealous or zealous for Jerusalem (Zech. 1:14), for Zion (Zech. 1:14; 8:2), and for His holy name (Ezek. 39:25). In those texts His zeal takes the form of protection of His people from their adversaries and restoring their peace and prosperity.

God takes pity on His people. The word for pity here belongs to the same conceptual field as the word translated "spare" in the immediately preceding prayer of 2:17. In fact the two words are sometimes used in parallel (Deut 13:8; Jer. 21:7; Ezek. 9:10). The Lord shows Himself here as *"gracious and merciful . . . He relents from doing harm"* (2:13) and spares His people from the threatened destruction.

Verse 19 states explicitly that the Lord has answered the prayer of His people. First, He promises to send grain, new wine, and oil—the trio of 1:10 which represents the sum of agricultural produce and was destroyed by the locust plague and the drought. Not only does He promise to send these staples again, but He assures the people that there will be sufficient quantity, that they will be *"satisfied"* or filled.

Next, in response to the prayer of 2:17, God promises that He will *"no longer make you a reproach among the nations."* The conqueror from the north who subjected God's people to shame will be driven away, defeated, and destroyed.

Mesopotamian armies bent on conquest in Palestine approached from the north. Jeremiah identifies the Babylonian conquerors with the north (Jer. 1:13–15; 4:6; 6:1, 22). The visions of Ezekiel about the future attack of Gog and Magog on Israel locate these nations in the north (Ezek. 38:6, 15; 39:2). The *"northern army"* in Joel 2:20 has sometimes been identified as the locust horde which came against the land or as a conquering nation, perhaps from the north (1:6). In view of the parallels in Jeremiah and Ezekiel the *"northern army"* here probably refers to the apocalyptic army of 2:1–11.[1] Perhaps the *"northern army"* connotes both the locusts and the apocalyptic army, just as the locusts foreshadowed the attack of the apocalyptic army.

The text uses a number of images to portray the defeat and destruction of the northern army. God will remove them far away so that they no longer threaten His people. He drives them into the desert, splits them apart and drives their *"face toward the eastern sea"* (Dead Sea) and their *"back toward the western sea"* (Mediterranean Sea). The sense of the Hebrew is better represented by the RSV: "and drive him into a parched and desolate land, his front into the eastern sea, and his rear into the western sea." Remaining unburied in disgrace, the stench of their dead bodies will rise, even though they had done *"monstrous things"* (literally "great things").

Thus, it appears that the answer of God in verses 19-20 deals with both the current disaster of the locusts and drought and with the future disaster of the day of the Lord with its threatening army. Verses 21-27 go on to address the details of the current agricultural situation, while verses 28-32 look into the more distant future and return again to the theme of day of the Lord.

Verses 21-24 seem to form a subunit. They consistently refer to God in the third person and share a common structure of exhortation to a specified audience followed by a reason, similar to the call to lament in 1:5-14. They address three subjects that encompass those affected by the disaster: the *"land"* (2:21), which was devastated by the locust plague and drought (1:10), the *"beasts of the field"* (2:22), who were groaning at the lack of food (1:18, 20), and the *"children of Zion"* (2:23), the people called to lament in 1:5-14 and to repentance and return in 2:12-17.

Verses 21-24 of chapter 2 are knit together also by repetition of the verbs used in the exhortations. The beginning address to the land has two exhortations, not to be afraid and to be glad and rejoice. The first exhortation (*"fear not"*) is repeated for the beasts in verse 22, while the second two-part exhortation *(be glad and rejoice)* recurs in addressing the *"children of Zion"* in verse 23. Mourning replaced joy during the locust plague and drought (1:12, 16), but now it is to return with the Lord's provision.

The reasons for ceasing to fear and for rejoicing in verses 21-24 show a pattern of development from very brief and general to longer and more specific. The reason given for the exhortations to the land is that *"the Lord has done marvelous things"* (literally "great things"), a summary of the Lord's great acts for the people, which will be spelled out in detail in the following verses. Verse 21 repeats the verbs of verse 20, perhaps drawing a contrast between the great works of the Lord, which will continue for His people, and the great works of the army, which temporarily threatened His people.

In this section the *"marvelous things"* that the Lord does concern restoration of the produce of the land. The terminology corresponds closely with 1:16-20. This section announces that the devastation described in 1:16–20 has been reversed. The beasts will enjoy growing and plentiful pastures, while the trees and vines will again bear fruit (2:22), in contrast to the devastated pastures and trees of 1:18–20. The Lord sends the rain (2:23), in contrast to the dry landscape of 1:17–20, and provides abundance at harvest time (2:24), in contrast with the failed harvest of 1:10–11, 16–17. The picture is one of the receptacles for the products of harvest filled to overflowing. The threshing floor, where the grain is separated from the straw, will be full of wheat. The vats, where the olive oil and grape juice collect after the fruit is crushed, will overflow.

God's provision of rain is highlighted in verse 23 for good reason. Most of Palestine was totally dependent on rain to provide the water necessary for growing crops. There was no great river for irrigation, such as those enjoyed by Egypt and Mesopotamia. Sufficient rainfall was a crucial gift of the Lord to His people.

A new subsection begins in verse 25 and extends through verse 27. Here the word of the Lord is quoted again, with references to God primarily in the first person. Now the Lord promises to restore the *"years"* eaten by the locusts, that is the annual harvests of those years devastated by the locust invasion. The four terms for locusts introduced in 1:4 are repeated here, though in a different order. The locust horde is identified as *"my great army which I sent among you,"* again connecting the locust invasion and the prefigured apocalyptic army of 2:1–11.

Verses 26 and 27 present the results of the restitution offered in verse 25. The harvests will again be plentiful enough for the people to eat and be satisfied. That the people will be satisfied and not be put to shame recalls the initial promise in 2:19. Yet these verses go on to describe further results of the new bounty. The people will then praise the name of the Lord, recognizing the source of their sustenance. Israel had been previously warned of the dangers of being satisfied: forgetting the Lord in complacency or presumption (Deut. 8:10–20).

A further result of the new bounty is found in verse 27: the people will confidently know God, His presence, and His uniqueness. They will know that He is in their midst, effectively present with them, that He is *their* God, active on their behalf and the One to whom they owe allegiance. They will know that there is no other God, that He alone is worthy of their worship and praise. It is only as the people live in the light of this knowledge of God that they can truly fulfill His design that they be a light to the nations.

Thus, the goal of the new agricultural bounty is not just full stomachs, though that is important. God's intention for the people of Joel's time and for us is much larger than that. The picture is one of restoration to health as whole people and as a healthy community, which depends on a righteous relationship with the Lord. It is a complete orientation around the Lord who is in their midst. This reorientation around the only God and sovereign Lord is certainly part of what is intended in returning to the Lord *"with all your heart"* (2:12). It is the sort of life orientation called for in Jesus' command, "Seek first the kingdom of God" (Matt. 6:33).

Verse 27 also provides a transition to the promises relating to the more distant future day of the Lord. The people will never again be put to shame, recalling the shame of foreign domination and the threatened conquest by the apocalyptic army. The more distant future is the subject of the rest of the book of Joel.

NOTES

1. Wolff, *Joel and Amos*, 62.

CHAPTER FIVE

New Life in the Spirit and Deliverance

Joel 2:28–32

> 28 "And it shall come to pass afterward that I will
> pour out My Spirit on all flesh; your sons and your
> daughters shall prophesy, your old men shall dream
> dreams, your young men shall see visions;
> 29 "and also on My menservants and on My maid-
> servants I will pour out My Spirit in those days.
> 30 "And I will show wonders in the heavens and in
> the earth: blood and fire and pillars of smoke.
> 31 "The sun shall be turned into darkness, and the
> moon into blood, before the coming of the great and
> awesome day of the Lord.
> 32 "And it shall come to pass that whoever calls on
> the name of the Lord shall be saved. For in Mount Zion
> and in Jerusalem there shall be deliverance, as the Lord
> has said, among the remnant whom the Lord calls."
>
> *Joel 2:28–32*

This passage has a special place in the proclamation of the church of Jesus Christ. The life, death, resurrection, and reigning power of the Son of God forced the apostles to read these texts with new eyes and to see fulfillments of these promises that Joel and his contemporaries could have expected only dimly. However, if we jump immediately to the fulfillment in Christ, we may miss something of the word of God to Joel's generation and to us as well. Thus, we shall attempt to explore the meaning of these texts for Joel's contemporaries in the light of the Scripture they had available before we turn to the New Testament understanding of these texts and what they can mean to us today.

The *"afterward"* of verse 28 is a signal that the gaze of Joel's prophecy moves from the near future with its promise of agricultural restoration to the more distant future. Israel will experience new wonders *"before the coming of the great and terrible day of the Lord"* (2:31). Verses 28–32 portray three aspects of this distant future: a new experience of God's Spirit (vv. 28–29), amazing signs in the heavens and earth (vv. 30–31), and the way of deliverance from the dangers of that time (v. 32).

In verses 28–29 the general promise is issued first, that God will pour out His Spirit on all flesh. Then the meaning of this is expanded, telling of the different groups of people affected and of the ways in which this outpouring of the Spirit will be manifested.

"All flesh" in the Old Testament can indicate all of humanity (Gen. 6:12; Isa. 40:5, 6) or even all of humanity and the animal kingdom (Gen. 6:17, 19; Ps. 136:25). However, in this context it is more likely that *"all flesh"* refers to all Israel. The term is clarified by the following subgroups. God is speaking reassurance to His frightened people in Jerusalem and refers to *"your sons and your daughters,"* *"your old men,"* *"your young men,"* *"My menservants, and . . . My maidservants."* The possessive pronouns and the context of the promise indicate that Joel and his listeners would probably have understood this as a promise to Israel alone. Moreover, the lot of the other nations as described in chapter 3 would seem to exclude them from this promise. Even if we limit the promise to Israel, it still represents a radical expansion of the experience of God's Spirit.

The root meaning of the Hebrew word for Spirit, *rûah*, is "wind," thus also "breath," and then "spirit" or "life principle." We see it as wind in Exodus 10:13; 15:10; and Jonah 4:8, and as breath in Genesis 6:17; Job 15:30. The combination of the ideas of wind and spirit is evident in the creation narrative (Gen. 1:2). In a general sense God's Spirit gives life to all living beings (Ps. 104:29–30; 37:14). Yet in Old Testament texts that talk about the Spirit of God coming upon humans, it is most often to specially equip an individual or small group for a great task, such as craftsmen (Exod. 31:3), prophets (Num. 11:17–29; 1 Sam. 10:6–10; 19:20–23), warriors (Judg. 3:10; 15:14), and leaders and kings (Judg. 6:34; 1 Sam. 11:6). Israel expected that the Spirit of God would rest upon the messianic king and servant (Isa. 11:2; 42:1).

With this promise in Joel, the movement of the Spirit encompasses the whole society, regardless of sex (sons/daughters), age (old men/

young men), or social status (servants). Joel was not alone in such a vision. In their picture of the future restoration of Israel, other prophets envisioned an immediate relationship with God that would be enjoyed by all of God's people and not just a select few. With terminology very close to Joel's, Ezekiel announces God's word, "I shall have poured out My Spirit on the house of Israel" (Ezek. 39:29). He also speaks of the new spirit and heart that God will place in His people enabling them to obey His commandments (Ezek. 36:26-27). In Jeremiah's vision of the new covenant, God proclaims, "I will put My law in their minds, and write it on their hearts; and I will be their God, and they shall be My people. No more shall every man teach his neighbor, and every man his brother saying, 'Know the Lord,' for they all shall know Me, from the least of them to the greatest of them" (Jer. 31:33, 34).

What would it mean for Israel that God's Spirit would be poured out on each person? Three specific manifestations of the Spirit are given: people will prophesy, dream dreams, and see visions. These are not really three unrelated phenomena but are related manifestations of an immediate and close relationship with the Lord where He communicates His word and understanding to individuals, who then communicate it to others. Throughout the Old Testament we find God communicating His word through dreams: from Jacob (Gen. 28:12-15), Joseph and Pharaoh (Gen. 37:5-10; 40:1-41:40), Solomon (1 Kings 3:5-15), to Daniel and Nebuchadnezzar (Dan. 2). The prophets of the Old Testament sometimes experienced visions (Dan. 8:1; Hos. 12:10) as vehicles of God's revelation, which then found their way into their speaking and writing to the people. Vision and prophecy are so closely linked that the writings of the prophets can be introduced as visions: "The vision of Isaiah" (Isa. 1:1); "The vision of Obadiah" (Obadiah 1:1); "The words of Amos . . . which he saw" (Amos 1:1, where the verb saw, *ḥāzâ*, has the same root as the word *vision, ḥāzôn*).

We miss the meaning of prophecy if we think of it primarily as *foretelling* the future. It may include that, but it is better characterized as *forth-telling,* that is, proclaiming God's word. The Old Testament prophets sometimes told what the future had in store for Israel and other nations, but this was based on more fundamental elements of their proclamation: a communication of the character of the Lord, His justice and righteousness, His grace and mercy, His love and compassion, His character in action through their history, and His special word to them in their situation, whether it be encouragement, comfort, challenge, or judgment. The future they proclaimed was most often a future determined in large measure by the response of the people to God's former communication.

On the human level we might look at prophecy as an ability to speak based on the understanding of two indispensable elements: a vital knowledge of God and a deep insight into the condition of the people. Yet it was not merely communication based on human analysis on the horizontal level. The prophets continually speak about the word of the Lord coming to them, a force from outside compelling them. God Himself gives the insight and the boldness with which to speak.

THE PROPHET IN YOUR SKIN

The great need of our day is for authentic prophets both in the pulpit and in the pew, leading the church, launching personal evangelism and social mission actions, and caring for people while grasping the Lord's vision for new strategies for winning the world. The gift of prophecy is for all the Lord's people. It is our rebirth right and responsibility. Our challenge as communicators is to present the privilege of being a prophet in a fresh and impelling way. The possibility of being a prophet may not be very attractive to people. They may think of eccentric graybeards of Old Testament times uttering mysteries of flaming judgment and woe. For this reason, I find it effective to begin a message on the calling of every Christian to be a prophet with the following five questions:

1. Would you like to have new love for people, be able to care for them profoundly, and become effective in helping them reach their full potential?

2. Would you like to have X-ray vision to be able to see beneath the surface of people to their deepest hopes and hurts?

3. Would you like to be able to discern what God wants to say to people through you?

4. Would you like to be able to speak the truth to them in love in a winsome, winning way?

5. Would you like to have a direct, personal experience of God's Spirit and become a Spirit-filled, Spirit-empowered person?

Any Christian who says "Yes" to these questions is ready to receive the call to be a prophet and receive the momentary, situational, relational spiritual gift of prophecy. The needs of people and groups before us will bring forth the gift of the Spirit from within us. Our responsibility is to "keep on being filled with the Spirit" (Eph. 5:18, note the present passive imperative of the Greek). The indwelling Spirit gives the gift when we get into challenges requiring the wisdom, insight, discernment, and boldness the gift provides. The gift of prophecy is neither a permanent endowment nor a private possession. It is equipment for ministry. We are to seek the Giver, the Spirit, get in over our heads in ministry, and then ask for and become equipped with prophetic power. One day's anointing is not sufficient for the next. I would not dare to preach on any Sunday without prayer with the laying on of hands by my elders or by the leaders of a church where I am a guest preacher.

The principle is no less applicable to the laity. Prayer for the gift of prophecy in each relationship, situation, or challenging circumstances is an hour by hour, moment by moment requirement for effective ministry.

Paul put the gift of prophecy next to the gift of love in importance among the spiritual gifts (1 Cor. 14:1). In fact, the two gifts are interdependent. The gift of prophecy gives us supernatural power to discern the inner meaning of what is happening around us and what God wants us to say with the companion gift of love. When caring for people, we are given X-ray vision to forth-tell the incisive thing God wants said. People are like islands: we need to row around before we know where to land. The Spirit shows us where and how.

Anyone who is in Christ is called into ministry. We are recovering in our day the biblical mandate of the ministry of the laity. Every member of our churches is to be an evangelist and a missionary. But there will be little effectiveness in personal witnessing and social action without the spiritual gift of prophecy.

The most dynamic one-to-one evangelists in my congregation are those who ask for and receive the gift of prophecy. They do not have canned monologues to bore people. Rather, they know how to listen, to care, to empathize with love. The Spirit gives them insight about what to say, timing for when to say it, boldness to be honest, personal, and incisive in helping people respond.

Prophets are no less needed in the church's mission in the community. We need church members who will take stands on social issues, speak out with fearlessness regardless of the cost, and become involved with their time and money and hands-on ministry.

I had breakfast recently with an executive who is deeply involved in our church's *Lord's Lighthouse Feeding Ministry* every Sunday afternoon on our church campus. One of the features of the program is that our members do not just serve the food, but sit down, eat, and talk with the hungry people who come from the streets of Hollywood. My friend said a remarkable thing about a radical change in his ability to care for those he helps feed. He heard a message I preached on the gift of prophecy. In response he made a commitment to pray for a fresh anointing of the Spirit each day and ask for the gift of prophecy for his ministry. "It's amazing!" he exclaimed. "I sit there wondering how to make contact, how to express love and what to say. Then I pray for the gift of prophecy to forth-tell the Gospel with clarity and empathy. Suddenly, I know what to say and how to say it. There's no way I could identify without the Spirit's twin gifts of love and prophecy. Now I'm praying the same prayer for the gifts to be able to share my faith at work. The Spirit is certainly innovative in giving me the discernment I need."

The gift of prophecy also is urgently needed as pastors and church officers lead the congregation in forming policy and programs. What a difference it would make if before and during meetings leaders prayed for the gift and then spoke forth the truth in love as the Lord revealed it. We can be equipped to dream God's dream for what He wants, see His vision for how it can happen, and forth-tell the hope. Churches become what the leaders envision. It is tragic when the vision is limited to human skills of planning without the Spirit's inspiration and power. A favorite question I repeatedly ask myself and other church leaders is, "What are you planning that was instigated by the Spirit *and* cannot be accomplished without His supernatural power?"

We live in the post-Pentecost era in which God's promise to pour out His Spirit now is being fulfilled. Christ lived, died, and was raised up to prepare new people on whom the Spirit could be poured. The Father appointed Christ to be the reigning Lord of the Church and the baptizer with the Spirit (Acts 2:33). The Spirit works in our lives to bring us to conversion and new life. "No one can say that Jesus is Lord except by the Holy Spirit" (1 Cor. 12:3). That is just the beginning. As we yield, regeneration follows. And then there comes a time when we realize we cannot live by talent and human skill alone. Then we are ready to live supernaturally, receiving the exact gift of the Spirit we need in each challenge. And one of the most needed of the gifts is prophecy. Moses expressed what is now the deep need of the Church: "Oh, that all the Lord's people were prophets and that the Lord would put His Spirit upon them!" (Num.11:29).

We are privileged to live in the era of the Spirit between Pentecost and the end times of the day of the Lord. It is to that awesome time that Joel looks in the conclusion of chapter 2. The Spirit is being poured out so that we might be among those who have called on the name of the Lord, have been delivered from the bondage of sin, and are saved. We repeat Paul's assurance to the Ephesians, with first person gratitude and praise, "In Him [Christ] I also trusted, after I heard the word of truth, the gospel of my salvation; in whom also, having believed, I was sealed with the Holy Spirit of promise, who is the guarantee of my inheritance until the redemption of the purchased possession, to praise of His glory" (Eph. 1:13–14).

DELIVERANCE

A new picture of the distant future appears in Joel 2:30–31 — cosmic upheavals that signal the coming day of the Lord. These will not be simple indicators of the time to come, but *"wonders,"* extraordinary events. The same word was prominent in the exodus narrative, describing the wonders that God did through Aaron and Moses, and in other texts remembering the exodus (Exod. 4:21; 7:3; 11:9–10; Neh. 9:10; Ps. 78:43; Jer. 32:20–21).

The wonders are located both in heaven and on earth. Those on the earth are described first: *"blood, fire, and pillars of smoke"* (Joel 2:30). Blood might refer to literal, massive bloodshed or to some extraordinary event such as the Nile turning to blood (Exod. 7:14–24). Fire and smoke were prominent parts of the awe-inspiring encounter of Israel with Yahweh at Sinai (Exod. 19:18), but also recall dramatic occurrences of God's previous judgment (Gen. 19:24; Deut. 4:24; 32:22;

Josh. 7:15). Joel's audience might also have envisioned an outbreak of terrible volcanoes or the fire and smoke of cities burning in warfare.

The heavenly bodies will be darkened, as already indicated in Joel 2:10. We have noted that darkness and cosmic upheaval are part of other texts on the day of the Lord (Isa. 13:10, 13; Amos 5:18–20; Zeph. 1:15). The sun turning to darkness and the moon to blood are apt descriptions of the appearance of solar and lunar eclipses, but here the images probably indicate more intense or persistent phenomena than simple eclipses, perhaps darkening due to the catastrophes on earth.

As in Joel 2:10, we are reminded that the day of the Lord will be *"great and terrible"* (2:31). That description in 2:10 prompted the question, *"Who can endure it?"* (v. 11). Here the answer is offered: *"Whoever calls on the name of the Lord shall be saved"* (2:32). The construction "to call on the name of Yahweh" did not mean merely to appeal to Yahweh for help in time of calamity, as if what one did the rest of the time did not matter. The clause is used for one who worships Yahweh (Gen. 4:26; 12:8; Ps. 116:17; Zeph. 3:9) and who acknowledges allegiance to Yahweh even among other nations (Ps. 105:1; Isa. 12:4; 41:25; Zech. 13:9). In Joel's situation it would be an encouragement to those who had followed his exhortation to return to the Lord that they would be saved from the destruction of the day of the Lord.

Joel's prophecy takes up other prophetic passages about deliverance at Jerusalem (Isa. 14:32; 28:16; 52:1; 60:1–22), with a nearly word-for-word correspondence to Obadiah 17. The message is also prominent in a number of Psalms (46; 48; 76; 125; 126). The following words, *"as the Lord has said,"* indicate clearly that Joel meant his audience to recall and take to heart God's previous promises about Zion.

The final clause of verse 32 is difficult, partly because it comes after what appears to be a concluding formula, *"as the Lord has said."* The NKJV and RSV offer two alternative translations of the Hebrew as we have it. NKJV: *"Among the remnant whom the Lord calls."* RSV: *"And among the survivors shall be those whom the Lord calls."* Either way it seems to be a further clarification about the extent and agency of the deliverance. The first part of the verse placed the stress on the people calling on Yahweh. Here the stress is on the corresponding and prior call of Yahweh to His people. Those who are delivered and survive do so based on Yahweh's call to return and their response to that call— their calling on Yahweh's name.

Joel's audience was still devastated by the locust plague and no doubt faced the prospect of the day of the Lord with terror inspired by the vision of 2:1–11. The section in 2:28–32 is an assurance that the repentant people of God will not only make it through the agricultural crisis, as promised in 2:19–26, but can look forward to a vibrant life with God, enjoying the immediacy of His presence as a whole community and not just through a few select individuals. Though the day of the Lord will still be terrible, they can trust that its destructive effects will not overwhelm those who call on the name of the Lord.

Jesus' apostles used these texts to interpret the coming of Christ and His action in their midst. The awesome picture of the cosmic upheavals before the day of the Lord found its way into New Testament descriptions of the last times (Matt. 24:29; Mark 13:24–25; Luke 21:25; Rev. 6:12). The promise of Joel 2:28–32 had a prominent place in the birth of the church, where Peter quoted nearly the full text (Acts 2:17–21, 39). He argued that the phenomenon of the disciples speaking in tongues to the gathered throng at Pentecost was none other than the pouring out of the Holy Spirit, as promised in Joel 2:28–29. In light of the saving work of Christ for the whole world, he applied the promises not only to the Jews but to all humanity, *"whoever* calls on the name of the Lord shall be saved"* (Acts 2:21). Paul uses this same text to argue the availability of salvation to both Jew and Greek (Rom. 10:12–13).

Since we are living in the new age of the Spirit, which has been poured out since that Pentecost nearly 2000 years ago, we have the awesome privilege of accepting the gift of prophecy to proclaim the Gospel and issue the same liberating deliverance, *"If you confess with your mouth the Lord Jesus and believe in your heart that God has raised Him from the dead, you will be saved" (Rom. 10:9).*

CHAPTER SIX

A Decision about Our Decisions

Joel 3:1–21

The third chapter of Joel, as well as the book as a whole, is a reminder that decisions matter. God makes a decision about our decisions. The only thing more important than our decisions is what God decides about them.

The people of Joel's day faced the decision whether to heed the prophet's call to repent and return to the Lord. The nations faced decisions about how to treat Judah as well as other neighbors. Their decisions determined how they would fare in the "Valley of Decision."

The theme of God's decisions about our decisions gives us a key for a contemporary exposition of Joel 3.

Recently, I overheard a conversation in a department store. A man was exasperated with his wife who could not decide which hat among many she wanted to buy.

"Decisions, decisions, decisions!" she exclaimed. "Oh, how I hate decisions!"

Her husband replied impatiently, "If you can't make a decision about a silly hat, how are you going to decide something that's really important?"

Deciding what's really important is the issue of life. Sometimes the multiplicity of choices immobilize us from making any decisions. We are like the sailor in the anonymous poem:

> There was an old sailor my grandfather knew
> Who had so many things he wanted to do
> That, whenever he thought it was time to begin
> He couldn't because of the state he was in.

But we have all discovered that making no decision is in itself a decision. That often is the wrong decision, and God will decide about our indecision in the "Valley of Decision."

Taking a lead from Winston Churchill's statement, "We build houses and houses build us," F. W. Buhreham, the late Australian preacher, said, "We make our decisions, and then our decisions turn around and make us."

A decisive question puts our decisions into perspective: "If we were to die today, would we have accomplished the purpose for which we were born?"

The three most important decisions involve our conversion, our daily commitment, and our consistent contritions. Our eternal destiny will be determined on the basis of our decision to accept Christ as Savior and Lord of our lives. But that decision will have little meaning unless we daily decide to seek first the kingdom of God and His righteousness. Richard Baxter gave us a prayer for that, "Lord, what Thou wilt, where Thou wilt, when Thou wilt." And the end of every day is filled with mocking reminders of our insubordination or just plain insensitivity to the guidance that was given through the day. That is when, before we sleep, a decision must be made to accept the Lord's forgiveness for the unguided, willful choices we may have made. Seldom a day comes to an end without regret over poor decisions, great and small. Then a crucial decision stares us in the face: will we justify ourselves or accept forgiveness so the next day will be different?

The Lord confronts us with a decision about our decisions in every area of life. Daily, and on that ultimate day. We are accountable to Him for our stewardship of our lives, our material wealth, what we give away to care for the poor and the hungry, and our impact on the soul-sized issues in our society. And when we get to heaven, who will be there to greet us because we introduced them to Christ, and whom will we leave behind living the abundant life because we made the decision to care profoundly?

Every hour we make decisions on whether or not to be to others what Christ has been to us. The Lord deemed that loving was so essential that He made love the password for receiving answers to our prayers. "And whatever you ask in My name, that I will do. . . . If you love Me, keep My commandments. . . . This is My commandment, that you love one another as I have loved you," (John 14:13–15; 15:12).

The Lord's word to us is never a homily for hermits. The Christian life is not just a walk in the garden alone. And so, He will make a decision about the decisions we have made as part of the church — the visionary decisions we had the courage to support or the feckless decisions we faithlessly tolerated.

Add to all those decisions the ones we have made about our communities and nation and we realize that there is a great deal the Lord will decide about our decisions in the "Valley of Decisions."

Decisions do matter. They affect our destiny, and they influence others. Thomas Carlyle set the agenda: "To see and dare, and decide; to be a fixed pillar in the welter of uncertainty."

Now we are ready to grapple with Joel, chapter 3. It is a tryst in the Valley of Jehoshaphat where "Yahweh judges" the nations. We are aware, too, as individuals and the church, that we cannot escape the valley's other name, the Valley of Decision, where God decides about our decisions.

JUDGMENT IN THE VALLEY

3:1 "For behold, in those days and at that time, when I bring back the captives of Judah and Jerusalem,

2 "I will also gather all nations, and bring them down to the Valley of Jehoshaphat; and I will enter into judgment with them there on account of My people, My heritage Israel, whom they have scattered among the nations; they have also divided up My land.

3 "They have cast lots for My people, have given a boy as payment for a harlot, and sold a girl for wine, that they may drink.

4 "Indeed, what have you to do with Me, O Tyre and Sidon, and all the coasts of Philistia? Will you retaliate against Me? But if you retaliate against Me, swiftly and speedily I will return your retaliation upon your own head;

5 "because you have taken My silver and My gold, and have carried into your temples My prized possessions.

6 "Also the people of Judah and the people of Jerusalem you have sold to the Greeks, that you may remove them far from their borders.

7 "Behold, I will raise them out of the place to which you have sold them, and will return your retaliation upon your own head.

8 "I will sell your sons and your daughters into the hand of the people of Judah, and they will sell them to the Sabeans, to a people far off; for the Lord has spoken.

9 "Proclaim this among the nations: Prepare for war! Wake up the mighty men, let all the men of war draw near, let them come up.

10 "Beat your plowshares into swords and your pruning hooks into spears; let the weak say, "I am strong."

11 Assemble and come, all you nations, and gather together all around. Cause Your mighty ones to go down there, O Lord.

Joel 3: 1–11

Joel looks again into the future and envisions the judgment on Israel's enemies, primarily on the basis of their treatment of God's people. We might view the chapter as an extended exposition of how God will fulfill the promise of 2:19, that the people will no longer be *"a reproach among the nations."* The final verses also portray the new peace and prosperity of Judah and Jerusalem. This chapter has much in common with sections of other prophetic books that deal with the future of Israel and the nations.

Verse 1 introduces the new theme with a time reference, *"in those days and at that time,"* continuing in the time frame of the distant future begun in 2:28. It is also characterized as a time when God will "bring back the captives" (NKJV) or restore the fortunes (RSV) of Judah and Jerusalem. The Hebrew allows for either translation, the more general sense being appropriate as a link with the restoration promises of 2:18–27 and 3:18–21, but the more specific sense of captives linking with the condition of Israel in 3:2–3.

At this time the Lord will gather all nations. The verb *gather* is commonly found in other texts where nations are gathered for judgment (Isa. 66:18; Ezek. 22:19–20; Mic. 4:12; Zeph. 3:8). He will bring them down to the Valley of Jehoshaphat, a location not otherwise mentioned in the Old Testament. Jehoshaphat means "Yahweh has judged" and was the name of a Judean king contemporary with Ahab of Israel in the ninth century B.C. (1 Kings 22; 2 Kings 3; 2 Chron. 17–20). The Valley of Jehoshaphat is most probably a symbolic name indicating an appropriate place for judgment. We cannot specify an exact geographical location, though tradition has identified it with the Valley of Hinnom and more often with the Kidron Valley near Jerusalem.

Here the Lord will *"enter into judgment"* (Joel 3:2) with the nations (see Jer. 25:31), bringing His lawsuit against them. The accusations against the nations concern their treatment of God's people and land. The possessive pronouns *("My people," "My heritage Israel," "My land")* are repeated four times in a short space, emphasizing the close relationship of God with the land and people, as we have already seen in Joel 1:6; 2:17-18, 26-27.

The first accusation is that they have scattered God's people among the nations. Joel probably recalls the Assyrian conquest of the northern kingdom and the later Babylonian conquest of the southern kingdom, when a significant portion of Israel and Judah were deported.

The next accusation is that they have divided up God's land. The land of Israel and Judah was God's possession, given to the people as part of His covenant with them (Gen. 12:7; Deut. 3:20; 17:14; 18:9; Hos. 9:3). The conquerors took possession of the land and divided it among other conquered peoples whom they had deported from their home-lands and brought to Palestine (2 Kings. 17:24; Mic. 2:4).

The final accusation concerns their abuse of the conquered people. The conquerors apportioned the people as slaves among themselves by casting lots. The slave trade then operated, as always, cheapening the value of human life, treating people as things. While slavery was not outlawed in Israel, kidnaping was punishable by death (Exod. 21:16), and slavery was regulated by some humanitarian restraints (Exod. 21:2-11; Deut. 15:12-18; 21:10-14). But the conquerors of God's people observed no restraints on cruelty or self-indulgence, selling a boy for the price of a harlot and a girl for wine (Joel 3:3).

But God did not ignore the faults of His own people while judging other nations. We should remember the broader context of Joel and of other books as well. Joel had envisioned Yahweh's great army coming against Jerusalem in 2:1-11, and deliverance could not be assumed just because they were God's people. They were under obligation to return to the Lord (2:12-13). It was only on that condition that the promises of restoration could be announced and appropriated.

Amos likewise accuses other nations of inhumane treatment of neighboring peoples (Amos 1:3-2:3). What is remarkable about these passages in Amos is that the acts condemned are atrocities committed not only against the people of Israel and Judah, but against other nations as well. Moreover, Judah and Israel stand under condemnation none the less (Amos 2:4-16). In fact, the inhumane treatment is denounced in words similar to Joel's: "Because they sell the righteous for silver, and the poor for a pair of sandals" (Amos 2:6).

While verses 1-3 of Joel chapter 3 treat the nations in general, listing their crimes against God's people, verses 4-8 condemn specific nations in close proximity to the people of Judah. The section begins by challenging them to account for their actions and assuring them of the consequences (v. 4). Verses 5-6 bring specific accusations against them. The section concludes in verses 7-8 with their punishment.

God calls Tyre, Sidon, and all the coasts of Philistia into account. Tyre and Sidon were the main cities of the Phoenicians, who had long been active in Mediterranean trade. The Philistines, another coastal people, also actively engaged in slave trade. Both came under condemnation in Amos for selling captives to Edom (Amos 1:6, 9), and Tyre's slave trade with Greece (Javan) among other nations is mentioned in Ezekiel 27:13.

God accuses them first of removing His silver and gold to their temples or palaces. The silver and gold of Judah are identified as God's precious possessions (Hag. 2:8), just as the people and the land have been in Joel. Not satisfied with material spoils alone, these nations carried off the people of Judah and sold them as slaves to the Greeks. The text notes specifically that this cruelly removes them *"far from their borders"* (3:6) with no hope of return and beyond the reach of any attempts to buy them back.

The punishment for these atrocities perfectly fits the crime. Not only so, but the victims become God's agents to carry out the punishment. Against reasonable hope, God will raise His enslaved people out of their places of slavery. Using the same terms as those describing the crime, God will *"sell"* the sons and daughters of Tyre, Sidon, and the Philistines to Judah, who will *"sell"* them as slaves *"to the Sabeans, to a people far off"* (v. 8). The Sabeans, whose land was sometimes called "Sheba" in the Bible, were famous traders known throughout Israelite history (1 Kings 10:1-10, 13; Job 6:19; Ps. 72:10, 15; Isa. 60:6; Jer. 6:20; Ezek. 27:22). Their home was in the southwest corner of the Arabian peninsula. This would be southeast of Judah, the opposite direction from the Greeks.

The principle of justice here is repeated in verses 4 and 7: God will return their deeds upon their own heads. Affirmed elsewhere in the Old Testament as a general principle of retribution, the wrongdoer's crime comes back upon himself (Ps. 7:14–15; Prov. 26:27).

After the interlude in verses 4–8 about specific nations, the focus turns back to all nations and to the scene of judgment introduced in 3:2. Verses 9–12 consist of exhortations to the nations to prepare for war and to gather in the Valley of Jehoshaphat.

The initial and general call is to prepare (literally "consecrate") for warfare. Then a series of specific steps are called for: rouse and gather the warriors and bring them to the site of battle (3:9), bring all the implements of war possible (3:10a), bring all the people possible (3:10b), and assemble together (3:11).

The summons to battle appears elsewhere in the prophetic literature. Sometimes it calls armies commissioned by God for judgment against His own or other peoples (Joel 2:1–11; Jer. 6:4). In other cases the summons is made to an army that Yahweh will oppose and certainly defeat (Isa. 8:9–10; Jer. 46:3–4, 9; Ezek. 38:7–8). Such is the case here.

Joel 3:10 contains a clear reversal of Isaiah 2:4 and Micah 4:3. There the prophet envisioned a future time of universal peace when the nations would convert their weapons into farming implements. Here the summons to battle exhorts the nations to beat their *"plowshares into swords"* and their *"pruninghooks into spears."*

That this is no ordinary battle is demonstrated by the exhortation: *"Let the weak say, 'I am strong.'"* The word translated "strong" can also mean "mighty man" or "warrior" (RSV). Here is a call even to the weak to become soldiers.

Verse 11 calls the nations to make haste and gather together. The final sentence of the verse is difficult to understand in the present context. The NKJV offers a straightforward translation of the Hebrew text: *"Cause Your mighty ones to go down there, O Lord."* In its present form it seems to be a cry for help during the battle. The ancient translations take different directions as do modern commentators, and all depend on slightly different Hebrew texts. The Septuagint has "Let the meek become a warrior," interpreting this in the light of verse 10. The Targum and the Vulgate describe the fate of the assembled army: "there Yahweh will break the power of their warriors."[1]

VALLEY OF DECISION

> 12 "Let the nations be wakened, and come up to the
> Valley of Jehoshaphat; for there I will sit to judge all
> the surrounding nations.
> 13 "Put in the sickle, for the harvest is ripe. Come,
> go down; for the winepress is full, the vats overflow —
> for their wickedness is great.
> 14 "Multitudes, multitudes in the valley of decision!
> For the day of the Lord is near in the valley of decision.
> 15 "The sun and moon will grow dark, and the stars
> will diminish their brightness."
>
> *Joel 3:12–15*

The exhortations in verse 12 repeat the summons to be awake or
aroused (v. 9) and then call the nations to come up to a location, which
we would expect to be the site of battle. The location given turns out
to be the location of judgment, the Valley of Jehoshaphat (3:2). The
picture is one of Yahweh enthroned as judge to pronounce sentence
on the nations that have gathered.

The imagery changes to harvest language in verse 13, where the call
comes to cut the ripe grain or grapes. Now those addressed are no
longer the nations to be judged, but God's agents for judgment on
those nations, probably the heavenly hosts of God. Next is the summons to *"come"* and *"tread"* (RSV; better than NKJV *"go down"*). The press
where the grapes or olives are put is full, and the vats that collect the
grape juice or olive oil are overflowing (2:24), an abundant harvest.
Here the harvest/slaughter is enormous *"for their wickedness is great."*
Harvest language is found in other texts to portray judgment of defeat
in battle (Isa. 17:4–6; 63:3; Hos. 6:11; Mic. 4:13).

Next the picture is of a great throng gathered in battle (Joel 3:14). The
root meaning for the word translated *"multitudes"* is "murmur, roar,
tumult," thus the noise of a great crowd, often of armies pitched in battle
(1 Sam. 14:19; 1 Kings 20:13; Isa. 13:4; 29:5–8). Now the site is called the
"valley of decision." Though the noun translated *"decision"* is found
nowhere else in the Hebrew Bible, the verb of the same root, with a basic
meaning "to cut," appears to describe a decision that has been determined or fixed (1 Kings 20:40; Job 14:5; Isa. 10:22–23; Dan. 9:26–27).

The day of the Lord, a primary theme of Joel, is mentioned here for
the last time in the book. It is drawing near in the valley of decision, a

time of judgment for the nations who have abused God's people. The day is described with the same images of terror that have been associated with it before in Joel. The heavenly portents connected with the day of the Lord in 2:10 and 2:31 appear in 3:15, in fact using the identical words of 2:10. The awesome voice of the Lord (3:16; 2:11) goes forth; the heavens and earth shake (3:16; 2:10).

RESTORATION AND KNOWLEDGE OF THE LORD

16 "The Lord also will roar from Zion, and utter His voice from Jerusalem; the heavens and earth will shake; but the Lord will be a shelter for His people, and the strength of the children of Israel.

17 "So you shall know that I am the Lord your God, dwelling in Zion My holy mountain. Then Jerusalem shall be holy, and no aliens shall ever pass through her again.

18 "And it will come to pass in that day that the mountains shall drip with new wine, the hills shall flow with milk, and all the brooks of Judah shall be flooded with water; a fountain shall flow from the house of the Lord and water the Valley of Acacias.

19 "Egypt shall be a desolation, and Edom a desolate wilderness, because of violence against the people of Judah, for they have shed innocent blood in their land.

20 "But Judah shall abide forever, and Jerusalem from generation to generation.

21 "For I will acquit them of the guilt of bloodshed, whom I had not acquitted; for the Lord dwells in Zion."

Joel 3:16-21

The last part of Joel 3:16 clarifies the contrast between the portrayal of the day of the Lord in 2:1-11 and in chapter 3. In chapter 2 the day of the Lord was a terror for the people of Jerusalem. It was only after they returned to Lord that the fury of the day retreated into the more distant future and was turned from them and toward their enemies who had oppressed them. Rather than being a terror to His people, the Lord is now their *"shelter"/"refuge"* and *"stronghold"* (RSV; better than NKJV *"strength"*). A number of memorable texts picture God as a refuge or impregnable fortress for His people (Ps. 27:1; 46:1-3; Isa. 17:10; 25:4; Nah. 1:7).

257

Israel will have a certain knowledge of Yahweh their God (3:17). The restoration of agricultural bounty in the near future would result in a new knowledge of Yahweh as the unique God in their midst (2:27). Even so, their deliverance and the judgment of their enemies in the more distant day of the Lord would result in the certainty that the One who spoke these words and performed these great acts is Yahweh their God, the One acting throughout their history.

Far from Jerusalem being faced with destruction as in 2:1-11, Jerusalem is now the place of Yahweh's dwelling. God pitches His tent or dwells there. The text uses that special word for dwelling, *šōkēn*, from which the word for God's tabernacle of the wilderness wanderings is derived (*miškān*, Exod. 25:9) and which was used to describe God's presence with His people at key times throughout their history (Exod. 25:8; 1 Kings 8:12-13; Ps. 68:16,18; Isa. 8:18; Ezek. 43:9). Zion is the Lord's holy mountain or the mountain of His sanctuary, and thus the city is holy or consecrated to the Lord (Isa. 52:1; 56:7; Ezek. 20:40; Obad. 16; Zech. 14:21). Desecrated and destroyed by enemies in the past, Jerusalem will now be free from aliens (Isa. 52:1; Nah. 1:15; Zech. 14:21).

It seems that the previous vision ended with a climax in 3:17, just as in 2:27. Now a new vision explores some of the implications of Yahweh's dwelling in Jerusalem. The land of Judah will know extraordinary fertility (3:18). While the former promises of agricultural prosperity in 2:19-26 described bounty that was well within the realm of the people's experience, the agricultural conditions in 3:18 are outside the envelope of normal conditions in Palestine. The conditions described here recall other passages of restoration: the stream flowing out of the temple in Ezekiel 47:1-12; the similar stream in Zechariah 14:8; the marvelously abundant produce of Amos 9:13-15.

In contrast to the well-watered and fertile land of Judah, their historical enemies, Egypt and Edom, shall become desolate wilderness areas (3:19). This is because of the violence done to the people of Judah. In numerous prophetic oracles about the nations, the judgment on Egypt and Edom is prominent, even in other texts about the day of Yahweh. (Egypt: Isa. 19; Jer. 46; Ezek. 30; Edom: Isa. 11:14; 34:5-17; Jer. 49:7-22; Ezek. 35; Amos 1:11-12; Obad. 1-16; Mal. 1:2-4)

As a result of their enemies being removed, Judah and Jerusalem can look forward to a peace and prosperity which will continue forever (3:20). When Yahweh dwells with His people (3:17, 21), then His people can dwell secure (3:18, 20).

The first part of verse 21 is handled in different ways by the ancient versions. For example, the RSV follows the Greek and Syriac, which depend on a slightly different Hebrew text: "I will avenge their blood, and I will not clear the guilty," a return to the judgment of Judah's enemies. The NKJV translation is faithful to the Hebrew text as we have it. The implication seems to be that Judah would be acquitted of any guilt that they had incurred. This would be an assurance that they no longer need to fear condemnation, as from previous judgment oracles.

The final chapter of Joel completes the promises of restoration begun in 2:18. Joel speaks to the people who had experienced and perhaps continued to experience cruel foreign domination, who were currently ravaged by the locust plague and drought, and who were confronted with the terrors of the coming day of the Lord. Joel communicates God's word to His people who have returned with all their heart to the Lord. We have seen the promises of agricultural prosperity and rescue from the terrors of the day of the Lord in 2:18–32. Chapter 3 completes the picture with the assurance that the day of the Lord will bring other nations to accountability for the violence done to God's people and that such violence will never be repeated, since the people will dwell secure in their land as Yahweh dwells with them forever. The assurance of eventual vindication and peace should enable Joel's contemporaries and their descendants to endure before full restoration is completed.

These promises of restoration were not completely fulfilled in Joel's time, in the time of Christ and the apostles, or to this day. The vision of the heavenly city Jerusalem (Rev. 21–22) builds on the Old Testament images of Ezekiel and Joel.

The Book of Revelation, like Joel, was addressed to God's people to encourage them to persevere through the difficulties they faced. They both attempt to lift the gaze of God's people from the immediate circumstances and give them a larger view of God's grand design, His eventual settling of accounts with those who had treated His people violently, and His eventual restoration of His people to full, abundant, and peaceful life. In this way these books retain their relevance for each generation, encouraging God's people to trust in the God who holds the past, present, and future in His hands.

NOTES

1. Wolff, *Joel and Amos*, 73.

Introduction to the Book of Amos

Amos and his contemporary Hosea were active in the middle of the eighth century B.C. Although Amos was from Judah, both prophets spoke primarily to the northern kingdom, Israel. A few years later Isaiah and Micah would address the southern kingdom, Judah, with a similar message.

Amos probably began his ministry a few years before Hosea and completed his prophecy within the reign of Jeroboam II of Israel. Hosea began his prophecy in the last years of that king and continued into the turbulent years leading up to the collapse of the northern kingdom. Hosea's ministry apparently ended near the destruction of Israel's capital, Samaria, in 722 B.C.

POLITICAL BACKGROUND

The long reign of Jeroboam II (786–746 B.C.) was a time of prosperity for Israel, as it was for Judah during the contemporary reign of Uzziah (783–742 B.C.). Israel and Judah were able to subdue neighboring nations and extend their borders nearly to the outlines of Solomon's kingdom (2 Kings 14:25; cf. 1 Kings 8:65). The larger powers of Egypt and Assyria were preoccupied with problems closer to home, so that Palestine was free from foreign domination, though this was soon to change.

With the extended territory and conditions of peace, Israel and Judah enjoyed increased trade and the revenue generated by controlling major trade routes. Archaeological evidence confirms the wealth of Samaria during this period. Israel and Judah were at their economic and political peak.

Such a climate was bound to breed optimism and a confidence in the prospects for the future. The nation doubtless regarded its prosperity as a sign of God's favor and a confirmation of their policies and practices. The prophets Amos and Hosea gave a vastly different evaluation of the situation and predicted the catastrophe which would come with surprising quickness.

After the death of Jeroboam II, Israel fell into political chaos. Jeroboam's son Zechariah was assassinated after only six months on the throne. His assassin, Shallum, ruled for one month before falling to the sword of Menahem.

In addition to the internal collapse, external conditions spelled disaster for Israel. The Assyrian king Tiglath-Pileser III (745–727 B.C.) proved to be a vigorous ruler, able to subdue enemies close to home and extend Assyria's influence far beyond. His conquests were also different in character from earlier Assyrian exploits, which were mainly tribute gathering raids. Now Assyria was bent on full conquest. Any nations that failed to submit faced deportation, a policy which Tiglath-Pileser III pursued more consistently than any previous ruler.

In 734 B.C. Tiglath-Pileser III attacked the Philistine cities, then moved against Israel, and took Damascus in 732 B.C. The Assyrians took most of Israel's land outside the Samaritan highlands and deported the population (2 Kings 15:29). At this time Hoshea murdered Pekah and surrendered to the Assyrians. A few years later Shalmaneser V (727–722 B.C.) became the new Assyrian king. Hoshea used the change of throne as an opportunity to withhold tribute. The Assyrian retaliation came in 724 B.C. Samaria fell in 722 B.C., the population was deported, and the northern kingdom of Israel was no more.

SOCIAL BACKGROUND

Contrary to the egalitarian tendencies of the covenant stipulations and the tribal league, conditions under the monarchy had brought extremes of wealth and poverty. This was particularly true in Israel, where the native Canaanite population with its feudal background had a much stronger influence than in Judah. Amos in particular rails against the breakdown of the social structure and the constant injustices.

RELIGIOUS BACKGROUND

Syncretism characterized the religious order of the day. The worship of the Canaanite god Baal diluted Israel's worship of Yahweh to a great extent. Baal, meaning "lord" or "husband," was the name commonly given to the Canaanite storm god, Hadad. He was often represented as a bull, the symbol of fertility. The bull images built by Jeroboam I at Dan and Bethel (1 Kings 12:28–33) no doubt provided another occasion for assimilating the worship of Yahweh to the worship of Baal.

Canaanite religion, like most in the ancient world, connected gods and goddesses with forces in the natural world and considered that their course could be influenced by the devotion and rituals of worshipers. Religion then takes on a magical quality as an attempt to manipulate the gods, which is characteristic of perverted religion in any place and time. Rituals aim to ensure the foundations for life, such as the rain necessary for crops in Palestine and the success of animal and human reproduction.

Along with this was the view that sexual relations between gods and goddesses are responsible for some of the initial and continuing processes in nature. Based on this idea and concept of imitative magic, sacred prostitution was a prominent part of the cult. Worshipers would engage in sexual intercourse with cult prostitutes at the shrines hoping to influence the gods to do likewise and thus ensure continuing fertility.

Religious devotion was hardly lacking in this age. The question was the quality of that devotion. Certainly the acts of Yahweh were celebrated in the cult, but too often these were taken as a sign of unconditional support for the status quo. The covenant obligations were either blurred or understood as completely fulfilled by the rituals (Amos 5:21–24).

On the specific conditions that Amos addresses, Wolff includes some helpful comments in his introduction to the book. Other commentators include similar portraits.

> After the military success in the early part of Jeroboam's reign, Israel experienced the period of economic prosperity which is assumed in many of Amos's oracles. Commerce became extremely active (8:5a), and trade was practiced on an international scale (3:9). Deceitful business practices increased profits (8:5b). Building activity flourished (3:15). Houses became more numerous and more substantial than ever before in Israel (3:15b; 5:11; 6:8), and they were elaborately furnished (3:10, 12b, 15b; 6:4a). Viniculture and cattle raising became geared to demanding

customers (5:11b; 6:4b) since the thirst for pleasure manifest in rollicking feasts had to be accommodated (4:1; 6:4, 6). New music was composed (6:5). Sexual immorality increased (2:7b). The cults participated in the economic boom: sacrificial offerings proliferated (4:4–5; 5:21–22); the feasts were celebrated with ebullient singing and instrumental music (5:23).

The converse of this development was social upheaval. The rich became richer while the poor became poorer. Such early capitalism quickly led to expropriation of the holdings of the smaller landowners. The ancient Israelite land rights were superceded by Canaanite practice. Slavery for debt took on vicious forms (2:6; 8:6). The socially underprivileged were exploited (2:7a; 4:1; 8:4). Their rights were violated through intimidation of witnesses and bribery of judges (2:7a; 5:10, 12).Thus in the shadow of world politics following the great foreign policy successes of Jeroboam II, luxury and injustice alike abundantly flourished; in the east, border incidents had once again begun to occur. Such is the time of Amos around 760.[1]

THE PROPHET AMOS

There is general agreement that Amos's ministry lasted for a relatively short time, sometime in the period of 760 to 750 B.C. Although it has been common to regard Amos as a fairly poor man, a shepherd who supplemented a meager income with seasonal work in western Judah, many scholars now take the position that he was an owner or a manager in the agricultural business.[2]

The name Amos, meaning literally "load, burden," is used for no one else in the Old Testament, and the prophet is not mentioned elsewhere. So we are totally dependent on the book of Amos itself for any information about the prophet.

Amos's home was Tekoa in the southern kingdom of Judah. The village and area called Tekoa was twelve miles south of Jerusalem and extended twenty miles east to the northwestern shores of the Dead Sea. The present name of the village is Tekua. The elevation was more than 2,700 feet above sea level and sank 4,000 feet to the east, into the chasm of the Dead Sea. It was a bleak area, a waste and a wilderness.

Sir George Adam Smith vividly described the conditions and atmosphere of the Tekoa territory.

> When you climb the hill of Tekoa, and, looking east, see those
> fifteen miles of chaos, sinking to a stretch of the Dead Sea, you
> begin to understand the influence of the desert on Jewish imagi-
> nation and literature. It gave the ancient natives of Judaea, as it
> gives the visitor of today, the sense of living next door to doom;
> the sense of how narrow is the border between life and death; the
> awe of the power of God, who can make contiguous regions so
> opposite in character. The desert is always in the face of the
> prophets, and its howling of beasts and dry sand blow mourn-
> fully across their pages the foreboding of doom.[3]

These were the geographical conditions of Amos's home area affecting both his personality and his perception.

Amos asserted that he was neither a full-time prophet nor a
prophet's son (7:14). That is, he was not a professional prophet as
others of his time. Rather, we glean three other things. He was a
shepherd (1:1), but note that the word used is not the common word
for shepherd but one used for a person in the sheep business who
owned flocks of sheep. He also was a cattleman. Here the Hebrew
word used in 7:14 implies one who had large herds in addition to
flocks. The third part of his vocation was growing and harvesting fig
trees that grew in the vicinity of the Dead Sea. Thus we see that Amos
was occupied with a threefold vocation when he received his call to
function as a prophet for a brief time, probably during a time when
his business travels took him to the northern kingdom of Israel.[4]

Though Amos was not professionally trained as a prophet, he was
specifically and specially called by God to speak His word to Israel.
He is an example of the biblical principle that the need before a God-
sensitive person blossoms into action from the gift of God within him
or her. Knowing Amos's background makes his prophetic excellence
all the more astounding as the work of God. The greatness of Amos
was that he was willing to allow God to use him as His mouthpiece.

THE BOOK OF AMOS

There are three distinct portions of the prophecy of Amos. The first
two chapters are a series of messages to foreign nations and concluding with an oracle of judgment focused on Israel. This coherent unit
employs the very effective method of rallying Amos's audience with

partisan feelings about other nations before his incisive "And as for you Israel" thrust of judgment on the northern kingdom. In the second section, chapters 3–6, the prophet's basic concerns about Israel were made clear. The people have exploited the poor. Dishonest business dealings by the merchants are abhorrent. The law and the courts have been corrupted. Surface religion hides the deeper loss of authentic faith. The third section of the prophecy of Amos, chapters 7–9, consists of a series of five visions. Between the visions are inserted oracles and the conflict between Amos and his adversary Amaziah, who speaks on behalf of the organized religion of the time. The book of Amos concludes with a short section, 9:11–15, containing positive messages of hope.

PREACHING AND TEACHING FROM AMOS

A few years ago the division in the church between the pietists and social activists was both pronounced and divisive. Today, dynamic local churches and effective denominations are discovering that this nonbiblical dichotomy is perilous. An in-depth preaching and teaching of Amos gives us an opportunity to speak to the irreverence of irrelevant personal faith that is insensitive to social injustice, but also to the need for social mission to be both motivated and empowered by God and not just political or humanitarian motives. The vivid similes, metaphors, and parabolic images of Amos provide the focus for impelling and imaginative communication of the Gospel. Contemporary communication of Amos gives us a propitious privilege of proclaiming the whole Gospel for the wholeness of honest personal faith and holy living that confronts and seeks to change the injustices of society.

Keeping in mind that this is primarily a commentary for preachers and teachers, I will divide the prophecy of Amos into sections that might well provide the content for a series of messages or classes. Some will cover a large portion of the material, while others will focus on shorter, more salient passages. The important thing is to keep the listener's attention with an arresting progression while at the same time making incisive application for our own day.

NOTES

1. Wolff, *Joel and Amos*, 89–90.

2. For example, Craigie, *Twelve Prophets: Volume 1*, 121; Stuart, *Hosea – Jonah*, 376–377; and Wolff, *Joel and Amos*, 90–91.

3. George Adam Smith, *The Historical Geography of the Holy Land*, 1894, as quoted in Craigie, *Twelve Prophets: Volume 1*, 121.

4. Craigie, *Twelve Prophets: Volume 1*, 121–122.

An Outline of Amos

CHAPTER ONE

The Voice and the Mouthpiece

Amos 1:1–2

> 1:1 The words of Amos, who was among the sheepbreeders of Tekoa, which he saw concerning Israel in the days of Uzziah king of Judah, and in the days of Jeroboam the son of Joash, king of Israel, two years before the earthquake.
>
> 2 And he said: "The Lord roars from Zion, and utters His voice from Jerusalem; the pastures of the shepherds mourn, and the top of Carmel withers."
>
> *Amos 1:1–2*

This superscription of the book of Amos provides the preacher/teacher an opportunity to do a character study of Amos. We immediately are struck by the unpretentious phrase, *"the words of Amos,"* contrasted with the voice of the Lord in verse 2. The gift of prophecy was given to one who was not a professional prophet to articulate the message of the voice of the Lord. At this point we are not given an account of Amos's call to prophecy. That comes later in 7:14–15. What we are told now is that he heard in his soul the roar of the Lord from Zion, the utterance of His voice from Jerusalem. What the Lord said to Amos, the judgments He roared in his consciousness, the visions He vividly portrayed in Amos's mind's eye, and the promises He graciously entrusted to Amos became the content of His message. With all that Amos could say with prophetic authority, *"Thus says the Lord"* (v. 3).

Now, let's consider what these introductory verses tell us about the man who became the mouthpiece for the voice of the Lord.

Amos was a layman. By his own admission, he was not a professional prophet born in the line of the prophets. Amos made his living in the sheep business as a herdsman. The Hebrew word *nōqēd* means more than a shepherd, *rō'eh;* it is used for one who owned flocks of sheep and was a sheep breeder. In 7:14 we learn that Amos also was a cattleman with large herds. In addition, he was a fruit farmer of a kind, growing and harvesting a type of fig that grew in the vicinity of the Dead Sea, in the eastern territory of Tekoa (7:14). As a sheep breeder, cattleman, and fruit farmer, he was certainly among the prominent men of the territory.

Amos's character and personality was shaped by the desolate, rugged territory of Tekoa. (Note material on Tekoa in the Introduction to Amos.) He did not spend his life in the relative comforts of city life or in the ambience of institutional religion. Devoid of either, his experience of Yahweh in the desert regions of Tekoa was rooted in the promises and demands of the covenant. Though Amos lived in the country, he was well educated in the Torah. From the Scriptures he drew a keen sense of loyalty to God, justice, morality, and righteousness. Many have suggested that he served as a jurist in deciding cases of justice in his small hometown. This explains Amos's language in presenting his case against Israel.

Amos's business took him to the northern kingdom where he sold his wool, cattle, and fruit. On these journeys he was disturbed by the evidences of dissolute living, dishonesty, and injustice. His visits to Bethel shocked his spiritual sensitivity. There he saw the evidence of Baal worship syncretized with Yahweh. The priesthood was corrupt and indifferent to the issues of justice. In the nation as a whole, the poor were getting poorer and the rich richer.

The phrase *"which he saw concerning Israel"* (1:1) means more than mere observation. The verb for "saw" is *hāzâ,* used for the reception of visions, designates the special insight of the prophetic mode of seeing. Amos saw what was happening in Israel from God's perspective and indignation.

On one of Amos's visits to Bethel, his God-sensitive indignation boiled over. The messages he delivered were later written down when he returned to Tekoa, after being driven from the northern kingdom. In Amos we meet a resolute man of God who had courage in the face of immense opposition. He lived up to his name. *Amos* means "Burden" or "Burden-bearer." The burden the prophet carried was that a holy God demands moral holiness from His people.

The date of Amos (see Introduction) is made clear by the references to *"the days of Uzziah king of Judah, and in the days of Jeroboam the son of Joash, king of Israel, two years before the earthquake"* (1:1). Scholars dispute the exact dates that these kings reigned, but the range of options is within one decade. The following picture uses the dates given by Wolff. The reigns of Uzziah and Jeroboam began about 787 B.C. Jeroboam II died in 747/46 B.C. and Uzziah about 735 B.C. In his later years, Uzziah became ill, and Jotham assumed the regency in 757/56 B.C. (2 Kings 15:5). The fact that Jotham is not mentioned in verse one indicates that Amos's prophetic ministry was during Uzziah's reign prior to Jotham. Also the references in Amos's oracles to the military successes of Jeroboam II and then to the threats of the Arameans and Amorites in 1:3 and 1:13 places the date of Amos's ministry around the end of the first three decades of Jeroboam II or about 760 B.C.[1]

Archaeological studies also affirm this date. "Two years before the earthquake," Wolff reminds us, "Stratum VI at Hazor shows evidence of destruction caused by a great earthquake, traces of which have also been uncovered in archaeological work at Samaria. Independently of the exegetical considerations . . . the excavators have dated this earthquake circa 760."[2] This would suggest a date somewhere around 762 B.C. for Amos's prophetic activity.

At that time of outward success and prosperity contrasted with spiritual apostasy, moral decay, and social injustice, Amos heard the voice of the Lord. The two poetic couplets of verse 2 emphasize that it was Yahweh Himself who spoke, and what He spoke spelled judgment and devastation. *"The Lord roars."* Usually in a Hebrew sentence, the verb comes before the subject. Amos reverses the order. The divine name comes first and then the verb, thus making it all the more emphatic who it is who roars. It is none other than Yahweh of the burning bush, of the parting of the Red Sea, of the pillar of cloud by day and fire by night in the wilderness, of Sinai, of the covenant, of the Law. Further, it is supremely Yahweh present in the holy of holies in the temple in Jerusalem. A God of mercy and forgiveness, yes, but also a God of righteousness. And His character was being denied and His holiness contradicted. His roar is one of condemnation and judgment. The people had gone too far. They mocked His covenant, denied His commandments, and habitually sinned against Him.

The Hebrew construction *nātan qôl* (literally "give voice") often implies thunder.[3] But instead of thunder that is the portent of rain, just the opposite will follow the thunder — like the roar of Yahweh. It will produce the judgment of a destructive drought. The devastation will be from the pastures to the plentiful forests of Carmel. The metaphor communicates the totality of the destruction of the nation. Samaria fell to the Assyrians in 722 B.C., a little more than three decades after Amos's preaching.

And so the book of Amos opens with an informative *who, where, when,* and an intimidating *why.* It is the *why* of Yahweh's roar that lingers. In fact, if we will listen, the same roar is sounded today. It is the roar of a holy God in righteous judgment on His people. His wrath and grace must never be separated. Both must be kept in balance as we study Amos. It is out of grace that God judges His people. And it is only after we have heard the roar of His judgment and repented that fresh grace can be received. What makes God roar in judgment of Christians and the church today? Or, more personally, in your life and mine? If we were to make a list, we would find some of the same things that made Him roar over Israel. That is what makes a study of Amos so relevant for today . . . and disturbing. And yet, if we will approach the study with honesty and openness, we will experience the grip of the Lord's holiness on us and will be able to change what needs to be changed.

NOTES

1. Wolff, *Joel and Amos,* 124.
2. Ibid.
3. Stuart, *Hosea – Jonah,* 301.

CHAPTER TWO

For Three Transgressions . . . and for Four

Amos 1:3–2:16

Recently, *Time* magazine featured a disturbing article entitled, "An Outbreak of Bigotry."[1] The subheading made an alarming statement and asked a searching question. "Everyone says it's only human nature to despise one's neighbor. If that's true, what can governments around the world do to control such hatred?"

The article took the reader on a soul-rending trip around the world illustrating the resurgence of prejudice and violence. As the world tour of contemporary hatred proceeded, I was dismayed by the epidemic of ethnic hatred sweeping the world. Jewish cemeteries in France and Italy are being desecrated. Turks in Bulgaria are the victims of persecution. Koreans in Japan are denied jobs, housing, and dignity. Africa's Hutu and Tutsi tribes continue to slaughter one another. In the South Africa Transvaal, right-wing white citizens are being trained to use weapons as part of the Afrikaaner Resistance Movement. They wear swastika-like insignias, salute Nazi style, and are preparing for a "holy war" if there is a black resurgence. In India a local custom called cruelty is reviving ancient animosity between the upper-caste and the untouchables with intensified brutalities.

I put the magazine down with "What is this world coming to?" indignation. There was no possibility of smacking my lips with American pride. We have made strides, to be sure. But fresh in my memory was a Friday evening spent empathizing with the congregation of a synagogue nearby that had been desecrated with swastikas. The same "Skinheads" who had done that also marched up and down the street outside the sanctuary of my church hollering obscenities during Sunday morning worship. The proclivity of human nature to feel superior to others and express hostility and even brutality is still around in every nation.

The contemporary resurgence of bigotry makes our study of the first two chapters of Amos more than a review of bygone ethnic hatreds. In fact, like Israel, we may be surprised to discover that the word of the Lord is not just meant for others, but for us!

Amos was a brilliant communicator. Under the influence of the Spirit of God, he knew how to win and then confront his audience. His inaugural message recorded in 1:3–2:16 needs to be considered as a whole. Only then do we sense the full impact on his audience. Some agree that it was delivered as a single address.

Step by step, Amos exposes the sins of the nations encircling Israel. We can imagine these exposures brought cheering approval. As he was winning their attention, we doubt that any of them realized he was moving closer and closer to them. The first three nations condemned were merely political enemies, the next three were closer kin, and finally the spotlight was on Israel herself! In God's evaluation His chosen people were no better than other nations when it came to inhumane cruelty and violence.

The eight oracles in Amos's initial message were delivered in what is called "messenger speech." The prophet proclaims what God gave him to say quoting Him verbatim in the first person. God is clearly identified in the repetition of the divine words. Eight times the *"Thus says the Lord"* punctuates Amos's message with divine authority (1:3, 6, 9, 11, 13; 2:1, 4, 6). Yahweh asserts His sovereignty over the world as the judge of the nations. Douglas Stuart reminds us that all the oracles in Amos's opening message

> rest on a shared theological assumption: there is one God, Yahweh, who has power over the whole earth, and whose righteousness will not tolerate unrighteousness on the part of any nation. In other words, Yahweh is not merely the God of Israel or Judah, but has an implicit covenantal relationship with all nations, through which he expects obedience to a basic sort of "international law" and in recognition of which He will enforce that covenant's sanctions against those who rebel against it.[2]

Yahweh has basic standards for human relations and will not forever tolerate any nation's barbarity and brutality. All nations will be held accountable for what has been done to deface His image in human beings. He has placed a conscience in all people and will judge all the nations regardless of whether or not they believe in Him.

Each of the eight oracles begins with the words, *"For three transgressions . . . and for four."* This phrase communicates the divine patience for repeated crimes that are piled on the judgment scale and then one that overloads and tips the scale making God's punishing intervention unavoidable. The fourth, the untenable sin, is exposed in each oracle. This sin forces God to say to the nation, *"I will not turn away its punishment,"* and declares a judgment which is irrevocable.

The term used for the punishable transgressions is *pĕsāʿîm*, meaning "crimes." Wolff suggests that the word serves as a legal technical term to characterize and summarize particular cases. In Amos these cases involve infraction of property and personal rights, deeds that deliberately violate communal standards.[3]

THE JUDGMENT OF DAMASCUS

3 Thus says the Lord: "For three transgressions of Damascus, and for four, I will not turn away its punishment, because they have threshed Gilead with implements of iron.
4 "But I will send a fire into the house of Hazael, which shall devour the palaces of Ben-Hadad.
5 "I will also break the gate bar of Damascus, and cut off the inhabitant from the Valley of Aven, and the one who holds the scepter from Beth Eden. The people of Syria shall go captive to Kir," says the Lord.

Amos 1:3–5

Damascus was the capital of the city-state of Aram in eastern Syria bordering Israel on the northeast. Aram was a constant foe of Israel in the border wars of the ninth and eighth centuries B.C. David conquered the Arameans (2 Sam. 8:6), but they subsequently broke free during Solomon's reign (1 Kings 11:23–25). The Arameans persistently antagonized Israel through the years.

What Damascus did to the Transjordan Israelite region to the south called Gilead was the "fourth" crime that tipped the scales of Yahweh's patience. The cruelty and violence of Damascus against Gilead is described by the metaphor of threshing. *"They have threshed*

Gilead" (1:3). The image describes the process of dragging a grinding sledge over the sheaves to separate the grain from the chaff. Yahweh uses this image to depict the savage methods of warfare. In Amos's day, the sledge was made of boards with the underside studded with metal prongs or knives. The image implies not only the crushing of Gilead by Damascus but the cruel treatment of those taken as prisoners.

Yahweh will send a devouring fire into the house of Hazael and the palaces of Ben-Hadad as punishment. The names signify contemporary eighth century B.C. Aramean rulers known under the dynastic names of Hazael and Ben-Hadad. In addition to the judgment conflagration, the inhabitants of Syria will be defeated and carried off into foreign exile. This actually happened when Tiglath-Pileser III sacked the area and deported those left alive. The Assyrian ruler's annals describe what took place. "I destroyed 592 towns of the 16 districts of the country of Damascus, rendering them like hills over which the flood had passed." [4]

As we reflect on this first oracle, several points need underlining. Yahweh is Lord over all the nations, not just His chosen people. His anger is especially roused by human cruelty. Disregard for the value and dignity of human life will not go unpunished. And Yahweh will use the unfolding drama of the struggle of nations to accomplish His purposes. Damascus crushed Gilead like sheaves under a threshing sledge, but as Longfellow reminds us,

> Though the mills of God grind slowly, yet they grind
>   exceeding small;
> Though with patience He stands waiting, with
>   exactness, grinds He all.[5]

With this first oracle Amos was off to a good start. We can picture the cheering affirmation his audience gave to this judgment of an ancient archenemy. So much for openers. Amos is just warming up.

THE JUDGMENT OF GAZA AND TYRE

6 Thus says the Lord: "For three transgressions of Gaza, and for four, I will not turn away its punishment, because they took captive the whole captivity to deliver them up to Edom.

7 "But I will send a fire upon the wall of Gaza, which shall devour its palaces.

8 "I will cut off the inhabitant from Ashdod, and the one who holds the scepter from Ashkelon; I will turn My hand against Ekron, and the remnant of the Philistines shall perish," says the Lord God.

9 Thus says the Lord: "For three transgressions of Tyre, and for four, I will not turn away its punishment, because they delivered up the whole captivity to Edom, and did not remember the covenant of brotherhood.

10 "But I will send a fire upon the wall of Tyre, which shall devour its palaces."

Amos 1:6-10

The judgment of Gaza and Tyre continues Yahweh's condemnation of man's inhumanity to man. This time the focus is on kidnaping people to be sold on the international trade market as slaves. Gaza represents not only the city, but the Philistine state, located between Palestine and Egypt in the southeastern corner of the Mediterranean. On the main trade route, it was in a position to engage in the profitable business of selling captured Hebrews to the Edomites. Tyre was a Phoenician coastal port city-state in the eastern Mediterranean and located northwest of Israel about 100 miles from Jerusalem. The Tyrians had despoiled Israelites of their goods and sold them to the Edomites (Joel 3:4-6).

The judgment against Gaza was *"because they took captive the whole captivity to deliver them up to Edom"* (1:6). *"Whole captivity," gālût šĕlēmâ,* refers to the total conscription of entire villages.[6] People were used as things, objects of trade with blatant inhumanity. This was clearly forbidden by Mosiac Law (Exod. 21:16). Now Yahweh judges Gaza for a sin outlawed among His chosen people.

Sinful Gaza will receive the same punishment as Damascus. The Philistine city's walls will afford no more protection than did the walls of the Syrian cities against the Assyrians. Ashdod and Ashkelon, two of the five chief Philistine cities, would fare no better. Ekron, the most northern of the principal Philistine cities, was also given a special dishonorable mention: *I will turn My hand against Ekron.* Yahweh's hand denotes overwhelming strength. This will be turned against the city. Most final is the fact that all the *"remnant of the Philistines shall perish"* (1:8).

277

Once again we check subsequent history to see how it all happened. Gaza was held siege by Alexander the Great for five months, and when it fell its inhabitants were slaughtered. Each time it was rebuilt, it was besieged, first by Jonathan Maccabeus, then by his brother Simon, and finally devastated by Alexander Janneus in 96 B.C. Subsequent revivals brought little relief from constant turbulence.

As for Ashdod, it was captured by the Assyrians in 711 B.C. Ashkelon also knew little peace. It was twice taken by Jonathan Maccabeus and subsequently set on fire by the Jews. It was the birthplace of Herod the Great. Ekron resisted Sennacherib in 701 B.C. in vain and was destroyed.

Tyre's sin was that it captured and sold Israelite slaves to Edom and *"did not remember the covenant of brotherhood"* (v. 9). This probably refers to the cooperative relationship that existed between the Phoenicians and the Israelites, established with Hiram by David (2 Sam. 5:11) and carried on by Solomon (1 Kings 5:1, 11) and Ahab (1 Kings 16:31). Instead of honoring that treaty, Tyre became a center for the trading of Israelite slaves to the Edomites. The punishment mentioned in verse 10 probably refers to the siege by Nebuchadnezzar which lasted thirteen years, 586–573 B.C. Also, it should be noted that in 332 B.C., when Tyre fell to Alexander the Great, 30,000 Tyrians were sold into slavery. What was done to the Israelites centuries before also happened to Tyrians!

These two oracles forcefully carried on the central thrust of Yahweh's concern for human rights and dignity. He did not create anyone to be a slave of another. He meant for none of His children to be in bondage. We shudder when we trace the history of slavery through the centuries and remember that a little more than a century ago a civil war was fought in our own nation over the issue of slavery! That is about twenty-six centuries after Amos and eighteen centuries after Christ. We learn so little, so late!

THE JUDGMENT OF EDOM AND AMMON

11 Thus says the Lord: "For three transgressions of Edom, and for four, I will not turn away its punishment, because he pursued his brother with the sword,

and cast off all pity; his anger tore perpetually, and he kept his wrath forever.

12 "But I will send a fire upon Teman, which shall devour the palaces of Bozrah."

13 Thus says the Lord: "For three transgressions of the people of Ammon, and for four, I will not turn away its punishment, because they ripped open the women with child in Gilead, that they might enlarge their territory.

14 "But I will kindle a fire in the wall of Rabbah, and it shall devour its palaces, amid shouting in the day of battle, and a tempest in the day of the whirlwind.

15 "Their king shall go into captivity, he and his princes together," says the Lord.

Amos 1:11–15

Amos now moves closer home with Israel from the Mediterranean coast to two nations east of the Jordan and the Dead Sea. Edom was east of the Jordan and south of the Dead Sea. Ammon was further north and directly east of Israel. The two nations were known for unusual cruelty and inhuman violence.

For a comprehensive survey of the background of the conflict between Edom and Israel, the descendants of Esau and Jacob, please see the commentary on Obadiah. It will be helpful to our listeners to have a review of the historic development of the intense hatred of Edom for Israel.

Here in Amos's oracle against Edom the main issue is fratricide: *"because he pursued his brother with the sword"* (1:11). Dating back to Esau and Jacob, Edom and Israel were "brother" nations. However, from the time the Edomites refused Moses passage through to the promised land, to the hostility and warfare that persisted through the years, Edom expressed wrath against Israel. The problem with the rough-hewn, fierce, and combative Edomites was not that they had other gods, but that they had no god at all. Without God and any moral accountability, they *"cast off all pity."* There was no expressed need for God's mercy and therefore no imperative to show mercy to others. Instead, Edom *"kept his wrath forever"* (v. 11).

There is a great difference between the wrath of God and the godless wrath of people. God's wrath is a part of His grace. He cares unreservedly and therefore confronts anything that robs us of our full

279

potential in our relationship with Him, our true selves created in His image, our relationship with others in which we are called to be to them what He has been to us, and our relationship to the natural world He has given us to enjoy as stewards. God's wrath does not smolder in lasting resentment; it flames with purity and gives us an opportunity to change.

Human wrath, however, smolders like a refuse dump heap in which the resentments and prejudices of the years have been layered. It is not a righteous indignation based on the soul-sized issues of justice and righteousness, but rather, a burning hatred rooted in collective memories of personal slights and hurts and in the codified hostilities of group prejudice. At its foundation is the assumption of the right to judge others and mete out punishments. Human wrath is playing God.

Smoldering wrath constantly seeks a costly revenge and retaliation. It usually does greater harm to us than to others. A more recent Amos underlined this in a radio routine for the comedy team of Amos and Andy. Andy proposed that he was going to get even with a person he didn't like who always slapped him across the chest.

Amos asked, "What are you going to do about it?"

Andy said that he was ready for his erstwhile friend. "I've put a stick of dynamite in my vest pocket," he said. "The next time he slaps me on the chest, he'll get his hand blown off."

Amos's silence made the point: Andy failed to see that the same charge that would blow off his enemy's hand would blow out his own heart. As Harry Emerson Fosdick commented to a lady filled with smoldering wrath for what her sister had done to her, "Hate is like burning your house down to get rid of a rat."

When I was a boy, I was given an Australian boomerang. It was fun flinging it out and watching it return. One time I made the mistake of not watching for the boomerang's return. Distracted momentarily, it returned and hit the back of my head with a painful thud.

The boomerang of Edom's wrath came in a succession of defeats that spelled the eventual demise of the Edomites as a people. From the late sixth to the fourth century B.C., the Nabateans, an Arab tribe, occupied Edom and its capital, Petra. In 312 B.C. Alexander the Great's general, Antigonus, conquered the Edomites. They were displaced and scattered throughout southern Palestine. Later, in the second century B.C., the Edomites endured further defeats from Judas

Maccabeus. Josephus accounts for the complete ruination by Alexander Janneus of the remaining Edomites who had settled in the Negeb, also known as Idumea. Origen, in the third century A.D., wrote of the Edomites as a people whose name and language had perished from history.

Ammon's wrath was even more ferocious than Edom. The "fourth" transgression that precipitated the punishment of Yahweh was that they executed pregnant women and tore them open to kill their fetuses. This was done not only to ensure no growth in the population of Gilead but to create panic in the remaining women about becoming pregnant.

A counterpart in our own day would be the careless practice of what might be called contraceptive abortion in which the unborn are murdered because of an unwanted pregnancy. The abortion clinic's scalpel is no less sharp than the Ammonite's sword.

The Ammonites were a vicious people who occupied the rugged territory on the edge of the deeper border on Gilead's east and south. They, too, were related to Israel, having descended from Ben-Ammi, Lot's second son. Since the days of the Judges, they had sought to take parts of the fertile land of Gilead. In Amos's day they were once again attempting aggressive incursion in border wars because of Jeroboam II's attempts to reestablish the borders between Gilead and Ammon (2 Kings 14:25, 28). The memory, however, of the atrocities of Ammon remained.

Yahweh's punishment will be decisive. Rabbah, the Ammonite capital, would be destroyed by fire, and the king and princes would be carried into exile. The prophecy came to pass when Ammon was crushed by the Assyrians and became a vassal state. The nation of Ammon collapsed under attack by the Babylonians in the sixth century B.C. and was virtually depopulated.

Craigie has a helpful summary of Ammon.

> Ammon's sin, like that of Edom, is an example of mankind's inhumanity to fellow human beings. And yet, for all the horror of Edom's acts, those of Ammon are even more reprehensible. They employed their violence against the defenseless and the unborn. And for all the macho bragging with which they must have celebrated their violent deeds, those Ammonites have survived in history as the exemplars of cowardice. Upon those without defense, they raised their bloodthirsty swords. And Amos is convinced that such cowards must stand under the judgment of God.[7]

The Judgment of Moab

2:1 Thus says the Lord: "For three transgressions of Moab, and for four, I will not turn away its punishment, because he burned the bones of the king of Edom to lime.

2 "But I will send a fire upon Moab, and it shall devour the palaces of Kerioth; Moab shall die with tumult, with shouting and trumpet sound.

3 "And I will cut off the judge from its midst, and slay all its princes with him," says the Lord.

Amos 2:1–3

From Amos's home territory of Tekoa, he could look southeast across the Dead Sea to the shores of Moab. It was bordered on the south by Edom. The Moabites were descendants of Moab, Lot's son, and therefore closely related to the Ammonites.

The Moabites' crime that provoked Yahweh occurred during a battle between them and the Edomites. The Moabites exhumed from a tomb the bones of a former Edomite king and burned them until they were lime powder. The totality of the destruction is stressed. Wolff follows the Targum in interpreting *laśśîd* ("to lime") to mean that the Moabites had turned these royal ashes into a substance to whitewash stones or buildings. Says Wolff, "The mere fact that the remains of a human being were so desecrated, that a man had been treated as material, was of itself sufficient cause for Amos's indictment."[8]

Just as the Ammonites committed an outrage against the unborn, the Moabites' offense was against the dead. The bones of the dead were a sacred memory of a person. The ultimate desecration of a person's memory was to exhume his bones and display them for ridicule. Moab had even gone further in burning the bones into calcium oxide.

We wonder if this paradigmatic crime was motivated by the widely held belief that the bones of the dead would be refleshed and resurrected. Perhaps the Moabites wanted to be sure that a formidable enemy might never return to do battle with them. Most likely, the motive was to hassle the living by desecrating their dead.

We are jarred out of our reflections of eighth century B.C. atrocities by what happened recently in Carpentras in southern France. Four vandals invaded a Jewish burial ground before dawn one day and dragged a woman's body halfway out of her grave and exhumed the corpse of an 81-year-old man recently buried and impaled it on an umbrella. Copycat crimes followed in a wave of anti-Semitism. We are happy, at least, that the desecrators had not read about and emulated the ancient Moabites.

Staying in the twentieth century for a moment longer, we can imagine the outrage if the Ku Klux Klan exhumed the body of Martin Luther King, Jr. and burned the remains in effigy. Feel the shock waves of rage that would follow because of the desecration of the memory of that great and courageous leader!

Now back to Moab. Yahweh's punishment again is fire. Kerioth, the site of the sanctuary of Chemosh, the god of the Moabites, would be destroyed. The people of Moab will die in tumult (2:2). *ša'ôn* signifies the "uproar" (RSV) of armies of attacking troops and the clashing of an attack. The judge, *šôpēṭ,* and the princes, *šārîm,* probably meaning the king and his court, will be slain (v. 3).

The issue of the Lord's judgment was not just the desecration of the bones of a dead king, but the inhuman assault on the feelings of the living. Inflicting pain on others by ridicule and maligning what is sacred to them is judged and punished by God.

JUDGMENT ON JUDAH

> 4 Thus says the Lord: "For three transgressions of Judah, and for four, I will not turn away its punishment, because they have despised the law of the Lord, and have not kept His commandments. Their lies lead them astray, lies which their fathers followed.
> 5 "But I will send a fire upon Judah, and it shall devour the palaces of Jerusalem".
>
> *Amos 2:4–5*

Now God, through the voice of Amos, really comes close to home. The noose twined so carefully around the necks of pagan enemies now twines around Judah, the southern kingdom. The oracle against Judah is different in several ways. It is shorter than all the previous ones except the accusation against Edom. Also, it represents a salient shift from sins against humanity to sins against Yahweh Himself, His covenant, and His commandments. And the Lord speaks not only in the first person but refers to Himself in the third person as the object of Judah's growing apostasy—to despise the Law of the Lord was to deny the Lord.

We can surmise that some in Amos's audience took prejudiced delight in hearing Judah included in the indictment of foreign nations. Since the division of the kingdom in Solomon's time, tension, criticism, hostility, and conflict had grown. Judah was quick to denounce the apostasy of Israel. Now Judah was being given its comeupannce. "Long overdue!" some of Amos's listeners probably said with pious self-justification.

The accusations of Yahweh against Judah could not have been more pointed. His chosen, called, and cherished people in Judah had come to the place where they despised the Law of the Lord. The crucial issue is covenant disobedience. This led to breaking the Torah and to idolatry. They followed after "fakes" kĕzābîm. For generations their fathers had followed pagan gods rather than trusting only in Yahweh.

The judgment of Yahweh on Judah will be the same as on pagan nations. *"I will send a fire upon Judah, and it shall devour the palaces of Jerusalem"* (2:5). The point is that Yahweh considered covenant disloyalty, idolatry, and apostasy as serious as the crimes of inhuman cruelty, slavery, killing of unborn children, and desecration of the bones of the dead. The destruction of Jerusalem finally came in 586 B.C.

Don't miss the fact that this oracle of judgment was delivered by a citizen of Judah. Amos was confronting the sins of his own people. This must have had an impact on his audience. It made what he had to say about Israel all the more difficult to evade.

JUDGMENT ON ISRAEL

6 Thus says the Lord: "For three transgressions of Israel, and for four, I will not turn away its punishment, because they sell the righteous for silver, and the poor for a pair of sandals.

7 "They pant after the dust of the earth which is on the head of the poor, and pervert the way of the humble. A man and his father go in to the same girl, to defile My holy name.

8 "They lie down by every altar on clothes taken in pledge, and drink the wine of the condemned in the house of their god.

9 "Yet it was I who destroyed the Amorite before them, whose height was like the height of the cedars, and he was as strong as the oaks; yet I destroyed his fruit above and his roots beneath.

10 "Also it was I who brought you up from the land of Egypt, and led you forty years through the wilderness, to possess the land of the Amorite.

11 "I raised up some of your sons as prophets, and some of your young men as Nazirites. Is it not so, O you children of Israel?" says the Lord.

12 "But you gave the Nazirites wine to drink, and commanded the prophets saying, 'Do not prophesy!'

13 "Behold, I am weighed down by you, as a cart full of sheaves is weighed down.

14 "Therefore flight shall perish from the swift, the strong shall not strengthen his power, nor shall the mighty deliver himself;

15 "he shall not stand who handles the bow, the swift of foot shall not escape nor shall he who rides a horse deliver himself.

16 "The most courageous men of might shall flee naked in that day," says the Lord.

Amos 2:6–16

Amos's audience may well have thought he was done when he finished with Judah. Just before they had time to applaud his message about the sins of other nations, he thrust further. We can almost sense the dramatic surprise when he said, "For three transgressions . . ." And the audience waited wondering, "Who's next?" The name "Israel" must have been like a clap of thunder. Amazement followed shock waves rippling across the crowd. Amos certainly had their attention when he went on with prophetic authority speaking the word of the Lord, " . . . *and for four, I will not turn away its punishment!*" (2:6).

The first charge is against selling the innocent and the poor into debt-slavery. *"Because they sell the righteous for silver, and the poor for a pair of sandals"* (v. 6). The word *righteous* (ṣaddîq) means "innocent," one who in a court of law has been declared not guilty. In the case in point, one accused of owing a debt is judged and found not guilty.

And yet, he is sold into debt-slavery. This requires either disregarding the judgment of the court or bribing a judge who, after finding the accused not guilty, would rule that he should be sold into debt-slavery anyway. In either case, justice would be denied and a farce made of the courts.

The poor did not fare any better than the innocent. The needy, *ʾebyôn,* signifies a person in need of help. Those who had incurred a debt of as little as the price of a pair of sandals could be indentured into debt-slavery. Again the courts were either totally ignored or the judges bribed.

The issue is the use of innocent and helpless fellow Israelites as things and not as persons. This kind of inhumanity was worse than the Phoenicians selling Israelites to the Edomites! Amos had prepared his audience well for that shocking implication.

Verse 7 continues the exposure of the exploiters of the poor. *"They pant after the dust of the earth which is on the head of the poor."* Regarding the initial verb, most commentators follow the Septuagint and read "they trample," taking the original Hebrew root here as *šûp* rather than *šāʾap.* The meaning is that the influential and rich trampled the head of the poor into the dust. *"And pervert the way of the humble."* To pervert, *nāṭâ derek (hiphil),* means to abrogate the course of justice, in this case, for the humble, *ʿănāwîm,* the oppressed. The perpetrators would be the proud and the arrogant. Proverbs 22:22 strikes the same note, "Do not rob the poor because he is poor, nor oppress the afflicted at the gate."

We pause to evaluate our own lives and our churches in the light of God's indictment of Israel. Our faith is measured by how we relate to the poor and oppressed. Christ came to preach the Gospel to the poor (Luke 4:18). He ministered to the disadvantaged, and He made our eternal life contingent on feeding the hungry and clothing the naked (Matt. 25:31–46). Throughout Christian history vital spiritual power has been linked with intentional care for the poor and needy. It is safe to say that no Christian is fulfilling his or her calling without an active involvement in ministry to the poor. In addition to financial contributions to agencies for organized relief and assistance, we all need to get directly engaged in the care, assistance, and rehabilitation of several individuals and families who are poor or oppressed by circumstances.

In my congregation in Hollywood many of the members have had their lives transformed by hands-on ministry with the hungry, homeless, and disadvantaged.

As I mentioned earlier, our *Lighthouse Ministry* feeds hundreds of hungry people every Sunday afternoon on the church campus. The food is prepared and served by members. But one of the secrets of the success of the program is that they sit down and talk with those they serve. Nameless street persons are now known by name and are cared for as persons. This is no "soup for a sermon" ministry. Rather, the Bread of Life is shared in deep conversations. Many who are fed physically and spiritually have become Christians. In addition to fulfilling the Lord's call to care for the poor, many of our members have found a new joy in their own walk with the Lord. This personal ministry has made us more committed to working to change the deeper causes of poverty and hunger.

In Israel, the mistreatment of the poor and oppressed was directly related to the people's misplaced worship and devotion. They put their trust in the fertility cults of Baal. A part of Baal worship was "sacred" prostitution. It was believed that copulation with the temple prostitutes would result in fertility in their flocks and herds as well as success in the growth of crops. As we discovered in our study of the book of Hosea, when the Israelites crossed over Jordan from the wilderness to claim the promised land, they were unprepared for agricultural life. They soon observed that the Canaanites depended on Baal worship for their prosperity and had shrines to the fertility god in their fields. Adopting Baal worship in combination with worship of Yahweh began the addiction to syncretism, which had become entrenched by Amos's time.

Cult prostitution flourished in this syncretism. This, too, has its contemporary manifestations. A shocking evidence of it was recently reported in the *Los Angeles Times.*

A Los Angeles couple was found guilty of prostitution, although they claimed they were following the tenets of the Church of the Most High Goddess. According to the woman, her sex acts with hundreds of men were her legitimate duties as high priestess of the allegedly 5,000-year-old Egyptian religion.

During the trial, the husband compared himself to Jesus Christ and Mormon leader Joseph Smith, who, he said, were persecuted because their beliefs contradicted social norms of their times. He said he revived the religion in 1984 after receiving a revelation from God.

The couple said that in their religion, the sins of men are absolved through sex with the church's priestess. They did not say how women's sins were absolved, however. Besides the absolution of sin through sex, a $150 donation to the church showed a man's allegiance to the church.

The practice of cult prostitution in Israel in confronted by Yahweh in verse 7b. *"A man and his father go in to the same girl, to defile My holy name."* This probably does not mean incest or a father and son off on a sexual foray, but that fathers and sons alike were engaged in using cult prostitutes in worship of Baal. The commandments and the covenant were being denied and Yahweh's name, His presence, power, and authority were being defiled.

Added to that (v. 8), clothes taken from the poor in pledge of the payment of a debt were being offered to the Baal gods on the pagan altars. The wine taken from those condemned to debt-slavery was being drunk in the temples.

Very significant. Baal worship had neither moral requirements or responsibilities. What Yahweh would not permit was flaunted in the temples of the permissive Baal gods. The same equivocation is perpetrated in every age by God's people when they find His spiritual and moral standards too stringent. Another god, an easy religion that strokes our proclivities and prejudices, is found to worship because there is no accountability.

In verse 9 Yahweh asserts that it was none other than He who has been scorned and denied. *"It was I who destroyed the Amorite before them."* *Amorite* is synonymous with *Canaanite.* Yahweh led the battle and gave victory over the Canaanites who were strong and well-rooted *"like the height of the cedars . . . as strong as the oaks."* As He led the conquering Israelites, He completely defeated the enemy, *"his fruit above and his roots beneath."*

In verse 10 Yahweh continues to review His acts in Israel's salvation history. He alone made possible the exodus, the provision and protection in the wilderness, and the possession of the promised land.

As the young nation settled in Canaan, the Lord not only sought to bless His people with their material needs as the source and sustainer of all, but He raised up prophets or Nazirites to be seers and guides for the people's development as a holy nation (v. 11). The name *Nazirite* means one separated, consecrated to God for a certain specified period. The detailed list of the requirements is found in Numbers 6. One requirement was to not drink wine or strong drink nor eat any product of the vine during the time of his separation.

Yahweh's charge against Israel is that the people blatantly resisted the authority of the Nazarites to prophesy and actually enticed them to drink (v. 12). All this was part of the rebellion that had infected His people.

The thrust of the oracle against Israel is now very clear. Yahweh actively showed His strength to help a weak people become strong. The tragedy was that they used their strength to oppress the weak. Yahweh was Israel's defender; now they exploited the defenseless.

Yahweh's punishment of Israel's rebellion is detailed in Amos 2:13–16. We need to look carefully at the translation of verse 13, *"Behold, I am weighed down by you, as a cart full of sheaves is weighed down."* The Hebrew verb in both clauses is active and not passive. The RSV thus translates, "Behold, I will press you down in your place, as a cart full of sheaves presses down." The rare verb, *ʿûq (hiphil)*, is rendered by Wolff as "break open," as a cart of sheaves breaks open the earth beneath its wheels, suggesting the image of an earthquake. Stuart thinks the verb more likely means "bog down," as a heavily loaded cart sometimes grinds to a halt.[9]

In any case, the time of Yahweh's punishment will be inescapable. The remaining verses of the oracle describe the plight. There will be no safe refuge even for fast runners, the strong will be weak, archers will not be able to take a stand, soldiers will not be able to defend themselves, and calvary troops (or charioteers) will not be able to save themselves. Even those with heart, *lēb* (in v. 16 denoting the vital center of strength and courage), will flee naked in sheer panic. This is a startling description of what actually happened in 722 B.C. during the siege of Samaria and the subsequent destruction of the northen kingdom by Assyria.

BACK TO WHERE WE STARTED

Now we come full circle back to our own times. The accounts of hatred, prejudice, and inhumanity in our day make Amos's inaugural message more than a study of eighth century B.C. history. Unfortunately, many of the relational sins described for the Israelites, we do also — we have not progressed very far.

We ponder what is the "fourth" sin of our own society. Then we reflect on what it is for the church as a whole and for your church and mine in particular. Like Israel, we will be held accountable in greater measure. Has our experience of salvation through Christ put people and their needs top on our agenda? Does our zeal for social righteousness outstrip the agnostic humanitarian or the nonbelieving social worker?

Any responsible teaching or preaching of this passage must lead to an even more startling conclusion than Amos's confrontation of Israel when his audience least expected it. There is a ninth oracle for our own audience today. In it we must list the relational and social sins of neglect in our own churches and in our own lives.

NOTES

1. "An Outbreak of Bigotry," *TIME*, May 28, 1990, 35–37.

2. Stuart, *Hosea – Jonah*, 308.

3. Wolff, *Joel and Amos*, 152–153.

4. Craigie, *Twelve Prophets: Volume 1*, 128.

5. Henry Wadsworth Longfellow, "Retribution," from *The Sinngedichte of Friedrick von Logau*.

6. Wolff, *Joel and Amos*, 129.

7. Craigie, *Twelve Prophets: Volume 1*, 136.

8. Wolff, *Joel and Amos*, 163.

9. Ibid., 171; Stuart, *Hosea – Jonah*, 319.

CHAPTER THREE

The Challenge and Cost of Being Chosen

Amos 3:1–4:3

We come now to the second and main unit of Amos's prophecy. This unit spans chapters 3–6 and contains the major themes of his message. It is a collection of oracles, unified around the central thrust that there is an awesome challenge and cost to being chosen. Amos 3:1–8 clearly establishes the cause and effect of Israel's election and her accountability to her God. Verses 1–2 serve as a kind of topic statement for the entire unit of chapters 3–6.

PRIVILEGE AND PURPOSE

> 3:1 Hear this word that the Lord has spoken against you, O children of Israel, against the whole family which I brought up from the land of Egypt, saying:
> 2 "You only have I known of all the families of the earth; therefore I will punish you for all your iniquities"
>
> *Amos 3:1–2*

The American Express Company has the slogan, "Membership has its privileges." In an ultimate sense, our election by God has life's greatest privileges. To be elected by the sovereign grace of God is to be chosen and called to be His person, to be the focus of His love, providential care, and timely interventions. The privilege of belonging to God also has rigorous responsibilities. We are elected to fulfill God's purposes. Our lives are to be a theocracy under His reign.

We are to seek first to know and to do His will and to glorify Him as Lord of all.

Israel was elected to be a nation of chosen people. Amos 3:1 summarizes the whole sweep of their salvation history. They were God's holy people, belonging first and foremost to Him. He called them out of Egypt, liberated them from bondage, blessed them with the exodus, and brought them to the promised land. However, through the years Israel forgot that her privilege was inseparably related to accomplishing God's purpose. The word of the Lord spoken by Amos against Israel was for their defection from that purpose.

Verse 2 puts the responsibility of election in the most personal language. *"You only have I known of all the families of the earth."* The word *know* implies the most intimate relationships. Yahweh cherished Israel with tender love and mercy. His saving grace establishes the ground for special accountability. Based on this accountability (*"therefore"*), the following statement communicates the certitude of punishment for all of Israel's iniquities. An iniquity is a long-standing, persistent, compulsive sin despite warnings and opportunities to change.

At base, Israel's sin was the refusal to be Yahweh's family and obey Him as Father of the nation. The nation was a rebellious child caught in the bind of a continuing tantrum against Yahweh's authority.

As Christians we, too, have a magnificent salvation history: liberation from bondage through the cross, an exodus to new life in Christ, a promised land of the abundant life, and countless blessings each step of the way. The danger is we can become so faithlessly familiar with all that is ours we forget we are not our own. We need Paul's bracing reminder, "For you were bought at a price; therefore glorify God in your body and in your Spirit, which are God's" (1 Cor. 6:20). Glorifying God is our vocation, our calling. This includes personal piety and social righteousness.

Churches can become proud of their heritage and miss the call to obedience now. This happens when great memories of what God did leads us to pride and precludes humbly discovering what He wants to do in and through us today. Focusing on our past experiences with God keeps us from experiencing God now. Life with God is a daily walk.

To Walk or Not to Walk?

3 "Can two walk together, unless they are agreed?

4 "Will a lion roar in the forest, when he has no prey? Will a young lion cry out of his den, if he has caught nothing?

5 "Will a bird fall into a snare on the earth, where there is no trap for it? Will a snare spring up from the earth, if it has caught nothing at all?

6 "If a trumpet is blown in a city, will not the people be afraid? If there is calamity in a city, will not the Lord have done it?"

Amos 3:3–6

These questions establish the relationship of cause and effect. The first, sixth, seventh, eighth, and ninth questions deal directly with Israel as God's chosen family, and the intervening four emphasize from nature the point that every visible effect has a cause.

"Can two walk together, unless they are agreed?" (3:3). The word *agreed* is really "met" in the Hebrew, *yā'ad (niphal)*. Two people who take a walk must meet together to begin the walk. There must be a starting place, a shared pace, and a shared destination. This is the cause of the effect of the walk.

Israel had been called as God's chosen family to walk with Him. He extricated His people out of Egypt so He could meet them at Sinai to begin to walk with them as His holy nation, His bride. The terms of that walk were clearly defined in the covenant and the commandments. The destination of the walk was not just the promised land, but consistent companionship with Him through history.

The simile of life in God being like a walk with God was a part of Israel's sacred history. Abraham, Enoch, and Moses were said to have "walked with God." Then after the meeting of Sinai, God said, "Walk in My statutes, walk in My commandments, walk in My way." Walking humbly with God meant walking attentively and responsively to what God said as He walked with His people. They were not to run ahead or lag behind, but to keep His pace with Him, moving toward His goal. The watchword was, "This is My way, walk in it."

Thus the question, "Can two walk together unless they have met?" stresses the point that Israel's daily walk with God was not being consistently renewed.

The starting place for a Christian's walk with God is Calvary. We meet Him at the foot of the cross. George Whitfield never forgot the place and time when he began his walk of faith. Whenever he returned to Oxford, he went directly to a certain tree where he first experienced grace and was born again. Wherever he was in England or America, his daily walk was renewed with the memory of that hallowed place of commitment. John Bunyan also consistently remembered how he began his walk with God. "I was made to see, again and again, that God and my soul were friends by His blood; yea, I saw that the justice of God and my sinful soul could embrace and kiss each other, through His blood. This was a good day to me; I hope I shall never forget it."

The old hymn expresses this liberating experience of beginning to walk with the Lord:

> At the cross, at the cross,
> Where I first saw the light,
> And the burden of my heart rolled away,
> It was there by faith
> I received my sight,
> And now I am happy all the day.[1]

The image of the Christian life being a walk is firmly rooted in the messages of Paul and John. Paul called the Ephesians "to have a walk worthy of the calling with which you were called, with all lowliness and gentleness" (Eph. 4:1–2). He called the saints to "walk by faith" (2 Cor. 5:7), to "walk in the Spirit" (Gal. 5:16), to "walk in love" (Eph. 5:2), and to "walk as children of the light" (Eph. 5:8). God in Immanuel is the companion of our walk. "As you have therefore received Christ Jesus the Lord, so walk in Him, rooted and built up in Him and established in the faith, as you have been taught, abounding in it with thanksgiving" (Col. 2:6–7).

For the Apostle John, walking in Christ meant walking in the light of truth. Fellowship with the Lord and with our fellow walkers in faith requires honesty and openness. "If we say that we have fellowship with Him, and walk in darkness, we lie and do not practice the truth. But if we walk in the light as He is in the light, we have fellowship with one another, and the blood of Jesus Christ His Son cleanses us from all sin" (1 John 1:6–7).

From the meeting place of Calvary, we walk in the light of the presence and truth of Christ, God with us, and daily our pace and direction is righted with confession and forgiveness. We must meet the Lord in the morning if we want to walk with Him through the day. And each day's walk will lead is on in the Lord's plan and purpose for our lives.

Recently, a friend asked me, "How's your walk? Is your walk consistent with your talk?" A good question to ask every day. It is easy to veer off on our own, breaking fellowship with the Lord, and heading off in a wrong direction.

James Sammis put it more poetically but no less directly in his poem that has been set to music of a favorite hymn:

> When we walk with the Lord
> in the light of His Word,
> What a glory He sheds on our way!
> While we do His good will
> He abides with us still,
> And with all who will trust and obey.

This was exactly what Israel refused to do. They had ceased to walk with Yahweh. They would not meet Him daily for a renewal of the true covenant. That was the cause of the effect that they no longer walked in His ways.

EXAMPLES OF CAUSE AND EFFECT

Now Amos draws on his rich experience with nature to drive home the inseparable linkage between this cause and its effect. He asks four questions. As a tender of sheep and a breeder of livestock, he knew the danger of a lion hungry for its prey. *"Will a lion roar in the forest, when he has no prey?"* (3:4). The roar frightens the prey away from the flock so the lion can corner it and kill it. The second question, *"Will a young lion cry out of his den, if he has caught nothing?"* The roar is the effect of the cause that the lion has secured the prey in its den and warns other animals to beware coming near. This is in keeping with the shepherd's old maxim, "If a lion roars, he has just made a catch."[2]

In verse 5, Amos uses ornithological metaphors but with the same cause and effect intent. *"Will a bird fall into a snare on the earth, where there is no trap for it?"* Stuart translates, "Does a bird fall into a ground trap if the snare has not been set?"[3] Wolff identifies the word *môqēš* as a wooden missile, a throwing stick that was used to ground a flying bird. "There is evidence," says Wolff, "that the boomerang and the throwing stick were common hunting weapons in the ancient Near East, being used primarily to catch birds."[4] Whatever the instrument, it was the cause of the effect of catching the bird.

The second device for catching birds was a net, *pah* (folding net). The point is the same: If the net was not set up, the bird would not be snared. *"Will a snare spring up from the earth, if it has caught nothing at all?"* Of course not. The bird in the net trips the closure of the net. But it had to be set — the cause — if it is to catch the bird — the effect.

Questions six and seven in verse 6 return to humankind and present the frightening effect of Israel no longer walking with God. *"If a trumpet is blown in a city, will not the people be afraid?"* Amos now moves closer to his central goal of alerting Israel to the danger of Yahweh's judgment on her apostasy. A trumpet blast by a city's watchman was to give warning and arouse the people of an approaching danger. The result follows the cause. Amos's prophecy was a trumpet blast of warning of the approaching accountability with Yahweh.

And now the key question: *"If there is calamity in a city, will not the Lord have done it?"* Yahweh will be behind the scenes in Israel's forthcoming calamity because she rejected the call to walk humbly with Him. He will use the course of events involved in Israel's international affairs to bring His judgment on His people.

Calamity in the city, in our lives, through other people, or because of our sins, are sometimes used by the Lord to alert us to the fact that we have refused to walk humbly with Him toward His destination for us. When trouble strikes, it is a trumpet call to reestablish our walk with Him. Of course, sometimes we get into trouble because we are walking with the Lord doing what love requires. But we know the difference between corrective trouble and persecution for righteousness sake. Our daily conversations during our walk with the Lord make that abundantly clear. The question, "Lord what are you trying to say to me in what's happening to me?" never goes unanswered — if we are listening.

Often I exercise on a walking machine. It goes at a steady pace, alternating the speed for aerobic results. You have to walk at the pace determined or you will fall off the machine. One day I thought, "How like walking with the Lord this is! We either go at His pace or not at all."

Toki Niyashina has written a version of the 23rd Psalm that should be a daily motto for those who want to walk with the Lord:

> The Lord is my Pace-setter, I shall not rush;
> He makes me to stop and rest for quiet intervals.
> He provides me with images of stillness,
> which restore my serenity.
> He leads me in the ways of efficiency
>   through calmness of mind.
> And His guidance is peace.
> Even though I have a great many things to
>   accomplish each day,
> I will not fret, for His presence is here.
> His timelessness, His all importance, will
>   keep me in balance
> He prepares refreshment and renewal in the
>   midst of my activity,
> By enriching my mind with His oil of tranquility.
> My cup of joyous energy overflows.
> Surely harmony and effectiveness shall be the
>   fruits of my hours
> For I shall walk in the pace of my Lord, and
>   dwell in His house forever.[5]

A CLEAR CALL AND A READY RESPONSE

> 7 "Surely the Lord God does nothing, unless He reveals His secret to His servants the prophets.
> 8 "A lion has roared! Who will not fear? The Lord God has spoken! Who can but prophesy?"
>
> *Amos 3:7–8*

The final couplet of questions (eight and nine) is given by Amos to witness to his own prophetic calling and ready response. Verses 7–8 are sometimes dealt with as a separate oracle unrelated to the seven previous questions. My view is that they serve as an example of creative cause and effect from the prophet's own experience. Unashamedly, he longs for all of Israel to respond to the cause of Yahweh's call with the effect of reverence and obedience. His statement is in defense of his prophetic authority but exemplifies the way all of Yahweh's people should walk with Him.

Amos asserts that the Lord does nothing without revealing both the *what* and the *why* to His servants, the prophets. Not a single thing, event, or certain matter, *dābār*, is done. Yahweh reveals His plan, *sôd*, to the prophets. He explains His actions and uses the prophets to interpret their meaning. Amos heard the roar of God's word. The prophet responded with authentic awe and true repentance. The Lord spoke to Him and revealed His judgment. He could not disobey the calling to prophesy to God's people of the impending danger.

As with any effective communicator, Amos lived his message. He asked Israel to do no more than he was willing to do himself. God called and he responded. God spoke and he delivered the message. Amos modeled the challenge and cost of being chosen. Nothing less was required of Israel. And from this side of Calvary even more is expected of us. Jesus said, "For everyone to whom much is given, from him much will be required; and to whom much has been committed, of him they will ask the more" (Luke 12:48).

THE MESSAGE COMMITTED TO AMOS FOR SAMARIA

9 "Proclaim in the palaces at Ashdod, and in the palaces in the land of Egypt, and say: 'Assemble on the mountains of Samaria; see great tumults in her midst, and the oppressed within her.

10 "'For they do not know to do right,' says the Lord. 'Who store up violence and robbery in their palaces.'"

11 Therefore thus says the Lord God: "An adversary shall be all around the land, he shall sap your strength from you, and your palaces shall be plundered."

12 Thus says the Lord: "As a shepherd takes from the mouth of a lion two legs or a piece of an ear, so shall the children of Israel be taken out who dwell in Samaria—in the corner of a bed and on the edge of a couch!

13 "Hear and testify against the house of Jacob," says the Lord God, the God of hosts,

14 "That in the day I punish Israel for their transgressions, I will also visit destruction on the altars of Bethel; and the horns of the altar shall be cut off and fall to the ground.

15 "I will destroy the winter house along with the summer house; the houses of ivory shall perish, and the great houses shall have an end," says the Lord.

4:1 Hear this word, you cows of Bashan, who are on the mountain of Samaria, who oppress the poor, who crush the needy, who say to your husbands, "Bring wine, let us drink!"

2 The Lord God has sworn by His holiness: "Behold, the days shall come upon you when He will take you away with fishhooks, and your posterity with fishhooks.

3 "You will go out through broken walls, each one straight ahead of her, and you will be cast into Harmon," says the Lord.

Amos 3:9–4:3

Amos 3:9–4:3 contains the message committed to the prophet to declare to Samaria, the capital city of the northern kingdom. The unit has four oracles closely intertwined around the central theme of the sins of the city.

We are immediately impressed by Amos's boldness and courage in the first oracle. The sheepherder of Tekoa was empowered by his encounter with the Lord and the word he was given to prophesy. With fearless authority Amos calls for messengers to be sent to the palaces of Ashdod,[6] a leading Philistine city, and to the palaces of Egypt. The summons is to come and see what is happening in Samaria. *"Assemble on the mountains of Samaria"* (3:9). The city was built by kings Omri and Ahab back in the ninth century B.C. on a mountain more than 300 feet above a plain. The plain also was encircled by other mountains or hills. Great fortification walls surrounded the city, known for its wealth and military strength. From Yahweh's perspective, Amos saw something more than the sumptuous security of the city. He sees *"great tumults in her midst, and the oppressed within her"* (v. 9b). Though the structures of the strongholds of Samaria were impressive, a closer look revealed great tumults, chaos, panic, and disorder. The construction great *tumults, mĕhûmôt rabbôt*, also can mean the confusion caused by unrestrained and wanton revelry as in orgies out of control. The oppression, *ʿăsûqîm*, was the subjugation of the poor and helpless by the powerful and rich. Samaria was Vanity Fair, Sin City, obsessed with sexual lust and sensualism.

Tragically, Samaria's leaders thought what they were doing was right! They had drifted so far from the covenant and the commandments that they were completely without moral standards. *"'For they do not know to do right,' says the Lord, 'who store up violence and robbery in their palaces'"* (3:10). Having lost all moral perspective, they filled their storehouses with the proceeds of their exploitation and robbery of the poor. Craigie comments, "The archeological excavations of Samaria have revealed great storehouses in the palace complex; perhaps the prophet mocks these structures in saying that the citizens of Samaria 'store up violence and robbery.'"[7]

Verse 11 declares Yahweh's judgment of people who contradicted so blatantly their calling as His people. An adversary will invade the whole land, and in Samaria the rich will have done to them what they were doing to the poor. Their houses will be plundered. It will be more than a *"calamity in the city"* (v. 6) but a total denuding and destruction. It is not revealed who the adversary will be. From the grim perspective of history, we know that it was Assyria.

The next oracle (vv. 12–15) is a mixture of the inevitability of God's judgment and what He will do to rescue some of His people from annihilation. Amos draws on his shepherd's experience to show the unavoidability of what will occur. *"As a shepherd takes from the mouth of a lion two legs or a piece of an ear, so shall the children of Israel be taken out"* (3:12). The example is based on a specific statute governing what should be done when a shepherd allows a sheep entrusted to his care by another to be killed by a beast of prey. The obligation of restitution is nullified as long as the shepherd can supply evidence (Exod. 22:10–13). Two pieces of bone from the legs or the tip of an ear was sufficient proof that the sheep was killed by a beast of prey and not stolen by the shepherd. The proof was to establish that the loss was unavoidable.[8]

The explanation of this example is easier than the application to Israel. What seems to be intended is the extent of the destruction of the nation will be total. Israel will die as a national power. What is left in the mouth of her adversary of prey will only be a remnant of the people. They will be taken out of Samaria in the exile.

The general sense of the next picture is clear, although the specifics are disputed. Concerning those who lived in luxury, only fragments of their wealth will be left. Those who had beds and couches while the poor slept and sat on the ground will be stripped of the accouterments of their acquisitive accumulation. They will go into exile with barely the clothing on their backs.

Next the people are reminded that they are *bêt ya'ăqōb*, the house of Jacob, under the bond of the covenant and Yahweh's people. Once again the theme of the challenge and cost of being chosen is sounded. Even though wealth and military might delude them into believing they were one of the great nations of the world, they would lose their assumed pride. They sinned against their God and would be punished. They wanted to be like other nations; soon they would be no nation at all.

The most serious of Israel's sins was Baal worship at the altars of Bethel (v. 14). Yahweh will destroy those altars on which pagan sacrifices were being made. The people thought of the altars as places of expiation and atonement. Now there would be neither. Even the horns of the altar will be cut off. The reference is reminiscent of an earlier practice of giving asylum to a fugitive who reached the sanctuary and grasped the horns of the altar. Now there would be no refuge. Israel would be treated as a murderer who, according to ancient covenant Law was to be taken by force away from the horns and executed (Exod. 21:12-14; cf. 1 Kings 1:50; 2:28). There will be no place for the people to flee. The altars on which they syncretized Baal with Yahweh would not help them.

A further judgment on the rich who gouged the poor would be the destruction of both their winter and summer houses (3:15). Seasonal residences were a sign of wealth. The great houses of Samaria were adorned with ivory. Ivory plaques were found in the archeological excavations of Samaria. These elegant houses were razed when the city fell in 722 B.C.

HOLY COWS

The next part of Amos's prophecy against Samaria probably took place in the palace precincts. He addresses the elite women of the upper crust of society of the capital city. They were the wives of wealthy landowners, court dignitaries, and businessmen. These women were pampered, overfed, and self-indulgent. What they forgot was that all they wore and owned actually belonged to God. They were holy women belonging to God though doing everything possible to deny their election and covenant responsibilities.

Now the shock. Amos addressed these high and mighty ladies as *"cows of Bashan"* (4:1). Background on the term heightens our appreciation of the wave of indignation that must have been like thunder and lightning rumbling and flashing through the self-satisfied ambience of Amos's audience.

As a cattle breeder, Amos knew about the cows of Bashan. The territory was a fertile plain situated in Transjordan on both sides of the middle and upper Yarmuk at an altitude of about 1,500 feet. The plateau lying east of the Sea of Galilee had lush pasture used for fattening cattle. Ezekiel 39:18 calls these cattle "fatlings." They demanded a great deal of special care, water, and pasture. To call a group of women fat cows certainly would get their attention and their wrath.

Perhaps these women were overweight while the poor and oppressed went hungry, but they also were pampered and coddled. While they were abusive to the poor and crushed the needy, they reveled in drunken debauchery. "Bring wine," they say, "and let's get drunk!" Amos announces that God took a solemn oath to punish them for how they denigrated their calling as holy women and dehumanized the less fortunate.

The judgment of Yahweh that Amos announces is that *"He will take you away with fishhooks, and your posterity with fishhooks"* (v. 2). Most translators assume an indefinite subject in this verse. Stuart translates, "When they will pick you up with hooks."[9] Although the NKJV translates both instruments with *"fishhooks,"* the Hebrew uses two different terms. Only the second clearly refers to fishing: the words *sîrôt dûgâ* indicate some type of fishing instrument, but hardly an angling hook. Probably what is meant is a type of harpoon or lance used like a cattle prod. That would fit the image of the cows of Bashan. The other term may refer to hooks used to move dead cattle or to ropes.[10] Then the picture is the removing of the dead bodies of the women after the siege and destruction of the city. Dead or alive the women along with others would be dragged out of the city. The meaning of *Harmon* in verse 4:3 is uncertain. It can mean the dumping place for dead bodies or life in the exile.

Our application is that covenant loyalty to God demands social responsibility for the needs of people. A vital part of being chosen means active involvement in ministry to the poor, hungry, and disadvantaged. There is no escape from this calling or from the Lord's judgment when we neglect it.

We are left with some haunting questions:

Have we claimed our calling?
Is God first in our lives?
Is our purpose to glorify Him in everything?
Are people and their needs top in our agenda?
If we were to ask a close friend or member of our family what he or she thinks are our top priorities, what would he or she say?
What tangible evidence is there in our lives that we have accepted the challenge and cost of being chosen?

NOTES

1. Isaac Watts, "Alas! And Did My Savior Bleed," *The Presbyterian Hymnal* (Richmond, Virginia: John Knox Press, 1960), hymn number 97.

2. Wolff, *Joel and Amos,* 185.

3. Stuart, *Hosea–Jonah,* 323.

4. Wolff, *Joel and Amos,* 185.

5. This rendering of the 23rd Psalm was given to me by a friend. All efforts to find it in current publications have been unfruitful.

6. Note commentary on Ashdod, Amos 1:8. It should also be noted that some translations use Assyria instead of Ashdod following the Septuagint. I favor using Ashdod because Amos has already referred to it and does not mention Assyria directly anywhere else in his prophecy. Some argue that the variant use of Assyria balances better with Egypt as a world power.

7. Craigie, *Twelve Prophets: Volume 1,* 149

8. I am indebted to Wolff's background on this verse, *Joel and Amos,* 197–198.

9. Stuart, *Hosea–Jonah,* 328.

10. Wolff, *Joel and Amos,* 206–207.

CHAPTER FOUR

Godless Worship and Worshipless Living

Amos 4:4–13

With the stark realities of the abusive social attitudes and behavior of the people of Samaria freshly imprinted on his mind, Amos left the city. Perhaps he was disbarred from the city for a time because of his confrontation with the self-indulgent establishment. Amos just could not divide faith from social responsibility. Now he saw that Yahweh's people had neither. Faith had been replaced by religious customs, and social responsibility by careless neglect and greedy misuse of the poor and needy. Amos's soul flamed with divinely inspired indignation. He could not tolerate the faithless religion of people who no longer knew Yahweh and who had no moral integrity. Everything he saw going on in Israel as a whole was judged in the light of the people's brash disregard for the basics of social justice.

We can empathize. Get in touch with the feelings you have when you talk with a pietistic Christian whose lifestyle totally contradicts his glib talk. We all have a few people like that in our lives. I know lots of them. One comes to mind. His relationships are strained, his marriage is in a shambles, and he owns a great deal of slum property from which he gets richer each year. When people cannot or will not pay their rent, he simply takes the front door off until they pay up. It is difficult for me to listen to this man talk about Jesus.

And we all have had experiences with churches that have little or no ministry to the disadvantaged. I spoke at one recently. It was a traditional denominational church with all the right liturgy, beautiful buildings, and slick programs for the already convinced. What is lacking is evangelism and mission. Large endowments sustain the budget, but the church is going to die unless it reaches out to the surrounding city. It was difficult for me to see anything right in a church that was so wrong in its disregard for people who desperately need Christ. It is a religious institution made up of people who do not really know the Lord.

Now multiply your feelings of indignation about Christians and churches like those I have mentioned by the acute compassion you feel about the suffering in our society, and you begin to allow your heart to beat with the passionate heart of Amos. With the sins of Samaria on his heart, he could not appreciate the carnival-like ceremonial celebrations at the sanctuaries of Bethel and Gilgal. The prophet was at one of those national sanctuaries when he gave the message contained in Amos 4:4-13, probably in Bethel. Verses 4-5 are what he said to the pilgrims as they entered the sanctuary. It was a seething parody on Psalm 95:6-7. Verses 6-13 represent the cohesive message he proclaimed to the teeming crowds gathered in Bethel for the festival that seems to be in progress.

This section of Amos provides the communicator an excellent opportunity to deal with two closely related themes: Godless worship and worshipless living.

GODLESS WORSHIP

> 4 "Come to Bethel and transgress, at Gilgal multiply transgression; bring your sacrifices every morning, your tithes every three days.
> 5 "Offer a sacrifice of thanksgiving with leaven, proclaim and announce the freewill offerings; for this you love, you children of Israel!" says the Lord God.
> *Amos 4:4-5*

Imagine yourself with Amos in Bethel, the holy place of the sanctuary in the south of Israel, directly north of Jerusalem. The area is teeming with pilgrims who traveled great distances for an annual festival. They brought with them animals to sacrifice as well as the tithes of their harvests as offerings. The atmosphere is a combination of the excitement of a convention, the hoopla of a carnival, and the raucous jostling of an overcrowded picnic. The air is electric with the enthusiasm of the people who had come to celebrate their traditions and ceremonies.

We enter into the excitement. Ah, to be at Bethel! The place where Jacob dreamed of a ladder reaching from heaven to earth and where he tithed his possessions in gratitude for his mysterious encounter with the God of Abraham and Isaac. Bethel had been a sacred place of Canaanite worship. But after the conquest of the promised land, it became a worship center for the Israelites (Judg. 20:18). Samuel judged there (1 Sam. 7:16), and after Solomon died and the kingdom was divided, it became the rival sanctuary of Jerusalem for the people of the northern kingdom. The royal family worshiped there, and it was called *"the king's sanctuary"* (Amos 7:13).

We stand with Amos outside the sanctuary watching the gathered crowd prepare to enter. At any moment we expect the priest to come and call the people to worship with the traditional words of Psalm 95:6–7:

> O come, let us worship and bow down;
> Let us kneel before the Lord our Maker.
> For He is our God,
> And we are the people of His pasture,
> And the sheep of His hand.

Before the priest appears to give this call to worship, which Amos knew would be a travesty of contradiction to what he knew was going on in Israel's defection from knowledge of God and faithfulness to Him in social righteousness, the prophet boldly steps forth and with commanding presence gives a more honest and realistic call. *"Come to Bethel and transgress, at Gilgal multiply transgressions"* (4:4). Again Amos shocked and stunned his audience. He could not have used a more harsh term than *transgress* to describe what the people were planning to do in the sanctuary. The word *transgress (pāšaʿ)* means "to break with."[1] It is the same root used to describe the plot of Joseph's brothers to kill him (Gen. 50:17) or for rebellion. Amos uses the word here to jar the people with the fact that it is a sin to carry on with rites and rituals, ceremonies and sacrifices, when they have not obeyed Yahweh. The religious observances were totally separated from true worship of Him and obedience to Him. Nothing is more godless than worship that follows traditional procedures without an encounter with God Himself or any accountability to His commandments or obedience to His moral requirements.

306

The rituals for the festival were firmly set. Amos lists them with a tone of disdain because the true spiritual and moral quality of the nation belittles the significance of the rituals. Sacrifices were made every morning. Three days after arriving at the festival, tithes of harvest were to be made (v. 4). In violation of Leviticus 2:11 and 6:14–17, leaven was burned in the burnt offerings. Free will offerings beyond the tithe were pretentiously presented to call attention to the generosity of the giver rather than praise to Yahweh. The festivities of slaughtering animals, burnt offerings, attention-getting tithes, and self-serving free will offerings in the sanctuary had little to do with dedication of the pilgrims' lives to Yahweh. Without truly seeking Him, the traditional rituals actually became an outward sign of transgression, breaking away from Yahweh. "And you love it!" Amos shouts.

"But where is your love for Yahweh expressed in obedience to Him?" Amos implies.

Suddenly we are jarred out of our experience with Amos at Bethel and brought back to the realities of our own time. Surely there is no application of what we observed in that bizarre festival to our personal or corporate worship! But can we be so sure? Are there times when we pray our prayers with rote regularity when our hearts and lives are A.W.O.L. from serving God? We all have known times when our disobedience to God's revealed will makes our prayers empty and trite. And we have experienced the dichotomy between saying He is Lord and not following His guidance in ministry to people's needs. We humans have an immense ability to tolerate contradictions between our faith and our actions. It becomes a way of life. We live in two worlds: the faith we talk and sing about and the life we live.

The other day I met with a group of businesspeople. We discussed the things in our lives that make it difficult to be faithful and obedient to Christ. The last man to share cut to the core of the issue. "I have too many commitments competing with my ultimate commitment. I'm going in a hundred directions. I think about the Lord only in a crisis. And when I do, I'm afraid I've developed the fine art of evading His scrutiny of my life. I guess I fear really opening myself by asking how much that I'm doing is what He wants me to do. Oh, I still go to church, but I feel distant from the very Lord I am supposed to be worshiping."

A woman confessed the same problem in a different way. "What do you do with wandering attention? When I pray, I can't keep my mind on God for more than a few minutes. I drift off into all sorts of worries, fears, and fantasies. Even in worship at church, I'm there but I'm not really there. Strange thing—my mind wanders off to the very things I resist turning over to God."

Another woman presented a very different perspective. She and her husband have accumulated great wealth. "I've suddenly grown very weary of our endless round of social activities. I want my life to count for something. I want to connect my faith to my life and then do something to make a difference in the problems of our community." She has made and is making a great impact with her giving and her leadership in organized efforts of Christian social mission. I cannot help but wonder why she is more of an exception than the rule for many today.

When we take Amos seriously we must evaluate the worship life of the church. Often our traditions, ordered liturgies, cherished procedures, familiar words, and stained glass sanctuaries give us a religious feeling that might be a substitute for an authentic encounter with God. We meet a god below God and not the Holy God to whom we are accountable. True worship must expose our deepest personal needs to healing and the aching social ills of our community to a call to ministry. Without the context of reality, there is no cutting edge, no application, no radical obedience. The ebb and flow between worship and life keeps worship from being simply an emotional mood triggered by familiar procedures.

WORSHIPLESS LIVING

6 "Also I gave you cleanness of teeth in all your cities. And lack of bread in all your places; yet you have not returned to Me," says the Lord.

7 "I also withheld rain from you, when there were still three months to the harvest. I made it rain on one city, I withheld rain from another city. One part was rained upon, and where it did not rain the part withered.

8 "So two or three cities wandered to another city to drink water, but they were not satisfied; yet you have not returned to Me," says the Lord.

9 "I blasted you with blight and mildew. When your garden increased, your vineyards, your fig trees, and your olive trees, the locust devoured them; yet you have not returned to Me," says the Lord.

10 "I sent among you a plague after the manner of Egypt; your young men I killed with a sword, along with your captive horses; I made the stench of your camps come up into your nostrils; yet you have not returned to Me," says the Lord.

11 "I overthrew some of you, as God overthrew Sodom and Gomorrah, and you were like a firebrand plucked from the burning; yet you have not returned to Me," says the Lord.

12 "Therefore thus will I do to you, O Israel; and because I will do this to you, prepare to meet your God, O Israel!"

13 For behold, He who forms mountains, and creates the wind, who declares to man what his thought is, and makes the morning darkness, who treads the high places of the earth—the Lord God of hosts is His name.

Amos 4:6–13

Up to this point in this unit, Amos has confronted Israel's godless worship. Now in a message that spans verses 6 through 13, he addresses worshipless living. The basic theme is that the people urgently needed to return to God and prepare to meet Him. They refused to see the connection of recent calamities to Yahweh's call to return to Him. The tragedies should have been a megaphone call to truly worship and serve the Lord again. In essence, Amos's prophetic message here is, "What will it take to wake you up? What disaster will it take for you to see the vital connection between what has happened and Yahweh's judgment on you?" Yahweh's text, which He repeats five times for emphasis and illustrates with vivid examples, is, *"Yet you have not returned to Me."* Let's briefly look at each of these five national calamities:

1. Verse 6: There had been a famine in the land. *"Cleanness of teeth"* means hunger. A lack of bread had hit *"all your places."* No particular famine is focused, but a general period of hard times. These times should have motivated Israel to return to (*šûb ʿad*) the Lord.

Stuart points out that the expression *šûb ʿad* is a synonym for *šûb ʾel*, "a standard expression for turning from idolatry and polytheism (Deut. 4:28) to orthodox faithfulness to Yahweh."[2]

2. Verses 7–8: Widespread and prolonged drought produced no more repentance than the famine. The cities that received rain did not

return to the Lord with gratitude, while those who had a drought did not connect it to Yahweh's judgment. The people had become insensitive to Yahweh's control of nature and their lives.

3. Verse 9: A blight from a hot east wind dried up the grain prematurely and caused the green grain to turn brown because of the invasion of worms. *"Blight* (or scorching) *and mildew"* are mentioned as part of the covenant warnings and invitation to repentance in Deuteronomy 28. The people did not heed the signs of the blight or of the attack of the locust on the vineyards, fig trees, and olive trees. Still they did not repent and return to Yahweh.

4. Verse 10: Israel also should have seen the dire warning of plagues and war. Both were clearly mentioned as covenant curses against those who break the covenant (Deut. 28:49–57). The plague *"after the manner of Egypt"* may refer to the exodus plagues sent on Egypt to force the Pharaoh to release the Israelites. *Plague* is also used in parallelism with *sword*. Here the young men of Israel, the elite troops, probably the chariot corps, fell by the sword along with their horses. The stench of the decay reached the nostrils of the people, but still they did not repent and return to the Lord.

5. Verse 11: In warfare some of the cities of Israel were overthrown like Sodom and Gomorrah (Gen. 19). However, like a log pulled away from a fire, the nation had been saved. And yet, these interventions of Yahweh did not change their stubborn infidelity to Him.

These five illustrations of Yahweh's judgment in the past prepare for the confrontation of verse 12. All that the Lord has been doing have been warnings. They have not produced repentance, and now, instead of a few miseries affecting only a few people, Yahweh will unleash full punishment of the whole nation. Therefore, *"Prepare to meet your God, O Israel!"* (4:12). If Israel will not meet God with humble repentance, she will meet Him in judgment. I think this was still a further appeal for the people to return to Him, like the call, *"Seek Me and live"* (5:4).

Verse 13 follows with a magnificent self-disclosure of Yahweh's might and majesty. He is in control of everyone and all things. He shapes the mountains, creates the spirit of man (*rûaḥ*, "wind," also "spirit, breath"), reveals His thoughts ("his plan," *śēḥô*), His will, and His law. Yahweh asserts His power above the false gods of the Baal cults. He alone can control the revolution of the earth around the sun for He is sovereign of the whole universe. The *"high places of the earth"* refer to claims made for Baal Shamem who was touted as taking the high places of the land. Yahweh, not a diminutive Canaanite false god, is Lord over all creation. *"The Lord God of hosts is His name."* Yahweh is not one god in the pantheon of syncretistic religion, but the only God of heaven and earth. When Israel lost the sense of awe and wonder of true worship, she began to lose everything else.

NOTHING HAPPENS WITHOUT GOD'S PERMISSION

This unit of Amos brings us again into direct confrontation with the God of the Bible. Nothing happens without His permission. He is not a helpless God who sits wringing His hands watching the affairs of the world. Nor is He impotent against the forces of evil or human rebellion. His ultimate will is that we know, love, and serve Him. The only way to live at peace with Him is to worship Him in the ups and downs, the joys and difficulties, the delights and the discouragements of life. God will never give us more than we can take while trusting in His strength. He will use our problems to help us grow as persons. When we become arrogant, He will break our pride by what we go through. Life's troubles can function as signpost warnings. Worshiping the Lord in all things opens us to receive judgment when that is needed. Consistent fellowship with the Lord helps us know what He is seeking to give us in the ever-changing drama of our lives. Daily, moment by moment, God-centered worship makes for worshipful living. God is constantly calling us to worship Him. This requires a contrite spirit and truthfulness about our lives. "The hour is coming, and now is, when the true worshipers will worship the Father in spirit and truth; for the Father is seeking such to worship Him" (John 4:23).

NOTES

1. Wolff, *Joel and Amos,* 218–219.
2. Stuart, *Hosea–Jonah,* 338.

CHAPTER FIVE

Requiem and the Remnant

Amos 5:1–17

5:1 Hear this word which I take up against you, a lamentation, O house of Israel:

2 The virgin of Israel has fallen; she will rise no more. She lies forsaken on her land; there is no one to raise her up.

3 For thus says the Lord God: "The city that goes out by a thousand shall have a hundred left, and that which goes out by a hundred shall have ten left to the house of Israel."

4 For thus says the Lord to the house of Israel: "Seek Me and live;

5 "but do not seek Bethel, nor enter Gilgal, nor pass over to Beersheba; for Gilgal shall surely go into captivity, and Bethel shall come to nothing.

6 "Seek the Lord and live, lest He break out like fire in the house of Joseph. and devour it, with no one to quench it in Bethel—

7 "you who turn justice to wormwood, and lay righteousness to rest in the earth!"

8 He made the Pleiades and Orion; He turns the shadow of death into morning and makes the day dark as night; He calls for the waters of the sea and pours them out on the face of the earth; the Lord is His name.

9 He rains ruin upon the strong, so that fury comes upon the fortress.

10 They hate the one who rebukes in the gate, and they abhor the one who speaks uprightly.

11 Therefore, because you tread down the poor and take grain taxes from him, though you have built houses of hewn stone, yet you shall not dwell in them;

you have planted pleasant vineyards, but you shall not drink wine from them.

12 For I know your manifold transgressions and your mighty sins. Afflicting the just and taking bribes; diverting the poor from justice at the gate.

13 Therefore the prudent keep silent at that time, for it is an evil time.

14 Seek good and not evil, that you may live; so the Lord God of hosts will be with you, as you have spoken.

15 Hate evil, love good; establish justice in the gate. It may be that the Lord God of hosts will be gracious to the remnant of Joseph.

16 Therefore the Lord God of hosts, the Lord, says this: "There shall be wailing in all streets, and they shall say in all the highways, 'Alas! Alas!' They shall call the farmer to mourning, and skillful lamenters to wailing.

17 "In all vineyards there shall be wailing, for I will pass through you," says the Lord.

Amos 5:1-17

Amos turned the festival at Bethel into a wake for a dead nation. Though his funeral address (5:1-17) was given three decades before the actual death of Israel, he speaks of the nation as if the final demise had taken place. And yet, in the midst of his verbal requiem there flashes hope for a remnant that will survive. Amos's prophecy alternates between the helplessness of that nation to avoid the end of the nation and the hope of a remnant being part of a new beginning. Israel may be finished, but God is not finished with His people.

THE DEATH OF THE NATION

Amos begins by announcing what he is going to say. His message will be a lament or elegy, *qînâ*, for Israel. A funeral sermon! Like his previous attention-arresting opening lines of previous oracles, he once again startles and jars his audience. Verse 1 is a call to announce a recent death. Then suddenly, the name of who has died is disclosed. The house of Israel! The audience is addressed as the corpse over whom the lament is to be given.

313

A similar method was used by a Highland Scots pastor who preached a funeral sermon for his church as his Sunday morning message. Without mentioning the name of the church, he extensively described why and how the church had died. At the end of his sermon he said, "The church of which I have been speaking is this church! And death will surely come unless we ask the Good Lord to revive us and give us a new beginning." The pastor's text was from Revelation 3:1, "You have a name that you are alive, but you are dead."

Amos held out no such hope for the revival of Israel as a nation. In verse two he speaks of Israel, once the virgin bride of Yahweh, as fallen; she will not rise as a national power again. She is forsaken. No one will be able to resuscitate the dead nation.

THE HOPE OF THE REMNANT

There will be no hope except for a small remnant that will be saved. Amos shifts into the messenger speech of prophesy in verse 3 to give this thin ray of hope. *"The city that goes out by a thousand shall have a hundred left, and that which goes out by a hundred shall have ten left to the house of Israel."* Those who go out are the people who will not survive the destruction at the end. Only a tenth will be saved to be part of the remnant.

In verse 4 Yahweh announces the only way to be part of that remnant. *"Seek Me and live"* has the ring of a final call to repentance and return to the Lord. The call is followed by a clear warning that He would not be found in the syncretistic shrines of Israel. If Amos gave this word from the Lord at Bethel, we can imagine the stir caused by the words, *"Do not seek [Me at] Bethel."* Yahweh was not there in the pretentious rituals, the polytheism, and the apostasy. Nor were the people to enter Gilgal in search for Yahweh. The very site that reminded the people of their inheritance of the promised land would be destroyed by an invader and the altar carried off as part of the victor's booty. Beersheba, once hallowed as the worship place of Abraham, Isaac, Jacob, and Joseph, was a place of assurance of the companionship of God. It, too, had fallen into the disgrace of apostasy. "Don't go to Beersheba looking for Me," Yahweh says.

The call to seek the Lord and not the degraded worship at the national shrines is reiterated in verse 6. Truly seeking the Lord was the only hope of surviving the devouring fire of the wrath of Yahweh that would destroy all of Israel including the shrine at Bethel.

Amos interrupts his prophetic announcement of the word of Yahweh to include a hymn sung at the festivals and familiar to his audience. He uses the hymn to establish the authority and power of the One for whom he is speaking. The hymn declares that Yahweh created the stars (Pleiades and Orion) and has power over life and death (5:8).

NO EULOGY

Amos then contrasts the glory of Yahweh with the sinfulness of His people (vv. 10-13). This is a strange twist for a funeral oration. Instead of dwelling on the laudable qualities of the deceased, Amos lists Israel's social unrighteousness. All the charges the prophet previously made are now exposed as the cause of the nation's death. The poor were exploited. They were taxed for the aggrandizement of the wealthy and powerful. It was an evil time of bribery and the passing of hush money for even the prudent to keep silent about the injustice. The rich who profited at the expense of the poor and oppressed built stone houses and planted desirable vineyards. But with the death of the nation, these unrighteous people will not live in their houses or drink of the wine from their vineyards.

After the panic-producing declaration, Amos again turns to the hope of a remnant surviving the destruction of the nation. Now the admonition is described differently to emphasize that seeking the Lord means departing from social evil. *"Seek good and not evil"* (v. 14). Seeking God and practicing social righteousness are inseparable.

Verses 16-17 conclude Amos's funeral address with a grim picture of the wailing over the death of the nation. There will be wailing in all the streets. The grief will be so profound that there will not be enough professional wailers to express the grief. Even farmers from outside the cities will be called to add their voices to the multitude of anguished cries.

The final words are most terrifying of all. *"'For I will pass through you,' says the Lord"* (v. 17). He will be the angel of death Himself. There will not be a passover as in Egypt. Instead of being protected, the people will be destroyed. No imagery could be more alarming and denigrating to Amos's proud listeners.

APPLICATION

Amos's funeral address has great preaching and teaching value for the Christian communicator. It vividly describes our condition prior to Christ, it sounds a call for repentance, and it gives us the authentic test of regeneration.

1. Like Israel of old, our human condition prior to conversion is death. We are the spiritually dead among the living. Paul described this to the Ephesians. "We were dead in trespasses" (Eph. 2:5).

2. Christ, the very life of God, came that we might have life. His whole message and ministry could be focused on the words, *"Seek Me and live"* (Amos 5:4). Through His death and resurrection and indwelling presence, He offers us abundant life now and eternal life forever. In response, we must repent, receive Him as Lord, and relinquish our own control. When Christ takes up residence in us, we truly come alive. We are resurrected out of the grave of sin. We are regenerated into new people, new creatures of the new creation.

3. The authentic test of our regeneration is that we *"seek good and not evil"* (5:14), we hate evil and love good and establish justice. Our righteousness is in Christ by faith. This is our liberating motivation for seeking righteousness in all our relationships and in society. The practice of righteousness is a sure sign that we have been born again. "He who practices righteousness is righteous, just as He is righteous" (1 John 3:7). Love is the litmus test. And that love is expressed by sharing our faith and working for social justice. The spiritual and physical needs of people become the passion of our lives.

CHAPTER SIX

No Place to Hide

Amos 5:18–27

Harry became a famous escape artist. He found that he could draw large crowds and eventually earn fame and fortune by his feats of escape.

He began with handcuffs, then straight jackets, then tightly nailed boxes, and finally vaults made by the best safe manufacturers in the world. Only after Harry Houdini's death in 1926 were his secrets disclosed by his assistants. Houdini's slogan was, "I only got into situations I could control and from which I could escape."

Most of us have a Houdini in our souls—the escape artist who at times seeks to escape from God. The Houdini Christian is one who looks like he or she is locked into commitment to God but always has an escape route.

ESCAPING A LION AND MEETING A BEAR

Amos spoke to Israel at a time when the people were seeking to escape God. As we have seen, they lacked evidence of justice and righteousness in their national life and in their daily living. They longed for the day of the Lord, thinking it would be an intervention of God to save them from their enemies. While trying to escape from the covenant claim of God on their national and personal lives, they took for granted the blessings of God. Amos warned them not to be so cocky about the day of the Lord.

> 18 Woe to you who desire the day of the Lord! For what good is the day of the Lord to you? It will be darkness, and not light.

19 It will be as though a man fled from a lion, and a
bear met him, or as though he went into the house,
leaned his hand on the wall, and a serpent bit him.
20 Is not the day of the Lord darkness, and not light?
Is it not very dark, with no brightness in it?

Amos 5:18–20

Yahweh was tracking Israel. The more the people tried to run from Him, the more they ran into Him. As they tried to escape from repentance for their personal and social unrighteousness, they would meet Him first as a lion. When they narrowly escaped that encounter and ran in another direction, they met him as a bear. Hosea uses the same images of a lion and a bear in Hosea 13:7–8. In Hosea the bear was one who had been denied her cubs, just as Yahweh was denied His people through their apostasy.

Amos adds a somber dimension to the pursuit by Yahweh. In the end, those who persistently ran from Him would be bitten by a serpent. The day of the Lord will be a day of accounting and judgment for the escape artists of Israel. But before that day of reckoning, Yahweh still pursued. "Seek God and live . . . do good and live!"

WHAT DOES THIS MEAN FOR US TODAY?

Again, we must ask the now familiar question of this commentary, "What does this mean to us?" The answer is, "Plenty! More than we might expect and probably more than we want." Few texts have as much to say *both* to the preacher/teacher and to the hearer.

Point one: We are all escape artists when it comes to God. Some of us have never really met Him and spend our lives trying to escape an encounter with Him. Others of us have met Him and yet want to avoid a complete surrender of our wills to Him. Still others of us have resisted the implications of really knowing Him. We fear the cost of being faithful and obedient disciples in our relationships and our responsibilities in the sores of suffering in our society. And then there are those of us who have heard a specific call to costly commitment and have been running away ever since.

We hear a lot about love/hate relationships. This passage of Amos confronts us with our love/escape complex when it comes to our relationship with God. We feel both the longing to know God and the fear of what His love will demand.

As a young boy, I huddled around the radio with my family to listen to the sportscaster give blow-by-blow accounts of the boxing matches of Joe E. Lewis. Some say he was the greatest boxer who ever lived. Late in the 1930s, he was challenged by Billy Kahn, a boxer from Pittsburgh. Kahn boxed by backing up and landing a punch at the most opportune time. His fellow boxers called him "the runner" because he would not stand and confront his opponent. Before Lewis's bout with Kahn, a sportswriter asked him if he would be able to beat Billy Kahn with Kahn's running technique. Lewis answered, "He can run, but he can't hide!"

The same is true for us. We can try to run from God, but we can't hide. Running from Him is like being in a hall of mirrors—everywhere we turn we see not our face but His!

NO PLACE TO HIDE

Point two: There is no place to hide. There is no escaping our inescapable God . . . no place to go where He will not be there waiting for us.

The psalmist experienced both the omnipotence and the omnipresence of God. He knew there was no place to hide from Him. He made the astounding discovery that the Lord of all creation knew Him personally. He also discovered that God pursued.

> O Lord, You have searched me and known me. You know my sitting down and my rising up; You understand my thought afar off. You comprehend my path and my lying down, and are acquainted with all my ways. For there is not a word on my tongue, but behold, O Lord, You know it altogether. You have hedged me behind and before, and laid Your hand upon me. Such knowledge is too wonderful for me; it is high, I cannot attain it. Where can I go from Your Spirit? Or where can I flee from Your presence? If I ascend into heaven, You are there; if I make my bed in hell, behold You are there. If I take the wings of the morning, and dwell in the uttermost parts of the sea, even there Your hand shall lead me, and Your right hand shall hold me. If I say, "Surely the darkness shall fall on me," even the night shall be light about me; indeed, the darkness shall not hide from You, but the night shines as the day; the darkness and the light are both alike to You.
>
> *Ps. 139:1–12*

Frances Thompson came to the same conclusion after a long run as a fugitive from God. He was raised in a Christian home but feared the cost of being a disciple of Christ. He studied for the priesthood, then medicine, flunking out of both because of laziness. The only thing he got out of his study of medicine was an addiction to narcotics. He would do anything to get his daily fix: hold horses, clean the dung off the streets, sell matches, or clean boots. And all the while, he was running from God.

However, Thompson had a hidden talent for putting his thoughts and feelings into poetry. One day, he sent off to a newspaper publisher one of his poems about God's pursuit of him. The publisher and his wife were so impressed that they began a search all over London for the anonymous poet—they had to find the genius who had written those lines. When they found him, they saw a man broken in body and spirit. He had no shirt under his rumpled coat. His worn shoes gave him little protection from the icy streets. He wore no gloves to protect his hands from the cold as he had written his lines. What he had written expressed his sense of the impossibility of escaping the inescapable God. Eventually, Frances Thompson became a Christian and is now recognized as one of the great poets of English literature. His poem, "The Hound of Heaven," has gained immortal status because it expresses the heart of every person who has run or is running from God.

> I fled Him, down the nights and down the days;
> I fled Him, down the arches of the years;
> I fled Him, down the labyrinthine ways
> Of my own mind; and in the mist of tears
> I hid from Him, and under running laughter.
> Up vistaed hopes I sped;
> And shot, precipitated,
> Adown Titanic glooms of chasmed fears,
> From those strong Feet that followed, followed after.
> But with unhurrying chase,
> And unperturbed pace,
> Deliberate speed, majestic instancy,
> They beat—and a Voice beat
> More instant than the Feet—
> "All things betray thee, who betrayest Me."[1]

The words, "all things betray thee, who betrayest Me," linger with uncomfortable impact. We meet God as lion and bear whenever we evade the demands of personal and social righteousness. Fleeing from the lion who confronts us with who we really are, we try to take refuge in religious activity. Sometimes what we do for God becomes our false god and an effort to escape Him. Then we meet the bear who tells us that nothing will work right without true righteousness. Helmut Thielicke once said, "Whoever lets God in only halfway is always the one who is cheated. He would be better off not to do it all." But God does not give up easily with the halfhearted. Just when we get settled into self-righteous complacency, we hear the demanding voice of the bear roaring through the prophet Amos from Bethel.

> 21 "I hate, I despise your feast days, and I do not savor your sacred assemblies.
> 22 "Though you offer Me burnt offerings and your grain offerings, I will not accept them, nor will I regard your fattened peace offerings.
> 23 "Take away from Me the noise of your songs, for I will not hear the melody of your stringed instruments.
> 24 "But let justice run down like water, and righteousness like a mighty stream.
> 25 "Did you offer Me sacrifices and offerings in the wilderness forty years, O house of Israel?
> 26 "You also carried Sikkuth your king and Chiun, your idols, the star of your gods, which you made for yourselves.
> 27 "Therefore I will send you into captivity beyond Damascus," says the Lord, whose name is the God of hosts.
>
> *Amos 5:21–27*

HIDING IN RELIGION

There is no more seemingly effective way to hide from God than in religion. When Amos came to Bethel, he called it for what it was — an evasion of righteousness. God was not impressed by the piping of pious songs and psalms while the people forgot their responsibilities to their fellow women and men, as they ground the poor into the mire and loaded the overburdened with misery. Burnt offerings that were to be an outward sign of total dedication to God were a religious mockery; peace offerings affirming fellowship with God were contradicted by the people's unwillingness to obey Him. What God wanted was inner righteousness, an inward moral commitment to do what He had declared was right. He demanded that this inward righteousness be expressed in justice, righteousness in action. And so, in the midst of Israel's covenant confidence that had led into complacency and complicity with social injustice, Yahweh roared, *"But let justice run down like water, and righteousness like a mighty stream"* (v. 24). Yahweh did not want a high mountain trickle or a little rivulet of righteousness and justice, but a rushing white-water river, running fast and pure.

And Yahweh wanted something more. He wanted Israel's worship cleansed of the pollution of foreign idols and false gods. Verse 26 identifies the gods of the Assyrians that the Israelites had added to the worship of Yahweh in an effort to pacify the potential invader. In that day, truce settlements were sealed by the dominant nation leaving behind images of its gods in the shrines of the subservient nation. Trying to buy time in her uneasy relationships with Assyria, Israel had placed at Bethel an image of Sikkuth, from the Assyrian tabernacle of Molach. Chiun, the star god of the Assyrians, was placed in Israel's constellation of gods along with Yahweh. And added to all that petulant polytheism was the ever present syncretism with Baal worship.

Now we can see why Yahweh was tracking down His people. What was happening in their lives and their society was directly related to their escape into false religion. The forms of their religion were keeping them from Him!

The same thing happens to us when we add our false gods to our worship of the Lord God. Our gods of success, affluence, materialism, popularity, political loyalties, and even our religious work compete for first place in our lives. Sometimes we even seek God's strength to continue our obligation to our secondary gods. Soon our lack of commitment to the Lord as our first love shows in our lack of love for others. That is when the Lord starts tracking us, meeting us at every turn of our fast-paced run from Him.

Life begins to fall apart in one setback after another. We go from pillar to post, failure to failure, difficulty to disappointment. We escape from one problem only to meet another. The lion and the bear confronting us with who we are! We thought we had closure with Him when we said we believed in Him, joined the church, and began acting religious. Like Houdini, we thought we had God in a box from which we could escape. We think we are finished with God, but He has only begun with us. He wants to remold our character, reshape our personalities, and reorder our priorities. Most of all He wants inner righteousness and outer justice. It is when we really see the demands God makes on His chosen people that we start running. We may stay in the same place, but our minds and hearts are running away. (We will have more to say about that in the commentary on Jonah.)

LOVED BY THE INESCAPABLE GOD

The fact that God meets us at the pass of every wrong path, every shrine to a false god, every misguided loyalty, and every expression of self-serving unrighteousness is really comforting. What if He did not care enough to pursue us; what if when we ran from God we were not caught?

T. S. Eliot wrote, "And at the end of all our exploring will be to arrive where we started and know the place for the first time."[2] And we will know something else. We will know that we are loved. Why else would God have dogged our steps, pursued us indefatigably? Life's greatest disappointment, the most monumental despair would be to think God would let us escape.

It is a sublime moment of truth with God that the metaphor of the lion, the bear, and the serpent is superseded with another image. Between us and the confrontive lion and the pursuing bear and the death-imposing serpent stand the Lamb. "Behold, the Lamb of God, who takes away the sin of the world!" And we look again at the faces of the lion and the bear and realize what we had not seen before. The face of the Lamb had always been there if we would only stop running long enough to see.

NOTES

1. Francis Thompson, "The Hound of Heaven," *The Poems of Francis Thompson* (London: Oxford University Press, 1960), 89.
2. T. S. Eliot, "Four Quartets," V, line 240.

CHAPTER SEVEN

A Judgment to Fit the Crime

Amos 6:1–14

We come now to the last segment of the second major section of Amos's prophecy. He has left the principal shrines of Israel and returned to Samaria. The last time he was in Samaria, he confronted the rich women of the establishment. In case we were tempted to think this was a chauvinist attack on women, we need to brace ourselves for what Amos says to their husbands. He speaks with decisive directness about their luxurious, self-indulgent, and irresponsible life-styles. Here is a picture of the rottenness at the core of Israel's leadership. The judgment of the exile would more than fit the crime.

> 6:1 Woe to you who are at ease in Zion, and trust in Mount Samaria, notable persons in the chief nation, to whom the house of Israel comes!
> 2 Go over to Calneh and see; and from there go to Hamath the great; then go down to Gath of the Philistines. Are you better than these kingdoms? Or is their territory greater than your territory?
> 3 Woe to you who put far off the day of doom, who cause the seat of violence to come near;
> 4 who lie on beds of ivory, stretch out on your couches, eat lambs from the flock and calves from the midst of the stall;
> 5 who sing idly to the sound of stringed instruments, and invent for yourselves musical instruments like David;
> 6 who drink wine from bowls, and anoint yourselves with the best ointments, but are not grieved for the affliction of Joseph.

7 Therefore they shall now go captive as the first of
the captives, and those who recline at banquets shall
be removed.

Amos 6:1-7

Amos never ceases to amaze us with his ability to catch the attention of his audience. Back in Samaria, he opens his message with a
woe to those who are at ease in Zion, Jerusalem. This appealed to the
national prejudice and rivalry of the leaders of Samaria against the
southern kingdom. Just about the moment they thought this fiery
prophet from Tekoa might not be so bad after all, Amos included
them in his woe and thrust his lance at these notable persons who
associated with Israel's monarchy either by family ties or by employment. They were the power brokers with the perks of power that
brought them authority, adulation, and the ability to fix and collect
taxes which they used for their own advantage. This power structure
was riding high, falsely secure in military power and victories over
Syria. People paid them obsequious attention, for nothing could happen without their approval. Amos came to them with an obsequy for
the impending death of the nation: *"Woe to you . . . who trust in
Samaria"* (6:1). The verb *trust (bāṭaḥ)* is used to expose the false optimism and sense of security and carefree arrogance of the leaders.
They were looking at themselves through their own clouded vision
and not the eyes of Yahweh, their God. Amos proclaimed to them
how the Lord of all nations saw the littleness of their assumed greatness.

Amos lumps Israel into a very unfavorable category of subjugated
city-states. Calneh and Hamath were Aramean city-states now under
Israel's power as major cities of conquered Syria. Judah controlled
Gath, one of the five principal cities of the Philistines. Now the
clincher rhetorical questions: *"Are you better than these kingdoms? Or is
their territory greater than your territory?"* (v. 2). The response of the
leaders probably was "Yes, of course!" Amos's response to his own
question is given in the rest of chapter 6. Israel will be invaded,
Samaria will be destroyed, and these proud leaders will be the first to
be carried off in an exile.

Verse 3 seems to be the prophet's response to the scoffing ridicule
and disbelief given by his audience to what seemed to them to be an
absurd comparison of Samaria to the subjugated city-states he cited.

325

Amos notices this and gives another woe in direct response. *"Woe to you who put far off the day of doom, who cause the seat of violence to come near."* Nādâ (piēl) means "to banish or cast out violently or hatefully." The leaders totally rejected Amos's prophecy. This lack of fear of oncoming doom allowed them to continue in their violence or abusive treatment of the poor and oppressed (5:12).

While they persisted in this mistreatment of the underprivileged, the leaders carried on their own lives of ease and affluence. Verses 4–6 paint the picture. They loll on beds of ivory. On these couches, they are sprawled out in a drunken stupor. Their diet is made up only of the tenderest meat from young lambs. *"Calves from the midst of the stall"* means veal meat from the calves kept in stalls for fattening. As they stuffed themselves with this gourmet food, the Samarian nobles noisily chanted their drinking songs with improvised musical instruments like zithers to add to the rollicking revelry. We assume that neither the instruments nor those who played them had the quality of David's instruments played by the gatekeepers in praise (1 Chron. 23:5). Wine is not even drunk with the refinement of goblets but straight from the bowls. Expensive ointments covered their soft bodies, the scents further exhilarating their senses.

But these senses were also dulled by the opulence. The notable leaders were not leaders at all. They grasped for political power but abdicated their responsibility as leaders. While they indulged themselves, the affliction (literally "ruin," šēber, cf. Lev. 26:13, 19, 26 for the same root in verbal form) of Joseph, Ephraim, caused them no grief or concern.

The leaders demanded preferential treatment and recognition. In verse 7, with his customary irony, Amos says that they will be recognized, indeed, by being the first to be led off as captives. They will be at the head of the defeat march into captivity.

True Leadership

Applying this passage to us prompts us to think about the awesome responsibility of leadership. A nation, church, or Christian movement can rise no higher than its leadership. Followers also seek the level of commitment of their leaders. They either rise to great heights or sink to terrible lows depending on the spiritual and moral quality of the leadership.

The despicable thing about the leaders of Samaria was not just their self-indulgent life-styles, but that they did not grieve for the affliction of their people. Their power could have been used to correct many of the causes of their suffering. The taxation system they imposed could have been relieved. They could have instituted programs to feed the hungry and to create work for the poor. They could have led the way for righteousness and justice in the land. But the apostasy and immorality in the nation was a reflection of their own antinomianism. Hosea later said, "like priest, like people." Amos would well have said, "Like leaders, like people."

Amos's description of the self-serving notables of Samaria contrasts with Jesus' requirements for leadership. His power for leadership is not squandered. It is given to those who will be servant-leaders. The Master was abundantly clear,

> You know that the rulers of the Gentiles lord it over them, and those who are great exercise authority over them. Yet it shall not be so among you; but whoever desires to become great among you, let him be your servant. And whoever desires to be first among you, let him be your slave—just as the Son of Man did not come to be served, but to serve, and to give His life a ransom for many.
>
> *Matt. 20:25–28*

Servant-leaders recognize they exist for their people's growth in greatness rather than their people existing to make them great. Too often in churches this gets turned around. Pastors sometimes act as if their churches belong to them and their congregations are to make them great. Rather, shepherds are to care for their sheep. Their safety and feeding is the shepherd's entrusted responsibility.

Early in my ministry a seasoned old saint asked me, "Would you rather be a great pastor or the pastor of a great congregation?" The question has been a good corrective through the years, especially in the heady atmosphere of the distorted "star" system of contemporary media ministry.

I will never forget a comment by a woman in a church I served years ago, "Ogilvie, we were here before you came, and we'll be here after you leave, and we'll follow your leadership with loyalty so long as we sense that you are following Christ. So lead us on to the next step of glory He has in store for us!" With her colorful way of putting things, this woman was right on all counts. I was there for their growth not my glory.

Reading the book of Amos at least once a year should be a required discipline for leaders of all kinds. It is a bracing reminder that leadership is by divine appointment and those He allows the privilege of positions of authority, He can also depose.

THE ROOT CAUSE

> 8 The Lord God has sworn by Himself, the Lord God of hosts says: "I abhor the pride of Jacob, and hate his palaces; therefore I will deliver up the city and all that is in it."
> 9 Then it shall come to pass, that if ten men remain in one house, they shall die.
> 10 And when a relative of the dead, with one who will burn the bodies, picks up the bodies to take them out of the house, he will say to one inside the house, "Are there any more with you?" Then someone will say, "None." And he will say, "Hold your tongue! For we dare not mention the name of the Lord."
> 11 For behold, the Lord gives a command: He will break the great house into bits, and the little house into pieces.
> 12 Do horses run on rocks? Does one plow there with oxen? Yet you have turned justice into gall, and the fruit of righteousness into wormwood,
> 13 you who rejoice over Lo Debar, who say, "Have we not taken Karnaim for ourselves by our own strength?"
> 14 "But behold, I will raise up a nation against you, O house of Israel," says the Lord God of hosts; "And they will afflict you from the entrance of Hamath to the Valley of the Arabah."
>
> *Amos 6:8–14*

Amos now moves from his own analysis of Israel's problem to deliver the words of the Lord about the real root of the evil among His people. Yahweh swears by Himself, for there is no higher authority.

He swears by His life, without which nothing can exist. He tells the people that the real cause of the problem is pride. *"I abhor the pride of Jacob."* *Jacob* here means the whole of Israel. It was the pride of the people manifested in arrogance that caused all of the other sins. Like a deadly cancer, pride ate away the soul of God's people. Pride motivated their defection from Him. In pride they put their confidence in other gods, military might, and the strongholds of Samaria. The Lord hates the palaces of the city because they are material signs of Israel's swaggering self-confidence. And this unacknowledged and unconfessed pride is the cause of Yahweh's abandonment of the people to the hands of an enemy He will use as the agent of His punishment.

Any great tragedy is best explained in how it effects one family. Amos does that (vv. 9–10) by showing how a particular family will go through the ordeal of the siege and invasion of the city. All the men in the house die. A kinsman (the Hebrew is "uncle"), will come to remove the bodies. He will ask a person still alive in the house if there are any others left alive. The answer is, "None." Another person overhearing the conversation will say, "Silence! For we dare not mention the name of the Lord." *Silence, hās,* was a word spoken at the approach of the Lord (Hab. 2:20; Zeph. 1:7; Zech. 2:13). The warning against speaking the name of the Lord is for the people to know that it is Yahweh who punished them, not just an invading army. This will be the awesome realization. They will not be able to escape Yahweh's judgment by blaming an enemy nation. The Lord will punish, and only He can forgive.

And the stark reality of Israel's pride is that the rich who live in great houses and the poor who live in little houses will all suffer alike (v. 11). All because of Israel's prideful denial of God's justice and righteousness. In so doing the people have contradicted the divine order of life. Amos points to their foolishness with two seemingly absurd questions in verse 12. Reading *babbāqār yām* for *babbĕqārîm,* the rhetorical questions are, *"Do horses run on rocks?"* *"Does one plow the sea with oxen?"* (RSV). The obvious answer to such foolish questions is, "No!" In the same way, it is utter folly and obdurate stupidity to go against what God has commanded. And yet that is exactly what Israel has done in substituting gall and bitterness for righteousness and wormwood, poison for justice. The people deranged God's order and went contrary to His design for humankind. If pride leads to

329

arrogance . . . stupidity is not far behind. In essence, Amos is saying that to deny righteousness and justice is like denying the law of gravity by jumping off a cliff.

Arrogance was also expressed in not giving God glory for military victories that He caused to prosper (v. 13). Two towns under Syrian rule were taken by Israel in a campaign by Jeroboam II. Lo Debar was in Gilead, about three miles east of the Jordan and twelve miles south of the Sea of Galilee. Karnaim was north and east in Bashan. We wonder why Amos selected these towns. Some commentators suggest that he was playing on the meaning of the names, lō᾿dābār implying "Nothing," and qarnāyim meaning "horns." Perhaps Amos was saying, "Your strength has been for nothing." What is certain is that the prophet was saying that Israel's pride in previous military victories will not help in the forthcoming invasion.

Verse 14 completes the ironic twist at the end of this section. Israel is proud of her military expansion. It happened just as the prophet Jonah had prophesied (2 Kings 14:25) from "the entrance of Hamath to the Sea of Arabah." Lebo-Hamath represented Israel's northern boundary and the Wadi Arabah at the south end of the Dead Sea the southern boundary.

These are exactly the extent that the invasion and occupation of the enemy will cover. Israel's entire territory will be captured in a complete defeat. And again, Yahweh will be behind it all. *"Behold, I will raise up a nation against you."* Israel functioned as if Yahweh was no longer in charge of her life. Her proud refusal to practice the basics of righteousness and justice, her rebellion, and her growing apostasy said she no longer took Him seriously. But Yahweh could not be set aside. Within about thirty years, Israel fell. Samaria was destroyed. Boastful arrogance was changed into baneful anguish.

Blessed is the nation whose God is the Lord, but woe be to the nation that substitutes pride for grateful praise. Or any person, church, or group today!

CHAPTER EIGHT

Visions That Demand a Response

Amos 7:1–17

The third and final section of the book of Amos, spanning the last three chapters, contains five visions and five promises. The five visions and the prophet's encounter with the Lord about them have an obvious and ominous progression. They more from grace, to Israel's rejection of that grace, to judgment, and then to punishment (Amos 7:1–9:10). Then the last five verses give the Lord's promises of hope for the restoration of His people.

The visions can provide the basis of one message or class session or can be presented as a series. I have done it both ways. When using the series approach, I have found it effective to do the first two visions as a unit, and each of the last three as separate units. Whatever the method, it is important to stress the flow of Amos's dynamic interaction with the Lord about Israel and the consequences of her refusal to repent and to accept His forgiveness. The visions are living proof of Amos's conviction that *"Surely the Lord God does nothing, unless He reveals His secret to His servants the prophets"* (Amos 3:7). These visions were given to Amos over the brief period he prophesied in Israel. Some of them became the content of messages. Sadly, the first two got no response, and the third received a violent response. The last two were proclaimed to deaf ears.

In the visions and the Lord's interpretations to Amos, we behold a mighty God of righteousness who is unable to wink at unrighteousness. He is willing to reverse His punishment because His prophet shares His compassion for His people, longing for them to repent and accept His grace. In the end He reluctantly metes out the necessary judgment. And after the visions, we sense that the Lord can hardly wait to reveal to His prophet that though Israel as the prophet knew

her was finished, He was not finished with her. The Lord always has a
plan for finally bringing the best out of the worst we have done.

GOD CHANGES HIS MIND

> 7:1 Thus the Lord God showed me: Behold, He
> formed locust swarms at the beginning of the late crop;
> indeed it was the late crop after the king's mowings.
> 2 And so it was, when they had finished eating the
> grass of the land, that I said: "O Lord God, forgive, I
> pray! Oh, that Jacob may stand, for he is small!"
> 3 So the Lord relented concerning this. "It shall not
> be," said the Lord.
> 4 Thus the Lord God showed me: Behold, the Lord
> God called for conflict by fire, and it consumed the
> great deep and devoured the territory.
> 5 Then I said: "O Lord God, cease, I pray! Oh, that
> Jacob may stand, for he is small!"
> 6 So the Lord relented concerning this. "This also
> shall not be," said the Lord God.
>
> *Amos 7:1–6*

Amos's first two visions and the prophet's prayer to the Lord about
them brought him to an awesome discovery. The Lord can change His
mind!

In the first vision, the Lord shows Amos the plague of locusts He is
preparing in punishment for Israel's apostasy and unrighteousness. It
is to be in the late spring after the first crop had been harvested. Since
the first harvest was in, the plague of the locust would not mean a
total devastation and complete famine. The full wrath of Yahweh was
not being unleashed. He was giving Israel a warning of what would
come unless the people repented.

In Amos's intercessory prayer to Yahweh, we see another dimension of the prophet. We feel his compassion and tenderness. He is
profoundly moved by what might happen to Israel. *"O Lord God, forgive, I pray! Oh, that Jacob may stand, for he is small!"* (7:2). Don't miss
the pathos, the heartrending anguish of that urgent intercession. And
most of all, don't miss Yahweh's response. He relented, changed His
mind, was converted from His original just punishment.

The next vision that prompted Amos's further intercession is of a fire of judgment on Israel. It is a sweeping conflagration of the land, a fire that would be so devouring that it *"consumed the great deep"* (v. 4). It would be inextinguishable. That means a fire that even water cannot put out. It would happen in midsummer when the fields were dry and would burn like a wildfire across all of Israel.

Once again Amos cries out to the Lord for merciful forgiveness. The words of the prophet's prayer are similar to those in response to the first vision. A second time the Lord relents and changes His mind.

Imagine the excitement in Amos's voice when he told Israel about these visions. Scholars have questioned whether these visions were really shared with the people or were simply pages from his diary. We know he retold the third vision about the plumb line. Why not the warnings of the first two and the monumental good news of another chance? News about God changing His mind would be hard to keep. It should have brought a nationwide repentance and a return to Yahweh. But the people's souls were calloused with pride. It was an evil time (Amos 5:13).

We pause to reflect about both the power of intercessory prayer and the forgiveness of God. In his fellowship with God, Amos became an agent of asking for what God wanted to give. God did not desire the destruction of His people. He consistently sought another way. God's change of mind does not indicate that He vacillates. He would not have put it into Amos's heart to ask for forgiveness for Israel if that had not been His greater desire all along.

Intercession for others is an expression of profound trust in God and love for them. We long to bring them and God together again. But effective intercessory prayer requires listening to God to know how to pray. After adoration, confession, and thanksgiving in our prayers, the next step is to spread out before the Lord the need of others. Then it is time to be quiet so He can clarify what He wants to give or do. After that, we can intercede boldly.

Even then, however, we have no assurance that people will want what God wants for them. And He will never cross the picket line of the will. If people do not want what He wills for them, He will not negate their freedom to choose not to be loved. Frightening, yes. But thank God for those who do respond.

Amos's prayer, *"O Lord God, forgive!"* was prayed centuries later by Christ on the cross. Then the Savior did what Amos could not do. He became the sacrifice in answer to His own prayer. The cosmic atonement of Calvary was the result. And now the suffering Savior is the living, reigning Lord who guides our prayers and intercedes on our behalf. We look back at Amos prior to the new dispensation and gratefully realize what an assurance it is to live on this side of Calvary and Pentecost. Only that makes it possible to see ourselves and others around us in the proud eighth century B.C. Israelites and know that for the same sins, if we will repent, forgiveness will be given. Amos's next vision helps us to see what may need to be confessed.

CROOKED SAINTS

7 Thus He showed me: Behold, the Lord stood on a wall made with a plumb line, with a plumb line in His hand.

8 And the Lord said to me, "Amos, what do you see?" And I said, "A plumb line." Then the Lord said: "Behold, I am setting a plumb line in the midst of My people Israel; I will not pass by them anymore.

9 "The high places of Isaac shall be desolate, and the sanctuaries of Israel shall be laid waste. I will rise with the sword against the house of Jeroboam."

Amos 7:7–9

The drawing of an ancient Egyptian plumb line (see next page) helps us to envision the kind Amos saw in his visions. He would have been familiar with this type of plumb line from his observation of masons at work. This drawing is based on an Egyptian original. Two ledges of wood were joined, one above the other, at right angles to a plank. The line was attached to the top of the plank and passed through a hole in the upper ledge. If the line touched the edge of the lower ledge when stretched taut by the weight of the plumb, the wall was properly built "in plumb." The plumb line was in use in Egypt as a builder's tool as early as the first half of the third millennium B.C. Reproduced in the other drawing are plumb weights from the time of the Twelfth Dynasty in Egypt (20th–18th century B.C.). Something like these plumbs were in use in Amos's day. The only refinement was that, following the Iron Age, the weights were made of metal.

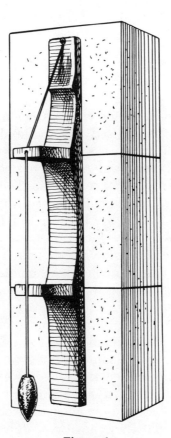

Figure 1

Adapted from *Views of the Biblical World: 3 Later Prophets*,
© 1960 by the International Publishing Company Ltd., Jerusalem.

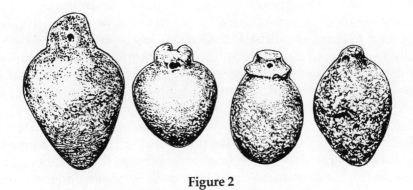

Figure 2

Adapted from *Views of the Biblical World: 3 Later Prophets*,
© 1960 by the International Publishing Company Ltd., Jerusalem.

Amos's vision was of the Lord standing on a wall that had been made with a plumb line. If the plumb line was anything like the ancient Egyptian one pictured in this drawing, then it was probably placed against the wall at the top where Amos saw the Lord standing. The plumb line was being used to test the alignment of the wall perpendicular to the horizon.

In the vision, the Lord asked Amos what he saw. The prophet's response was, *"A plumb line."* Then the Lord's words were decisive, *"Behold, I am setting a plumb line in the midst of My people Israel; I will not pass by them anymore"* (7:8). Why? Because Israel was out of plumb. It was not perpendicular to the horizon of the Lord's covenant and commandment. The wall of Israel was not straight according to righteousness and justice. The symbolism was pointed. Israel was leaning so far out of the plumb of God's will that the "wall" was dangerous. It must be destroyed for safety.

I have entitled this section of our commentary "Crooked Saints," purposely creating a double entendre to get at the deeper meaning of this vision of Israel . . . and of some churches and Christians today. A saint is a person who is chosen and called by God to be His person. *Saint* means "holy, belonging to God." But saints can also be crooked, out of plumb, dangerously leaning away from being perpendicular to the horizon of God's will. They can also be downright crooked in the usual meaning of dishonest, and still be saints. But not without the Lord's plumb line being lowered.

Sometimes at the end of a radio or television drama an announcer will say, "Any resemblance to persons living or dead is purely coincidental." My words introducing a message on the plumb line and crooked saints would be, "Any resemblance to persons in eighth-century B.C. Israel or Christians today is clearly intended!" *Crooked* really means "not straight; leaning; out of plumb, or not straightforward in conduct, tricky, dishonest irregular." So a crooked saint is someone who belongs to God but whose life is inconsistent with his or her beliefs. That takes in just about all of us.

Every day, every moment, in each situation and in every relationship God stands by the wall with a plumb line in His hand; and every day He notes any divergence from plumb, from the straight. Is the divergence getting worse? When is the wall of our life dangerous for others?

Search me, O God, my actions try
and let my life appear
As seen by Your all searching eye
to mine, my ways make clear.

The first note of the kingdom of God is righteousness. How do our walls stand by that plumb line? Are they in line or off the straight, out of the perpendicular. We need to see what we are, what we could be, and realize that we need not stay the way we are.

The plumb line of God exposes the leaning of dichotomy between being blessed and being a blessing, between outward worship of God and true knowledge of God, between our faith and our works, and between being holy and holy living.

God set a living, ever-present plumb line in history in the Incarnation. Christ is our plumb line. And the walls of our lives are constantly being measured by Him. He is both the Chief Cornerstone and the One who measures us by His plumb line of absolute love, forgiveness, service, purity, and honesty. The good news is that He is the Master Builder of our character and not only shows us what is out of plumb but helps us straighten the wall. We do not have to remain as crooked saints. But sometimes we refuse to admit our wall is crooked.

I have often wondered if the reason that God decided not to pass by Israel again was that the thing He found most out of plumb was the people's lack of response to the first two visions. They would not repent when He offered to relent. The worst thing ever to be out of plumb for a saint is the unwillingness to accept forgiveness. That pride, coupled with the refusal to return to righteousness and justice, brought forth announcement that the wall of Israel would be destroyed.

SEALING OF THE OPPOSITION

10 Then Amaziah the priest of Bethel sent to Jeroboam king of Israel, saying, "Amos has conspired against you in the midst of the house of Israel. The land is not able to bear all his words.

11 "For thus Amos has said: 'Jeroboam shall die by the sword, and Israel shall surely be led away captive from their own land.'"

12 Then Amaziah said to Amos: "Go, you seer! Flee
to the land of Judah. There eat bread, and there
prophesy.

13 But never again prophesy at Bethel, for it is the
king's sanctuary, and it is the royal residence."

14 Then Amos answered, and said to Amaziah: "I
was no prophet, nor was I a son of a prophet, but I was
a sheepbreeder and a tender of sycamore fruit.

15 "Then the Lord took me as I followed the flock,
and the Lord said to me, 'Go, prophesy to My people
Israel.'

16 "Now therefore, hear the word of the Lord: You
say, 'Do not prophesy against Israel, and do not spout
against the house of Isaac.'

17 "Therefore thus says the Lord: 'Your wife shall be
a harlot in the city; your sons and daughters shall fall
by the sword; your land shall be divided by survey
line; you shall die in a defiled land; and Israel shall
surely be led away captive from his own land.'"

Amos 7:10–17

When Amos told Israel about the vision of the plumb line and
especially about the implications for the destruction of the sanctuaries
and the sword against King Jeroboam II, the prophet's opposition was
sealed in determination to get rid of him. Amaziah, the high priest,
had been waiting for his moment. The prophet had gone too far this
time. He not only had threatened the high priest's position at Bethel,
the king's sanctuary, but had made a treasonous threat against the
king. Never mind that the prophet claimed to be speaking the word of
the Lord. Strange. Of all the people in Israel who should have been
alarmed by a direct word from Yahweh, it should have been the head
of the religious establishment. But then, down through history
religious leaders from popes to pastors have sometimes been the
least responsive to revival or reform—these threaten their vested interests.

Amaziah was quick to get word to Jeroboam II about the fiery
prophet from Judah and his judgment against the king. Note how he
twisted Amos's announcement of the Lord's words that He would
rise with the sword against the house of Jeroboam. That could mean
Jeroboam's court or his posterity in years to come (Israel's final king
Hoshea was, indeed, of the lineage of Jeroboam II). But Amaziah's

carefully reworded message to the king was, *"Jeroboam shall die by the sword, and Israel shall surely be led away captive from their own land"* (7:11). Amazing how we can misconstrue things when we want a desired response.

We are not told whether Amaziah's inflammatory message earned him an audience with the king. What we do know is that the high priest of Israel's polluted religion confronted Amos with authority as if he spoke for the crown. *"Go, you seer! Flee to the land of Judah. There eat bread, and there prophesy. But never again prophesy at Bethel, for it is the king's sanctuary, and it is the royal residence"* (7:12-13). In other words: "Go back to where you belong, you foreigner! Let the people of Judah support you as one of their professional prophets, but don't ever appear at Bethel again with your prophecies. Be careful, Bethel is the king's sanctuary, and he's liable to be there to deal with you himself." Strong words from a power-hungry priest who did not know Yahweh.

But Amaziah met his match in Amos. The prophet was not only a good communicator but an excellent debater. He immediately took the wind out of puffed-up Amaziah. One by one, Amos deflated the priest's accusations. He said he never had claimed to be a professional prophet. What he had claimed was that the Lord "took" him, grasped him, and conscripted him to prophesy in Israel. He was there by Yahweh's authority, not his own. Then, right there, eyeball to eyeball with Amaziah, Amos began to prophesy.

Amaziah had tried to silence Amos with ridicule and fear. Amaziah's name meant "The Lord is strong." And yet the priest had done everything he could to weaken the Lord's cause in Israel. Deluded with syncretism and polytheism, he polluted Israel's faith. Amaziah did not want God's truth and demands for righteousness proclaimed in Israel. What he had not counted on was a word from Yahweh Himself. And what a scathing word it was!

After the forthcoming defeat of Israel and the destruction of Bethel, Amos said, Amaziah would be sent into exile. His wife, left with no resources to continue the sumptuous lifestyle he had provided, would fall into prostitution. The priest's sons and daughters would be killed during the invasion, and he would languish in the captor's land (v. 17). Not a pretty picture. It fits with Amos's previous prophecy that Israel's leaders would be the first in the defeat march of exiles out of their own land.

THE AMAZIAH COMPLEX

We all know people with an Amaziah complex. The complex is made up of a combination of control, defensiveness, and pride. People who have this complex are master manipulators and power brokers and will use people against one another to get their own way. Many of those who suffer from this spiritual malady are religious but do not know God or have a deep communion with Him. They usually say they believe in Him, but they resist His claims on their lives. And when the demands of righteousness are proclaimed, they can cheer if it does not invade their own priorities. There are always a few Amaziahs in most churches. Often, they seek positions of leadership.

But before we begin to single them out, we need to get in touch with the ways the complex may have invaded our own psyches. A good test is to question how we might have responded to Amos's visions, especially the plumb line. The only sure antidote to the Amaziah complex is to let the plumb line fall on our lives every day in honest, open prayer. Then our cry will be, "Lord, forgive!" That is the one thing Amaziah would not do; and the one thing we will never outgrow. We are called to be saints in plumb with a new commitment to pray for opportunities to practice our gift of righteousness. As Elizabeth Barrett Browning said, it is a "gift with a gauntlet in it."

CHAPTER NINE

When Hypocrisy Becomes a Habit

Amos 8:1–14

Amos's visions follow the seasons of the year. The vision of the locust depicted late spring, and the vision of the conflagration was set in summer. The third vision of the plumb line came soon after, measuring, in addition to Israel's overall condition, the lack of repentance in response to the Lord's warnings and willingness to relent of His just punishment of His people. The account of Amaziah's efforts to get rid of Amos illustrated just how out of plumb Israel was leaning. That the high priest of the land wanted to silence the voice of God through the prophet shows the extent of the nation's apostasy and rebellion.

Now the fourth vision of the basket of ripened fruit points to early fall, late August or early September. The purpose of the vision is to show that Israel's sin had ripened and the spoilage was inevitable. The famine of hearing is the Lord's judgment on this ripened rebellion. And the cause of it all was an insidious spiritual hypocrisy.

THE RIPENED END

8:1 Thus the Lord God showed me: Behold, a basket of summer fruit.

2 And He said, "Amos, what do you see?" So I said, "A basket of summer fruit." Then the Lord said to me: "The end has come upon my people Israel: I will not pass by them anymore.

3 "And the songs of the temple shall be wailing in that day," says the Lord God—"Many dead bodies everywhere, they shall be thrown out in silence."

4 Hear this, you who swallow up the needy, and make the poor of the land fail,

5 saying: "When will the New Moon be past, that we may sell grain? And the Sabbath,

6 "that we may trade our wheat? Making the ephah small and the shekel large, falsifying the balances by deceit, that we may buy the poor for silver, and the needy for a pair of sandals—even sell the bad wheat?"

7 The Lord has sworn by the pride of Jacob: "Surely I will never forget any of their works.

8 "Shall the land not tremble for this, and everyone mourn who dwells in it? All of it shall swell like the River, heave and subside like the River of Egypt.

9 "And it shall come to pass in that day," says the Lord God, "that I will make the sun go down at noon, and I will darken the earth in broad daylight;

10 "I will turn your feasts into mourning, and all your songs into lamentation; I will bring sackcloth on every waist, and baldness on every head; I will make it like mourning for an only son, and its end like a bitter day.

Amos 8:1–10

In this fourth vision the Lord shows Amos a basket of ripened fruit. The *kĕlûb* was a wicker basket filled with *qāyiṣ*, ripened fruit. The word *qāyiṣ* does not mean "summer" as it is rendered in most English translations. Only by implication can we call it "summer fruit," fruit that has been ripened in the summer and harvested in early fall. The word is used in Jeremiah 40:10–12 as the yield of the harvest. The vision was probably of a basket of ripened figs with which Amos was familiar.

Amos is asked what he saw. "A basket of ripened fruit," he replied. The Lord's interpretive statement introduces a homonymic play on words. *"The end has come upon My people Israel"* (8:2). *End, qēṣ,* comes from the root *qāṣaṣ,* "to cut off," and was pronounced identically with *qāyiṣ,* "ripened fruit." Though the words came from different roots, they sounded identical. Diphthongs had contracted by Amos's time.[1] So the point of the vision was to declare that Israel's rebellion had ripened. The harvest of their disobedience was the judgment of Yahweh. When *qēṣ* is used for people it means the end of life. A fig removed from the tree was dead and would eventually spoil. Israel's refusal to return to the Lord now had brought her to the point of no return. Yahweh's word of judgment is pronounced with finality, *"I will not pass by them anymore."*

342

Verse 3 underlines the finality of death. The songs in the temple will turn into the wailing of funereal lamentation. There will be so many corpses that the cemeteries will not be able to contain them, and the judgment of death will be even greater by the shame of no burial.

The implications of this vision for us today must be communicated with utmost care. When is an individual, a church, or a ministry ripened fruit? Does resistance to God finally result in an irreversible end?

Certainly physical death ends the possibility of repentance and new life. We will spend eternity separated from God unless we accept His love, forgiveness, and eternal life through Christ before our physical demise. The frightening thing is that it is possible to resist the overtures of God's love so long that our wills can become hardened. We need to teach and preach the danger of becoming ripened fruit by never confessing Christ as Lord. Whenever I have risked sounding old fashioned by asking people if they are sure where they will spend eternity, I have usually had some very modern nonbelievers on the verge of becoming ripened fruit respond, repent, and accept the gift of eternal life.

Often when we preach or teach, there are traditional church people present who have never surrendered their lives to Christ. Years of running their own lives place them in the danger of duality – pretending to be Christians on the outside but unconverted on the inside. We need to take seriously the plight of agnostics in our churches – people who do not know Christ personally.

Then, too, there are people who have consistently resisted the Master's mandate of ministry. His words startle and shock us: "Not everyone who says to Me, 'Lord, Lord,' shall enter the kingdom of heaven, but he who does the will of My Father in heaven" (Matt. 7:21). Our pious claims of righteousness by faith must be combined with seeking and doing His will in our relationships and in responsibilities to care for the poor, hungry, and disadvantaged.

Some years ago, I talked with a pastor in the Midwest about his urban parish. He had been called to a church that was almost dead. Few people attended worship, the church school had dwindled, giving was down, and there was no evidence of care for the unreached people in the neighborhood. The church officers resisted the pastor's new leadership and vision. When we met, he was brokenhearted and filled with a sense of failure. "My officers simply do not want Christ to be Lord of their lives or their church!" he said with discouragement.

343

After several long visits, we prayed that the Lord would raise up new officers who would be open to lead the church in a dynamic new thrust of evangelism and mission. We also prayed that the pastor would have the courage to boldly preach the two-legged Gospel of personal commitment and social righteousness. He returned to his parish determined to do that.

Four years later I visited the church to lead a renewal conference. I was amazed at the revived spirit of the church. The church officers I saw were alive in Christ and on the move. The church had become a beacon of hope in its urban surroundings. People from the neighborhood were being reached by an effective program of personal evangelism and caring programs to meet their social needs.

"What made the difference?" I asked.

"A whole new breed of leaders," the pastor replied. Then his face darkened with sadness. "There's only a few of the officers left who were here four years ago. I feel very sad that I was not able to penetrate their hardened hearts. All I did was preach the Gospel and the biblical calling of the church. It was more than some of them wanted. Many of them have gone to other churches, and others are sitting on the sidelines. There was never a typical church battle or split. They simply said 'No' to renewal and to the city. I really love them and wish I had been able to reach them. The more I tried, the more entrenched they became. So, one by one, the congregation, now filled with new life, elected officers who were Christ-centered and filled with hope for the future of this church."

This is not a church renewal success story. It is a contemporary account of how some church leaders almost buried their church. The church might have become one more urban parish with an empty church building standing in a changing neighborhood as a monument to past glory. We all know churches where this has happened because religious people who did not know God or even want Him said "No" to Him too long.

And think of the parachurch movements that have fizzled out because the lodestar leader became a falling star. They did not heed the warning of the Lord or friends. There was a time when the spiritual sickness could have been healed, but not without the leadership admitting they were out of touch with the Lord and reality. Resistance to the Lord took a long time to ripen, but in the end the movement was a basket of ripened fruit. When we do not heed the Lord's warnings and the exposure of what is wrong by His plumb line, we face the eventuality of becoming *qāyiṣ* who are brought to the *qēṣ*. It is crucial for us to face the danger of resisting God's best for us for too long.

THE RIPENING OF HYPOCRISY

We run the danger of becoming ripened fruit through the long process of persistent hypocrisy. Israel's religious hypocrisy ripened and now would be cut off. The image of the ripened fruit is hypocrisy at its final stage. Spoilage and putrefaction began. Decomposition was not far off. The vision of the basket of ripened fruit suddenly hits home with contemporary force. We all suffer from the danger of duality, of pretending to be pious while our actions contradict our words.

In Amos's time, religious hypocrisy had ripened into blatant rebellion. Verse 4 begins a series of indictment oracles in which the vision of the ripened fruit is illustrated by specific charges of this hypocrisy. The initial imperative *"Hear this,"* or "Listen to this," introduces this unit and covers various indictments for breaking the covenant that led to a fully ripened hypocrisy.

The first indictment repeats a previous charge. Those who pretended to be religious were the very ones who *"swallow up"* or "trample" (RSV), *šā'ap* ("exploit"), the needy with the result, as we have observed previously, that the poor were made to *"fail"* (i.e., dying of starvation, being sold into slavery, or living in an impoverished state). The sin was against Yahweh's people, thus, against Him.

These hypocrites were those who strictly kept the New Moon festival and the Sabbath (v. 5). The festival was a covenant holiday (see Num. 10:10; 28:11; 1 Sam. 20:24-25; 2 Kings 4:23; Isa. 1:13; Hos. 2:11). During the New Moon festival, just as on the weekly Sabbath, no business was to be conducted. While this prohibition was kept impeccably, these religious hypocrites cheated the poor as soon as the festival or the Sabbath was over. They used exploitive methods strictly forbidden by the Law (Lev. 19:35-36; Deut. 25:13-15).

Weights and measures, so crucial to the economic order of the nation, were being falsified in the sale of grain, wheat, and produce. The ephah, a dry measure of 36.92 liters, or 65 pints, or about the size of our bushel today, was distorted by placing an object in it other than the commodity being weighed. If grain was being measured, the ephah would therefore contain less grain. The shekel (not to be confused with the coin by the same name) was a weight used on a scale. It was a limestone ball flattened at the bottom that weighed about 11.46 grams. If these weights were enlarged or made heavier, the purchase price would be fraudulently raised. The shekels were no longer "just weights" (Lev. 19:36) but had become "deceitful weights" (Deut. 25:13, 15). *"Falsifying the balances by deceit"* (Amos 8:6) meant to bend out of shape the cross beam of the scale, thus tampering with the scales themselves. All this was done to take advantage of the buyer, especially the poor and needy. The merchants sold contaminated wheat from the bins mixed in with the good wheat. Furthermore, profiting at the expense of the poor, the rich merchants used the money they had earned dishonestly in dealings with the poor to buy them for slavery.

In verse 7, Yahweh swears by an oath that He will never forget these practices of the hypocrites. In Amos 4:2 Yahweh swore by His holiness, and in 6:8 He made an oath by Himself. Here in 8:7 He swears *"by the pride of Jacob,"* (*ga'ôn ya'ăqōb*). The phrase can mean one of two things. It could refer to the land of Israel (Ps. 47:4), the promised land. Or, it could mean the arrogance of Israel, in which case Yahweh's oath was more unchangeable than Israel's persistent, unchanging refusal to reform. In either case, Yahweh's oath is definite: He will not forget what His people had done to distort the privilege of being chosen and called to be His people.

The consequence of Yahweh's oath is made clear in a rhetorical question in verse 8: *"Shall the land not tremble for this, and everyone mourn who dwells in it?"* Israel's end will be like an earthquake, the land will swell up, heave, and subside like the rising and falling of the River Nile. The judgment also will be like the eclipse of June 15, 763 B.C., which was still fresh in the memories of Amos's hearers. The sun will *"go down at noon"* and the earth *"will darken in broad daylight"* (v. 9). There will be profound fear and anxiety as the earth trembles and day is turned into night. The whole cosmos will seem to be in opposition to the people who turned away from the Almighty Creator and Lord of all Creation.

Israel's arrogant hypocrisy will be turned into funereal lament (v. 10). Feasts that celebrated the light of God's truth and sovereignty will be turned into dark dirges of despair. Festal robes will be replaced by sackcloth. Instead of shaving only the forelock, the men will shave their entire heads as a sign of grief. The anguish will be like a family that loses its only son and knows that the blessing of posterity has been taken away. Further, the day of judgment will be like the end of a bitter day in which not even the morning will bring relief from the remorse.

A Famine of Hearing the Words of the Lord

11 "Behold, the days are coming," says the Lord God, "that I will send a famine on the land, not a famine of bread, nor a thirst for water, but of hearing the words of the Lord.

12 "They shall wander from sea to sea, and from north to east; they shall run to and fro, seeking the word of the Lord, but shall not find it.

13 " In that day the fair virgins and strong young men shall faint from thirst.

14 "Those who swear by the sin of Samaria, who say, 'As your god lives, O Dan!' and, 'As the way of Beersheba lives!' They shall fall and never rise again."

Amos 8:11–14

By far the greatest manifestation of the judgment of God on Israel's unrepentant hypocrisy will be a famine of hearing the words of the Lord. Note that it will not be a famine of the words of the Lord, but a famine of hearing. Hypocrisy has ripened to the place that the people no longer seek God's words, nor do they listen when He speaks. A virus of unresponsiveness has debilitated the audio nerve in the souls of the people. For years the people did not want to hear God; now He will grant their desire. This is a tragic state for a people who had believed that "man shall not live by bread alone; but man lives by every word that proceeds from the mouth of the Lord" (Deut. 8:3). Through the centuries, God fed His people with the nourishment of His guidance and correction. He satisfied their spiritual hunger with His presence and power. By the middle of the eighth century B.C. they were determined to live by bread alone, much of it gained by unrighteous methods and at the expense of the poor. The judgment of God would be that they will know the worst famine of all — not being able to hear His words when He does speak.

In this famine of hearing, the people will react like starving people. Verse 12 is a vivid description of how people react when they are physically starving.

Television news programs bring into homes and hearts the stark reality of people who are starving. As we watch the tragedy of physical hunger, particularly in parts of Africa, we are forced to see the stages of starvation. The progression is frightening to watch. It starts with agitation and a frantic search for even a scrap of food. Acrimony

347

grows between people. Then the hungry move from place to place desperately looking for some source of food and water. Soon apathy sets in. An absent stare is seen in eyes that are set in dark, hollow sockets. As apathy takes over, the starving people sink to the ground. Atrophy begins. Then the terrible grip of the monster of hunger causes them to writhe in pain. And finally, there is death.

Now note the similarity of the spiritual starvation of the Israelites when the famine of hearing the words of God. *"They shall wander from sea to sea, and from the north to east; they shall run to and fro, seeking the word of the Lord, but shall not find it"* (v. 12). Wolff comments,

> The range of the roaming is described in the most far-reaching terms. "From sea to sea" surely does not here mean from the Dead Sea to the Mediterranean, but is intended to designate the uttermost boundaries of the earth, as in Ps. 72:8 and Zech. 9:10. If the intention here were to delimit the boundaries of Palestine, one would not expect "from the north to the east" in the parallel colon. One must rather think here of those vast regions into which the people of God were scattered. The peculiar combination of north and east is most easily understood in this way.[2]

Verses 13–14 spell out further implications and the deeper causes of the famine of hearing in Israel. The vigorous youth of the people will faint from thirst, and thus the future of the nation will be in jeopardy. The cause of the famine is that young and old swear by and give loyalty to false gods. The issue is that images to false gods are worshiped in Israel's shrines. The leaders of Samaria had fostered this sin. The reference to Dan, a shrine in the north of Israel, probably means the bull images set up there (1 Kings 12:29). Beersheba was a worship shrine in Judah visited by pilgrims (Amos 5:5) where syncretism of Yahweh with Canaanite gods was practiced. This finally caused the famine of hearing.

We can identify the famine of hearing in our own time. Mark the similarity to the famine of food. When people substitute hypocrisy for a dynamic relationship with God, there is an unsatisfied spiritual hunger. They go through the same process as in physical starvation. First agitation, then acrimony, followed by criticism and negativism. They run to and fro in search of meaning. Every religious movement, cult, cause, or activity is sought after as a source of feeding the terrible emptiness inside. Then there is the hollow look of discouragement and despair. And, long before the pulse stops, there is spiritual death.

The phrase *"words of the Lord"* is synonymous with both communion with Him and communication from Him. We cannot live without either. But we try. We seek to fill our spiritual hunger with substitutes. Our needs are great. We long for affirmation, but our real need is for love. We yearn for recognition, but our greater need is for an assurance that we belong to God. We lust after the material blessings of life, but our most profound need is to know that we are a blessed child in our heavenly Father's family. We search for meaning in a satisfying vocation, but our real need is to know that we are called by God to live for Him. Beneath all our surface needs is the one great need for God Himself. Only communion with Him and communication from Him will give us security, stability, and strength.

Does God send a famine of hearing today? Is it possible to block the ears of our minds and of our hearts to His words of grace and guidance, His demands of righteousness and justice in our personal lives and society for so long that we become spiritually deaf for a time? I think so. God gave us freedom of will. We can debilitate our spiritual audio nerve by disuse or misuse. Or it can be harmed by the din of the demanding noise of people who become diminutive gods or by the clamor of a frantic life. We simply do not take time to listen to God anymore. When a spiritual hunger gnaws at our inner being, we begin to try to stuff the emptiness with nutritionless food. Then as the anxiety grows, we panic as spiritual starvation sets in. That is the critical moment when we either keep on starving ourselves or cry out to God for the healing of the plugged ears of our souls and ask Him to feed us again with His words.

Thankfully, the same God who sent a famine of hearing because Israel refused to repent, came in Jesus Christ, the Bread of Life. The Savior gave us an awesome promise, "Blessed are those who hunger and thirst for righteousness, for they shall be filled" (Matt. 5:6). When we want God as much as a starving person longs for food and a parched person for water, we will be satisfied. If our dominant desire is for righteousness with God and His righteousness in all our relationships and responsibilities, He will answer our prayer. Our self-imposed famine of hearing need not cause our spiritual death. Righteousness with God through the atonement of Christ's blood is a gift. We do not need to starve to death spiritually. Accepting the gift by faith opens us to the continual feeding through the Word of God, Christ Himself, God with us. He promises to satisfy our deeper spiritual hungers. In daily, moment-by-moment prayer, He enables us to glorify the Father and baptizes and anoints us with the Spirit. We hear the words of the Lord in study of the Scriptures. He leads us in radical obedience to righteousness. Our heart ears are constantly sensitized to His commands. We can avoid a self-imposed hunger by a daily quiet time. We will starve without it.

Many do starve when spiritual food is available. There is not a famine of the words of God in America. We can turn on the radio at almost any time, day or night, and hear a biblical exposition. Christian television, despite the eccentric practices of some televanglists, offers the words of God. With varying degrees of effectiveness, the Gospel is being preached and taught in all kinds of churches. Bible study groups are available. Daily devotional guides are in abundance. Yet, many people starve for the words of God.

The difficulty is in the willingness to hear. This portion of Amos gives us an opportunity to help people identify their hunger and evaluate why they may not be listening. We may fear hearing what the Lord has to say. The words of the Lord may call for a greater commitment to righteousness than we are ready to live. We may not be ready to do what love demands. Our task as communicators is to portray the true satisfaction of having our spiritual hungers satisfied and lead our people in specific prayers of healing of the audio nerve of their souls.

Recently, I met with a group of people who knew they were spiritually starving and desperately wanted to be fed by the words of the Lord. They were a vivid contrast to many audiences I speak to around the nation where people look like they are listening but are suffering from a self-imposed famine of hearing. I spoke to the inmates of the Chino Women's Prison at Chino, California. My message was about how Christ meets our deepest needs and how to turn our lives over to His Lordship. After my brief talk, I began to give an invitation, but before I finished, the women were out of their seats streaming down the aisles to give their lives to Christ. They knew they were spiritually hungry. Failure and brokenness had unplugged their ears.

How unlike the famine of hearing among so many self-satisfied, self-righteous people who would rather starve to death spiritually than admit their need. Inner agitation and anxiety grow as the spiritual hunger pangs intensify. Outward personality patterns develop, and relationships are filled with stress and strain. The call of obedient discipleship is resisted. There is no peace, serenity, or vision.

At this point in our exposition of Amos, it is helpful to pause to assist our listeners to get in touch with their spiritual hungers and to sound a recall to the daily disciplines of Bible study and prayer and to faithfully live the guidance the Lord gives.

Some time ago, when I preached on this portion of Amos, I put the following morning commitment and evening evaluation in the bulletin for people to begin and end the days of the following week.

> *Morning commitment:* As a person made right with God by grace through Christ, I commit today to be a day of righteous living. My dominant desire, above all else, will be to seek first the kingdom of God and His righteousness in my decisions, ethics, and morality. I am willing to be made willing to prayerfully listen to the Lord for guidance for what I am to say and do. Lord, heal my heart ears!
>
> *Evening evaluation:* Today, did I express righteousness or deny it? In what ways did I listen intently for the Lord's clarification of what righteousness demanded? Did I balk at the Lord's guidance or blunder on in running my own life? I accept forgiveness for any willful independence so that tomorrow can be different. Tomorrow is another day and a fresh chance to trust and obey. As the Lord gives the day, He will show the way. He will fill my hunger and thirst for righteousness.

In a class setting or small group discussion it is creative to give people an opportunity to report on what happened to them with this experiment of listening. Or, with a congregation, to request that members write us sharing their experiences. Also, it is effective to have someone witness in a worship service about the difference intentional listening has made in his or her life.

Our challenge is to expose the warning of the vision of the ripened fruit and the impairment of the audio nerve of the soul. A sermon or class lesson on the eighth chapter of Amos should include both, but with an incisive application to our time, coupled with practical steps of what our people can do to avoid what happened to Israel. This will make eighth century B.C. history a startling call to repentance and new commitment today. If we do not learn from the failures of the past, we will repeat them.

NOTES

1. Stuart, *Hosea – Jonah*, 379.
2. Wolff, *Joel and Amos*, 330–331.

CHAPTER TEN

Behold Your God

Amos 9:1–15

Hope does not exist in a vacuum. It is not rootless optimism, unfounded yearning, or ungrounded wishing. Authentic hope comes from God. It is based on His nature and promises.

Amos chapter 9 gives us a basis of lasting hope. As you scan the chapter, you may think I am referring to the last five verses on the five promises of the restoration of Israel. Not so. The entire chapter animates hope. We behold God who makes and keeps His promises. He follows through on His promises of judgment as well as His subsequent promises of a new beginning. His righteousness and grace are inseparable. God is absolutely reliable in both. Because He is, we have a solid source of profound hope.

There is a unity to this final chapter of Amos. We are called to behold our God. We behold Him as a God with whom we cannot trifle, a God who is inescapable, a God who is sovereign over all nature and all nations. A God who is Lord of the future.

GOD KEEPS HIS PROMISES

9:1 I saw the Lord standing by the altar, and He said: "Strike the doorposts, that the thresholds may shake, and break them on the heads of them all. I will slay the last of them with the sword. He who flees from them shall not get away, and he who escapes from them shall not be delivered."

Amos 9:1

Amos's fifth vision is of the Lord who keeps His promises. He had promised judgment if Israel would not heed His warnings and repent. Now in this final vision He stands at the altar, the very center of the nation's life. It was there that Israel's primary loyalty to God had been compromised with pretense, hypocrisy, and apostasy. Syncretism with foreign gods had disavowed their historic monotheism. The altar should have been a place where they claimed their peace with the one true God. It was meant to be the dynamic center of the nation's total life. Instead, it had become the emanating source of the pollution of the moral, economic, and political life of the nation. The altar of the vision symbolized the rotten core of an apostate people. The Lord had patiently and repeatedly issued His recall for His people to return to Him, but with obdurate petulance they had not returned. The result is that the altar, the temple, and the nation itself will be destroyed.

The Lord stands on (*niṣṣāb ʿal;* cf. 7:7) the altar, symbolizing His supremacy over the false and distorted worship of Israel. Note that Amos uses the word *Adonai, ʾǎdōnāy,* rather than the name *Yahweh.* This probably expresses the prophet's reverence for the invisibility of God and communicates his vision of a manifestation of the presence of God. *Adonai* means "sovereign" and "king." Perhaps Amos wanted to underline the supremacy of God, the Sovereign One, over Israel's kings who offered sacrifices on the altar.

We are not told what the manifestation of God looked like. What we are told is what He said to Amos. The top of the central pillar would be shaken, as in an earthquake. *Kaptôr* means the pillar top, and *sippîm* means the stone bases of the door posts. The temple would be demolished from the top of the key pillar to the foundations. It would fall on the heads of all worshipers and priests. The co-mingling of worship and feasting inside the temple following the Canaanite custom is implied as opposed to the prescribed orthodox Israelite tradition of feasting outside in the temple courts.[1] Even if some of the reveling worshipers escape when the temple topples, they will not survive. The judgment of the Lord, which begins with the temple, will pervade the land.

The heart of Israel's problem was the heart. The distortion of their worship of God had permeated the heart of the nation. Greed, unrighteousness, and injustice was pumped like a virulent poison into the bloodstream of an apostate people. Outward conduct was caused by contradicted convictions. Everything was wrong because the nation was not right with God. Nothing works right when we alter the worship of the altar. It is true for us as individuals and for our churches. God demands absolute obedience.

The severity of God's judgment of the temple may shock us. Actually, it is a source of hope. God gave Israel repeated opportunities to repent and return to Him. He had told the people what would happen if they refused. What kind of God would we have if He nagged His people with warnings He never meant to enforce?

Or, to put it more personally for us, what if we presume on the grace of God because we do not really think He will judge? He becomes an indulgent grandfather whom we think we can manipulate. We smile at His stern warnings but think He will never hold us accountable. We operate on the assumption that there will never be a reckoning in this life or beyond.

We become like a teenager I talked to recently. He resists authority at every level. "My dad's been threatening me with punishment for years, but he's too soft to follow through. So I just listen, let what he says go in one ear and out the other, and go do what I want." His attitude is like many people's response to God. And sadly, that attitude is not just the problem of the pagan but also the proclivity of some Christians.

When we lose all accountability to God, we also lose a sense of hope. If we assume that God does not mean what He says when He holds us to His best for us, how can we be sure that His promises of blessings will be reliable? True security is submitting to God's authority, committing each day to discern and do His will, accepting His corrective judgment, and claiming His forgiveness. And that is exactly what Israel refused to do.

GOD IS INESCAPABLE

2 "Though they dig into hell, from there My hand shall take them; though they climb up to heaven, from there I will bring them down;

3 "and though they hide themselves on top of Carmel, from there I will search and take them; though they hide from My sight at the bottom of the sea, from there I will command the serpent, and it shall bite them;

4 "though they go into captivity before their enemies, from there I will command the sword, and it
shall slay them. I will set My eyes on them for harm
and not for good."

Amos 9:2–4

Further interpreting Amos's vision, the Lord declares that His judgment is inescapable. There will be no place to hide, as we noted earlier.
Verses 2–4 are an awesome contrast to the psalmist's assurance in
Psalm 139 of the omnipresence of God. What eighth century B.C. Israel
would not say was, "Search me, O God, and know my heart . . . and see
if there is any wicked way in me, and lead me in the way everlasting"
(Ps. 139:23–24). Mark the same progression of thought about trying to
escape an inescapable God in the Psalm and in Amos 9:2–4.

As a result of the refusal to repent, there would be no eluding of the
grasp of Yahweh's judgment. Hell, Sheol, the place of the departed
dead, would provide no protection. Note Proverbs 15:11, "Hell and
Destruction are before the Lord; So how much more the hearts of the
sons of men." Death will be no escape from the Lord. Nor will an
ascent into the farthest regions of the cosmos. The hand of Yahweh,
the power that controls everything, will bring the unrepentant down.
The top of Mount Carmel will not be a safe hiding place from the
indefatigable searching pursuit of the Lord. Mount Carmel was
falsely thought to be the realm of the Canaanite god, Baal Carmel.
Elijah had exposed the erroneous belief in Baal's power (1 Kings
18:17–46). And the false god would be equally impotent to hide the
defectors from the Lord in the eighth century B.C. northern kingdom.
The bottom of the sea will offer no protection, and even the sea serpent
will be subject to Yahweh's command. And finally, being carried
away into captivity by an invading enemy will provide no safety.

As we will see in our commentary on Jonah, some of the Israelites
had a funnel-like concept of providence, that Yahweh's power was
limited to the geographical territory of Israel and Judah. We can
imagine that some of the people said, "What's the worst that can
happen? Defeat and captivity? At least then we will be out of the
sphere of Yahweh's judgment." Serious miscalculation. Yahweh was
going to use even Israel's enemy to execute His judgment.

Israel's apostasy and rebellion have gone so far that the Lord says
these soul-shaking words, *"I will set My eyes on them for harm and not
for good"* (v. 4). Years later, similar words were spoken to Jerusalem

through the prophet Jeremiah (Jer. 21:10). Both prophets sounded these words of judgment before the exile of their respective nations. It was after the fall of Jerusalem and years of exile passed that the Lord said to the remnant of Judah,

> After seventy years are completed at Babylon, I will visit you and perform My good word toward you, and cause you to return to this place. For I know the thoughts that I think toward you, says the Lord, thoughts of peace and not of evil, to give you a future and a hope. Then you will call upon Me and go and pray to Me, and I will listen to you. And you will seek Me and find Me, when you search for Me with all your heart.
>
> Jer. 29:10–13

Today, this magnificent Jeremiah text of hope needs to be used in context. It is a promise for those who have accepted the Lord's judgment and have repented. God has plans, a future, and a hope for those who have gone through failure or have endured trials and have come to trust in Him completely.

I had repeated Jeremiah 29:11 for thirty-five years and had preached on it often, but I heard it sound in my soul with greater power one day when I was alone, flat on my back and helpless after a hiking accident on the northwest coast of Scotland. My leg was badly crushed, and my cries for human help had gone unheeded as I dragged myself for nearly three hours. When I gave up and accepted that I might not be rescued, my pleas for the Lord's help were answered when, with the ears of my heart, I heard this verse as if for the first time. Prior to hearing the Lord's word, I had surrendered my plans and dreams for my life, confessed my failures, and praised the Lord for all He had done. Whether I made it or not, I knew I was the Lord's forever. "I have plans for you . . . a future . . . a hope!" I heard as I drifted into the blur of excruciating pain and then unconsciousness. Sometime after, I was found by a doctor who "happened" to be out walking with his son and daughter. I had experienced authentic hope when I was helpless.

The long months in bed convalescing and then the tedious process of learning to walk again were both used by the Lord to help me continue the deepening process that had begun in my fresh encounter with Him after the accident. My own plans for my work for Him had to be surrendered so I could hear His plans. False gods of professional pride, success, and control had to be faced and removed from subtle syncretism with the Lord. We all get sucked into the seduction of the secondary, all the good things we do for the Lord that eventually compete with Him for first place in our lives. Busyness for the Lord is a beguiling false god if it keeps us from daily, hourly, communion with Him and moment-by-moment guidance in His plans for us. Sometimes He uses our problems and difficulties to get our attention. We get the most out of suffering when it brings us to deeper trust and a new commitment to Him as our only hope. For that we need a fresh vision of the majesty and might of the Lord.

OUR GOD IS MIGHTY

5 The Lord God of hosts, He who touches the earth and it melts, and all who dwell there mourn; all of it shall swell like the River, and subside like the River of Egypt.
6 He who builds His layers in the sky, and has founded His strata in the earth; who calls for the waters of the sea, and pours them out on the face of the earth — The Lord is his name.

Amos 9:5–6

God is not only inescapable, He is mighty. Amos follows the Lord's disclosure of His omnipresence with a magnificent declaration of His omnipotence. Israel's faith had degenerated until Yahweh was little more than a cult deity. Their vision of God was too small, limited, constricted. Amos uses a familiar hymn of praise to Yahweh to soar in exaltation, extolling His power over nature and the events of history. He is *"the Lord God of hosts"* (v. 5). He is the Commander of the armies (ṣĕbā'ôt) of angels who carry out His plans. The words, *"He who touches the earth and it melts"* meant that Yahweh's power could be displayed in an earthquake that causes people to mourn. With the earthquake comes the undulation of the earth like the annual rising and subsiding of the Nile River of Egypt (cf. Amos 8:8). Yahweh controls His creation because He is builder and founder of both heaven and earth. Creation is likened to a house or palace in which *ma'ălâ*, a kind of "upper room," is used for heaven, and *'ăguddâ*, or "storeroom," is used for the earth.[2] By Yahweh's power water is drawn from the sea and is poured out on the earth in rain. Who is this mighty God? The hymn ends with the refrain, *"the Lord is His name"* (v. 6).

This hymn may not impress our sophisticated ears so used to seismographic calculations of earthquakes, refined predictions of the tides, and seeding of rainless clouds so they will burst in a rainstorm. And yet, the more we understand the more we should be motivated to praise the Creator and Sustainer of the earth and universes within universes. Most wondrous of all, He created us to know and love Him. And the greatest miracle of all is our transformation through Christ, His cross, the resurrection, and His indwelling presence. This should lead us to unfettered praise and not unbending pride.

FALSE PRIDE AND FALLACIOUS PREJUDICE

> 7 "Are you not like the people of Ethiopia to Me, O children of Israel?" says the Lord. "Did I not bring up Israel from the land of Egypt, the Philistines from Caphtor, and the Syrians from Kir?
> 8 "Behold, the eyes of the Lord God are on the sinful kingdom, and I will destroy it from the face of the earth; yet I will not utterly destroy the house of Jacob," says the Lord.
> 9 "For surely I will command, and will sift the house of Israel among all nations, as grain is sifted in a sieve; yet not the smallest grain shall fall to the ground.
> 10 "All the sinners of My people shall die by the sword, who say, 'The calamity shall not overtake us nor confront us.'"
>
> *Amos 9:7–10*

We sense that Amos repeated this then familiar hymn to prepare his listener for the bracing truth that follows in verses 7–8. Yahweh, who is Lord of all creation, is also the Lord of all nations. And Israel, having denied both its privilege and responsibility, will be judged more severely than other nations. Stuart comments decisively, "In effect Amos says, 'That hymn you love shows how Yahweh controls the universe and metes out His judgment among the nations. But you have wrongly assumed that this judgment would always benefit you and harm others. Now you must realize that you also deserve the wrath of which the hymn speaks."[3]

Two rhetorical questions in verse 7 put Israel in her place. In essence, the Lord asks first, "Are you more important to Me than the people of Ethiopia?" The Nubians (*kušiyyîm*) were a small, obscure black nation in Africa. And second, "You are proud of your exodus from Egypt? Your enemies the Philistines and the Syrians each had one too." The Philistines came from Caphtor on Crete, and Kir is unknown. It must have been shocking for the Israelites to hear that Yahweh had been involved in the history of two nations they had categorized as their enemies. Perhaps they could not be so sure of Yahweh's protection. The questions were a carefully placed blow to the people's pride. Were they not the darlings of the Almighty?

Verse 8 makes it clear that Israel is the focus of Yahweh's attention alright, but as a sinful kingdom deserving destruction. Amos alone uses the term *"the sinful kingdom."* The article stresses the apostasy, unrighteousness, and rebellion of the northern kingdom. However, there is a thin ray of hope that pierces the darkness of the judgment. There will be a remnant saved. Some scholars suggest that the *"sinful kingdom"* refers to the monarchy and the house of Jacob to the people. What is most significant, however, is that Yahweh had a future planned for His people. He always has plans for working His purposes out in ways beyond our imagination. This, too, is a basis of hope.

The theme of the remnant is carried on in verses 9–10 in the metaphor of a sieve. Yahweh will sift His people as *"in a sieve"* (rare word, *kĕbārâ*). What is sifted is *ṣĕrôr*, translated in the NKJV as "grain" and in the RSV as "pebble." The metaphor is somewhat confusing since, on a threshing floor, the grain falls through and the stubble remains. That would make the image of the pebble more likely. In that case the pebbles remain and the grain would fall through. What remains in the sieve will be saved. What is important is the point of the metaphor: a remnant will be saved from death, but sinners, transgressors, will die by the sword. These are the people who have refused to heed Yahweh's warnings, saying, *"The calamity shall not overtake us nor confront us"* (v. 10). The basic meaning of the word for sin, *ḥāṭā³* — to miss the mark, is implied. It is the unwillingness to submit to God's call to righteousness and justice, and having heard His judgment still persist both in the sin and a determination not to acknowledge it and repent.

Again, the theme of hope gleams through the dark clouds of Israel's judgments. God offers grace to those who confess their sins.

The greatest sin is to persist in saying we have no sin. This was the problem of the Pharisees. After healing the man born blind, Jesus spoke about spiritual sight with the Pharisees as His target audience. "For judgment I have come into this world, that those who do not see may see, and that those who see may be made blind" (John 9:39). Those who could not admit that they needed spiritual sight, therefore would remain blind. "Are we blind also?" the Pharisees asked, seeking to trap Jesus. He responded, "If you were blind, you would have no sin; but now you say, 'We see.' "Therefore your sin remains" (John 9:41). The desire to see ourselves as Christ sees us and to allow Him to put His finger on what needs to be changed is the secret of spiritual power for personal growth and exhilarating discipleship. He is never finished with us nor are we ever finished growing.

Amos has confronted us with the danger of pride, arrogance, and self-righteousness. He calls us to live on the growing edge of absolute honesty and humble repentance in the never-ceasing challenge of living out our righteousness with God in our relationship and responsibilities for justice in our society.

PROMISES OF HOPE

11 "On that day I will raise up the tabernacle of David, which has fallen down, and repair its damages; I will raise up its ruins, and rebuild it as in the days of old;

12 "that they may possess the remnant of Edom, and all the Gentiles who are called by My name," says the Lord who does this thing.

13 "Behold, the days are coming," says the Lord, "When the plowman shall overtake the reaper, and the treader of grapes him who sows seed; the mountains shall drip with sweet wine, and all the hills shall flow with it.

14 "I will bring back the captives of My people Israel; they shall build the waste cities and inhabit them; they shall plant vineyards and drink wine from them; they shall also make gardens and eat fruit from them.

15 "I will plant them in their land, and no longer shall they be pulled up from the land I have given them," says the Lord your God.

Amos 9:11–15

These five promises of the restoration of Israel pulsate with hope-animating power. The same God who promised judgment for those who would not repent promises a new beginning for a remnant. After the exile, the people will be restored to their land and will live in prosperity and plenty.

Before we consider these promises, we must acknowledge that many scholars do not consider these last five verses to be a part of Amos's original prophecy. It is reasoned that, because of what seems to be a change in tone and theological content, this section was a later addition, probably from a Judean source. In addition to the change in tone, this conviction is based on the reference to *"the tabernacle of David"* (9:11) and to the possession of the remnant of Edom that occurred after the Babylonian exile of Judah.

None of these arguments seem conclusive. There is an obvious change of tone, from judgment to hope. However, if the Lord *"took"* (7:15) Amos to prophesy judgment on Israel with precise vision about how that judgment would be carried out years later, why should it be difficult to accept that the Lord could also reveal to the prophet the vision of the restoration? I think Amos was charged with both tasks and having accomplished prophecy of judgment with unswerving incisiveness, went on to predict aspects of the restoration. Amos spoke in the context of Yahweh's covenant relationship with Israel, and that restoration was necessary to accomplish His long-range purpose for His people. Without this we must assume that Yahweh only revealed His wrath to Amos and nothing of His plan for after the exile. This seems unlikely, especially when the prophet was given the vision of the remnant.

As for the Judean authorship, we must not forget that Amos was from the southern kingdom. Amos displayed extensive knowledge of international affairs, and, except for the brief time he prophesied in the northern kingdom, spent his life in Judah. His prophecy against Judah (2:4–5) reveals his knowledge of the growing spiritual apostasy in his own land. As a part of that prophesy Amos did, in fact, predict the destruction of Jerusalem (2:5).

That brings us to the reference to *"the tabernacle of David"* in verse 11 of the closing passage. The Hebrew word translated here as *"tabernacle"* is *sukkâ*, meaning "booth." Its use here could mean the temple, the dynasty of David, the role of the king as intercessor in the Festival of Booths, and, as Stuart suggests, the city of Succoth, a pivotal center in David's military operations. A good case can be made for the temple, and if so, it would be possible that Amos, who had a vision of the destruction of Jerusalem, could also have had a vision of the rebuilding of the temple. *"The tabernacle of David, which has fallen down"* is in a participial form and can also be translated "the falling tabernacle (booth) of David." If the booth means the Davidic dynasty, it was already in a decrepit, tottering condition in Amos's time.

Along with the other prophets, Amos shared the Jerusalem traditions of the fulfillment of the Davidic ideal. Undoubtedly, he, too, looked forward to the coming David.

The mention of the possession of Edom in verse 12 is used as a further argument for a later authorship of the final section of Amos. This is based on the reference in Obadiah 19. It should be noted, however, that the possession of Edom is predicted in Numbers 24:18.

These reasons are in strong support of Amos's authorship of 9:11–15. In the last analysis, however, what is most important is that it is part of the Bible, and the hope it contains is God's word for us.

There are five promises in this final section of Amos. The first is the tabernacle or booth of David. We have discussed some of the possible meanings of this term. Of these, the most plausible is that there will be a new day in which the northern and southern kingdoms will be reunified under a new David. Beyond the judgment of the exile, there will be a new time of rebuilding. The brokenness of the chosen people would be healed.

The second promise is that the new kingdom will *"possess"* or have power over all old enemies. *"That they may possess the remnant of Edom, and all the Gentiles who are called by my name"* (v. 12). Edom had been an old and constant enemy of the Israelites. The Edomites would finally be subdued and distress Israel no more. You will find a complete discussion of the Edomite problem and how this promise was fulfilled in the commentary on Obadiah.

Here in Amos 9:12 the name Edom is a kind of synecdoche for the phrase *"all the Gentiles,"* or, more accurately, "all the nations" *(kol-haggôyim)* which parallels it. The phrase *"called by My name"* means, "which I control." In the course of Israel's defeat, Yahweh had displayed His power over the nations to effect His purposes and judgment. Now He will restore to Israel the blessing of power over these nations.

The third promise is on prosperity and bounty for the land. *"When the plowman shall overtake the reaper, and the treader of grapes him who sows seed"* (v. 13). In the restored kingdom the land will be so fruitful that as the reaper is cutting grain the plowman will be preparing the ground for a new planting. At the time of harvesting the grape crop, before the harvesters finish, the next crop will be planted. Harvesters and planters will get in each other's way as the land yields an almost constant harvest. Leviticus 26:5 will have come to pass, "Your threshing shall last till the time of vintage, and the vintage shall last till the time of sowing; you shall eat your bread to the full, and dwell in your land safely." The success of the grape harvest will be so great that it will seem like the mountains will drip and the hills will flow with grape juice. All of the hyperbolical statements convey the unlimited blessing of Yahweh.

The judgment will be past. So the fourth promise is that the captives will be brought back to the land. The cities that have been devastated will be reinhabited and rebuilt. The people will settle down to a peaceful life able to pursue normal agriculture without fear of invaders and danger. Yahweh will make it all possible—*"I will bring back. . . ."* He is the source and sustainer of the restoration.

The first person intensity of the promises is repeated in the fifth and final promise. *"I will plant them in their land, and no longer shall they be pulled up from the land I have given them"* (v. 15). The pronouns "I" and "their" communicate the bliss of the reestablished covenant between Yahweh and His chosen people. Once again the people will know that all they have and are is a gift from their *only* God.

LIVING WITH HOPE

The entire ninth chapter of Amos helps us behold our God and live with hope rooted in His promises. He is the God of righteousness who demands that we live righteously, and He is our judge. He will not accept second place in our lives or second-rate discipleship. He promises that there will be an accounting, daily, and at the end of our physical lives. We are accountable to Him for what we do with the blessings He bestows on us. His judgments and punishments are never an end in themselves. Our God is more concerned with reconciling us to Himself than retribution. He follows judgment with the promise of a new beginning.

Amos has brought us to a renewed awareness of the cost of being chosen. We have been called to be saints, God's holy people, and we have been appointed to live holy, righteous lives. The prophet brings us to the realization of the impossibility on our own of attaining righteousness with God or living righteously. After studying Amos, we are prepared to behold our God with new awe and wonder, for He has intervened to make us right with Himself and give us the power to live righteous lives. Now we behold God incarnate in Christ. His death on the cross establishes the righteousness with God we could never earn or deserve

Amos brings us to Calvary with humility and repentance, for the righteousness the prophet proclaimed is now ours. And the fearless man of Tekoa has also put a warrant in our souls to live that righteousness with greater intentionality, without hypocrisy and pretense. Amos forces us to look in the mirror and repent and then to behold God in the face of Jesus Christ our righteousness.

NOTES

1. Stuart, *Hosea – Jonah*, 392.
2. Ibid., 393.
3. Ibid., 392.

Introduction to the Book of Obadiah

Obadiah is the shortest book in the Bible. It also is one of the most neglected books of the Bible in contemporary preaching and teaching.

When friends learned that I was writing this commentary on the Minor Prophets, they wondered what preaching and teaching values I would find in Obadiah. One pastor went so far as to exclaim, "I'm anxious to read what you will do with grim ol' Obadiah. Can't imagine preaching anything positive or creative out of that angry tirade. Obadiah is 'minor' not only in length, but also in any inspiration for discipleship today!"

I disagree. An exposition of Obadiah provides an excellent basis for treating three subjects of great importance and urgency.

First, Obadiah forces us to identify our enemies. A vital aspect of spiritual maturity is having the right enemies. I find it helpful to begin a class lecture or a sermon on Obadiah with the question, "Who are your enemies?" The question leads naturally into some introductory paragraphs about the difference between people who are categorized as enemies simply because of what they have done or said to us and those who are enemies of God.

There was no question in Obadiah's mind about who was his enemy. The twenty-one verses of his prophecy are focused on the judgment of the Edomites. The ancient, smoldering animosity between the Israelites, the descendants of Jacob, and the Edomites, the descendants of Esau, were flamed into a blaze because Edom had aided an invader in the sacking of Jerusalem. The first sixteen verses of Obadiah's message deal with condemnation of Edom in general and judgment for refusing to aid Israel in particular. A discussion of these first sixteen verses gives the expositor an opportunity to trace the feud between Israel and Edom.

A necessary companion to Obadiah's verses is Jesus' teaching on enemies in the Sermon on the Mount. The Master did not tell us we should not have enemies but rather that we should love them, bless them, and pray for them. How can we do that? We cannot without a transformation. We need deliverance.

The second major thrust in Obadiah's prophecy is a prediction of a deliverance on Mount Zion. *"But on Mount Zion there shall be deliverance, and there shall be holiness; the house of Jacob shall possess their possessions"* (v. 17). The deliverance prophesied was the return of the exiles to Jerusalem. An exposition of all the dynamics of that deliverance is a precursor of an ultimate deliverance that would take place on the cross. In that deliverance, the dividing wall of division between us and our enemies will be broken down. Most crucial of all, we will be given deliverance from the power of our real enemy—Satan. Christ defeated the enemy so we could be free to love our enemies.

The third and final theme of Obadiah is that judgment and punishment is God's prerogative. Edom will be destroyed. The last phrase of verse 21 provides a triumphant motto for our battles with *the* Enemy and our enemies: *"The kingdom shall be the Lord's."* This is our hope, strength, and confidence in conflict. God always has the final word, the decisive judgment, and the ultimate victory.

We will develop all three of these themes in our verse-by-verse exposition of Obadiah. For now, my hope is that taking this approach to Obadiah will help you see how preaching and teaching from this little book can be a dynamic experience for both you and your listener.

WHO WAS OBADIAH?

We know little about Obadiah. There are thirteen Obadiahs mentioned in the Old Testament. Since no kings are mentioned at the beginning of the prophecy, it is difficult to identify him with certainty as one of the ones listed. Depending on the dating of Obadiah's prophecy, four of the thirteen seem possible. An early dating would make a good candidate of the Obadiah who was an officer in Ahab's house and hid prophets in a cave (1 Kings 18:3–4). Another possibility would be the Obadiah who was sent out by Jehoshaphat to teach the Law in the villages of Judah (2 Chron. 17:7). Also, there was an Obadiah who participated in repairing the temple in Josiah's time (2 Chron. 34:12). A later date after the exile would suggest the priest named Obadiah during the reconstruction of Jerusalem under Nehemiah (Neh. 10:5). The fact that Obadiah's father is not mentioned indicates that the prophet was not from a priestly or kingly line.

What we do know about Obadiah is that he was fearlessly faithful to Yahweh and Israel, passionately abhorred the enemy of Edom, and firmly believed in the ultimate judgment of godless nations. His central conviction is that God's justice will triumph and be vindicated.

DATE OF OBADIAH

The date of Obadiah's prophecy is widely disputed. The invasion of Jerusalem mentioned in verses 10–14 provides the only assistance in the prophecy itself concerning the date. The discussion of the date of Obadiah has revolved around which invasion of Jerusalem that Obadiah refers to. Some scholars suggest Shishak's invasion of Jerusalem in 926 B.C. during the reign of Rehoboam. However, this is unlikely because Edom was not independent of Judah at that time and therefore could not have been part of the plundering of the temple and palace. A second possibility is the invasion and looting of Jerusalem by the Philistines and Arabians during the reign of Jehoram (848–841 B.C.). The Edomites had revolted and were bitter antagonists of Judah at this time. A third theory is that the invasion cited was the invasion by Jehoash of Israel in 790 B.C.

The fourth option seems correct. In 586 B.C. Nebuchadnezzar invaded Jerusalem, and destroyed the palace and temple and razed the walls. The historic enmity between Israel and Edom reached a climax when the Edomites not only refused to help when the Babylonians crushed the city, but actually aided in the destruction and expressed their delight in the defeat of their centuries-old archenemy.

Psalm 137, written in the Babylonian exile following the destruction of Jerusalem, provides a helpful cross reference. Edom is clearly identified as cheering participants in the razing of the holy city. "Remember, O Lord, against the sons of Edom the day of Jerusalem, who said, 'Raze it, raze it, to its very foundation!'" (Ps. 137:7).

Therefore, the approach we will take to Obadiah's prophecy will be in the context that it was delivered after the 586 B.C. destruction of Jerusalem and during the Babylonian exile.

An Outline of Obadiah

I. A Vision of the Enemy (1–16)
    A. Identifying the Enemy
    B. The Anatomy of the Enemy
    C. The Judgment of the Enemy
II. Deliverance from the Enemy (17–18)
    A. Deliverance on Mount Zion
        1. After the Exile
        2. After the Cross
    B. The Character of the Delivered
        1. Holiness
        2. Holy Living
    C. Possessing our Possessions
        1. Possessing the Prepossessor
        2. Claiming What Is Ours
    D. Fire and Flame
        1. The Fire that Destroys
        2. The Fire that Purges and Illuminates
III. Victory Over the Enemy (19–21)
    A. Judgment is the Lord's
    B. The Kingdom is the Lord's

CHAPTER ONE

A Vision of the Enemy

Obadiah 1–16

It is not wrong to have enemies. In fact, our spiritual maturity can be evaluated by the kind of enemies we have. The Bible does not condemn us for having enemies, but it does challenge us to be sure that our enemies are the self-appointed enemies of God.

Often our enemies are simply those who have hurt us personally. When someone opposes us, disagrees with us, or thwarts what we want to do, he is categorized as an enemy. We have all had experiences with people who have misunderstood, misjudged, and misused us. We make enemies of people who do not like us or have gossiped about us. Sometimes, we slate as our enemies those who hold different political views, denominational backgrounds, cultural values, or life-styles. Our obsession with petty enmity can keep us from confronting the true enemy.

Our real enemy is the collusive force of evil rampant in the world. Jesus identified Satan as that enemy. He also exposed those who were possessed by Satan or ploys of his diabolical schemes. Satan is the anti-God spirit constantly seeking to recruit people and organize movements to oppose God and His purposes of righteousness and justice.

Sometimes we feel that the enemy is winning, and we become discouraged in the seemingly endless battle against his virulent influence in society through godless people. We shudder as we read the daily paper, which shows us the destructive power of evil seen in individual violence, organized crime, and atheistic materialism. Every day we observe from the close-range focus of television the ravages of pride, selfishness, and hatred. We cry out in our prayers, "How long, O God, how long, must we wait for you to banish evil and bring justice?"

During those times of anguish it is helpful for us to look back over history and rejoice in God's interventions. He has toppled arrogant despots, crushed godless nations, exposed the proud, and destroyed evil movements. God is still in charge and is working out His purposes. And towering over the wrecks of time is the ultimate intervention of the cross and the assurance that "though the wrong seems oft so strong, God is the Ruler yet."[1]

Our conviction is strengthened through a careful study of Obadiah. The final verse of this short book thunders the truth, *"The kingdom shall be the Lord's."* Our God reigns — He always has the final word. On time, and in time, God constantly asserts His sovereignty and vindicates His people who humbly trust in Him. From this positive perspective we approach our exposition of Obadiah. We are reminded that our enemies are those who are determined to be God's enemies, and we can claim deliverance far greater than the prophet envisioned.

Leslie Allen underlines this positive perspective of the prophecy of Obadiah.

> The Christian, with a faith which sets value on loving one's enemies, will at first sight find Obadiah an unwelcome teacher. It must be remembered that the New Testament continually upholds the principle of love, in tension with a concern for moral order and justice which eventually involves the destruction of God's enemies (see Luke 19:27; 2 Thess. 1:7–10; Rev. 6:9–11). In the Old Testament the notion of a last judgment is brought forward into history and presented as something that God is doing now. Indeed, Obadiah gives the impression that Judah is living near the end time, as his use of "the day of the Lord" indicates. Moreover, for Obadiah what was at stake was not simply political rights or wrongs but religious ones; God was called upon to vindicate Himself even as He vindicated Judah. Vengeance wasn't the point but vindication of God and of His oppressed people was. Nevertheless, feelings against Edom not unnaturally ran high in Judah. Here the prophet, in God's name, is assuring frustrated and emotionally battered Jews that God cares and will put things right.[2]

No less an assurance is given to us in the twentieth century. Obadiah, when read through the focused lens of Calvary, helps us to trust in God's moral government and justice.

THE VISION

The prophecy of Obadiah begins with the words, *"The vision of Obadiah. Thus says the Lord God concerning Edom (we have heard a report from the Lord, and a messenger has been sent among the nations, saying: 'Arise, and let us rise up against her for battle')"* (v. 1). The vision given to Obadiah is not a pictorial one but a verbal account of what would take place in the destruction of Edom.

At this point, it is helpful to retrace the origin and identity of the Edomites and their antagonism to the Israelites, which takes us back to Isaac and Rebekah and their twin sons, Jacob and Esau. Esau was born first, and Jacob second, but only moments apart, for Jacob came out of the womb with his hand holding Esau's heel.

From the beginning Esau was his father's favorite, growing up to be a hunter, a man of the field. Like Isaac, Esau loved the thrill of the hunt, the freedom of adventure, the taste of game. By contrast, Jacob was Rebekah's favorite. The Scripture tells us he was a peaceful man living in tents. Perhaps Esau was free in his spirit to emulate his father's interests because Isaac had taken time to affirm Esau while Jacob hung around home longing to receive Isaac's affirmation.

The fundamental issue in Isaac's family was which of the sons would have the birthright—the right of primogeniture. The firstborn was to assume his father's place, property, and authority as the ruling member of the family at the time of his father's death. Along with the birthright went with the father's blessing.

Rebekah's passionate wish was that both the birthright and the blessing be given to her favorite, Jacob, instead of Esau. She inbred her desire in Jacob so that he joined her in her plan to get him the birthright. One day when Esau came in from the fields famished after a day's work, Jacob was cooking stew, and Esau, with youthful impetuosity, demanded some of it—saying that he would die if he did not eat immediately.

"First sell your birthright," Jacob retorted to Esau. Esau's nonchalant attitude toward the birthright is indicated by his response. "Behold, I am about to die; of what use is a birthright to me?" So, Esau sold the birthright and got a dish of stew—red stew. Edom means "red" . . . "Therefore his name was called Edom" (Gen. 25:30).

The plot intensified some time later when Isaac sensed he was dying and wanted to give his blessing to Esau. He sent his firstborn out on a hunt for game for a savory dish. "Bring it to me that I may eat, that my soul may bless you before I die" (Gen. 27:4). Rebekah was listening. The moment she had been waiting for had come. Quickly she told Jacob to kill a choice kid from the flock, prepare the dish Isaac wanted, and receive the blessing and birthright intended for Esau. Together Rebekah and Jacob staged a deception. Jacob dressed in Esau's clothes and put goat skins on his neck and hands so Isaac would think he was Esau. Jacob served Isaac the meal and duped Isaac into blessing him rather than Esau. Jacob received the birthright instead of Esau.

> Therefore may God give you
> Of the dew of heaven,
> Of the fatness of the earth,
> And plenty of grain and wine.
> Let peoples serve you,
> And nations bow down to you.
> Be master over your brethren,
> And let your mother's sons bow down to you
> Cursed be everyone who curses you,
> And blessed be those who bless you!
>   *Gen. 27:28–29*

When Esau returned home he discovered what his mother and brother had done against him, and he begged for some blessing from Isaac. "Have you only one blessing, my father? Bless me, even me also, O my father!" (Gen. 27:38).

It is difficult to understand the severity of Isaac's depreciation of Esau's destiny. And yet what he predicted for Esau came true:

> Behold, your dwelling shall be of the fatness of the
>   earth,
> and of the dew of heaven from above.
> by your sword you shall live,
> and you shall serve your brother;
> and it shall come to pass, when you become restless,
> That you shall break his yoke from your neck.
>   *Gen. 27:39–40*

Thus a terrible grudge became the riverbed for the flow of competition, hatred, and jealousy between Jacob and Esau. Esau made plans to kill his brother as soon as Isaac died. Fortunately, Esau never succeeded. Later, the two brothers negotiated a solicitous, surface peace, which was never shared by their descendants. While the descendants of Jacob were called Israelites, the descendants of Esau were called Edom, or Edomites, from the name of the red pottage for which Esau had traded his birthright.

Esau settled in a place called Mount Seir (Gen. 36:8–9). This was not just one mountain but a mountainous region inhabited by the Horites. It extended from the south of the Dead Sea to the Gulf of Aqabah. Eventually, the descendants of Esau dispossessed the Horites (Deut. 2:12).

The Edomites became a people to match the rocky, ragged crags and serrated ridges of the Seir territory. They were a hard, earthy people, proud, cruel, and fierce. There is no evidence that they had any religion. Their problem was not syncretism with other gods; they had no gods at all. The only things that bordered on religious fervor was their concentrated, persistent, bitter hatred against Israel. They fostered and perpetuated an implacable feud with the descendants of Jacob that was expressed repeatedly throughout the evolving history of the two nations.

During the wilderness wanderings of the people of Israel, Moses appealed to the Edomites to allow them to pass through their territory. With angry threats the Edomites refused. The animosity between the peoples deepened (Num. 20:14–21).

Intermittent conflict ensued. Balaam prophesied Edom's defeat (Num. 24:18). Later, Saul led Israel against the Edomites (1 Sam. 14:47), and David conquered them (2 Sam. 8:13–14; 1 Kings 11:15–16). The Edomites rose to strength in the ninth century B.C. and, in confederation with the Ammonites and the Moabites, raided Judah while Jehoshaphat was king (2 Chron. 20:1–2). Then again, during the reign of Jehoram, they rebelled against Judah (2 Kings 8:20–22). The angry bitterness between Edom and the people of Israel remained during the eighth century B.C. Amaziah recaptured Edom with great slaughter (2 Kings 14:7). Subsequently, during Ahaz's reign the Edomites raided Judah, taking captives.

After 734 B.C. Edom was a vassal nation of Assyria and later of Babylonia. It was during the Babylonian invasion of Jerusalem in 586 B.C. that the longstanding enmity with the Edomites reached a climax. The Edomites aided in the destruction of the city. It is in response to this that Obadiah prophesied judgment on Edom. He wrote in the early portion of the exile following the destruction of Jerusalem.

Commenting on the date of Obadiah's prophecy, Douglas Stuart says, "It is the exilic period, particularly the early exile (580s or shortly thereafter) that meets the criterion best. Most importantly, four other Old Testament passages from the same early sixth-century period reflect the same sort of situation and perspective found in Obadiah: Ps. 137:7; Lam. 4:18–22; Ezek. 25:12–14; 35:1–15. These parallels echo the furious resentment expressed in Obadiah at the way the Edomites took advantage of Jerusalem's subjugation by the Babylonians."[3]

1 Esdras 4:45 blames the Edomites for burning the Jerusalem temple. Though Esdras is not a reliable source, the composite evidence is that the Edomites shared in the destruction of Jerusalem and profited from it by looting and by taking southern Judean land.

With that background, we are ready to consider Obadiah's vision concerning Edom's judgment. The word *vision (ḥāzôn)* is a term for communication from God. The substance of the vision indicates that God's message came to the prophet in the form of words. *"We have heard a report from the Lord"* (v. 1). It is not just Obadiah's indignation over Edom that we are to hear, but God's judgment. He had already judged His own people for their apostasy. Now as Lord of all nations, He levels His condemnation on the people of Edom.

That is important to keep in mind. Otherwise we might well ask, "In the light of the bloodshed Judah had caused in Edom over the years, what right did Obadiah have to judge them or what they did to Jerusalem?" The fact that it is God who speaks through Obadiah, one who has experienced His judgment, gives a ring of reality to the prophet's words. God was not playing favorites. As Peter Craigie points out,

> The essence of the book is that it contains the Lord's word. And God was not partial; He had already judged His own people for their evil, and no less would He judge other nations. The essence of the theology throughout is that God is the Lord of human history; the evil acts of any nation, regardless of affiliation or national faith, invite divine judgment. And that theme, though delivered in Obadiah's time, contains a timeless truth.[4]

It is significant that the word of the Lord to Obadiah is a call to the nations to rise up against Edom. *"Arise, and let us rise up against her for battle."* There are times when God rallies the nations to put down a nation that has become an enemy of His righteousness.

In the case of Edom, some five years after they aided the Babylonians in razing Jerusalem, they fell under the yoke of the Chaldeans. Malachi 1:3–4 and Jeremiah 49:7–22, along with the records of Josephus, make this plain. From the late sixth to the fourth century B.C., the Nabateans, an Arab tribe, occupied Edom and its capital, Petra. In 312 B.C. Alexander the Great's general, Antigonus, conquered the Edomites. They were displaced and scattered throughout southern Palestine. Later, in the second century B.C., the Edomites endured further defeats from Judas Maccabeus. Josephus accounts for the complete ruination by Alexander Janneus of the remaining Edomites who had settled in the Negeb, also known as Idumea. Origen, in the third century A.D., wrote of the Edomites as a people whose name and language had perished from history. What God had told Obadiah in his vision of words came true.

The Anatomy of an Enemy of God

Analysis and close examination of Obadiah 2-14 gives us a clear picture of the component elements of what made Edom an enemy of God. The review provides a startling warning to nations today, but also serves as a stark reminder of what God abhors in us as individuals and as the church. Looking at Obadiah's prophecy from this perspective broadens our exposition beyond a mere historical analysis of the sins of Edom.

There is a series of oracles in verses 2–14 portraying the aspects of what God judges in Edom: (1) verses 2-4, pride and arrogance; (2) verses 5-6, greed and plunder; (3) verses 7-8, loss of wisdom and understanding; (4) verses 10-14, violence and gloating over suffering of others. These form a natural progression for preaching and teaching this section of Obadiah.

PRIDE AND ARROGANCE

David Baker entitles the first oracle against Edom as, "Pride Goes Before Destruction."[5] This is an apt description of what caused Edom's demise. *"The pride of your heart has deceived you"* (v. 3). That inner pride was based on outer securities and lack of accountability to God or any moral requirements.

The outward cause of the pride of the Edomites was their assumption that their rocky, mountainous territory was impenetrable. *"You who dwell in the clefts of the rock, whose habitation is high; you who say in your heart, 'Who will bring me down to the ground?'"*

In travels in this territory, I could see why the Edomites might have developed a sense of security against attack. As I rode on horseback, I could see how the rocks, clefts, chasms, and corridors between perpendicular sandstone rocks offered military protection for towns and outposts. The site of the fortress city of Petra can be reached only by passing through long narrow gorges in the impenetrable high rock formations. The pink hew to the sandstone makes the territory breathtakingly beautiful.

We can imagine that the fortress and fortifications about 3,800 feet above sea level felt like the security of a soaring eagle. *"'Though you ascend as high as the eagle, and though you set your nest among the stars, from there I will bring you down,' says the Lord"* (v. 4).

Note the progression in the word picture. First, there is the soaring eagle reaching great heights. Then we picture the way an eagle relaxes and is carried almost motionless by the jet stream to even greater heights.

We were created to soar like eagles. But Isaiah underlined the secret of the strength to really soar. *"Those who wait on the Lord* shall renew their strength; they shall mount up with wings like eagles" (Isa. 40:31). My observation of eagles is that they rest in their nests, then mount up with the strength of their great wings and soar to greater heights.

The one thing the Edomites never did was wait on God, much less believe in Him. The author of Hebrews speaks of Esau as a "profane person" (Heb. 12:16). His descendants followed in his footsteps. Some scholars maintain that not only did the Edomites refuse to acknowledge Yahweh, but they had no gods at all. The psalmist refers to the fool who says in his heart there is no God (Ps. 53:1). Edom seems to have been a nation of fools. Their god was themselves, their nation, and their fierce might. That is why pride reigned in their hearts as they cried, "Who shall bring me down?" G. Campbell Morgan said of the Edomites, "They were the very embodiment then of practical defiant godlessness, expressing itself in the deification of self, and the conviction that self was sufficient, and that the fortresses which it had made for its own protection were enough to protect it against all opposition."[6]

We think of the contemporary Edomites where deification of self leads to pride. Arrogance rules their lives. They are the materialists whose security is in human power and possessions. Accountable to no one but themselves, they perpetuate the cult of humanism. Bloated egoism results. There are no rules except those they set to control others. People are manipulated as things; accumulated accouterments of success are touted as the meaning of life. Their motto is, "What's good is what makes me feel great." These are the truly dangerous people. The real enemies of God. And our enemies too, because their lack of accountability to anyone greater than themselves makes them willing tools of the archenemy, Satan. He is the instigator of the pride that eventually blocks out God and His righteousness.

Yet it is the practical atheists who are even more dangerous. These are the people who simply live as if God does not exist. Life is lived on a flat horizontal level. They set their own goals and seek to achieve them on their own strength. Where the hard-core atheist is often a perpetrator of evil, the practical atheist is a passive participant.

But God is not mocked. He brings down the arrogant, if not in their lifetime, in their death and in history's evaluation of them. Louis XIV of France called himself "the great" and made the infamous assertion of pride, "I am the state!" His court was the most magnificent in Europe at the time. When he died, his funeral was spectacular. He had left behind orders to dramatize his greatness. He was placed in a gold coffin. The cathedral was dimly lit, with only one candle placed above his coffin. Thousands waited in hushed silence as Bishop Massilon was about to give an appropriate eulogy. Instead, slowly reaching down, he snuffed out the candle and said, "Only God is great!"

Greatness is not measured in our achievement for our own glory but in the measure that we glorify God. Without that, life is an empty quest for human greatness.

Mark Schorer's analysis of Sinclair Lewis points up the emptiness of Lewis's life without God. "In flight from himself, he tried to compensate by his immense vaudeville talent. He never got around to connecting his talent and his life so that he knew who he was. There was no inner certainty, no balance, no serenity, nothing between heaven and earth to which he could withdraw for quietude and healing. Because he never knew himself, he outraged himself."

The only lasting antidote to pride is praise. But without someone greater than the aggrandized self, there is no one and no thing to praise. Such was the condition of the Edomites and the basic cause of their lack of accountability to anyone, least of all God.

Reinhold Niebuhr calls this the primal sin of pride in man. "His inclination to abuse his freedom, to overestimate his power and become everything is understood as the primal sin. It is because man is inevitably involved in this primal sin that he is bound to meet God first of all as judge, who humbles his pride and brings his vain imagination to naught."[7]

PLUNDER, DESTRUCTION, AND DEFECTION

The second oracle (vv. 5–7) predicts a plunder and destruction of Edom such as they had participated in doing to Judah and Jerusalem. Two rhetorical questions in verse 5 focus the completeness of Edom's destruction by contrasting it to partial loss: Will not a robber steal until he has all he wants? Doesn't a grape harvester leave some grapes? But in the ravage of Edom everything will be despoiled, and the land will be stripped bare. In contrast to the thief and the harvester's denunciation, in Edom's case the plunder will be total. Verse 6 says that the Edomites will be ransacked, and no hidden treasure will remain undiscovered by the conqueror. Baker points out the fact that in verse 5 God speaks *to* Edom but *about* him in verse 6, as one who is no longer there. The progression of the description is broken by laments starting with *"Oh, how" (ʾêk)*, expressing shock and amazement over the extent of the judgment.[8]

Added to the physical destruction will be the defection of trusted friends. *"All the men of your confederacy will force you to the border; the men at peace with you shall deceive you and prevail against you. Those who eat your bread shall lay a trap for you. No one is aware of it"* (v. 7). Edom's *"confederacy"* or "allies" (RSV, NIV) and friends (Hebrew, "men of peace") will turn against her. Her armies will be deceived and will be lured out of their strongholds. The treacherous Edomites will suffer treachery by the hands of those on whom they had depended because of a quid pro quo established in the covenant-making ceremonies of eating bread together. This is an obvious play on words. The same Hebrew consonants in the word for "bread" *(lḥm)* are also found in another word meaning "do battle." Edom's allies who have covenanted by breaking bread to fight *with* her would now fight *against* her. As we have noted, the Babylonians and later the Arab tribes turned against Edom.

The Lord of the nations is able to turn His enemies against one another as part of His judgment.

LOSS OF WISDOM AND UNDERSTANDING

The third oracle presses the judgment of Edom even further. Everything in which Edom had false pride will be brought down—her fortification, the resources of her land, her security in allies, and now in this oracle, her wise men. Edom was noted for her wise men who were seers distinguished in folklore, the mysteries of life, and magic. An example of such wise men would be one of Job's counselors, Eliphaz of Teman. His counsel to Job could be applied to his own nation. "Those who plow iniquity and sow trouble reap the same. By the blast of God they perish, and by the breath of His anger they are consumed" (Job 4:8–9).

The trouble with Edom's wise men in the sixth century B.C., however, was that they did not use their wisdom to check their leaders and their military arrogance. The wise men were to be seers and advisors to the *"mighty men"* (warriors) of Teman. (Teman was one of the chief cities of Edom, about five miles east of Petra.) Their supposed wisdom had become captive of the nationalistic spirit of Edom's leaders. This vaunted wisdom devoid of reverence and understanding without knowledge of God had approved of violence against Israel. In the day of judgment these wise men of Edom would be deposed along with the warriors.

VIOLENCE AND GLOATING

The next oracle deals with the specific acts of violence in, and gloating over, the destruction of Jerusalem. *"For your violence against your brother Jacob"* (v. 10). The list of evils done to Judah and the people of Jerusalem is tantamount to a form of fratricide against Jacob—that is, all of Israel. We are reminded of the historic conflict between these two brother nations reaching back to the progenitors in Jacob and Esau.

The *"shame"* of Edom is that she *"stood on the other side"* (vv. 10–11). The Edomites did not lift a hand to help when the Israelites were carried off into exile and as the Chaldeans cast lots for the spoils of the city. With hateful complicity, the Edomites acted as if they were *"one of them."* The implication is that they gleefully aided in the looting of the city.

The insult added to the injury was that the Edomites gloated over the captivity of the people of Judah in Babylon and the continuing destruction of the city. With mean spitefulness, they *"gazed on their affliction"* (v. 13).

But the catalogue of the sins of the Edomites reaches a climax with the description of how they stood at the crossroads outside Jerusalem and captured the fleeing citizens of the city and turned them over to the invaders. Added to this, the Edomites apparently acted as quislings to the Chaldeans in rounding up the Israelites who were still hiding in the city. No mercy was shown by the Edomites.

THE DAY OF THE LORD FOR EDOM

The day of the Lord, the day of judgment, on all nations was close at hand. Verses 15 and 16 focus that day for Edom. The talion law of tit for tat will be applied to the Edomites: *"As you have done, it shall be done to you; your reprisal shall return upon your own head."* The awesome thing is that the punishment of Edom matched their intent. They intended the complete destruction of the Israelites and that is what eventually happened to them.

The imagery of verse 16 communicates that the destruction of Edom will be complete. *"For as you drank on my holy mountain, so shall*

all the nations drink continually; yes, they shall drink, and swallow, and they shall be as though they had never been." Jeremiah 25:15–28 explains the cup that is drunk. It is the cup of the Lord's wrath against the nations in opposition to Him, first for Judah's apostasy and then for the pagan nations. "For thus says the Lord God of Israel to me: 'Take this wine cup of fury from My hand, and cause all the nations, to whom I send you, to drink it'" (Jer. 25:15).

In the light of that cross-reference we can understand Obadiah's word of judgment for Edom. Because of what she had done, she was given the cup of God's wrath to drink and swallow. And the prophecy that she would be as though she had never been came true in subsequent years.

In these first 16 verses of Obadiah, we have been stirred by the awesome sovereign power of God over all nations. As Lord of history, He towers above individuals and nations. Any person or nation opposing Him in personal or nationalistic pride will be judged and punished. When we seek to identify our true enemies as the proud enemies of God, we also must admit that at times we are among them. Any review of the catalogue of the sins of Edom stirs within us an honest confession of pride in human strength, accomplishments, intellect, and learning. And we, too, have shared in the selfish glee over others's weaknesses and failures. The hurt we have inflicted on others haunts us. What would happen to any of us if at this moment the talion law were leveled on us, "As you have done it, it shall be done to you!" We shudder as we think about that! It is then that we cling to the cross and our Deliverer and cry:

> Father look upon His anointed face
> And look on us only as seen in Him
> Look not upon our misusing of Your grace
> Our prayers so languid, our faith so dim,
> For between our sins and their reward
> We place the cross of Christ our Lord.

NOTES

1. Maltbie D. Babcock, "This Is My Father's World," *Hymns for the Living Church* (Carol Stream, Ill.: Hope Publishing Co.), 58.

2. Leslie Allen, *Hosea–Malachi* (London:Scripture Union, 1987), 56.

3. Stuart, *Hosea–Jonah,* 404.

4. Peter Craigie, *Twelve Prophets: Volume 1,* 199.

5. David W. Baker, "Obadiah", *Obadiah, Jonah, and Micah,* Tyndale Old Testament Commentaries (Downers Grove, Ill.: InterVarsity Press, 1988), 31.

6. G. Campbell Morgan, "The Kingdom Shall Be the Lord's," vol. 8, *20 Centuries of Great Preaching,* (Waco, Tex.: Word Books, 1971), 16.

7. Reinhold Niebuhr, *The Nature and Destiny of Man* (New York: Scribner's, 1949), 92.

8. Baker, "Obadiah," 34.

CHAPTER TWO

Deliverance from the Enemy — Then and Now

Obadiah 17–18

17 "But on Mount Zion there shall be deliverance, and there shall be holiness; the house of Jacob shall possess their possessions.

18 "The house of Jacob shall be a fire, and the house of Joseph a flame; but the house of Esau shall be stubble; they shall kindle them and devour them, and no survivor shall remain of the house of Esau," for the Lord has spoken.

Obad. 17–18

Deliverance on Mount Zion! We read the words of this promise of liberation through the longing eyes of the captives in exile and then through our dilated vision of the ultimate deliverance on Calvary.

A comparison of these two deliverances gives us an excellent opportunity to do justice to the Obadiah text, and at the same time show how its promise is a precursor of the lasting deliverance of the cross.

The two deliverances are separated by more than 500 years. The post-exile deliverance resulted in further wrath against Israel's enemies; the deliverance of Calvary resulted in liberation from the wrath of God. The first produced an occasion for restitution of land taken by the enemy; the second affected a reconciliation to God. One issued in a holiness of reestablished traditions, the other the holiness of authentic God-centered character. The late sixth-century B.C. deliverance gave the Jews power to subdue their enemies; the deliverance of A.D. 33 overcame the influence of the arch-enemy, Satan, and gave the new Israel—the church—power to fulfill the command to love human enemies. With the initial deliverance, the house of Jacob and

Joseph became a fire and a flame to burn the stubble of the enemy. In the final deliverance, the new creatures of the new creation are filled with the Light of the World and experience the passion of the fire of His Spirit.

THE FIRST DELIVERANCE

Verse 17 begins with the transitional conjunction *but*. It introduces the contrast of the judgment of Edom with the restoration of Israel. In the very place the Israelites were helpless refugees (*pĕlêṭîm*) at the hands of the Edomites, there will be deliverance (*pĕlêṭâ*) by the intervention of the mighty hand of God. The clause of this promise is a direct quotation of Joel 2:32. Not only will there be a deliverance of the captives in exile, but there will be a deliverance of Mount Zion, the Temple, and the holy city from the occupation of the Babylonians and the demeaning subjugation of the Edomites. Out of goodness and mercy, Yahweh will honor His covenant with Israel and restore His people.

"And there shall be holiness" (v. 17). This can mean that God's holy presence will return to the holy of holies of the reconstructed Temple, or it can mean a holiness in God's people as a result of the deliverance. The masculine is used so the meaning is most likely a reference to the holiness of Mount Zion, not to Israel, where the feminine would have been used. It is the Temple which was sanctified with the return of the presence of Yahweh. Regretfully, there was a distinct lack of renewed holiness, the sanctification of character, among the returning exiles, as Ezra attests.

Their major concern was to claim the promise that they would *"possess their possessions."* The word *môrāšêhem*, "their possessions," is sometimes repointed as *môrîšêhem*, "their dispossessor." "Pointed thus," Allen says, "it provides a better link with the reference to the nations in the previous stanza and to Edom in the next.[1] A similar phrase is used in Jeremiah 49:2 where the word is translated in the NKJV as "inheritance": "Then Israel shall take possession of his inheritance."

Actually, Israel will possess both the dispossessors and the possessions taken by them, as the rest of the Obadiah prophecy promises. The dispossessor of Israel will be dispossessed, and the people of God will once again possess the inheritance of the promised land. This interpretation is supported by the textual variation in the Septuagint and in the Hebrew manuscript discovered at Murabbaat near the Dead Sea. Thus Allen translates, "The community of Jacob will regain territory from those who took it from them."[2]

The covenant, which had been broken by Israel's apostasy resulting in the punishment of Jerusalem's fall in 586 B.C., would be restored. This actually took place under Zerubbabel in 537 B.C. when the people were returned to Jerusalem and in 515 B.C. when the Temple was rebuilt.

Verse 18 returns to Obadiah's theme of the judgment of Edom. The remnant of the house of Jacob and Joseph, Jacob's most distinguished son (i.e., the tribes of Judah), will be a fire and a flame for the burning of the stubble of Edom. The conflagration of the ancient foe will blaze until the destruction is complete, without survivors. In the Scriptures, the wicked are often compared to stubble, the cut stalks of grain left sticking up after a harvest which are burned off before replanting season. After the burning, the scorched ground leaves no trace of the consumed stubble. "For Yahweh has spoken," says Obadiah, as if to assert the guarantee of the prophecy.

DELIVERANCE ON CALVARY

Without unduly spiritualizing verses 17 and 18, we are given a magnificent progression for a review of the cosmic deliverance of Calvary. Alexander Maclaren, a great expositor of another generation, said of passages like this,

> Prophesies which were susceptible of . . . a historical and approximate fulfillment in the restoration of the Jews from Babylonian captivity, have a higher and broader and more real accomplishment in that great deliverance wrought by Jesus Christ, of which these earlier and partial and outward manifestations were themselves prophecies and shadows. So I make no apology for taking them as having their only real accomplishment in the office and working of Jesus Christ.[3]

In a similar way we could approach Micah 2:13, "The one who breaks open will come up before them; they will break out, pass through the gate, and go out by it; their king will pass before them, with the Lord at their head." Or, Psalm 68:18, "You have led captivity captive," when seen in the light of Paul's reference to Christ in Ephesians 4:8: "When He ascended on high, He led captivity captive, and gave gifts to men."

COMPARISON OF THE TWO DELIVERANCES

The comparison of the post-exilic deliverance on Mount Zion and the deliverance of Calvary leads us into a vivid description of the liberating power of Christ's atonement. He came to preach deliverance to the captives (Luke 4:18) and delivered us from the power of sin and Satan.

Through the shedding of His blood, Christ the Liberator has delivered us from the wrath of God, His judgment upon all nations and peoples. In God's heart, wrath and atonement are two sides of the same reality—His grace. He had to find a way of judging sin and justifying the sinner. Justification is the complete and unconditional exoneration of the sinner. The only way for God to accomplish that was to provide a just recompense for sin and an effective reconciliation of the sinner. He came in the Messiah, the suffering Servant, the Lamb of God. On Calvary, sin was judged and paid for. Christ suffered in humankind's place for the primal sin of pride expressed in the arrogance of the Edomite and the rebellion of the Israelite, in all people separated or estranged from Him.

THE JUST AND THE JUSTIFIER

In Christ we meet God as both just and justifier. This is the exciting news Paul wrote to the Christians in Rome.

> All have sinned and fall short of the glory of God, being justified freely by His grace through the redemption that is in Christ Jesus, whom God set forth to be a propitiation by His blood, through faith, to demonstrate His righteousness, because in His forbearance God had passed over the sins that were previously committed, to demonstrate at the present time His righteousness, that He might be just and justifier of the one who has faith in Jesus.
>
> *Rom. 3:23–26*

Note the progression: righteousness, the just, the justifier, and faith. God's righteousness is the consistent expression of His nature. He must judge any denial of His love, untruth in any form, and all distortions of His plan and purpose for humankind set forth in the Commandments. He cannot abdicate being just, the judge of all manifestations of pride that separate us from Him, that cause our gross misuse of others, and that wreak havoc in His creation. What can God do? The just must also be the justifier. We cannot help ourselves either through self-justification or self-punishment. Without denying His nature as the just, God must become the justifier. Out of unqualified and undeserved grace, our righteous God makes us right with Himself by both demanding atonement and providing it. He is both the just and the justifier in the sacrifice of Calvary.

THE ONLY QUALIFICATION

Faith is the only qualification for accepting and enjoying the free gift of this deliverance. But even that cannot be deserved or earned. It, too, is a gift. The same Lord who is just and the justifier is also the giver of the ability to respond. God enables us to accept our justification and claim our righteousness in Him. The primary gift of His Spirit at work in us is faith. By faith alone we claim that we are forgiven and reconciled with God.

Now we can see the great difference between the deliverance of Obadiah 17 and the deliverance of Calvary. We do not escape the wrath of God only to delight to see it turned on our enemies. "He has delivered us from the power of darkness and translated us into the kingdom of the Son of His love, in whom we have redemption through His blood, the forgiveness of sins" (Col. 1:13). Instead of living in the *gaols* of self-centeredness, we are delivered to live out God's *goals* for our lives.

THE SECOND MAJOR DIFFERENCE

So we see the second major difference between the two deliverances we are considering. God's primary goal for our lives is to make us like His Son. He has assigned that responsibility to the Son Himself. When we confess Christ as Lord of our lives and invite Him to take up His post-resurrection residence in us, we begin the process of authentic holiness. Holiness is belonging to God, receiving the character transplant of His Son into our nature, and expressing His implanted nature summarized in the fruit of the Spirit: "love, joy, peace, longsuffering, goodness, kindness, gentleness, faithfulness, self-control" (Gal. 5:22–23).

The holiness manifested in the post-exilic deliverance was primarily the presence of God returned to the holy of holies of the reconstructed Temple. Now, through the deliverance of Calvary, we are called to be the living temple of God in whom He dwells in the Spirit of His Son.

THE THIRD DRAMATIC DIFFERENCE

The third dramatic difference between the two deliverances is that we can claim both interpretations of the promise to possess our possessions.

Consider the first: we can possess our dispossessor. Our dispossessor is really Satan. He is the one who seeks to demean our calling and our potential, discourages us in our efforts to be faithful and obedient to the Lord, disrupts our relationships with anger and hostility, and deranges life into chaos. He tries to rob us of peace, constantly directing us to no-exit cul-de-sacs of disobedience. Satan is the hassler, the huckster of disagreements with others, and the harbinger of self-condemnation. He wants to get us down on ourselves. He knows that soon we will transfer self-depreciation to blaming others.

Satan is delighted when we make people our enemies. He gains a powerful position of anonymity and laughs with glee when we battle people rather than fighting for truth.

On the cross Christ dispossessed Satan as our dispossessor. He defeated his ruling power. Now there is One Name that he cannot abide, one sign and symbol He cannot resist: the name of Jesus Christ and the cross. With both we can possess our archenemy, the dispossessor, Satan.

Having done that, the alternative interpretation of possessing our possessions can be realized. We can claim all that is ours in Christ's deliverance: atonement, assurance that we are forgiven even before we ask, freedom from guilt, the indwelling Spirit and His gifts (1 Cor. 12), daily and hourly guidance, peace in life's chaos, and the assurance that death will only be a transition in our eternal life. Paul encouraged the Corinthians to possess their possessions: "All things are yours: . . . the world or life or death, or things present, or things to come – all are yours. And you are Christ's, and Christ is God's" (1 Cor. 3:21–23).

CLAIMING WHAT IS OURS

Claiming all our possessions, we are empowered to confront our real enemy, Satan, and follow Christ's call to love our enemies. He delivered us on the cross so we could live His revolutionary admonition to love and forgive with His divine "I AM" authority. He gave us a new commandment:

> You have heard that it was said, "You shall love your neighbor and hate your enemy." But I say to you, love your enemies, bless those who curse you, do good to those who hate you, and pray for those who spitefully use you and persecute you, that you may be sons of your Father in heaven; for He makes His sun rise on the evil and on the good, and sends rain on the just and on the unjust. For if you love those who love you, what reward have you? Do not even the tax collectors do the same? And if you greet your brethren only, what do you do more than others? Do not even the tax collectors do so? Therefore you shall be perfect, just as your Father in heaven is perfect.
>
> *Matt. 5:43–48*

The stark difference between this challenge and Obadiah's startles us. But only through the power of His deliverance and His indwelling Spirit are we able to live Christ's awesome challenge. When we dare to try, our efforts are undergirded by His new law of multiplying returns:

> But love your enemies, do good, and lend hoping for nothing in return; and your reward will be great, and you will be sons of the Highest. For He is kind to the unthankful and evil. Therefore be merciful, just as your Father also is merciful. Judge not, and you shall not be judged. Condemn not, and you shall not be condemned. Forgive, and you will be forgiven. Give, and it will be given to you: good measure, pressed down, shaken together, and running over will be put into your bosom. For with the same measure that you use, it will be measured back to you.
>
> *Luke 6:35–38*

Who can live that way? No one . . . that is, apart from a consistent flow of God's mercy through Christ. We cannot give what we do not have or have been unwilling to receive. But to have received mercy and forgiveness and not share them is to eventually come to a place of not being able to receive. It is here that the Minor Prophets and Jesus are of one voice. We dare not overlook Jesus' words near the close of the Sermon on the Mount.

> Not everyone who says to Me, "Lord, Lord," shall enter the king-dom of heaven, but he who does the will of My Father in heaven. Many will say to Me in that day, "Lord, Lord, have we not prophesied in Your name, cast out demons in Your name, and done many wonders in Your name?" And then I will declare to them, "I never knew you; depart from Me, you who practice lawlessness!"
>
> *Matt. 7:21–23*

According to Matthew 25, our salvation is dependent on what we do to the hungry, thirsty, strangers, naked, sick, and imprisoned. "Inasmuch as you did not do it to one of the least of these, you did not do it to Me. And these will go away into everlasting punishment, but the righteous into eternal life" (Matt. 25:45–46). We have seen this mandate for mission in Amos and the other Minor Prophets.

THE FIRE OF LOVE

The sure sign that we have experienced the deliverance of Calvary is that we have a fire of love burning in us. This brings us to the final contrast of the deliverance in Obadiah and the deliverance of the cross. The fire and flame of the house of Jacob were used to destroy Edom; the fire of Christ's Spirit in us gives us a holy passion for a righteousness expressed in sacrificial service to others. Near the end of His ministry, He said, "I came to send fire on the earth, and how I wish it were already kindled! But I have a baptism to be baptized with, and how distressed I am till it is accomplished" (Luke 12:49–50).

Jesus envisioned a new creation of people who would abide in Him and in whom He would abide. He knew that before that could happen He would have to go to the cross to die for the sins that keep people from both abundant and eternal life. Then He would rise from the dead in victorious defeat of death and Satan's power. He would be loosed on the world as the ubiquitous, omnipresent Lord of the new creation He had come to establish. He knew that the love and forgiveness of His cross would raise His followers out of the graves of doubt, fear, and reservation. They would be ready for the fire He would set ablaze in their minds and hearts with His Spirit. It is significant that two of His followers who met Him as resurrected Lord exclaimed, "Did not our heart burn within us while He talked with us on the road, and while He opened the Scriptures to us?" (Luke 24:32). Like physical fire, Christ's Spirit purifies, refines, radiates from us, and brings warmth to others through us. Christ's fire sets us ablaze with convictions we cannot deny, with the will to obey that we cannot resist, and with love we cannot withhold.

It is the fire of Christ's Spirit that empowers us to love our enemies. At the same time His fire blazes in us with social righteousness. We do not become eccentric firebrands, but effective disciples branded with the fire of Christ's character and concern for people who suffer. We have been delivered to be involved with Christ in changing people and battling injustice in our society.

NOTES

1. Leslie C. Allen, *The Books of Joel, Obadiah, Jonah, and Micah*, The New International Commentary on the Old Testament (Grand Rapids, Mich.: William B. Eerdmans Publishing Company, 1976), 163.

2. Ibid.

3. Alexander Maclaren, *Expositions of Holy Scripture: Ezekiel, Daniel, and the Minor Prophets* (Grand Rapids, Mich.: Baker Book House, reprinted 1982), 207.

CHAPTER THREE

The Kingdom is the Lord's

Obadiah 19–21

The final three verses of Obadiah's prophecy at first review seem to hold little for fruitful preaching and teaching. But look again. The last clause of the closing verse offers a key to the exposition of these three verses and for a dynamic message on the kingdom of God. It is a shout of acclamation, an outburst of triumphant faith. *"The kingdom shall be the Lord's!"*

THE FIRST CONVICTION

First of all, this statement expresses Obadiah's confidence that the prophecy he just made about the repossession of the land occupied by Edom and others will be accomplished. We look back over verses 19–21 from our perspective of history and realize that the prophet's assurance was well-founded. All that he prophesied came true. God provides for what He guides.

While the Israelites were enduring the captivity of the exile, the Edomites occupied the towns of the Negeb, the southern portion of Judah. The very people who had been occupied by the Edomites later succeeded in conquering the Edomite territory.

The Israelites of the lowlands (*šĕpēlâ*) will drive out the Philistines and overcome Philistia as well (v. 19). Note Zephaniah 2:5 as a cross reference, "The word of the Lord is against you, O Canaan, land of the Philistines: 'I will destroy you; so there shall be no inhabitant.'" It happened!

But there's more. The next conquests listed were accomplished in the second century B.C. when the Jews were under the Maccabees. The

Israelites did indeed possess the "fields of Ephraim," central Palestine, the district of Samaria and Benjamin took Gilead to the east. The returning exiles of the northern kingdom occupied the Canaanite territory, north to Zarephath, between Tyre and Sidon.

The Jews who had been in captivity in Sepharad, or Sardis, the capital city of Lydia in Asia Minor, took possession of cities of the south, the Negeb.

Verse 21 prophesies that *"saviors"* will rule over Edom from Mount Zion. The word *saviors* means judges who will lead the conquests and act as rulers.

THE SECOND CONVICTION

The second great conviction expressed by the assurance that *"the kingdom is the Lord's"* is: our God reigns as Lord over all the nations. He composes and disposes. Yahweh is judge of all the nations. He used Edom and Babylonia to execute His judgment upon Jerusalem when, after repeated warnings, the people of Judah refused to repent. Yet, at the same time, He was faithful to His covenant with the Israelites and gave them a new beginning—He used the Israelites to bring down Edom.

THE THIRD CONVICTION

A third stirring conviction arising from the statement that *"the kingdom is the Lord's"* is all that we have belongs to the Lord. This includes not only our possessions, but our projects, our relationships, and our responsibilities. *God owns what we falsely enthrone.* We all have our little kingdoms, our realms of responsibility. It is our proclivity to think that ultimately we are in charge and in control. What God seeks to do through us, we shift and want to do for Him and subtly place under our control. Soon pride and willfulness take over, and our service becomes a projection of our prideful egos. We want God's help only to do things in *our* way. Soon we begin expressing, at least in attitude, "Lord, what's Yours is mine," then, "What's mine is mine!"

When I was a boy in Kenosha, Wisconsin, I used to play "King of the Mountain" on a hillside in a park. Whoever could maintain supremacy over the top of the hill was king of the mountain. One of the lads by the name of Arthur, a scrawny little guy with a lisp, never wanted to be king of the whole hillside. He marked off a small spot off to the side and would shout, "It's not very big, but it's mine!"

Arthur's words have come back to me often as I talked to husbands or wives who acted as if they owned their spouses, or parents who clutched at control of their children, while raising them and long after they became adults. I also hear the same possessiveness in Christians about tasks they believe God has given them to do. Church officers sometimes act as if their churches belong to them. Clergy are constantly in danger of forgetting that Christ is Lord of the church.

The reminder that *the kingdom is the Lord's* is actually a source of great relief. He provides the strength and wisdom to do His work. And He constantly shifts His strategy. Too often, we get into trouble when we insist on doing things the way we have always done them. But, under His control, He closes doors and opens others—He begins movements, and He ends them when they have accomplished His purpose. Frequently, we try to prop up and keep alive what He may have deemed no longer useful in His kingdom business.

We are in the kingdom to do the King's will. Staying in close communion with the King of our lives enables us to know what He wants, when He wants it, and how He wants it done. Prayer is not preying on God to tell Him what we want Him to do, but listening attentively to His orders. *God inspires what He desires.*

The Fourth Conviction

Finally, Obadiah's description of assurance that *the kingdom is the Lord's* is a petition of supplication for God's reign on earth. The prophet joins with the other minor prophets in prophesying the kingdom of God as His ultimate plan and purpose for history. Joined with these prophesies were the predictions and longing expectations for the Messiah to come and reign as Lord of history.

John the Baptist, as a forerunner of the Messiah's ministry, declared, "The time is fulfilled, and the kingdom of God is at hand. Repent, and believe the gospel" (Mark 1:15).

The central thrust of Jesus' message was the kingdom of God. It was the theme of His parables. He taught His disciples to pray, "Thy kingdom come" (Matt. 6:10). He proclaimed the kingly rule, sovereignty, and Lordship of God over His people and all creation. The reign of God through Immanuel was manifested in Jesus' deeds and miracles manifested in His power over the demons and healing the sick.

When John the Baptist sent emissaries to Jesus to ask, "Are You the Coming One, or do we look for another?" Jesus answered, "Go and tell John the things you have seen and heard: that the blind see, the lame walk, the lepers are cleansed, the deaf hear, the dead are raised, the poor have the gospel preached to them" (Luke 7:20, 22).

The kingdom of God present in the Messiah was God's thrust into history to break the power of evil and establish His reign in people's hearts.

Jesus taught that the kingdom was present in Him and yet coming; within us and yet in the midst of our lives; to be entered at the cost of total surrender and yet of more value than a pearl of great price.

The Messiah went to the cross in full assurance that as suffering Servant and Lamb of God atoning for the sins of the world He would be raised up, be glorified, and return as King of the kingdom which He had taught and which was manifested in His ministry.

And so we, in the post-resurrection, post-Pentecost period, are to repeat Obadiah's ancient clause, *the kingdom is the Lord's,* as a confession of faith in Christ as our Lord and a commitment of our lives to be a specific realm of His rule and of our hearts as the throne of His reign as controlling King of our intellect, emotions, and wills. From that command post, He guides us as we seek first the kingdom of God and His righteousness.

Introduction to the Book of Jonah

As expositors of the Scriptures, we all enjoy passages with a clear story line. And so do our listeners and readers. A historical account, a parable, or a dramatic encounter between a biblical character and God are welcome changes of pace. We can get inside the skins of people and identify with their struggles and discoveries with "you are there" intensity.

Revelation of truth can be imparted relationally. Application, that ever present challenge to a communicator of the Scriptures, comes more readily. Our words are given wings. Outlines flow more freely giving us uncontrived pegs on which to hang the progression of thought that comes naturally. Of course, if we limited our expositions to passages with a story line, we and our listeners would be denied the richness of the etymological studies and theological formation provided by verse-by-verse exposition of the words of the Lord or the teaching of the prophets and apostles. These verses and passages become the cross-references for an in-depth interpretation of the story-line passages.

The book of Jonah is one of those accounts of a person's encounter and struggle with God that is power packed with theological truth and practical implications for people in every age. As we follow the story line, we find that analyzing Jonah is a look in the mirror, and we may not like what we see. We all have run away from God or His explicit guidance. And we all have run back to Him in times of need. We also remember the delight of running with God. But who hasn't run ahead of Him, trying to use our prayers to tell Him what is best for us, others, and situations?

THE PROPHET JONAH

Jonah is mentioned only once in the Old Testament outside the book of Jonah. 2 Kings 14:25 identifies him as the son of Amittai and as a prophet during the reign of Jeroboam II (786–746 B.C.) in the northern kingdom. He lived in Gath-hepher in the Zebulun territory, better known as Galilee. The town is identified with Khirbet ez-Zurra, three miles northeast of Nazareth. Jonah's prophecy expresses his nationalistic fervor. He prophesied that Jeroboam II would restore "the territory of Israel from the entrance of Hamath to the Sea of the Arabah." The king's accomplishment of this expansion provides the occasion for the reference to Jonah in 2 Kings 14:25.

The name *Jonah* means "dove." A character and personality profile from the book of Jonah suggest that perhaps the name *hawk* better describes him. He was an ardent nationalist and an isolationist. His truncated theology restricted the providence of God to the Israelites. The call to preach to the Assyrians was abhorrent to Jonah.

THE BOOK OF JONAH

There are varied and sharply differing theories of the nature of the book of Jonah. Some suggest that it is simply a parable written by an unknown author and the use of the name for the principal character is coincidental. Others assert that an unknown author wrote it as a parable and simply used the name of the most obscure prophet he could find. The theory that the book of Jonah is only a parable is often directly associated with the account of Jonah being swallowed by a whale. Those who discount this possibility reason that the whole book must be a parable with no actual historical roots. The book of Jonah is handled in the same way as the parable of the Good Samaritan.

Some disavow any historical grounds for the book because it is so different from conventional prophetic narratives. This theory may support the conviction that Jonah himself was not the author. If he were, the book is a very honest self-exposure, even confession, but the ending of the book indicates no transformation of Jonah's obdurate resistance to God. If the prophet Jonah wrote it, he admitted denying his prophetic calling not only in his rebellion against God, but also in his reluctance to forth-tell what God had told him about His mercy. It is unlikely that an eighth century B.C. prophet would make himself the ploy of an account of disobedience and leave his reader dangling.

My own theory is that the book of Jonah was written by an unknown author about the historical prophet Jonah who lived in the eighth century B.C. This writer's purpose was didactic, to impart spiritual and moral truth in biographical form. If the author had set out to write only a parable, chances are that he would have selected another name for his central character just so his readers would not confuse him with Jonah from Gath-hepher. So I would classify the book of Jonah as didactic biography.

However, it is the message of the book of Jonah that is most important. Frankly, if as much time were spent interpreting the message as has been spent over the centuries debating in which literary category the book belongs, we would be closer to living the mercy and mission of God. The message of the book of Jonah is one that is urgently needed in the church today. The book is more than just a whale of a story! The central theme is God's nature of mercy for all humankind.

The Date of Jonah

Since the book of Jonah contains no list of kings, its date has been open to conjecture and no small amount of debate among scholars. Dates they have suggested range from the eighth to the third centuries B.C. The prophet Jonah lived during the first half of the eighth century B.C. during the reign of Jeroboam II, as we have noted, so the date would not have been before that. And its inclusion in the Book of the Twelve means that it could not have been later than the end of the third century B.C. Nineveh was conquered and destroyed by the Babylonians and the Medes in 612 B.C., so even a parable citing *"that great city"* (Jon. 1:2) seems untenable after that date.

My conclusion is that the historical Jonah was called to go to Nineveh before the middle of the eighth century, and the book of Jonah was written as a didactic biography sometime after that, but before 733 B.C., when Tiglath-Pileser III began his assaults on the northern kingdom, deporting captives to Assyria (2 Kings 15:29). It would have been difficult for a Hebrew prophet to prophesy in Nineveh. If the book had been written later, the *"wickedness"* of Nineveh would probably have been focused on the Assyrian captivity.

In the final analysis, the message of Jonah is not dependent on the date when it was written. It is sufficient to say that Nineveh was a symbol of wickedness, an enemy of Israel, and the last place Jonah would expect the Lord to send him to express mercy.

A homiletical outline of the content of the book of Jonah may be divided into four parts. These four sections may be used for a four-part message or lesson series or as the four major points of one sermon or class on the book of Jonah.

As with the exposition of the other four prophets in this volume, our focus will be on communicating Jonah to contemporary congregations and classes. There are aspects of the reluctant prophet in all of us and in the contemporary church as a whole. The Lord will expose this raw nerve and heal it with His mercy.

An Outline of Jonah

I. Running Away from God (1:1-16)
   A. Jonah's Call and Our's
   B. Tarshish and Nineveh—Rebellion or Response
   C. The Inescapable Presence
   D. When Narcissism Turns to Masochism
   E. Intervention
II. Running Back to God (1:17-2:10)
   A. Jonah's Prayer
   B. Jonah's Deliverance
   C. Back to the Beginning
III. Running with God (3:1-10)
   A. Recall to Missions
   B. The Success of the Mission
   C. The Results of the Mission
IV. Running Ahead of God (4:1-11)
   A. A Petulant Prophet
   B. A Merciful God
   C. Oh, For Pity's Sake!

CHAPTER ONE

Running Away from God

Jonah 1:1–16

> 1:1 Now the word of the Lord came to Jonah the son of Amittai, saying,
>
> 2 "Arise, go to Nineveh, that great city, and cry out against it; for their wickedness has come up before Me."
>
> 3 But Jonah arose to flee to Tarshish from the presence of the Lord. He went down to Joppa, and found a ship going to Tarshish; so he paid the fare, and went down into it, to go with them to Tarshish from the presence of the Lord.
>
> *Jon. 1:1–3*

Focus in your mind's eye the people you find it most difficult to love. On the screen of your consciousness flash the faces of the persons, the types, and the groups of people of whom you are most critical and judgmental. Think of the personalities you dismiss, hoping to have little contact with or responsibility for them. These are people who have become enemies because of what they do, say, or believe. Now if these people or groups have declared themselves to be enemies of God or their behavior is blatantly anti-God, we feel all the more justified in our judgment of them and writing them off.

That is what happened to Jonah. *"The word of the Lord came to Jonah the son of Amittai"* (Jon. 1:1). So far so good. This sounds similar to other openings for the books of the Minor Prophets. Like the rest, Jonah received the word of the Lord. More than words, this was a profound experience of the Lord's presence and power. Surely he shuddered with awe and wonder. Jonah's call to be a prophet was reaffirmed and validated, his faithfulness and loyalty to Israel confirmed.

Then, before Jonah could revel in his new encounter with God, shock waves exploded in his mind, his heart sank, and his strong will resistantly stiffened. The Lord told him what he was to do: *"Arise, go to Nineveh, that great city, and cry out against it; for their wickedness has come up before Me"* (1:2).

"Nineveh, Lord?" he must have replied. "Surely you don't mean that?! The capital city of the Assyrians? The center of Israel's worst Gentile enemy?" A contest of wills between the prophet and Yahweh began.

Jonah's nationalistic fervor had been delighted by his previous assignment from the Lord. He prophesied that Jeroboam II would restore "the territory of Israel from the entrance of Hamath to the sea of Arabah" (2 Kings 14:25). And Yahweh empowered Jeroboam to do it. Jonah witnessed the faithfulness of Yahweh firsthand Why, then, would he be so shocked that the Lord would send him to Nineveh? Because Jonah believed that Yahweh was the exclusive God of the Hebrews. Palestine was His realm. Jonah could readily agree about the wickedness and sin of Nineveh. But what concern was that to him?

And yet, there was a deeper reason Jonah balked at God's call to go to Nineveh. He describes later what was going on in his mind: "For I know that You are a gracious and merciful God, slow to anger and abundant in lovingkindness, One who relents from doing harm" (4:2). These are an almost exact duplicate of the words Yahweh spoke to Moses about His nature (Exod. 34:6). Jonah knew his Scripture. The prophet stiffened his back against Yahweh's command to go to Nineveh because he suspected that if they responded and repented, God would be merciful to them. This was the inner core of Jonah's resistance. The last thing Jonah wanted to do was become an agent for the salvation of his arch enemies.

THE PROPHET OF THE POCKET VETO

Jonah was the prophet of the pocket veto. He was a strong-willed man who was now engaged in a power struggle with God. His pocket veto was not in his cloak but in his heart. Jonah was a faithful prophet as long as God wanted what Jonah wanted. But when God's marching orders went contrary to Jonah, he would not do what he was told.

We can empathize. Leslie Allen wrote, "A Jonah lurks in every Christian heart, whimpering his insidious message of smug prejudice, empty traditionalism and exclusive solidarity."[1]

Let us consider what we struggle with God about. What is the command we find most difficult to hear? What instructions from God panic us? What prompts us to say, "Anything but that Lord!"? If He told us to go communicate His mercy to some person, some group, some type of human need, what assignment causes us to dig in our heels?

TARSHISH OR NINEVEH?

Jonah did arise as he had been told by the imperative of Yahweh. But when the prophet stepped out of his house at Gath-hepher, three miles north of what is now Nazareth, he had a choice. If he turned one way, it was about five hundred miles northeast to Nineveh, the abhorred capital of Israel's Gentile enemy, Assyria. Or, Jonah could turn in the other direction, head west for Joppa on the Mediterranean coast, and catch a ship going to the farthest place from Nineveh he could imagine—and from the Lord.

Jonah headed for Joppa and attempted to sail to Tarshish, a little fishing village around Gibraltar on the Atlantic coast of Spain. Nineveh or Tarshish? Obedience or escape?

Nineveh was situated on the east bank of the Tigris River, north of the confluence of the Tigris and the Upper Zab. Modern excavations indicate a city of great size—the walls were eight miles in circumference. The broader reaches of the city, also thought of as part of the megalopolis, included Calah, eighteen miles south, Rosen, between Calah and Nineveh, and Rehoboth-ir, which means "broad places of the city."

For Jonah, Nineveh simply meant the center of Assyrian power—the place from which ruthless armies moved out to subdue and conquer. Assyria loomed as a threat to Israel's safety and survival. Nineveh was the epitome of everything Jonah hated in the Gentile world. It was a synonym for godless tyranny. It was an idolatrous, sin-ridden city in Jonah's mind, and nothing was more repulsive or repugnant than going there to preach repentance. Jonah's theology was dominated by a funnel concept of providence—that God's power and control were limited to Palestine and the covenant people.

Tarshish, on the other hand, represented for Jonah a place where he could escape Yahweh's call. At Joppa he probably asked, "What's the next ship to the farthest place you sail?" When he learned that one was about to sail for Spain, no price was too high to get a ticket and go on board. The quiet little village symbolized escape and freedom from the call and presence of God. At that time, a sea voyage to Tarshish took almost a year with stops at ports of call on the way. "What difference?" Jonah thought as it carried him further from Nineveh. He was in flight from Yahweh and any responsibilities.

Most of us have our own Nineveh and Tarshish. One is the city of faithfulness and obedience; the other is a place of escape and equivocation. Our Ninevehs are those clear revelations of the will of God. Also, whatever or whomever our judgments have focused on as our enemy can be our Nineveh. Nineveh can be simply the Lord's urging that we change our behavior or do some obedient action that demands more than we are ready to give. Whatever else, Nineveh is the call of God sounding in our hearts to put Him first, be His person, and accept our vocation to be servants in mission.

But running off to our Tarshish can happen in our soul long before we physically head for a Joppa or board a ship to Spain. Some run away from God without ever leaving their geographical location. We can run away by so filling our lives with activities that time for God is squeezed out and ministry to people and involvement in social programs He has placed on our agendas are set aside. Some of us are running off in all directions but are not under God's direction.

At a class in our church in which I was teaching Jonah, I asked the people to write a short paragraph about their Ninevehs. For many, it meant being God's faithful lay ministers where they were and expressing love, forgiveness, and reconciliation to others and specific involvement in mission in our city.

One man was very direct as he confessed, "I've spent most of my life running away from God! I believe in Him and attend church regularly. You know of my giving and attendance at meetings like this class. People think of me as a 'good Christian.' But inside, deep in my heart, I think I may be trying to escape really doing His will. I live a frantically busy life, but this class on Jonah has made me wonder if I'm running in the wrong direction." Tarshish can be inside our own souls!

One couple wrote their response together: "Our marriage is our Tarshish. Help!" And a woman wrote, "Every time the announcement is made about the need for people to work on the AIDS Taskforce, I feel called, but it means giving up some deep-seated prejudices."

We dare not miss the startling implications of the call that sent Jonah running away from God. When we become Christians, God begins a character transformation of our narcissistic self-concern. He seeks to deploy us in the central business of the kingdom, to get us moving with Him in loving people and sharing our hope. We are all missionaries. We cannot clutch the Gospel as our own private possession to help us accomplish our uncommitted goals. He has targeted us for personal evangelism and mission to the social pain and suffering of our cities. Life has its special times on the Joppa wharf when we decide whether or not to persist in going to our Tarshish.

John Oxenham has put our choice of Tarshish or Nineveh into poetic but penetrating words:

> To every man there openeth
> A way, and ways and a way
> And the high soul climbs the highway
> And the low soul gropes the low
> And in between, on the misty flats
> The rest drift to and fro
> But to every man there openeth
> A high way and a low
> And every man decideth
> The way his soul shall go.

RUNNING AGAINST THE WIND

4 But the Lord sent out a great wind on the sea, and there was a mighty tempest on the sea, so that the ship was about to be broken up.

5 Then the mariners were afraid; and every man cried out to his god, and threw the cargo that was in the ship into the sea, to lighten the load. But Jonah had gone down into the lowest parts of the ship, had lain down, and was fast asleep.

6 So the captain came to him, and said to him, "What do you mean sleeper? Arise, call on your God; perhaps your God will consider us, so that we may not perish."

7 And they said to one another, "Come, let us cast lots, that we may know for whose cause this trouble has come upon us." So they cast lots, and the lot fell on Jonah.

8 Then they said to him, "Please tell us! For whose cause is this trouble upon us? What is your occupation? And where do you come from? What is your country? And of what people are you?"

9 So he said to them, "I am a Hebrew; and I fear the Lord, the God of heaven, who made the sea and the dry land."

10 Then the men were exceedingly afraid, and said to him, "Why have you done this?" For the men knew that he fled from the presence of the Lord, because he had told them.

11 Then they said to him, "What shall we do to you that the sea may be calm for us?" —for the sea was growing more tempestuous.

12 And he said to them, "Pick me up and throw me into the sea; then the sea will become calm for you. For I know that this great tempest is because of me."

13 Nevertheless the men rowed hard to return to land, but they could not, for the sea continued to grow more tempestuous against them.

14 Therefore they cried out to the Lord and said, "We pray, O Lord, please do not let us perish for this man's life, and do not charge us with innocent blood; for You, O Lord, have done as it pleased You."

15 So they picked up Jonah and threw him into the sea, and the sea ceased from its raging.

16 Then the men feared the Lord exceedingly, and offered a sacrifice to the Lord and made vows.

Jon. 1:4–16

Jonah thought he was finished with God, but God was not finished with the defecting prophet. The rebellious missionary bet his life on the false idea that he could flee the presence of God. He lost. After he had boarded the ship for Tarshish, he immediately went below to anesthetize himself with sleep. What he had forgotten was that Yahweh was Lord of the sea as well as the promised land. The broad reaches of the Mediterranean were as much under His control as Jonah's beloved Israel.

Verse 4 tells us that *"the Lord sent out a great wind on the sea." Sent* is much too mild for *hēṭîl. Threw* or *hurled* like a javelin (1 Sam. 18:11; 20:33) would be better. The wind the Lord threw on the sea caused it to rage violently. The sea became tumultuous with white-capped, turbulent waves breaking over the ship.

The mariners all cried out, each one to his own god (v. 5). Yahweh, the only and true God, was not implored to help because none of the sailors knew Him. The only person on board who did know Yahweh was asleep in the hull trying to sleep off the calling he had rejected. As Jonah slept, the sailors threw the cargo overboard in a frantic attempt to save the ship. When the various gods of the seamen did not help, the captain remembered the passenger who boarded at Joppa. He went below to find Jonah (vs. 6). With a sea captain's directness he said, "What are you doing down here, you sleeper, get up and pray to your God. We've tried everyone else's gods; maybe yours will consider our plight and keep us from perishing." Desmond Alexander notes the close similarity of the captain's summons and Jonah's summons from God.[2] The words must have mocked the runaway prophet.

Meanwhile, the sailors cast lots to find out who was the guilty person on board, who was the cause of the storm (v. 7). The idea behind this was that it was obvious that some god or gods were angry about someone on the ship, and they were all being punished because of him.

Even though the casting of lots clearly identified Jonah as the culprit, the sailors asked a series of questions (vs.8) that sounds like a prescribed interrogation of a ship's court, as if the answers were to be duly entered in the log.

Notice in verse 9 that Jonah bypasses the questions about his occupation, town, and country. He especially evades answering the question about his occupation as a prophet. In his own mind, he disqualified himself from that high calling.

What follows is a sad exposure of a believer before pagans. Jonah told the ship's crew that he was a Hebrew who feared God. Here *fear* has the meaning of worship and affiliation, much like a person today might say he is a Christian with little more meaning than that he is not a Buddhist or a Muslim. But Jonah does draw on his heritage to speak about Yahweh. There is a note of irony and pathos in the words he chooses to explain Yahweh. It is almost as if he spoke of the attributes of his God while at the same time feeling that he could not claim them for himself in the present crisis because of his defection. The declaration,

"The Lord, the God of heaven, who made the sea and the dry land," contradicted Jonah's own assumption that he could escape God.

The sailors latched onto Jonah's declaration about his God and must have implored him to call on this God who made and controlled the sea. That brought a full disclosure from Jonah that he was running away from his God because he refused to obey his call to go to Nineveh. A contemporary wording of the sailor's response (vs. 10) might be, "With a God like you have described, why would you want to do that?"

What a great evangelism opportunity Jonah missed. I have often speculated what might have happened if Jonah had repented of his defection right there on the spot and called for Yahweh to save him, the crew, and the ship. If he had, it is most likely that Yahweh would have intervened and calmed the storm. Everyone on the ship no longer would have had any other gods before Yahweh. The ship could have put into the next port, and the grateful sailors could have sent Jonah on his way to Nineveh. But that is exactly what Jonah did not want. For Jonah to call on God for help would surely mean that He would reissue the call the prophet had vehemently turned down back at Gath-hepher only days before.

It is tragic when refusal to do God's will puts us out of commission spiritually. Great opportunities to witness to our faith are missed. And when the failures of Christians to live what they have previously said they believed are publicly exposed, there is a remarkable sadness in the secular world. As a man said recently during the media exposure of a prominent Christian leader, "I was starting to listen to what that guy said. It's really disappointing to see that he couldn't live it out in his own life."

By contrast to Jonah's missed opportunity, we think of Paul centuries later on a ship floundering off the coast of Malta. There was no equivocation expressed by the apostle in the crisis. He took command of the situation and declared that God would save all those on board. Unashamedly he said that they would be saved because he had a mission to accomplish in Rome. He witnessed to what the angel of the Lord had said to him, "Do not be afraid, Paul; you must be brought before Caesar; and indeed God has granted you all those who sail with you." Then Paul gave hope to the crew, "Therefore take heart, men, for I believe God that it will be just as it was told me" (Acts 27:23–25).

Courage like that comes from consistent communion with God. That is what Jonah lacked because of his disobedience. If Jonah knew that the storm was God's judgment on him, why didn't he either set things right with God or get off the ship? Instead, Jonah made the sailors responsible. *"Pick me up and throw me into the sea; then the sea will become calm for you. For I know that this great tempest is because of me"* (vs. 12). His narcissism on the ship was a hairbreadth from masochism, as it would be later in his life as well. When we spend our lives thinking only about ourselves and the times we cannot get our way, we tend to manipulate people to fulfill our self-defeating prophecy by inflicting pain on us.

Note that the ship's crew tried everything before complying with Jonah's request to be thrown overboard. They tried to row to shore, but the sea got even more tempestuous (vs. 13). Then it was they, not Jonah, who prayed to Yahweh (vs. 14). It was an amazing prayer of confession and contrition to the Lord. After they did throw Jonah overboard, the sea ceased raging (vs. 15). Then they knew that Yahweh was, indeed, sovereign of the sea. The sailors shuddered with awe and wonder, then made a sacrifice to Yahweh and followed it with vows. Seamen who had previously worshiped a sundry of false gods became people who worshiped Yahweh and vowed to serve Him. Strange twist. Jonah would not go to Nineveh to prophesy to the Gentiles there, but he is caught in a situation in his escape in which Gentile sailors believed in Yahweh because of his brief witness that Yahweh, the God of heaven, made the sea and the dry land. God intended to use the prophet regardless of his resistance. There was no escape.

NOTES

1. Leslie Allen, *The Books of Joel, Obadiah, Jonah and Micah*, The New International Commentary on the Old Testament (Grand Rapids, Mich.: William B. Eerdmans, 1976), 235.

2. Desmond T. Alexander, "Jonah," *Obadiah, Jonah, and Micah*, Tyndale Old Testament Commentaries, (Downers Grove, Ill.: InterVarsity Press, 1988), 103.

CHAPTER TWO

Running Back to God

Jonah 1:17–2:10

During a review of what a fifth-grade church school class had studied, the teacher asked, "What is the book of Jonah about?"

"It's about a whale," one boy answered.

This response would be the answer of most Christians, young and old. It would also be the answer of both ultra-conservative and liberal biblical expositors who are obsessed with proving or disproving the whale of the book of Jonah. Elaborate arguments are arranged on both sides of the issue. The book of Jonah, however, is much more than a whale of a story!

DELIVERANCE

"Now the Lord had prepared a great fish to swallow Jonah. And Jonah was in the belly of the fish three days and three nights" (Jon. 1:17).

The subject of the first sentence is not the great fish, but the Lord. The point the author wants to make is that God provided a way of delivering Jonah. The salient thing is God's intervention to save Jonah and reconscript him with the original call to go to Nineveh. This point is often lost in the volumes of scholarship on the book of Jonah.

On the one hand are the amateur ichthyologists who present extensive material on whales and the size of the stomachs of sperm whales, to prove that Jonah could have been swallowed by a whale and could have existed there for three days. The annals of maritime history also are searched extensively to find a nonbiblical example of someone who was swallowed by a whale and later survived to tell about it.

Anyone who has read the commentaries of the past 100 years knows the frequent repetition of the account of James Bartley, who in 1891 claimed that he had fallen overboard from the "Star of the East" whaling ship, was swallowed by a whale, and, after a day and a night, escaped to recount his experience. What is missing is a record in the ship's log or testimony from his shipmates that he did, indeed, fall overboard. But even if that account could be validated we would be no closer to the central theme of the book of Jonah. My own studies of sperm whales indicate that a very large one could have swallowed Jonah, but an intervention from God would have been necessary to provide adequate oxygen and keep the stomach juices of the whale from beginning the decomposition of the digestive process. If the *"three days and nights"* is a Hebraism for a period of time and not necessarily seventy-two hours, it could be possible.

But, after I finished my research, I asked myself: "What have I proved? That God delivered Jonah?" I already believed that before I began my time-consuming study.

On the other hand, a large segment of biblical scholarship begins with the assumption that no one could survive in the belly of a whale for seventy-two hours. With equal vigor to those who try to prove that he could have survived, scholars have busied themselves with voluminous research to find data to prove that it would have been impossible. All this to support a deeper presupposition that the book of Jonah is only a parable.

I think the debate about whether or not Jonah was swallowed by a whale has swallowed up biblical expositors at both ends of the spectrum. Unfortunately, God's deliverance of Jonah becomes secondary to the debate.

The survival of Jonah after he was thrown overboard was miraculous. My breakthrough in accepting miracles occurred because God gave me the faith to accept the three greatest miracles of history: the cross for the atonement and reconciliation of humankind; the resurrection for the defeat of the power of death and Satan; and Pentecost for our transformation and regeneration. Accepting the Bible as the authoritative, inspired Word of God came as a result of a faith relationship with God Himself. But early on, I understood that what was more important than the miracles themselves was the power of God they revealed. God, who is Lord of all life, established the laws and order of nature and can supersede them. My limited observation of cause and effect must never limit what I think God could have done.

And can do now! That is the crucial issue. The Father has entrusted all power to the reigning Christ, who continues to do today what He did as Jesus of Nazareth and as the baptizer with the Spirit in the apostolic age. The new birth, transformation, and regeneration are still the component parts of His greatest miracles today. And as part of Christ's role as glorifier of the Father (Eph. 3:21), He continues to perform miracles of healing, intervention, and arrangement of circumstances. We are to expect miracles, never demand them, rejoice when, out of greater wisdom than ours, the Lord performs them, and resist the temptation to become so engrossed in analyzing the details of the miracles that we forget the Lord who graciously performed them for the Father's glory and our growth.

In this context, we can interpret Jonah 1:17 with the emphasis on God and His intervention to deliver Jonah. The circumstances of the miraculous intervention are not nearly as important as the far greater miracle God planned to perform in Nineveh.

The miracle would not have been less astounding if Jonah was rescued by a large board floating by that served as a life raft to get the prophet safely to shore. And the basic thrust of verse 17 would have no less impact if we were told that the Lord gave Jonah supernatural strength to swim to shore. At one point the sailors on the boat thought they might be able to row to land (1:13), indicating that perhaps the ship was coasting near to land. But lest someone start to develop this into a full-blown theory, let me hasten to add that if Jonah swam to shore, it would have been God's miracle, like the supernatural strength He entrusted to Samson. And even when our studies of sperm whales reveal that an exceptionally large one could have been the way Jonah was rescued, we need to resist the pride involved in thinking that we have preserved God's reputation or the authority of the Bible. Again, the point is that God delivered the prophet Jonah.

And for good reason. The miracle of Jonah's rescue was not just to save the prophet before he drowned but to save Nineveh from drowning in sin. God's miracles in our lives are for a greater purpose than our personal comfort or even survival, but so that we can get on with His agenda of serving Him and pressing on with evangelism and mission.

RUNNING TO GOD IN PRAYER

2:1 Then Jonah prayed to the Lord his God from the fish's belly.

2 And he said: "I cried out to the Lord because of my affliction, and He answered me. Out of the belly of Sheol I cried, and You heard my voice.

3 "For You cast me into the deep, into the heart of the seas, and the floods surrounded me; all Your billows and Your waves passed over me.

4 "Then I said, 'I have been cast out of Your sight; yet I will look again toward Your holy temple.'

5 "The waters surrounded me, even to my soul; the deep closed around me; weeds were wrapped around my head.

6 "I went down to the moorings of the mountains; the earth with its bars closed behind me forever; yet You have brought up my life from the pit, O Lord, my God.

7 "When my soul fainted within me, I remembered the Lord; and my prayer went up to You, into Your holy temple.

8 "Those who regard worthless idols forsake their own Mercy.

9 "But I will sacrifice to You with the voice of thanksgiving; I will pay what I have vowed. Salvation is of the Lord."

10 So the Lord spoke to the fish, and it vomited Jonah onto dry land.

Jon. 2:1–10

Jonah had tried to run away from God. Now he ran back to God in prayer. The psalm of Jonah 2:1–9 describes his prayer. It is filled with moving expressions similar to the Psalms and the devotional sayings of his people. The psalm expresses Jonah's rediscovery of Yahweh's omnipresence and His grace to those who turn to Him in their distress.

We have all known those desperate "God help me, please!" times when we have tripped and fallen flat on our faces while running away from Him. We make a mess of things. Life tumbles in on us. The Lord from whom we have been trying to escape becomes our only hope.

We do not deserve His intervention or a second chance, but there is nothing left but to cry out for His help. Jonah's prayer guides us as we admit our need for God in our distress. It is both a prayer of thanksgiving and a prayer for deliverance.

Jonah was rescued from drowning, but he was not yet safely on shore. First, the prayer shows us how to pray in the midst of failure, when our distress has been caused by our own disobedience. Often that is when it is most difficult to pray because our self-condemnation makes us think that either we have no right to call on God or if we did, He would not listen. If an errant rascal like Jonah could pray while he was in affliction that he brought on himself, so can we. God meets us even in our self-imposed trouble.

The second thing we learn from Jonah's psalm is to thank the Lord for confronting us with our disobedience. The storm at sea convinced Jonah that he could not escape God. His rebellion was exposed. Actually it is a great source of hope for us to know that He will not let us continue forever in our personal brand of rebellion. It would be the worst possible bad news if we thought God did not care enough to catch us when we run from Him (note the commentary on Amos 5:19).

Jonah honestly confesses that he is in the *"belly of Sheol"* (2:2) because of God's intervention. The prayer he prayed was as he was drowning. Jonah expresses gratitude that instead of perishing in the storm caused by his efforts to escape God, he was cast into the sea so he could see the error of his ways and confess. Notice that there is no doubt in Jonah's mind who was behind the storm or his being cast overboard. Yahweh did it. *"For You cast me into the deep, into the heart of the seas, and the floods surrounded me; all Your billows and Your waves passed over me"* (v. 3). It was Yahweh's action and Yahweh's sea. When we are confronted by God's exposure of some problem in our lives we have brought on our-selves, it is crucial to thank Him for loving us enough to do whatever was necessary to make us face what we have been doing. There is a measure of relief when things are brought to a crisis point, when we can no longer avoid them. It is like those times in a human relationship when conflict is finally recognized and addressed. We can see things as they are, out in the open, and do something about our part in the conflict. More profoundly, God does precipitate circumstances that expose us to what we are doing in our rebellion against Him or His will for us. But that does not mean an immediate release from the remorse.

Jonah continues in verses 4–6a to relate what went through his mind as he was thrashing in the sea and eventually began to drown. He feels the abject despair of being cast hopelessly away from God's presence and the despair of never again knowing the joy of worship in His presence in the temple. *"I have been cast out of Your sight"* means that God would condemn him to final judgment and death. The word *ʾāk*, "yet," should be amended to read *ʾêk*, "how." "How will I look again toward Your holy temple?" This rendering is more consistent with Jonah's despair as the deadly peril of drowning builds up. In verse 5, the waters encompass or surround the prophet. The verb *ʾāpap*, "surround," is found in Psalm 18:4 and 116:3—surrounded by the cords of death. Plants at the bottom of the sea twisted around Jonah's head.

Verse 6 reveals Jonah down on the floor of the sea. *"I went down to the moorings of the mountains."* The words *"moorings of the mountains,"* *qiṣbê hārîm*, mean the very foundation of the mountains as they existed under the primeval waters (note Deut. 32:22; Job 28:9; Ps. 24:2 for foundations or roots of the mountains). Jonah feels that he has reached the depths of Sheol from which there is no release. *"The earth with its bars closed behind me forever."* It was believed that the world of the dead had an imprisoning door that once closed behind a person there could be no extrication. Jonah went down for the third time and gave up. The grave of the sea had him, or so he thought.

Before we go on in the psalm of Jonah, we need to identify with the prophet's despair in the depths of the sea. If we move to the next portion too quickly, we will miss what the psalm has to teach us about the treasures of the depths. God tracks us down and stops us in our run-away path from obedience, then confronts us with what we are doing. He also allows us to go through a time of death of our willfulness. As we pray we are aware of the hopelessness of changing either ourselves or the problem we created. This moment of hopelessness puts us through a death to self and in a good sense we give up. There is nothing we can do. We hit rock-bottom. And when we do, our surrender to God and His mercy is more than words. We cast ourselves into the arms of everlasting Mercy. That is when resurrection to a new beginning can happen.

When Jonah gave up hope of surviving and could sink no lower, God intervened and saved him. *"Yet You have brought up my life from the pit, O Lord, my God."* Jonah uses words reminiscent of the familiar language of Psalm 103:4, "Who redeems your life from destruction" (*miššaḥat*, "out of the pit"). No wonder the psalmist said, "Bless the Lord, O my soul" (Ps. 103:1), and Jonah, "*O Lord, my God*" (Jon. 2:6). The prophet received the mercy that he was unwilling to preach about in Nineveh. *"When my soul fainted within me, I remembered the Lord; and my prayer went up to You, in Your holy temple"* (2:7). Out of mercy, the Lord allowed Jonah to get to the point of fainting, *hitᶜaṭṭēp*, when his life was ebbing away and he was about to lose consciousness, so that the prophet could desire Him more than life itself.

I am reminded of a young man who went to Buddha to ask how to find God. Buddha took him down to the river. The young man thought the teacher was going to perform a ritual cleansing. Instead, Buddha immersed his head in the water for a dangerously long time while the young man thrashed in the water. Then Buddha let him up. "What were you thinking about when I held your head under water?" the teacher asked.

"Air, air!" the novitiate gasped.

"When you want God as much as you wanted air, you will find him."

Our conception of God is quite different. He finds us, and we search for Him because He has already found us. He brings us to the place where we admit we have no other hope but Him and no possibility of making it through a self-imposed major crisis unless He intervenes. He allows us to discover the gift of the darkness, death to self-willfulness, before He resurrects us out of our tomb. God did not heal Jonah's spiritual sickness before the prophet realized just how sick he was.

In verses 8–9, Jonah shares the treasures of what he learned in the depths. He was confronted with his willfulness and disloyalty. In the style of a prophet, he uses the third person *they*. It serves as a contrast to his own new commitment in verse 10. Verse 8 needs careful interpretation as it consists of only five words in the Hebrew: *"Those who regard worthless idols forsake their own Mercy." "Worthless idols,"* hablêšāwĕʾ, is a compound also found in Deuteronomy 32:21 and Psalm 31:6 that carries a superlative impact—"uselessly worthless deceit"—and stands for *idol*.[1] *"Forsake,"* ᶜāzab, applies particularly to the people of God. And *"mercy"* here is ḥesed, "steadfast love" or "loyalty." *"Mercy"* is properly capitalized in the NKJV because it is used here as a synonym for God. So the lesson Jonah learned is that his disloyalty became an idol and it almost cost him his relationship with his God, who is consistently loyal and steadfast in mercy.

It is a new Jonah who confesses loyalty to his God in verse 9. He will sacrifice to Yahweh, express his thanksgiving and pay his vows. His scrape with death brought him running back to God. With personal intensity he could say salvation is of the Lord. He was ready to obey and share with Nineveh the mercy he had experienced. *"So the Lord spoke to the fish, and it vomited Jonah onto dry land"* (v. 10).

We picture Jonah standing on the beach shuddering with awe because of what he had been through, the stench of the whale clinging to his clothes. One likely to sway the sophisticated, secular pagan of Nineveh? Not without Yahweh's power and mercy.

NOTES

1. Hans Walter Wolff, *Obadiah and Jonah: A Commentary* (Minneapolis: Augsburg Publishing House, 1986), 137–38.

CHAPTER THREE

Running with God

Jonah 3:1–10

3:1 Now the word of the Lord came to Jonah the second time, saying,

2 "Arise, go to Nineveh, that great city, and preach to it the message that I tell you."

3 So Jonah arose and went to Nineveh, according to the word of the Lord. Now Nineveh was an exceedingly great city, a three-day journey in extent.

4 And Jonah began to enter the city on the first day's walk. Then he cried out and said, "Yet forty days, and Nineveh shall be overthrown!"

5 So the people of Nineveh believed God, proclaimed a fast, and put on sackcloth, from the greatest to the least of them.

6 Then word came to the king of Nineveh; and he arose from his throne and laid aside his robe, covered himself with sackcloth and sat in ashes.

7 And he caused it to be proclaimed and published throughout Nineveh by the decree of the king and his nobles, saying, "Let neither man nor beast, herd nor flock, taste anything; do not let them eat, or drink water.

8 "But let man and beast be covered with sackcloth, and cry mightily to God; yes, let every one turn from his evil way and from the violence that is in his hands.

9 "Who can tell if God will turn and relent, and turn away from His fierce anger, so that we may not perish?"

10 Then God saw their works, that they turned from their evil way; and God relented from the disaster that He had said He would bring upon them, and He did not do it.

Jon. 3:1–10

Charles Spurgeon said, "Faith and obedience are bound up in the same bundle. He who obeys God, trusts God; and he who trusts God, obeys God." When God first called Jonah to go to Nineveh, the son of Amittai simply could not trust that Yahweh was right in extending His mercy by giving the enemies an opportunity to repent. Jonah did not trust that God knew what He was doing.

We have no reason to assume that Jonah had changed his basic prejudices about the Ninevites when his second call came. His harrowing scrape with death in the deep forced the prophet to trust God for his survival. The "death-water" conversion shocked Jonah into promising that he would obey God. And so, God began again with Jonah. The willful prophet ran away from God and, in a terrible crisis, ran back to God. Now for a time at least, Jonah ran with God doing what he was told. Chapter 3 shows us the magnificent results that can happen when we cooperate with God. There is only one way to do anything—God's way. Obedience is the secret of spiritual power.

A Second Time

Chapter 3 opens with Jonah's recall to mission. In 1:1 he was identified as Jonah *"son of Amittai."* Here his parentage is dropped and *"the second time"* put in its place—the need for a second call is emphasized. The call has a different preposition. Previously Jonah was charged to cry *against* the city (1:2). Now he is instructed to preach *to* it (3:2). Perhaps Jonah's experience at sea prepared him to communicate more mercy than before. While God did not change, He did have a somewhat more cooperative prophet to use now. This is indicated by the emphasis that Jonah *"arose and went"* (3:3), whereas before he *"rose to flee"* (1:3). This makes us wonder about ourselves: Has life, and particularly the discipline of God, made us more or less obedient, more or less flexible, to receive orders and run with Him?

The Lord told Jonah that He would give Jonah the message to preach. The Lord promises the same for us today. He wants to guide the planning, the preparation, and the preaching of our messages. When we openly seek His direction He leads us to portions of Scripture and inspires the development of the sermon. He keeps us off our hobbyhorses and presses us to proclaim the truth to our people. I am always amazed and delighted when a message planned the previous summer prompts a remark in February such as, "How did you know what we were going through this week? Have you bugged our home?"

THE GREATNESS OF NINEVEH

Verse 3 reminds us again that Nineveh was a *"great"* city; vs. 1:2 is expanded here to *"an exceedingly great city."* The words literally mean "a great city to God." Our mission to our own cities should be motivated by the same designation. Through Jeremiah, God called the displaced Judeans in exile to seek the peace of their city, for in its peace they would find their peace (Jer. 29:7). Jesus wept over Jerusalem, and through the centuries of Christian history the cities have been a neglected mission field. William Booth said, "When I got the poor of London on my heart and a vision of what Christ could do, I decided He would have all of William Booth that there was." Nineveh was important to God.

Nineveh also is described as *"a three-day journey in extent"* (3:3). This phrase has been widely discussed. Some suggest that a day's journey was about twenty-two miles, and therefore the reference is to the metropolitan district of Nineveh comprising Nineveh itself and the suburban cluster of villages of the city-state. Other scholars think that *"three-day journey"* could mean the custom of a three-day visit to a city: one day for arrival, followed by a day of visiting and business, and a day of departure. I much prefer the first theory because excavations of the walls of Nineveh itself have estimated a circumference of the city of at most seven and a half miles. In circumference the larger metropolitan area of Nineveh was more like sixty miles, or what might be called a three-day journey.

This fits with verse 4a, *"And Jonah began to enter the city on the first day's walk."* This means that he began to preach when he arrived at the great metropolis, on the very first day. He did not delay announcing his divinely appointed message.

This message is condensed into only five Hebrew words in 4b. *"Yet forty days, and Nineveh shall be overthrown!"* Surely Jonah's message was longer than this, but the emphasis here by the book's author is that the prophet got right to the point. Jonah preached his decisive message as he walked into the center of the city, announcing what

Yahweh gave him to say. He did not bother to discern whether people liked him or approved of his message.

But look more closely at Jonah's basic theme. *"Forty days"* had religious significance. It alerted Jonah's listeners of a divinely appointed waiting time. The prophet's declaration of what was to happen at the end of those forty days would have an effect of a ram's horn warning of an approaching danger. Nineveh will be overthrown.

Some commentators remind us that the verb *hāpak,* "overturn," can also mean "return, turn around, transform, or repent." Wolff calls this changing of Jonah's message into an equivocal oracle impermissible and asserts that Jonah's message was an unambiguous announcement of judgment that would be made by divine wrath.[1] A message promising transformation to proud Nineveh would hardly have brought sackcloth and ashes. However, it must be noted that the author of Jonah was writing in Hebrew for readers who would catch the play on the word *hāpak* throughout chapter 3. I think Jonah's message included both the warning of the overthrow of the city and a call to repentance.

The account of Jonah's encounter with Nineveh moves fast with crisp sentences that require us to read between the lines. Jonah must have been an imposing, fiery character to be able to stride into a sophisticated, powerful city like Nineveh and proclaim Yahweh's message of judgment upon the sin and the wickedness of the city. But it was not the prophet's rhetoric or oratory that swayed the city but Yahweh working through him. This is encouraging for us as communicators since the response to our messages is not our doing, but a gift of God's Spirit. Yahweh does great things when we leave the results to Him.

The response to Jonah's terse, incisive message was astounding. The people believed God! Jonah's message must have had a "Don't argue with me; what I'm saying is Yahweh's word to you" ring about it. Jonah was not in Nineveh to win a popularity contest! The Hebrew text clearly says that the Ninevites put their trust in God. The same words are used in Exodus 14:31 to describe Israel's response for what Yahweh had done to release them from Egypt's bondage. Faith is a gift only God gives, it is not a human achievement. The account of the endowed faith of the Ninevites would have had a profound impact on the readers of the book of Jonah. They would be forced to see that faith in Yahweh was not their exclusive gift and it would expose their lack of faith. This is exactly what the author of the book of Jonah intended!

And the Ninevites put their repentance into action. Jonah's message, empowered by the Spirit of Yahweh, must have been preached directly to the king in addition to the broad reaches of the city-state. The king led a city-wide movement of repentance of *"the greatest to the least"* of Nineveh (3:5). He sent out a decree calling all the people, including his court, to fast. The fast also included all the herds and flocks. The clarity of the king's decree reflects that Jonah must have had personal influence on the monarch. The words of the decree echo exactly what Jonah's expanded message must have been. *"Cry mightily to God; yes, let every one turn from his evil way and from the violence that is in his hands. Who can tell if God will turn and relent, and turn away from His fierce anger, so that we may not perish?"* (3:8–9).

Who was this king? Douglas Stuart identifies Assur-dan III (773–756 B.C.), a contemporary of Jeroboam II of Israel, as a likely candidate. He concludes,

> There is, of course, absolutely no way to identify with confidence the king mentioned in Jonah 3:6. On the other hand, a king such as Aššur-dan III, during whose reign an agonizing confluence of omens and disasters (eclipse, earthquake, famine, rioting) had occurred, whose capital . . . may have been Nineveh, though this cannot be proved, and who was beset by international problems including continuing military failures again Urartu, was certainly the sort of king (among others) who might well have been predisposed to receive Jonah's message sincerely as a chance for respite from his troubles. The Ninevites of the time of Assur-dan were certainly no strangers to "trouble" (*r ʿh*; 1:2).[2]

Following this line of speculation, if the book of Jonah was written near the end or clearly after Jeroboam II's time in Israel, it would have been a stark comparison between the Assyrian king's court and the court of Samaria that vigorously rejected Amos's call to repentance (note page 000 of the commentary on Amos).

What is especially important for us to note is the influence of the king of Jonah chapter 3 on the people. It causes us to reflect on our personal time with decision-makers in our congregations and communities. In addition to proclaiming the Word of God from our pulpits and classrooms, we need to spend quality time with leaders to listen to their needs and help them accept their ministries and discern how God wants to use them in their spheres of influence. There is no lasting renewal in a parish if we bypass these leaders and gravitate to others who might respond more readily. Also, high profile leaders in entertainment, politics, and business can be used by God to influence others. But they need encouragement.

A president of a company needed this kind of caring. He had trouble connecting his faith with some of the policies of his company that were a contradiction to the Gospel. A message I preached on corporate unrighteousness got under his skin. He asked me to come to his office. It was the first of many visits. Eventually the man took a righteous, but very unpopular, stand that caused shock waves in his industry. His decision encouraged Christians who worked for him, but also other executives who were given courage to take a stand.

A well-known actor had never publicly acknowledged his Christian faith. He was a closet Christian. At the same time he was unsettled about his denial of his Lord. One evening at a community gathering, he broke free of his resistance and talked about what Christ meant to him. After the meeting he said to me, "Thought it was about time people knew where I stood. Thanks for helping me see my responsibility." I had spent lots of personal time with him and had encouraged him to freely discuss his faith in Christ. Other Christians in the movie industry were challenged to speak out, and the man's witness prompted his fans to think about what they believed.

As spiritual leaders we have all had experiences with people of influence who resisted our help. Richard Nixon did not lack for spiritual counselors. If he had listened to some of them during the days of Watergate, he might have made the kind of open confession that would have rallied the support of the American people and led his party and the nation in repentance and spiritual renewal. But even this negative example is the flipside of the power of influence.

In that vein, just imagine what would have happened to Jonah in Nineveh if the king had refused the stirrings of the Spirit of God in him? Jonah would probably have landed in jail.

A KING'S THEOLOGY

We are thankful for whatever personal or political crises the Assyrian king might have been facing that made him receptive to Jonah's message. Jonah gave the king some profound theology during the prophet's time with him. Jonah must have told him that repentance goes two ways: to Yahweh and from Yahweh. If the king and the people repented, turned from their wicked ways, God would turn from His just decision to overthrow the city. Only this kind of careful instruction in the theology of repentance could account for the amazingly insightful possibility the king held out to the people. *"Let every one turn from his evil way. . . . Who can tell if God will turn and relent, and turn away from His fierce anger, so that we may not perish?"* (vv. 8–9). The same word is used for the people's repentance and Yahweh's repentance. God changed His mind in response to the people's repentance.

God is against sin but for us. We cannot fly in the face of His righteousness and justice. He warns us and persists in confronting us until we turn away from sin and accept His forgiveness.

But even more awesome is that God instigates our ability to turn around and return to Him. So His repentance precedes as well as follows our repentance. And while this three-step process of election, repentance, and forgiveness is offered, we *can* reject it. In the instance of the king and the people of Nineveh, the full circle of repentance took place. Jonah was strategic in the process because he ran with God. What joy that must have given the prophet. Or did it? Jonah neither expected nor desired the response his preaching and teaching on repentance produced.

NOTES

1. Wolff, *Obadiah and Jonah,* 149.
2. Stuart, *Hosea-Jonah,* 492.

CHAPTER FOUR

Running Ahead of God

Jonah 4:1–11

Jonah suspected it all along. That is why he disobeyed the Lord's call to go to Nineveh in the first place. Now the runner who ran away from God, who ran back to Him in the ocean depth, who ran with God in proclaiming His message to Nineveh, now ran way out ahead of God in questioning Yahweh's forgiving mercy for the Ninevites.

The son of Amittai never really tore up his pocket veto. He was back to his idolatrous ways. Jonah's idol was Jonah! He was more committed to his concepts of how God should act than he was to God Himself. And all his protestations of love for Israel were only a projection of his devotion to himself. Clinging to the prejudiced presupposition that Yahweh was the exclusive God of the people of Israel, Jonah developed a theology that he would not even let God change. Jonah's theology became an expression of his indomitable will. In essence, the hard inner core of Jonah said, "This is what I believe about God and not even He is going to change it!"

This put Jonah in deep water indeed. In dire danger he called out for help, and the Lord rescued him. The prophet confessed his need but did not really repent. Looking back at his psalm in chapter two, we realize that Jonah said almost all the right words, but he continued to object to God extending His mercy to the Gentiles. At no point did Jonah say, "Yahweh, I was in terrible error when I objected to going to Nineveh. You are Sovereign, and I acknowledge Your power to do whatever you decide and to give your mercy to whomever You will." Jonah's problem was that he wanted to control God! And what do we do when we cannot get our own way? We get angry. Very angry.

JONAH'S ANGRY PRAYER

> 4:1 But it displeased Jonah exceedingly, and he be-
> came angry.
> 2 So he prayed to the Lord, and said, "Ah, Lord,
> was not this what I said when I was still in my coun-
> try? Therefore I fled previously to Tarshish; for I know
> that You are a gracious and merciful God, slow to
> anger and abundant in lovingkindness, One who re-
> lents from doing harm.
> 3 "Therefore now, O Lord, please take my life from
> me, for it is better for me to die than to live!"
> *Jon. 4:1–3*

Jonah's prayer in 4:2–3 shows that he is just as willfully stubborn as he was when God called him back at Gath-hepher. What Jonah says to God is more of a diatribe than an expression of devotion. Repeating the words of Exodus 34:6 that he was taught from childhood becomes the basis of his audacity and not adoration. He knows God's nature is immutable and that his punishments are mutable. Out of *ḥesed*, "lovingkindness," He would relent from *rā̄â*, "harm," because the Ninevites repented. The strange, satiric twist is that Jonah feels that God's repentance in response to Nineveh's repentance is a great harm to him! Jonah's anger was caused by his realization that he could not manipulate God. Jonah could not get the Almighty to repent, to change His mind, and to carry out Jonah's will that the Ninevites be destroyed for their wickedness.

For a willful, controlling person, there is nothing so abhorrent as not being able to control God. And so, he ran ahead of God. But out there alone, destructive anger turns into self-destructive despair. The only thing left that Jonah can control is whether he lives or dies.

Jonah tries to exercise this last vestige of willfulness by pronouncing his own judgment on himself and demanding that God carry out the prophet's self-inflicted sentence. *"Therefore now, O Lord, please take my life from me, for it is better for me to die than to live!"* (4:3). Even in this,

426

Jonah is trying to tell God what is best and what God should do about it. And that is idolatry at its worst.

A THREE-WORD QUESTION

> 4 Then the Lord said, "Is it right for you to be angry?"
>
> 5 So Jonah went out of the city and sat on the east side of the city. There he made himself a shelter and sat under it in the shade, till he might see what would become of the city.
>
> 6 And the Lord God prepared a plant and made it come up over Jonah, that it might be shade for his head to deliver him from his misery. So Jonah was very grateful for the plant.
>
> 7 But as morning dawned the next day God prepared a worm, and it so damaged the plant that it withered.
>
> 8 And it happened, when the sun arose, that God prepared a vehement east wind; and the sun beat on Jonah's head, so that he grew faint. Then he wished death for himself, and said, "It is better for me to die than to live."
>
> 9 Then God said to Jonah, "Is it right for you to be angry about the plant?" And he said, "It is right for me to be angry, even to death!"
>
> *Jon. 4:4–9*

The Lord responds to Jonah's death wish not with a long rebuke but with a question drenched in tender kindness that called the suicidal prophet to self-examination of his imperious willfulness. The question has only three words in it, eight in the English translation: *"Is it right for you to be angry?"* (4:4). God did have the right and cause to be angry with the Ninevites and chose to offer forgiveness. But who is Jonah to express anger when Yahweh chose not to destroy Nineveh? "Vengeance is Mine" (Lev. 19:18; Deut. 32:35). We play god when we continue to be angry at people and groups when God has pronounced His forgiveness. We take their punishment into our own hands. Whether in negative attitudes, vindictive words, or hostile destructive actions, we run out ahead of God in meting out what we think justice demands. And He asks, "Is that your right?" The question has only one answer, "No Lord, that is Your right, not mine!"

Jonah would not answer the Lord's question. His defiant attitude and actions indicate his reply. He went out to the east side of Nineveh and built himself a shelter and sat under it, peering out over the city hoping that the Lord might reverse His clemency. We should note the contrast between the sulking Jonah under a leafy booth and the king in the city fasting in sackcloth and ashes. We suspect that Jonah sat watching the city confident that the king and the people would soon return to their wickedness and this time the Lord would really destroy them.

Yet, the Lord persists in His kindness to Jonah despite Jonah's angry silence to His question. Yahweh causes a plant to grow to give the prophet further shade from the blasting sun. The plant was probably a caster oil tree that grows quickly and provides large leaves. The purpose of the shade tree is for more than Jonah's comfort. The words *"to deliver him from his misery"* (4:6) can be interpreted in two ways. The verb *deliver* can be also rendered "to shade," and *misery* can be translated "wickedness" or "trouble" as it is rendered elsewhere in Jonah (1:2 and 1:8).

Alexander observes, "Consequently, it is possible to interpret the phrase as meaning either, 'to shade him from his distress,' referring to the sun (cf. RSV, GNB, NIV), or, 'to deliver him from his wickedness,' referring to Jonah's unjustified anger (cf. JB)."[1] So the gift of kindness in the shade tree was not only to keep Jonah out of the sun but to remind him of the goodness of God. Jonah is delighted with the shade but still is no more compassionate to Nineveh despite this evidence of God's compassion for his *"misery"* or "wickedness." We are struck with the irony.

Since Jonah was unwilling to connect God's graciousness to him with God's graciousness to Nineveh, the Lord prepared a worm to attack and destroy the plant. When the sun rose, an east wind blew, reminiscent of the wind when Jonah was at sea. As the day proceeded, the sun grew in intensity until the prophet became faint. Jonah was angry over the loss of the plant, and once again he expresses his death wish. *"It is better for me to die than to live"* (4:8).

The gift of the plant was God's way of helping Jonah answer His penetrating question, *"Is it right for you to be angry?"* (4:4). The plant clearly symbolized to the prophet God's mercy on Nineveh. God wanted Jonah to understand how wrong it was for him to be angry about His intervention to save the city. The death of the plant symbolized the removal of God's mercy from Jonah in the blasting sun, just as he might have removed His mercy from Nineveh if He had followed the prophet's desires. Jonah was thankful for the plant and should have been thankful for the kindness of God to Nineveh. Although he was angry when the plant died, he would have been delighted if the mercy of God would have been denied to Nineveh. God was trying to show Jonah just how confused his thinking was.

The Lord's new question really puts Jonah on the spot. *"Is it right for you to be angry about the plant?"* (v. 9). However the prophet answers, it should reveal to Jonah how wrong he is. If he says "no" it would be an admission that his anger over God's mercy to Nineveh was wrong. If he said "yes" he would have to empathize with the Ninevites if the kindness of God was removed from them.

Jonah's answer, *"It is right for me to be angry, even to death,"* shows that he is not willing to live with a God who can give or take away grace to Gentile or Israelite alike. A terrible ambivalence in Jonah's soul is revealed. He cannot abide the thought of God's grace being extended to the Ninevites, and yet, he sees that he cannot live without that grace himself. He now sees that God will not let him have it both ways: mercy for Israel and judgment for the Gentiles. Since Jonah could not convince God that His kindness to all people who repent is wrong, the prophet wants to die. Jonah insists on winning the final round of his power struggle with the Lord. Jonah would rather die than admit he was wrong.

Some years ago, I counseled a woman in profound grief. After years of conflict in her marriage, her husband committed suicide. He left a note saying that he killed himself because of her. She was left to live with the grief of his death and the imposed guilt he put on her. This was a terrible way to win the battle for control. If the man could not control his wife in life, he would control her in his death.

Jonah saw his death as the only way to get away from God. Fleeing to Tarshish did not work. But Jonah thinks that death will give him separation from the God of pity whom he has now come to abhor because he could not control on whom that pity would be shown.

FOR PITY'S SAKE

> 10 But the Lord said, "You have had pity on the plant for which you have not labored, nor made it grow, which came up in a night and perished in a night.

11 "And should I not pity Nineveh, that great city,
in which are more than one hundred and twenty thousand persons who cannot discern between their right
hand and their left, and much livestock?"

Jon. 4:10-11

Yet, mercifully God does not give up on Jonah even though Jonah gave up on Him. In verses 10–11, God persists with a further attempt to communicate the contrast between the prophet's lack of pity and His pity on Nineveh. Jonah's pity on the plant was clearly a projection of his own self-pity. If he thought he had a right to this pity for himself, did not God have a right to pity Nineveh?

Once again Nineveh is referred to as *"that great city."* The size of the city is given as 120,000 persons. Some commentators suggest that the reference is to children — thus leading to population estimates ranging up to 600,000. Whatever the size, the whole population was indeed like children when it came to their religion. They could not distinguish between their many gods on their left hand and Yahweh on their right. These Gentiles were spiritual minors compared to the more mature Israelites. The Ninevites were wicked because they did not know the Law of Yahweh. God showed pity on them. Should not those spiritually mature in Israel have the same pity? Or, had God's people regressed into childlike behavior? In the person of Jonah, it was obvious they could not weigh truth and justice, God's gracious nature and their call to have mercy on Gentiles, their belief in Yahweh as sovereign of the universe and the inclusiveness of His love for all people.

In the final analysis, Jonah was so engrossed in self-pity that he had none to spare. Most of all, the prophet needed God's pity. Yahweh's pity, *ḥûs,* corresponds to His *ḥesed* that Jonah said he knew about in 4:2. The issue was that the prophet wanted none of Yahweh's *ḥûs* if it meant that he would have to express it to the Gentiles. The pity Nineveh needed from God, Jonah now needs even more because of his pitiless attitudes. His judgmentalism, issuing in petulant anger, was the result of not realizing that he, too, was being judged by God. If Jonah could have accepted God's sovereign right to show pity on whomever He chose and repented of his efforts to control God, the prophet could have received the precious pity he lacked so much. The book of Jonah ends abruptly without that crucial repentance from the unwilling prophet. What should have happened to Jonah?

Jonah's biographer left that question for Israel to answer. It is obvious that the author focused Israel's exclusivism and blind nationalism in the prophet. He wanted the people of Israel to take an honest look in the mirror he provided and see themselves. Their own idolatry made them no better than the polytheistic Assyrians. They were blessed to be a blessing to the nations. They were denying both.

The book of Jonah deserves its place among the books of the Minor Prophets. Many of the same themes are declared: Yahweh is Sovereign of all the nations. His *hesed* is not just for Israel. Nor is His judgment limited to other nations. Israel's syncretism is as abhorrent as Assyria's polytheism. And yet, to know Yahweh and not obey Him would seem to deserve a greater punishment and deeper repentance. The more profound the confessed sin, the more abundant would be the pity and mercy. That is what Jonah refused to acknowledge and what his biographer did not want Israel to miss.

The application of the book of Jonah to our personal lives and to the church as a whole is pointed and poignant.

On the personal level, the book of Jonah forces us to see our own power struggle with God. What has God called us to be or do that puts us into a contest of wills with Him? What challenges of obedience in our own inner spiritual formation or call to ministry have set us running away? Where are we right now? Are we in a Tarshish of escape or in a Nineveh of obedience?

And what about the hard inner core of ego that has never been given over to God's control? Was our conversion a radical transformation from self-centered willfulness or an effort to recruit God to help us accomplish our goals? Have the harrowing experiences of life broken our inner core of proud individualism, or are we essentially the same people we always were? After the crises are past, are we any more flexible and willing to discern and do God's will? Are there people we resist loving or caring for because of their contradiction of our values, beliefs, or life-style? Who are our personal Ninevites? If the Lord said, "Arise, go . . . ," what would be most difficult to obey? Do we ever get so committed to our predictions of what some people or groups deserve that we take on the responsibility, actively or in thought, to program their punishment? Do we know anyone in a power struggle like Jonah's? Are there vestiges of that struggle in us? For what do we need God's pity? Who in our lives needs God's pity through us?

The book of Jonah is no less challenging to the contemporary church. Often we desire to stay in the holy huddle when the next play calls for energetic evangelism and costly mission. Either our congregations are in mission or they are still a mission field.

The little book of Jonah packs a big punch into our exclusivism and judgmentalism about the pagan world. The Gospel is not our private possession. Evangelism and mission are not an aspect of a well-rounded congregational program; they are the reason for all we do in worship, education, and fellowship.

Churches, like individuals, can run away from God. It happens when traditions and customs become more important than our calling. We can get introverted into our own programs, buildings, and budgets. In every town or city there are hundreds, thousands, millions who do not know Christ. Our members must be called and equipped to be winsome, winning evangelists. And we dare not run away from the call of the city—your city or mine—that is as great to God as Nineveh of old. It is good to ask ourselves, then church officers, and then those vision shapers who determine how our congregations respond to obeying the Lord, "Where are we as a congregation? Back at Gath-hepher still wrestling with the call of God? In the hull of the ship asleep? In the depths trying to placate God so we can keep our agenda intact? Or, have we reached our Tarshish and think we're in Nineveh?" There is nothing worse for a congregation than to have the mind-set of Tarshish in Nineveh. The question is: "Do we love the people of Nineveh?"

What happens in our churches determines what happens throughout the city. The preaching and teaching of the grace of God can make the congregation a healing center, a place of authentic pity where people are loved and forgiven and set free of guilt and fear. Every time that liberating message is communicated, it should be coupled with a call to ministry for all members to be disciples of hope rather than controlling religious people who refuse to witness in Nineveh. A penetrating study of Jonah helps us get at our own and our people's power struggle with God for control and what could happen if, instead of running away from Him or ahead of Him, we run with Him.

Stephen Neill said, "The only reason for being a Christian is the ever-growing conviction that the Christian faith is true."[2] This happens when we meet Christ personally and experience His pity, His grace. Our power base changes from our will to His will for us. The hard inner core of self-control is surrendered to His control. When we invite Him to live in us, we experience the power of His indwelling Spirit and are free at last from our use of manipulative human power to evade His call. He not only shows us our Nineveh but gives us a continuous flow of grace to share there. The "greater than Jonah" will never leave us alone.

A final thought: Michelangelo's painting on the Sistine Chapel at the Vatican portrays the prophets, apostles, and patriarchs. Of all the faces he painted, none has a more radiant countenance than Jonah. We wonder if Michelangelo knew something we do not about what happened to Jonah after the sudden close of his biography. Or, perhaps the artist hoped that Jonah did indeed accept God's pity and became a communicator of grace. We do not know. But what we do know is that our own portrait is not finished. And what it will be is dependent on the mercy we receive and give away in our Nineveh.

NOTES

1. Alexander, "Jonah," 128.
2. Stephen Neill, *Call to Mission* (Philadelphia: Fortress Press, 1970), 10.

Bibliography

Hosea

Andersen, Francis I. and Freedman, David Noel. *Hosea*. Anchor Bible. Garden City, N.Y.: Doubleday, 1980.

Bright, John. *A History of Israel*. 2d ed. Philadelphia: Westminster, 1972.

Buss, Martin J. *The Prophetic Word of Hosea: A Morphological Study*. Berlin: Töpelman, 1969.

Childs, Brevard S. *Introduction to the Old Testament as Scripture*. Philadelphia: Fortress, 1979.

Fohrer, Georg. *Introduction to the Old Testament*. Translated by David E. Green. Nashville: Abingdon, 1968.

Hubbard, David Allan. *With Bands of Love: Lessons from the Book of Hosea*. Grand Rapids, Mich.: Eerdmans, 1968.

Kidner, Derek. *Love to the Loveless: The Message of Hosea*. Downers Grove, Ill.: InterVarsity, 1981.

Knight, George A. F. *Hosea*. Torch Bible Commentaries. London: SCM, 1960.

Mays, James Luther. *Hosea*. Old Testament Library. Philadelphia: Westminster, 1969.

Phillips, Harold Cooke. *The Interpreter's Bible*, vol. 6. Nashville: Abingdon, 1956.

Smith, George Adam. *The Book of the Twelve Prophets*, vol. 1. New York and London: Harper and Brothers, 1928.

Stuart, Douglas. *Hosea–Jonah*. Word Biblical Commentary. Waco, Tex.: Word, 1987.

West, James King. *Introduction to the Old Testament*. 2d ed. New York: Macmillan, 1981.

Wolff, Hans Walter. *Hosea*. Hermeneia. Translated by Gary Stansell. Philadelphia: Fortress, 1974.

Joel

Bright, John. *A History of Israel*. 2d ed. Philadelphia: Westminster, 1972.

Childs, Brevard S. *Introduction to the Old Testament as Scripture*. Philadelphia: Fortress, 1979.

Craigie, Peter C. *Twelve Prophets*. vol. 1. Philadelphia: Westminster, 1984.

Fohrer, Georg. *Introduction to the Old Testament*. Translated by David E. Green. Nashville: Abingdon, 1968.

Stuart, Douglas. *Hosea–Jonah.* Word Biblical Commentary. Waco, Tex.: Word, 1987.

West, James King. *Introduction to the Old Testament.* 2d ed. New York: Macmillan, 1981.

Wolff, Hans Walter. *Joel and Amos.* Hermeneia. Translated by Waldemar Janzen, S. Dean McBride, Jr., and Charles A. Muenchow. Edited by S. Dean McBride, Jr. Philadelphia: Fortress, 1977.

Amos

Bright, John. *A History of Israel.* 2d ed. Philadelphia: Westminster, 1972.

Childs, Brevard S. *Introduction to the Old Testament as Scripture.* Philadelphia: Fortress, 1979.

Craigie, Peter C. *The Old Testament: Its Background, Growth, and Content.* Nashville: Abingdon, 1986.

———. *Twelve Prophets.* vol. 1. Philadelphia: Westminster, 1984.

Fohrer, Georg. *Introduction to the Old Testament.* Translated by David E. Green. Nashville: Abingdon, 1968.

Knierim, Rolf P. "'I Will Not Cause It to Return' in Amos 1 and 2." In *Canon and Authority: Essays in Old Testament Religion and Theology,* edited by George W. Coats and Burke O. Long, pp. 163–175. Philadelphia: Fortress, 1977.

LaSor, William S., Hubbard, David A., and Bush, Frederic W. *Old Testament Survey.* Grand Rapids, Mich.: Eerdmans, 1982.

Stuart, Douglas. *Hosea–Jonah.* Word Biblical Commentary. Waco, Tex.: Word, 1987.

West, James King. *Introduction to the Old Testament.* 2d ed. New York: Macmillan, 1981.

Wolff, Hans Walter. *Joel and Amos.* Hermeneia. Translated by Waldemar Janzen, S. Dean McBride, Jr., and Charles A. Muenchow. Edited by S. Dean McBride, Jr. Philadelphia: Fortress, 1977.

Obadiah

Allen, Leslie. *The Books of Joel, Obadiah, Jonah, and Micah.* The New International Commentary on the Old Testament. Grand Rapids, Mich.: Eerdmans, 1976.

———. *Hosea–Malachi.* London: Scripture Union, 1987.

Baker, David W. "Obadiah." In *Obadiah, Jonah, and Micah.* Tyndale Old Testament Commentaries, pp. 19–44. Downers Grove, Ill.: InterVarsity, 1988.

Childs, Brevard S. *Introduction to the Old Testament as Scripture*. Philadelphia: Fortress, 1979.

Craigie, Peter C. *The Old Testament: Its Background, Growth, and Content*. Nashville: Abingdon, 1986.

——. *Twelve Prophets*. vol. 1. Philadelphia: Westminster, 1984.

Fohrer, Georg. *Introduction to the Old Testament*. Translated by David E. Green. Nashville: Abingdon, 1968.

LaSor, William S., Hubbard, David A., and Bush, Frederic W. *Old Testament Survey*. Grand Rapids, Mich.: Eerdmans, 1982.

Maclaren, Alexander. *Expositions of Holy Scripture: Ezekiel, Daniel, and the Minor Prophets*. Grand Rapids, Mich.: Baker, 1982 reprint.

Stuart, Douglas. *Hosea–Jonah*. Word Biblical Commentary. Waco, Tex.: Word, 1987.

West, James King. *Introduction to the Old Testament*. 2d ed. New York: Macmillan, 1981.

Wolff, Hans Walter. *Obadiah and Jonah*. Translated by Margaret Kohl. Minneapolis: Augsburg, 1986.

Jonah

Allen, Leslie. *Hosea–Malachi*. London: Scripture Union, 1987.

Alexander, T. Desmond. "Jonah." In *Obadiah, Jonah, and Micah*. Tyndale Old Testament Commentaries, pp. 45–131. Downers Grove, Ill.: InterVarsity, 1988.

Childs, Brevard S. *Introduction to the Old Testament as Scripture*. Philadelphia: Fortress, 1979.

Craigie, Peter C. *The Old Testament: Its Background, Growth, and Content*. Nashville: Abingdon, 1986.

——. *Twelve Prophets*. vol. 1. Philadelphia: Westminster, 1984.

Fohrer, Georg. *Introduction to the Old Testament*. Translated by David E. Green. Nashville: Abingdon, 1968.

LaSor, William S., Hubbard, David A., and Bush, Frederic W. *Old Testament Survey*. Grand Rapids, Mich.: Eerdmans, 1982.

Stuart, Douglas. *Hosea–Jonah*. Word Biblical Commentary. Waco, Tex.: Word, 1987.

West, James King. *Introduction to the Old Testament*. 2d ed. New York: Macmillan, 1981.

Wolff, Hans Walter. *Obadiah and Jonah*. Translated by Margaret Kohl. Minneapolis: Augsburg, 1986.